1,000,000 Books

are available to read at

Forgotten Books

www.ForgottenBooks.com

Read online
Download PDF
Purchase in print

ISBN 978-1-331-13635-4
PIBN 10149126

This book is a reproduction of an important historical work. Forgotten Books uses state-of-the-art technology to digitally reconstruct the work, preserving the original format whilst repairing imperfections present in the aged copy. In rare cases, an imperfection in the original, such as a blemish or missing page, may be replicated in our edition. We do, however, repair the vast majority of imperfections successfully; any imperfections that remain are intentionally left to preserve the state of such historical works.

Forgotten Books is a registered trademark of FB &c Ltd.
Copyright © 2018 FB &c Ltd.
FB &c Ltd, Dalton House, 60 Windsor Avenue, London, SW19 2RR.
Company number 08720141. Registered in England and Wales.

For support please visit www.forgottenbooks.com

1 MONTH OF FREE READING

at

www.ForgottenBooks.com

By purchasing this book you are eligible for one month membership to ForgottenBooks.com, giving you unlimited access to our entire collection of over 1,000,000 titles via our web site and mobile apps.

To claim your free month visit:

www.forgottenbooks.com/free149126

* Offer is valid for 45 days from date of purchase. Terms and conditions apply.

English
Français
Deutsche
Italiano
Español
Português

www.forgottenbooks.com

Mythology Photography **Fiction**
Fishing Christianity **Art** Cooking
Essays Buddhism Freemasonry
Medicine **Biology** Music **Ancient Egypt** Evolution Carpentry Physics
Dance Geology **Mathematics** Fitness
Shakespeare **Folklore** Yoga Marketing
Confidence Immortality Biographies
Poetry **Psychology** Witchcraft
Electronics Chemistry History **Law**
Accounting **Philosophy** Anthropology
Alchemy Drama Quantum Mechanics
Atheism Sexual Health **Ancient History**
Entrepreneurship Languages Sport
Paleontology Needlework Islam
Metaphysics Investment Archaeology
Parenting Statistics Criminology
Motivational

THE HARP OF PERTHSHIRE

A COLLECTION OF

Songs, Ballads, and other Poetical Pieces

CHIEFLY BY LOCAL AUTHORS

WITH NOTES
EXPLANATORY, CRITICAL, AND BIOGRAPHICAL

BY

ROBERT FORD

Author of "Thistledown," and Editor of "Auld Scots Ballants," etc.

THE AULD HOUSE OF GASK

ALEXANDER GARDNER
Publisher to Her Majesty the Queen
PAISLEY; AND PATERNOSTER SQUARE, LONDON

1893

PHELAN

ERRATA.

Page 78, line 43—*for* " to " *read* " by."
Page 112, line 30—*for* " Lyndoch " *read* " Lynedoch."
Page 398, line 21—*for* " master-place " *read* " muster-place."
Page 438, line 39—*for* " Aberdeen " *read* " Glasgow."

832864

PREFACE.

It has been remarked by more than one writer whose attention has been led to the subject that Perthshire has not produced any one who, in the loftier sense of the word, may be described as a great poet. And this is no doubt true. But, verily, there is only one shire in all Scotland that can, with uplifted head, claim for itself such rare distinction. And if Perthshire has not produced a Robert Burns, or any poet that may be ranked within measurable distance of the "glorious Ayrshire ploughman," the County, methinks, that can name as its own the gifted lady of Gask, who, next to the National Poet, has given more songs of enduring fame to the world than any other single singer that Scotland has seen; the County that gave birth to, and nurtured the early genius of Robert Nicoll, of Tullybeltane; James Stewart, of Dunkeld; Charles Spence, of Rait; and many another singer of scarcely less merit that might be named; whose scenes of natural beauty, and types of female loveliness, have attracted the Muse of nearly every poet of note in the land—as witness the Perthshire songs of Burns, Scott, Hogg, and Tannahill —has distinct claims to consideration in the matter of its Poets and Poetry.

The home poets of Perthshire, indeed, as we hope this work will satisfactorily demonstrate, have neither been few in respect of numbers, nor contemptible in regard to merit. Reviewing them in their chronological sequence, as the reader will find examples of their work arranged in the succeeding pages, from the time of Gavin Douglas, of Dunkeld, down to the present day, we discover a galaxy of authors of whom any County or district may be reasonably proud, and such a large number of songs and poems of more than parochial fame, the most of them by Perthshire writers, as will more than justify the publication of a work such as is here presented. Following the illustrious Bishop of Dunkeld, who flourished in the end of the fifteenth and in the beginning of the sixteenth centuries, and in addition to "The Palace of Honour," and "King Hart," and other works of a strikingly original and highly poetical character, "gave," as Scott in *Marmion* reminds us, "rude Scotland Virgil's page," we find Henry Adamson, the author of "The Muses Threnodie," whose writings in 1637 attracted the favourable notice of Drummond of Hawthornden, who recommended their publication, because, as he said, "longer to conceal them will be to wrong your Perth of her due honour, who deserveth no less of you than that she should be thus blazoned and registrate to posterity." Next comes into view Alexander Robertson, of Struan, with his curious medley of verses, serious and satiric—the great "Struan"—who fought under Dundee at Killiecrankie, under Mar at Sheriffmuir, and under Prince Charlie at Culloden; who is followed by the Rev. John Barclay, the founder of the Bereans, a native of Muthill, who wrote a rhymed version of the Psalms, and is the reputed author of one of the various ballads extant which celebrate the historic battle of Sheriffmuir. Then comes David Malloch, or Mallet, of the same fertile district, with his imperishable song of "The Birks of Invermay," and his beautiful and pathetic ballad of "William and Margaret," the latter of which, on its original publication in Aaron Hill's *Plain Dealer*, in 1724, set literary London positively by the ears. A few years later we discover Dugald Buchanan, of Balquhidder, the well known Gaelic poet, who is followed by Duncan Ban Macintyre, still dear to Breadalbane and the hills of Glenorchy; Andrew Sharpe, of Bridgend, the author of "Corunna's Lone Shore," and Alexander Campbell, of Tombea, editor of *Albyn's Anthology*, and the author of "Row weel, my Boatie, row weel." Following these in their course we are brought down towards the end of the eighteenth century, when the lyric muse of Robert Burns was making glorious the very hill tops of Scotland, and the "Flower of Strathearn"—as yet unseen—was blossoming into song in the "Auld House" of Gask, and surreptitiously adding to the "Land o' the Leal," the "Laird o' Cockpen," and many of her finest lyrics. And now comes into view Charles Spence, of Raitt, with his songs of "The Twa Bumbees" and "Linn Magray," etc., who is followed by David Drummond and his "Bonnie Lass o' Levenside;" William Clyde, with "St. Johnstoun's Bells;" David Webster, with "Tak' it, Man, Tak' it;" James Beattie, of Leetown, with his poems of "The Spring Lark," and "The Rainbow," and other songs of delicate beauty and tender emotion. Next we see James Stewart, of Dunkeld, with his graphic and clever character songs of "Our Little Jock," "Fouscanhaud," and "The Tailor o' Monzie;" and William Wilson, of Crieff, with "Jean Linn," and "Auld Johnny Graham."

Now we catch a glimpse of the bright morning star of Tullybeltane—Robert Nicoll—with his "Bonnie Bessie Lee," "The Folk o' Ochtergaen," "The Toun where I was Born," and many other familiar songs and poems. At his elbow is his younger brother, William, with one or two thoughtful pieces. Then comes David Millar, with his long and loving poem of "The Tay;" Caroline Oliphant, the younger; dear old Mrs. Sandeman, of Bonskeid and Springland—worthy grand-niece of the authoress of "The Land o' the Leal"—with her good and gifted daughter, Mrs. Barbour, recently deceased, and still more highly gifted grandson, the late Rev. Robert W. Barbour, each with songs of exalted fancy, richly imbued with spiritual suggestiveness.

Conspicuous among a number who follow each other in rapid succession towards the middle of the current century, there is discovered just behind Alexander Maclagan, the author of "A Cronie o' Mine," and "Hurrah for the Thistle," the giant form of the Rev. George Gilfillan, the one eloquent expounder of mysterious "Night;" Dr. Charles Mackay, author of "Cheer Boys, Cheer," who was a native of Perth; the late Sir William Stirling Maxwell, of credit and renown, for many years the County's able representative in Parliament; the Rev. Dr. J. R. Macduff, of Bonhard, a voluminous writer in prose and verse; Dr. John Anderson, the revered and gifted minister of Kinnoull; the Rev. Dr. William Blair, of Dunblane; the late Peter Norval, of Collace; D. H. Saunders, of Blairgowrie, the well known "Christian Democrat;" Duncan Macgregor Crerar, familiarly known as "The Breadalbane Bard," for many years resident in America; the Rev. Peter Anton, of Kilsyth, who is a native of the Carse of Gowrie; James Ferguson, of Stanley ("Nisbet Noble"); and many more.

From among those we have named, it will be seen there are not less than a dozen who enjoy a literary reputation that is co-extensive with the language in which they wrote and sang: while of the others, with the forty to fifty more, notice of whom will be found in the body of the work, it may, we think, be said without prejudice or fear of contradiction, that they have each produced something worthy of at least local preservation.

The anonymous muse has also made contributions to Perthshire literature, which cannot be overlooked in a popular collection; some of them being of great beauty, and not a few possessing considerable historic interest. And the inclusion of the more prominent of these—"The Weary Coble o' Cargill," "Bessie Bell and Mary Gray," "Killiecrankie," the various ballads celebrating the Battle of Sheriffmuir, and "The Lass o' Gowrie," etc., with the notes which accompany them—may prove to many readers not the least interesting feature in the book.

In addition to all these, we have embraced, in a separate department, the more notable Perthshire songs of Burns, Scott, Hogg, and Tannahill, and others, because, by reason of their own inherent merit, as well as the subjects they variously celebrate, they have come to be esteemed as essentially a part and parcel of our local literature. Much more might have been included; many more local authors might have found representation in the work; and many more poems and songs by outside writers, bearing upon local subjects, might have found admittance. To make, however, anything like an exhaustive collection of the poetry of Perthshire, not one, but a number of volumes would be required. At the same time, we think it will be generally admitted that all that is best and of most vital interest in the poetical literature of our beautiful and well beloved County has found a place in these pages.

The work of collecting and arranging the material has been to ourselves, in large measure, a labour of love, and we look for our reward mainly in the pleasure which we anticipate the book will afford to natives of Perthshire at home and abroad, many of whom have manifested the keenest interest in the progress and completion of the undertaking.

In the matter of size and general construction only may the present work be said to be uniform with its illustrious prototype, *The Harp of Renfrewshire*. The first series of that earlier work, which rose under the capable hand of William Motherwell, contains many poems and songs which have no connection with Renfrewshire, either in the matter of subject or authorship; but here not a single verse will be found that has not a claim to a place in the volume by the one good reason or the other. Perhaps a higher uniformity of merit could have been maintained had we chosen to ransack Scottish literature for gems wherewith to adorn the brow of our native County; but we preferred to "pick and wale" only among such effusions as belong to Perthshire by titular or native right. And herein lies the chief value of the book to those whom we expect to be moved by it. It is all our own; and is the first earnest attempt to afford a fairly comprehensive and popular representation of the poetry of the richly song-favoured and restricted district to which the title applies. The selections are not all of equal merit (this were next to impossible in a work of the kind), but a fair standard of excellence has been set up, and, we think, has been honourably maintained throughout. Such differences in quality as will be found existing, may be compared to the beauty of one flower, or the stately elegance of one tree, as contrasted with another, and will give a charm of variety to the work, which perhaps a stricter uniformity of tone and colour would fail to yield.

If into these pages, forsooth, we have been able to gather an abundant harvest of poesy—much of it, too, of excellent quality—and we think we have—it is surely not more than might be expected from the field that has yielded the crop. Perthshire is rich beyond measure in such scenery as is best calculated to inspire the beholder to articulate song. "Among all the provinces in Scotland," says Sir Walter Scott, "if an intelligent stranger were asked to describe the most varied and the most beautiful, it is probable he would name the County of Perth. . . . The most picturesque, if not the highest, hills are to be found here. The rivers find their way out of the mountainous region by the wildest leaps, and through the romantic passes connecting the Highlands with the Lowlands. . . . Its lakes, woods, and mountains may vie in beauty with any that the Highland tour exhibits; while Perthshire contains, amidst this romantic scenery, and in some places, in connection with it, many fertile and habitable tracts which may vie with the richness of merry England herself."

> "'Behold the Tiber!' the vain Roman cried,
> Viewing the ample Tay from Baiglie's side;
> But where's the Scot that would the vaunt repay,
> And hail the puny Tiber for the Tay?"

Now, enough by the way of preface. We will be joining the reader here and there in the notes throughout the volume, and for a more lengthened period in the biographical notices at the close. Until that longer meeting he will form many new friendships, and revive a good many old ones, and, we hope, will spend many a pleasant half-hour.

Our thanks are due, and are gratefully recorded, to the various authors and publishers who have readily granted permission to make extracts from copyright works, and to the ladies and gentlemen who have furnished books and manuscripts for the purpose of making selections.

To Miss Stewart, the sole surviving niece of Lady Nairne—who at the advanced age of ninety-eight is, happily, still hale and well—we have to express our special thanks. It is to her kindly disposition that the reader, as well as the publisher and editor, is indebted for the *fac-simile* of the original MS. of "The Land o' the Leal."

ROBERT FORD.

GLASGOW, 1893.

CONTENTS.

POEMS AND SONGS.

		PAGE
A Cronie o' Mine,	Maclagan,	206
A Dialogue between Will Lickladle and Tom Clean Cogue,	Barclay,	59
A Highland Funeral,	R. W. Barbour,	354
Allan Mac Allan Dhu,	Stewart,	157
Allan Water,	R. M. Fergusson,	365
Alma, Countess of Breadalbane,	Crerar,	293
A Legend of the Daisy,	Whittet,	277
A May Song,	W. Robertson,	330
"A Midsummer Nicht's Dream,"	Jessie M. King,	371
Answer to "I'm Wearin' awa', John,"	Gray	123
A Prelude,	Whittet,	276
Archy o' Kilspindie,	Finlay,	417
Around Benchonzie's Purple Crest,	Edwards,	361
A Soliloquy,	Sim,	98
A Tale o' Kirrie,	Geddes,	339
Athol Cummers,	Hogg,	405
Auld Johnny Graham,	Wilson,	163
Auld Johnny Shaw,	M'Culloch,	235
Autumn Thoughts,	Jessie M. King,	372
A Valentine,	Cromb,	319
Aye Fen' for Yersel',	White,	195
Bessie Bell and Mary Gray,	Anon.,	46
Bewitched,	Young,	271
Biggin' a Nest,	Ford,	318
Blythe, blythe and merry was She,	Burns,	394
Bonnie Bessie Lee,	Nicoll,	167
Bonnie Ochtertyre,	Kippen,	286
By Allan Stream,	Burns,	396
Caledonia's Blue Bells,	Crerar,	292
Caller Herrin',	Baroness Nairne,	111
Cam' ye by Athol?	Hogg,	403
Charming Phillis,	Nicol,	87
Corunna's Lone Shore,	Sharpe,	91
Craigie Hill,	Clyde,	137
Cromlet's Lilt,	Anon.,	30

CONTENTS.

		PAGE
Death,	*M. F. Barbonr,*	260
Donald Gunn,	*Webster,*	141
Donald Macinroy,	*Saunders,*	290
Duncan Ker,	*Stewart,*	159
Dunsinane,	*Ferguson,*	308
Elegiac,	*Sir W. S. Maxwell,*	243
Epistle to Tammas Bodkin,	*J. Campbell,*	201
Epitaph on Alexander Robertson of Struan,	*Nicol,*	88
'Es 'Αει,	*R. W. Barbour,*	353
Fair Helen and Lord William,	*Shain,*	178
Fallen Leaves,	*Fraser,*	374
Farewell,	*W. Nicoll,*	177
Farewell to Aberfoyle,	*Richardson,*	75
For Lack of Gold,	*Austin,*	74
Fouscanhaud,	*Stewart,*	153
Gilderoy,	*Anon.,*	42
Glen Ogil,	*D. M. Smith,*	326
Glentulchan's Sweet Flower,	*Mercer,*	214
Golden Gorse,	*Blair,*	280
Hail to the Chief,	*Scott,*	399
Hansel Mononday,	*A. M. Scott,*	385
Hereafter,	*Steven,*	266
Her Reply,	*Anon.,*	32
Hey the Rantin' Murray's Ha',	*Baroness Nairne,*	112
Home in Heaven,	*Oliphant,*	185
Hurrah for the Thistle,	*Maclagan,*	209
Hymn to Fire,	*Gilfillan,*	219
In the Gloaming,	*M. B. White,*	382
It's a' Owre,	*Dryerre,*	324
Jean Linn,	*Wilson,*	162
Jeanie Brown,	*James Craig,*	349
Jenny Whitelaw,	*Gairns,*	190
Kate o' Gowrie,	*Reid,*	119
Kilbryde Kirkyard,	*Blair,*	279
Killiecrankie,	*Anon.,*	51
King Hart,	*Douglas,*	11
Kinnaird,	*A. M. Scott,*	386
Kinnoull Cliff,	*F. Buchanan,*	263
Kitty Reid's House,	*Baroness Nairne,*	109
Lady Keith's Lilt,	*Drummond,*	64
Lassie wi' the Yellow Coatie,	*Duff,*	131
Life is short, but Love is long,	*R. M. Fergusson,*	365
Linn-Ma-Gray,	*Spence,*	128
Lord Ruthven; or the Waes o' Dupplin' Field,	*Pyott,*	340
"Love of Right and Scorn of Wrong,"	*Macduff,*	244
Lumbago,	*Young,*	267
Maggie Lyle,	*F. Buchanan,*	263
Mary Morrison,	*Wilson,*	165

CONTENTS.

XV.

		PAGE
Mary of Sweet Aberfoyle,	*Glen,*	135
Mary of Tombea,	*Scott,*	397
Mary Rose,	*Stewart,*	160
Maternal Night,	*Jacque,*	192
Morning in May,	*Douglas,*	7
Morning Musings in the Highlands,	*Robertson,*	191
Mount Pilatus,	*Gilfillan,*	222
My Auld Grannie's Leather Pouch,	*Maclagan,*	209
My Auld Scottish Bonnet,	*Peacock,*	238
My Bairn,	*Imrie,*	203
My Bonnie Bit Lassie.	*Anderson,*	386
My Bonnie Rowan Tree,	*Crerar,*	295
My Father an' my Mither,	*John Paul,*	351
My First Saumon,	*Graham,*	148
My Friend,	*Murray,*	288
My Grannie's Bible,	*James Paul,*	363
Neil Gow's Farewell to Whisky,	*Lyon,*	410
Now Winter's Wind Sweeps,	*A. Campbell,*	94
Och, Hey, Hum,	*Mitchell,*	375
Oh, Never! No, Never!	*Oliphant,*	184
Oor Auld Wife,	*Ford,*	317
Oor Hoose at E'en,	*S. J. Stewart,*	313
Ossian's Grave,	*Wordsworth,*	416
Our Last Flittin',	*White,*	197
Our Little Jock,	*Stewart,*	151
Pibroch of Bonnie Strathearn,	*Kippen,*	286
Piper M'Nee,	*Farquharson,*	216
Piscator Dolorosus,	*Anton,*	332
Poor Anne,	*Lewis,*	407
Pursuit o' Prince Charlie,	*Spence,*	125
Quitting the Manse,	*Sandeman,*	186
Receive, Resign, Restore,	*M. F. Barbour,*	261
Rob Roy's Grave,	*Wordsworth,*	412
Row Weel, my Boatie,	*A. Campbell,*	94
Ruth,	*Sir W. S. Maxwell,*	240
St. Johnstoun's Bells,	*Clyde,*	136
Scotland, Land of Liberty,	*Edwards,*	359
Scottish Song of Victory,	*Macnaughton,*	231
Shallum,	*Sir W. S. Maxwell,*	243
Since Loyalty is still the Same,	*Robertson,*	49
Sing, Little Bird,	*Steven,*	265
Sir James the Rose,	*Anon.,*	37
Song of the Royal Highland Regiment,	*Maclaggan,*	89
Song of the Tay,	*Ferguson,*	307
Sonnet: Scottish Heather,	*M. B. White,*	384
Sonnet: To a favourite Evening Retreat,	*Main,*	332
Sonnet: To Chaucer,	*Main,*	331
Strathallan's Lament,	*Burns,*	395
Sunlicht an' Munelicht,	*Pyott,*	344
Tak it, Man, Tak it,	*Webster,*	139

CONTENTS.

		PAG
Tayis Bank,	Anon.,	1
That Horn Spoon the Tinkler made,	Mitchell,	37
The Athol Gathering,	Anon.,	6
The Auld Carle's Courtship,	Norval,	28
The Auld Craw's Lament,	Taylor,	29
The Auld House,	Baroness Nairne,	10
The Banks of Allan Water,	Lewis,	40
The Battle of Corriemuckloch,	Anon.,	24
The Battle of Luncarty,	Vedder,	42
The Battle of Sheriffmuir,	M'Lennan,	5
The Birks of Aberfeldy,	Burns,	39
The Birks of Invermay,	Mallet,	6
The Birks o' Invermay,	Anon.,	7
The Blind Exile's Return,	Macnaughton,	23
The Bonnie Banks o' Fordie,	Anon.,	2
The Bonnie Burnie,	Mackay,	22
The Bonnie Earl of Moray,	Anon.,	4
The Bonnie Lass o' Levenside,	Drummond,	13
The Bonnie Wee Rose Bud,	Agnew,	14
The Bower of Tay,	Hogg,	40
The Braes abune Stobha',	Ford,	31
The Braes o' Balquhither,	Tannahill,	40
The Braes o' Mount Blair,	A. Fergusson,	30
The Braes roun' aboot Auchterairder,	Neish,	38
The Brooch of Lorn,	Scott,	40
The Burnie's Sang,	Neish,	38
The City Pent,	W. Nicoll,	17
The Croaker,	James Paul,	36
The Darwinian Theory,	Young,	26
The Deil and M'Ommie,	Sim,	9
The Deil's Stane,	D. M. Smith,	32
The Duke o' Athol's Nurse,	Anon.,	3
The Eirlic Well,	Crerar,	26
The English Knight,	Norval,	28
The Faithful Swain,	Spence,	1
The Fate of the Looking-Glass,	Robertson,	
The Flower o' Dunblane,	Tannahill,	4
The Folk o' Ochtergaen,	Nicoll,	1
The Forsaken,	Nicoll,	1
The Frozen Burn,	Whittet,	2
The Garb of Old Gaul,	Sir Harry Erskine(?)	
The Garb of Old Gaul,	Anon.,	
The Gathering of the Hays,	Anon.,	
The Goldfinch's Nest,	Beattie,	1
The Graces' Spell,	Tovani,	3
The Gude Wallace,	Anon.,	
The Hero of Barossa,	Duff,	1
The Hills o' Breadalbane,	Maclagan,	21
The Holocaust of the Witch of Monzie,	Blair,	28
The Hundred Pipers,	Baroness Nairne,	11

The Iron Horse,	*Balfour,*	246
The Kilted Hielandmen,	*J. Campbell,*	198
The Laird o' Cockpen,	*Baroness Nairne,*	102
The Lament of Benedict, the Married Man,	*Nicoll,*	172
The Land o' the Leal,	*Baroness Nairne,*	99
The Lass o' Glenshee,	*Anon.,*	146
The Lass o' Gowrie,	*Anon.,*	116
The Lass o' Gowrie,	*Col. Ramsay,*	117
The Lass o' Gowrie,	*Baroness Nairne,*	118
The Last Adieu to the Hills,	*Macintyre,*	84
The Lauch in the Sleeve,	*Anton,*	335
The Lofty Lomonds,	*Norval,*	282
"The Lord is my Shepherd,"	*Macduff,*	245
The Macgregor's Gathering,	*Scott,*	402
The Maiden wha shore in the Bandwin' wi' me,	*W. Robertson,*	328
The Maid of Isla's Lament,	*A. Fergusson,*	302
The Muir o' Gorse and Broom,	*Nicoll,*	169
The Muses Threnodie,	*Adamson,*	1
Then and Now,	*Sandeman,*	187
The Old Hearse,	*Jacque,*	193
The Past,	*Anderson,*	258
The Poet's Grave,	*W. Nicoll,*	175
The Power of Love,	*Anderson,*	257
The Priest o' Kinfauns,	*Millar,*	182
The Queen's Visit,	*S. Fergusson,*	272
The Rainbow,	*Beattie,*	145
The Romance of the Rose,	*Anderson,*	369
The Rose,	*Richardson,*	76
The Rowan Tree,	*Baroness Nairne,*	113
The Scottish Plaid,	*Murray,*	287
The Skull,	*Buchanan,*	81
The Spring Lark,	*Beattie,*	143
The Summons of Love,	*Cromb,*	320
The Sunday Cough,	*Anderson,*	259
The Sunny Side,	*S. J. Stewart,*	314
The Sun's on the Heather,	*James Craig,*	350
The Tailor o' Monzie,	*Stewart,*	155
The Tay,	*Millar,*	180
The Tollman's Lament,	*John Craig,*	345
The Toun where I was Born,	*Nicoll,*	166
The Twa Bumbees,	*Spence,*	126
The Valley of the Earn,	*Nelson,*	204
The Valley of the Shadow,	*Geddes,*	336
The Viking's Bride,	*R. M. Fergusson,*	366
The Weary Coble o' Cargill (*Old*),	*Anon.,*	21
The Weary Coble o' Cargill (*Modern*),	*Anon.,*	24
The Weaver's Bairn,	*Pringle,*	356
The Wheel of Life,	*Robertson,*	48

CONTENTS.

		PAGE
The Wifie o' Cargill,	A. Fergusson,	301
The Windy Gowl,	J. Smith,	304
The Wisdom o' my Granny,	Farquharson,	218
The Witch on the Brae,	W. Stewart,	250
The Wounded Soldier,	J. J. S. Stewart,	303
The Wraith o' Garry Water,	Mackay,	227
Tibby and the Laird,	Maclagan,	212
To Wordsworth,	M. B. White,	384
Tullymet,	Ferguson,	309
Turlum,	Dryerre,	321
Twa Auld Fouk,	Dryerre,	323
Twilights,	R. W. Barbour,	355
Wearied and Worn,	J. Campbell,	199
"Weel thro' the Valley,"	Mitchell,	377
We'll Hunker Doon to Nane,	J. Smith,	306
We'll mak' the Warld better yet,	Nicoll,	174
We're a' a'e Mither's Bairns,	Peacock,	236
Whaur Shaggie Sings,	Edwards,	360
When ye gang awa', Jamie,	Anon.,	121
William and Margaret,	Mallet,	71
Willie's Hay Stack,	Gairns,	188
Will ye go to Sheriffmuir,	Anon.,	63
Wi' the Pipers,	Taylor,	298
Ye'll Mount, Gudeman,	Baroness Nairne,	107

BIOGRAPHICAL NOTICES OF PERTHSHRIE POETS.

	PAGE
ADAMSON, HENRY,	429
AGNEW, PETER,	431
ANDERSON, Rev. JOHN, D.D.,	432
ANDERSON, JOHN,	434
ANTON, Rev. PETER,	434
BALFOUR, CHARLES,	435
BARBOUR, Mrs. M. F.,	436
BARBOUR, Rev. ROBERT W.,	438
BARCLAY, Rev. JOHN,	439
BEATTIE, JAMES,	440
BLAIR, Rev. GEORGE,	441
BLAIR, Rev. WILLIAM, D.D.,	441
BUCHANAN, DUGALD,	442
BUCHANAN, FRANCIS,	443
CAMPBELL, ALEXANDER,	444
CAMPBELL, JOHN ("Will Harrow,").	445
CLYDE, WILLIAM,	446
CRAIG, JAMES,	447

CONTENTS.

	PAGE
CRAIG, JOHN,	447
CRERAR, DUNCAN MACGREGOR,	448
CROMB, JAMES,	450
DOUGLAS, GAVIN,	451
DRUMMOND, DAVID,	452
DRYERRE, HENRY,	452
DUFF, JAMES,	454
EDWARDS, THOMAS,	454
FARQUHARSON, FINLAY,	455
FERGUSSON, ALEXANDER,	456
FERGUSON, JAMES,	457
FERGUSSON, Rev. R. M., M.A.,	458
FERGUSSON, Rev. SAMUEL,	459
FORD, ROBERT,	461
FRASER, PETER GALLOWAY,	461
GAIRNS, ROBERT,	462
GEDDES, JAMES Y.,	463
GILFILLAN, Rev. GEORGE,	464
GRAHAM, WILLIAM, LL.D.,	466
GRAY, CHRISTIAN,	467
IMRIE, DAVID,	468
JACQUE, Rev. GEORGE,	468
KING, JESSIE MARGARET,	469
KIPPEN, DUNCAN,	469
M'CULLOCH, JOHN,	471
MACDUFF, Rev. J. R., D.D.,	471
MACINTYRE, DUNCAN,	472
MACKAY, CHARLES, LL.D.,	474
MACLAGAN, ALEXANDER,	475
MACLAGGAN, JAMES,	476
M'NAUGHTON, PETER,	476
MAIN, DAVID M.,	477
MALLET, DAVID,	478
STIRLING-MAXWELL, Sir WILLIAM, Bart.,	480
MERCER, GRÆME REID,	481
MILLAR, DAVID,	482
MITCHELL, Rev. D. G.,	484
MURRAY, WILLIAM,	485
NAIRNE, CAROLINA BARONESS,	486
NEISH, WILLIAM,	489
NELSON, JOHN,	489
NICOL, ALEXANDER,	489
NICOLL, ROBERT,	491
NICOLL, WILLIAM,	494
NORVAL, PETER,	495
OLIPHANT, CAROLINE, The Younger,	496
PAUL, Rev. JAMES,	497
PAUL, JOHN,	497
PEACOCK, JOHN MACLEAY,	498
PRINGLE, ALICE,	499

	PAGE
PYOTT, WILLIAM,	499
RICHARDSON, WILLIAM,	500
ROBERTSON, ALEXANDER,	500
ROBERTSON, WILLIAM (p. 192),	501
ROBERTSON, WILLIAM (p. 330),	501
SANDEMAN, MARGARET STEWART,	502
SAUNDERS, D. H.,	504
SCOTT, ALEXANDER M.,	504
SHAIN, JAMES C.,	504
SHARPE, ANDREW,	505
SIM, JAMES,	505
SMITH, DAVID MITCHELL,	506
SMITH, JOHN,	507
SPENCE, CHARLES,	508
STEVEN, THOMAS,	509
STEWART, JAMES,	510
STEWART, JOHN JOSEPH SMALE,	512
STEWART, SARAH JANE,	512
STEWART, WILLIAM,	513
TAYLOR, JOHN,	514
TOVANI, WILLIAM THOMAS,	515
WEBSTER, DAVID,	515
WHITE, M. BUCHANAN,	516
WHITE, JOHN, LL.D.,	516
WHITTET, ROBERT,	517
WILSON, WILLIAM,	517
YOUNG, JOHN,	519

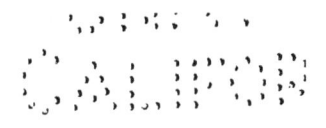

THE HARP OF PERTHSHIRE.

THE MUSES THRENODIE.

AN EXTRACT.

Now must I mourn for GALL, since he is gone,
And ye, my Gabions, help me him to mone;
And in your courses sorrow for his sake,
Whose matchless Muse immortal did you make.
Who now shall pen your praise and make you knowne?
By whom now shall your virtues be forth showne?
Who shall declare your worth? Is any able?
Who dare to meddle with Apelles' table?*

Ah me! there's none: And is there none indeed?
Then must ye mourn, of force, there's no remeed:
And I, for my part, with you, in my turne,
Shall keep a doleful consort whilst ye mourne:
And thus, with echoing voice, shall howl and cry,
Gall, sweetest Gall, what ailèd thee to die?

Now first my Bowes begin this dolefull song:
No more with clangors let your shafts be flung

---

* Apelles was a celebrated painter in the days of Alexander the Great, who would allow no other painter to draw his portrait; he lelt an imperfect picture of Venus; no painter would venture to finish it.—*Cant.*

In fields abroad, but in my cabine stay,
And help me for to mourn till dying day.
With dust and cobwebs cover all your heads,
And take you to your matins and your beads:
A requiem sing unto that sweetest soul,
Which shines now sainted above other pole.
And ye, my clubs, you must no more prepare
To make your balls flee whistling in the air:
But hing your heads, and bow your crooked crags,
And dress you all in sackcloath and in rags
No more to see the sun, nor fertile fields,
But closely keep you mourning in your bields;
And for your part the treble do you take,
And when you cry, make all your crags to crake,
And shiver, when you sing, alas! for Gall!
Ah! if our mourning might thee now recall!

And ye, my loadstones of Lednochian lakes,*
Collected from the loughs, where watrie snakes
Do much abound, take unto you a part,
And mourn for Gall, who loved you with his heart.
In this sad dump and melancholick mood,
The burdown ye must bear, not on the flood
Or frozen watrie plaines, but let your tuning
Come help me for to weep by mournfull cruning.
And ye, the rest, my Gabions less and more,
Of noble kind, come help me for to roare!
And of my woefull weeping take a part,
Help to declare the dolour of mine heart:
How can I choose, but mourne? when I think on
Our games, Olympick-like, in times agone.
Chiefly wherein our cunning we did try,
And matchless skill in noble archerie.
In these, our days, when archers did abound

---

* Lednoch is situated about four computed miles north from Perth, on the banks of Almond river: about this place the best curling-stones were found. The gentlemen of Perth, fond of this athletic winter diversion on the frozen river, sent and brought from Lednoch their curling-stones.—*Cant.*

In Perth, then famous for such pastimes found :
Among the first, for archers we were known,
And for that art our skill was loudly blown :
What time Perth's credit did stand with the best
And bravest archers this land hath possesst.*
We spar'd nor gaines nor paines for to report
To Perth the worship, by such noble sport ;
Witness the links of Leith, where Cowper, Grahame,
And Stewart won the prize, and brought it home ;
And in these games did offer ten to three
There to contend : *Quorum pars magni fui.*

I mourn, good Gall, when I think on that stead,
Where yee did hail your shaft unto the head ;
And with a strong and steadfast eye and hand,
So valiantly your bow yee did command ;
A sliddrie shaft forth of its forks did fling,
Clank gave the bow, the whistling air did ring,
The bowlt did cleave the clouds, and threat the skyes,
And thence down falling to the mark it flies.
 *   *   *   *   *
What shall be said of other martial games ?
None was inlaking from whence bravest stemmes ;
Victorious trophees, palmes, and noble pynes,
Olives, and lawrels, such as aunceint times
Decor'd the Grecian victors in their playes,
And worthie Romanes in their brave assayes,
For tryal of their strength each match'd the other,
Whose beauty was, sweat mixed with dust together :
Such exercises did content us more,
Than if we had possess'd King Crœsus' store.
But O ! ye fields, my native Perth neerby,

---

* Archerie, of which the gentlemen of Perth were great masters, was made an indispensable article of education from the days of James the First. (Guthrie's History). This most accomplished and wise prince passed an act, forbidding the favorite diversion of foot-ball, substituting in its place that of shooting with bows and arrows. Every boy, when he came to the age of thirteen, was obliged at stated times to practice archerie at certain bow-marks : there is a piece of ground without the north port, on the left of the road leading to Huntingtower, called the Bow-butt, where this exercise was practised.—*Cant.*

Prays you to speak, and truly testifie:
What matchless skill we prov'd in all these places,
Within the compass of three thousand paces
On either side, while as we went a-shooting,
And strongly strove who should bring home the booting,
Alongst the flowrie banks of Tay to Almond :
Ay when I hit the mark I cast a gamound ;
And there we view the place where sometime stood
The ancient Bertha, now o'erflow'd with flood
Of mighty waters, and that princely hold
Where dwelt King William, by the stream down rol'd,
Was utterly defaced, and overthrown,
That now the place thereof can scarce be known : *
Then through these haughs of fair and fertile ground,
Which, with fruit trees, with corns and flocks abound,
Meand'ring rivers, sweet flowres, heavenly honey,
More for our pastime than to conquesh money :
We went a-shooting both through plain and park,
And never stayed till we came to Lows-wark :
Built by our mighty Kings for to preserve us,
That henceforth waters should not drown, but serve us ;
Yet condescending, it admits one rill,
Which all these plains with christal brooks doth fill ;
And by a conduit, large three miles in length,
Serves to make Perth impregnable for strength,
At all occasions when her clowses fall,
Making the water mount up to her wall.

---

* About the year one thousand, two hundred and ten, Berth, or Bertha, which stood near to the river Tay, about two English miles north from Perth, was destroyed in the night-time by a very great inundation. So violent was the torrent, that the whole town was undermined, the houses levelled, and many persons of both sexes lost their lives. The royal palace did not escape. The King's youngest son John, with his nurse, were carried down the river and drowned, with about fourteen of the King's domesticks. William the First, surnamed the Lyon, did not long survive the catastrophe, for he dyed A.D. 1214. He laid the foundation of the present town of Perth, and endowed it with ample privileges, which were confirmed by the succeeding monarchs, with many additional privileges, and was the first royal burgh of the kingdom. The Kings of Scotland preceding James the Second were crowned at Scone, and resided at Perth, as the metropolis of the nation.—*Cant.*

When we had viewed this mighty work at Randon,
We thought it best these fields for to abandon.*
And turning home, we spared nor dyke nor fowsie,
Untill we came unto the Boot of Bowsie ; †
Alongst this aqueduct, and there our station
We made, and viewed Balhousie's situation.

O'erlooking all that spacious pleasant valley,
With flowers damasked, levell as an alley,
Betwixt and Perth, thither did we repair,
(For why the season was exceeding fair :)
Then all alongst this valley did we hye,
And there the place we clearly did espye,
The precinct, situation, and the stead,
Where ended was that cruel bloody fead
Between these cursed clans Chattan and Kay,
Before King Robert John, upon the day
Appointed, then and there, who did convene
Thirty 'gainst thirty, matched upon that greene,
Of martial fellows, all in raging mood,
Like furious Ajax, or Orestes wood ;
Alonely arm'd with long two-handed swords,
Their sparkling eyes cast fire instead of words ;
Their horride beards, thrown browes, brustled mustages,
Of deadly blows t' inshew, were true presages.

Thus standing, fortunes event for to try,
And thousands them beholding, one did cry,
With loud and mighty voice, " Stay ! hold your hands !

---

* Lowswark, about half-a-mile north-west from Ruthven Castle, now Huntingtower, is a very fine stone building which turns part of the river into an aqueduct that descended and washed the walls of Perth. The citizens of Perth, on any emergency, by means of sluices, filled the ditch without the walls to a great height, and rendered the city almost impregnable before the invention of fire-arms. The aqueduct serves to turn the flower, barley, malt, and snuff-mills of the town of Perth. —*Cant.*

† The boot, or boult of Balhousie, is a strong stone-work on the east bank of the aqueduct, in which is a round hole with a ring of iron at both ends, thirty-two inches round, for conveying water from the aqueduct to the mill of Balhousie, by contract and agreement betwixt the Eviots of Balhousie and the town of Perth.—*Cant.*

A little space, we pray, the case thus stands:
One of our number is not here to-day."
This sudden speech did make some little stay
Of this most bloody bargain, th' one party fight
Would not, unless the number were made right
Unto the adverse faction; nor was any
That would take it in hand among so many
Beholders of all ranks, into that place
On th' other side; none would sustain disgrace,
To be debarred from his other fellowes,
He rather hung seven years upon the gallawes.

Thus, as the question stood, was found at length
One Henrie Winde, for tryal of his strength
The charge would take; a sadler of his craft,
I wot not well, whether the man was daft;
But for an half French crown he took in hand
Stoutly to fight so long as he might stand;
And if to be victorious should betide him,
They should some yearly pension provide him.
The bargaine holds; and then with all their maine
Their braikens buckled to the fight again;
Incontinent the trumpets loudlie sounded,
And mightilie the great bagpipes were winded:
Then fell they to 't as fierce as any thunder,
From shoulders arms, and heads from necks they sunder,
All raging there in blood, they hew'd and hash'd,
Their skincoats with the new cut were outslashed;
And scorning death, so bravely did outfight it,
That the beholders greatlie were affrighted;
But chiefly this by all men was observed,
None fought so fiercely, nor so well deserved
As this their hired souldier, Henrie Winde,
For by his valour victory inclinde
Unto that side; and ever since those dayes
This proverb current goes, when any sayes-
How come you here? this answer doth he finde,
I'm for mine owne hand, as fought Henrie Winde.
So finely fought he, ten with him escap't,

And of the other but one, in flood who leap't
And sav'd himself by swimming over Tay,
But to speak more of this we might not stay.*
HENRY ADAMSON.

MORNING IN MAY.

As fresh Aurore, to mighty Tithon spouse,
Ished of her saffron bed and ivor house,
In cram'sy clad and grained violate,
With sanguine cape, and selvage purpurate,
Unshet the windows of her large hall,
Spread all with roses, and full of balm royal,
And eke the heavenly portis chrystalline
Unwarps braid, the warld till illumine;
The twinkling streamers of the orient
Shed purpour spraings, with gold and azure ment.
Eons, the steed, with ruby harness red,
Above the seas liftis furth his head,
Of colour sore, and somedeal brown as berry,
For to alichten and glad our emispery;
The flame out-bursten at the neisthrils,
So fast Phaeton with the whip him whirls.

---

* Buchanan informs us that, in the sixth year of the reign of Robert the Third, there was irreconcilable enmity betwixt the M'Intoshes and M'Kays, two powerful and fierce clans. The King sent the Earls of Dunbar and Crawfurd with an army to reduce them to order. They wisely tried to make up the matter, by proposing to the chiefs to pick out thirty men on each side, and decide the quarrel on the North Inch of Perth, in presence of the King, and they undertook that the conquering party should be honoured by him. They accepted the proposals, thirty on each side were chosen by their chieftains; they met in a place surrounded by a deep trench, around which galleries were built for the spectators. When they were ready to engage, one of the M'Intoshes was seiz'd with a panick and hid himself. This accident stop'd them, till Henrie Winde, a sadler in Perth, advanced and offered to supply his place for half a French gold-dollar. The terms were accepted: the combat began, and was carried on with redoubled fury on both sides, untill twenty-nine of the M'Kays were killed. The remaining one unwounded, wisely judging that he could not resist the impetuosity of Henrie Winde, and ten M'Intoshes who were left alive, jump'd into the River Tay, swam to the other side, and escaped.—*Cant.*

·　　　·　　　·　　　·　　　·　　　·
While shortly, with the bleezand torch of day
Abulyit in his lemand fresh array,
Forth of his palace royal ishit Phœbus,
With golden crown and visage glorious,
Crisp hairs, bricht as chrysolite or topaz,
For whase hue micht nane behald his face.

　　·　　　·　　　·　　　·　　　·
The auriate vanes of his throne soverane
With glitterand glance o'erspread the occane:
The largè fludes, lemand all of licht,
But with ane blink of his supernal sicht.
For to behald it was ane glore to see,
The stabled windis, and the calmed sea,
The soft season, the firmament serene,
The loune illuminate air and firth amene.

　　·　　　·　　　·　　　·　　　·
And lusty Flora did her bloomis spread
Under the feet of Phœbus' sulyart-steed;
The swarded soil embrode with selcouth hues,
Wood and forest, obnumbrate with bews.

　　·　　　·　　　·　　　·　　　·
Towers, turrets, kirnals, and pinnacles hie,
Of kirks, castles, and ilk fair citie,
Stude painted, every fane, phiol, and stage,
Upon the plain ground by their awn umbrage.
Of Eolus' north blasts havand no dreid,
The soil spread her braid bosom on-breid;
The corn-crops and the beir new-braird,
With gladsome garment revesting the yerd.

　　·　　　·　　　·　　　·　　　·　　　·
The prai besprent with springand sprouts despers
For caller humours on the dewy nicht,
Rendering some place the gerse-piles their licht;
As far as cattle the lang summer's day
Had in their pasture eat and nip away:
And blissful blossoms in the bloomed yerd,
Submit their heids to the young sun's safe-guard.
Ivy leaves rank o'erspread the barmkin wall;
The bloomed hawthorn clad his pikis all;

Furth of fresh bourgeons the wine grapes ying
Endland the trellis did on twistis hing;
The loukit buttons on the gemmed trees
O'erspreadand leaves of nature's tapestries;
Soft grassy verdure after balmy shouirs,
On curland stalkis smiland to their flouirs.

 . . . . .

The daisy did on-breid her crownal small,
And every flouer unlappit in the dale.

 . . . . .

Sere downis small on dentelion sprang,
The young green bloomed strawberry leaves amang;
Jimp jeryflouris thereon leaves unshet,
Fresh primrose and the purpour violet;

 . . . . .

Heavenly lilies, with lockerand toppis white,
Opened and shew their crestis redemite.

 . . . . .

Ane paradise it seemed to draw near
Thir galyard gardens and each green herbere
Maist amiable wax the ameraut meads;
Swarmis souchis through out the respand reeds.
Over the lochis and the fludis gray,
Searchand by kind ane place where they should lay.
Phoebus' red fowl, his cural crest can steer,
Oft streikand furth his heckle, crawand cleir.
Amid the wortis and the rutis gent
Pickand his meat in alleys where he went,
His wivis Toppa and Partolet him by—
A bird all-time that hauntis bigamy.
The painted powne pickand with plumes gym,
Kest up his tail ane proud plesand wheel-rim,
Ishrouded in his feathering bright and sheen,
Shapand the prent of Argus' hundred een.
Amang the bowis of the olive twists,
Sere small fowls, workand crafty nests,
Endlang the hedges thick, and on rank aiks
Ilk bird rejoicand with their mirthful maiks
In corners and clear fenestres of glass,
Full busily Arachne weavand was.

To knit her nettis and her wobbis slie,
Therewith to catch the little midge or flie.
So dusty powder upstours in every street,
While corby gaspit for the fervent heat.
Under the bowis bene in lufely vales,
Within fermance and parkis close of pales,
The busteous buckis rakis furth on raw,
Herdis of hertis through the thick wood-shaw.
The young fawns followand the dun daes,
Kids, skippand through, runnis after raes.
In leisurs and on leyis, little lambs
Full tait and trig socht bletand to their dams.
On salt streams wolk Dorida and Thetis,
By rinnand strandis, Nymphis and Naiadis,
Sic as we clepe wenches and damysels,
In gersy graves wanderand by spring wells;
Of bloomed branches and flouirs white and red,
Plettand their lusty chaplets for their head.
Some sang ring-songes, dances, leids, and rounds,
With voices shrill, while all the dale resounds,
Whereso they walk into their caroling,
For amorous lays does all the rockis ring.
Ane sang, "The ship sails over the salt faem,
Will bring the merchants and my leman hame."
Some other sings, "I will be blythe and licht,
My hert is lent upon so goodly wicht."
And thoughtful lovers rounis to and fro,
To leis their pain, and plein their jolly woe.
After their guise, now singand, now in sorrow,
With heartis pensive the lang summer's morrow.
Some ballads list indite of his lady;
Some livis in hope; and some all utterly
Despairit is, and sae quite out of grace
His purgatory he finds in every place.

. . . .

Dame Nature's menstrels, on that other part,
Their blissful lay intoning every art.

. . . . . .

And all small fowlis singis on the spray,
Welcome the lord of licht, and lampe of day,

Welcome fosterer of tender herbis green,
Welcome quickener of flourist flouirs sheen,
Welcome support of every rute and vein,
Welcome comfort of all kind fruit and grain,
Welcome the birdis bield upon the breir,
Welcome master and ruler of the year,
Welcome wellfare of husbands at the plews,
Welcome repairer of woods, trees, and bews,
Welcome depainter of the bloomit meads,
Welcome the life of everything that spreads,
Welcome storer of all kind bestial,
Welcome be thy bricht beamis gladdand all.

. . . . .

GAVIN DOUGLAS.

KING HART.*

AN ALLEGORICAL POEM.

(Extract from Canto First.)

KING HART, into his cumlie castell strang,
   Closit about with craft and meikill ure,
So seimlie wes he set his folk amang,
   That he no doubt had of misaventure;

---

* This was the celebrated Bishop of Dunkeld's first work of any extent, and it is impossible, as Mr. Fraser Tytler remarks, to give an analysis of it in more striking language than the author's own. "The hart of man," says he, "beand his maist noble part, and the fountain of his life," is here put for man in general, and holds the chief place in the poem under the title of "King Hart." This mystical king is first represented in the bloom of youth, with his lusty attendants, the attributes of qualities of youth. Next is pictured forth the Palace of Pleasure, near by the castle of King Hart, with its lovely inhabitants. Queen Pleasance, with the help of her ladies, assails King Hart's castle, and takes him and most of his servitors prisoners. Pity at last releases them, and they assail the Queen Pleasance, and vanquish her and her ladies in their turn. King Hart then weds Queen Pleasance, and solaces himself long in her delicious castle. So far is man's dealing with pleasure; but now, when King Hart is past mid-eild, comes another scene. For Age, arriving at the castle of Queen Pleasance, with whom King Hart dwelt ever since his marriage with her,

So proudlie was he polist, plaine, and pure,
With youtheid and his lustie levis grene;
So fair, so fresche, so liklie to endure,
And als so blyth, as bird in symmer schene.

For wes he nevir yit with schouris schot,
Nor yit our run with rouk, or ony rayne;
In all his lusty lecam nocht ane spot;
Na never had experience into payne,
But alway into lyking mocht to layne;
Onlie to love, and verrie gentilnes,
He wes inclynit cleinlie to remane,
And woun under the wyng of wantownes.

Yit wes this wourthy wicht king under ward;
For wes he nocht at fredom utterlie.
Nature had lymmit folk, for thair reward,
This gudlie king to governe and to gy;
For so thai kest thair tyme to occupy.
In welthis for to wyne for thai him teitchit;
All lustis for to love, and underly,
So prevelie thai preis him and him preitchit.

First war thair *Strenth*, and *Rage*, and *Wantounes*,
Grein *Lust, Disport, Jelosy,* and *Invy;*
Freschnes, New Gate, Waist-gude, and *Wilfulnes,*
Delyvernes, Full-hardenes thairby:

---

insists for admittance, which he gains. So King Hart takes leave of Youthheid with much sorrow. Age is no sooner admitted than Conscience comes also to the castle and forces entrance, beginning to chide the King, whilst Wit and Reason take part in the conference. After this and other adventures, Queen Pleasance suddenly leaves the King, and Reason and Wisdom persuade King Hart to return to his own palace: that is, when pleasure and the passions leave man, reason and wisdom render him his own master. After some other matters, Decrepitude attacks and mortally wounds the King, who dies after making his testament.

"King Hart" abounds with much noble poetry, and one often forgets, in the vivid descriptions and stirring incidents, the moral aim of the author.

Gentrice, Fredome, Pitie, Privy espy
Want-wit, Vaingloir, Prodigalitie,
  Unrest, Nicht-walk, and felon *Gluttony ;*
Unricht, Dyme-sicht, with *Slicht,* and *Subtiltie.*

Thir war the inwarde ythand servitouris,
  Quhilk governours war to this nobil king;
And kepit him inclynit to thair curis.
  So wes thair nocht in erde that evir micht bring
  Ane of thir folk awa fra his dwelling,
Thus to thair terme thai serve for thair rewarde;
  Dansing, disporting, singing, revelling,
With *Bissines* all blyth to pleis the lairde.

This folk, with all the femell thai micht fang,
  Quhilk numerit ane milyon and weil mo,
That wer upbred as servitours of lang,
  And with this king wald woun, in weil and wo,
  For favour, nor for feid, wald found him fro;
Unto the tyme thair dait be run and past;
  That gold nor gude micht gar thame fro him go;
Nor greif, nor grane, suld grayth thame so agast.
                                        GAVIN DOUGLAS.

TAYIS BANK.*

QUHEN Tayis bank was blumyt brycht,
  With blosumes brycht and bred,
By that river that ran doun rycht
  Vndir the ryss I red;

---

*This is perhaps the oldest Perthshire ballad extant, and, like the minstrelsy of the olden time generally, is probably more a thing of actual history than a creature of the poet's imagination. It belongs to the latter end of the fifteenth or the early years of the sixteenth century, and is one of the most perfect lyrical specimens of its time. Its authorship has been attributed to King James IV., and the ascription is backed by some show of probability; the poetic fire was in his blood—the verses contain evidence of a high paternity—and whether himself the "makkar" or not, his Majesty is obviously the

The merle meltit with all her mycht
 And mirth in mornying maid,
Throw solace, sound, and semely sicht,
 Alswth a sang I said.

Vndir that bank, quhair bliss had bene,
 I bownit me to abyde;
Ane holene, hevinly hewit grene,
 Rycht heyndly did me hyd;
The sone schyne our the schawis schene
 Full semely me besyd;
In bed of blumes bricht besene
 A sleip cowth me ourslyd.

About all blumet was my bour
 With blosumes broun and blew,
Orfret with mony fair fresch flour,
 Helsum of hevinly hew;
With shakeris of the schene dew schour
 Schynnyng my courtenis schew,
Arrayit with a rich vardour
 Of natouris werkis new.

Rasing the birdis fra thair rest,
 The reid sun raiss with rawis;
The lark sang loud, quhill, liycht nycht lest
 A lay of luvis lawis;
The nythingall woik of hir nest
 Singing the day vpdawis;
The mirthfull maveiss merriest
 Schill schowttit throw the schawiss.

---

first person in the ballad. The ill-fated "Bonnie Margaret Drummond" is as obviously the heroine of the verses; and the beautiful banks of the river Tay in the vicinity of Stobball will henceforth possess an additional attraction for all who may here meet with the effusion for the first time. Our royal wooer, we can well imagine, while a guest at Stobhall, had stolen unobserved from the Castle to keep tryst with his *inamorata* in the sweet, inviting seclusion afforded by the wooded bank of the river, and impatient to enjoy unfettered admiration of his "dyament of delyt," as he calls her, within "that semely schaw," he had gone early, and wiled away the laggard moments inditing verses to his mistress's eyebrows.

All flouris grew that firth within,
    That cowth haif in mynd;
And in that flud all fische with fyn,
    That creat wer be kynd;
Vnder the rise the ra did ryn,
    Our ron, our rute, our rynd,
The dvn deir dansit with a dyn,
    And herdis of hairt and hynd.

Wod winter with his wallow and wynd,
    But weir, away wes went;
Brasit about with wyld wodbynd
    Wer bewis on the bent;
Allone vndar the lusty lynd
    I saw ane lusum lent
That fairly war so fare to fynd
    Vnder the firmament.

Scho wes the lustiest on lyve,
    Allone lent on a land,
And fairest figuor, be set, Syve,
    That evir in firth I fand,
Her comely cullour to discryve
    I dar nocht tak on hand;
Moir womanly borne of a wyfe
    Wes neuer, I dar warrand.

To creatur that wes in cair,
    Or cauld of crewelty,
A blicht blenk of her vesage bair
    Of baill his bute mycht be;
Hir hyd, her hew, her hevinly hair
    Mycht havy hairtis uphie;
So angelik vnder the air
    Neuir wicht I saw with E.

The blosumes that were blycht and brycht
    By hir wer blacht and blew;
Scho gladit all the foull of flicht
    That in the forrest flew;

Scho mycht haif comfort king or knicht
    That ever in cuntre I knew,
As waill, and well of warldly wicht
    In womanly vertew.

Hir cullour cleir, hir countinance,
    Hir cumly cristell ene,
Hir portratour of most plesance,
    All pictour did prevene.
Off every vertew to avance
    Quhen ladies prasit bene,
Rychtest in my remembrance
    That rose is rutit grene.

This myld, meik mensuet Mergrite,
    This perle polist most quhyte,
Dame Natouris deir dochter discreit,
    The dyament of delyt;
Never formit wes to found on feit
    Ane figour more perfyte.
Nor non on mold that did hir meit,
    Mycht mend hir wirth a myte.

This myrthfull maid to meit I went,
    And merkit furth on mold;
Bot sone within a wane sho went,
    Most hevinly to behold;
The bricht sone with his bemys blent
    Vpoun the bertis bold,
Farest vnder the firmament
    That formit wes on fold.

A paradyce that place but peir
    Wes plesant to my sicht;
Of forrest, and of fresch reveir,
    Of firth, and fowll of flicht,
Of birdis, bath on bonk and breir,
    With blumes breck and bricht
As hevin in to this erd doun heir,
    Hertis to hald on hicht,

So went this womanly away
    Amang thir woddis wyd,
And I to heir thir birdis gay
    Did in a bonk abyd ;
Qubair ron and ryss raiss in aray
    Endlang the reuer syd ;
This hapnit me in a time in May
    In till a morning tyd.

The reuer throw the ryse cowth rowt,
    And roseris raiss on raw ;
The schene birdis full schill cowth schowt
    Into that semely schaw ;
Joy was within and joy without,
    Vnder that vnlenkest waw,
Quhair Tay ran down with stremis stout
    Full strecht vnder Stobschaw.

                                  ANONYMOUS.

THE GUDE WALLACE.*

WALLACE wicht upon a nicht,
    Cam' riding ower a linn ;
And he has to his leman's bouir,
    And tirl'd at the pin.

"O sleep ye, or wake ye, lady ?" he cried,
    "Ye'll rise and let me in."
"O wha is this at my bouir-door,
    That knocks, and knows my name ?"
"My name is William Wallace,
    Ye may my errand ken."

---

* The heroic Wallace was doubtless the subject of many ballads and songs that have been lost in the lapse of ages. A fragment of the present one originally appeared in Johnson's *Museum*. The subject will be found in the filth book of Blind Harry's *Wallace*, where Lochmaben, in Dumfriesshire, is cited as the scene where the incidents occurred. Perth, where the liberator was much in evidence, may, nevertheless, be the real ground of the ballad.

"The truth to you I will rehearse—
　　The secret I'll unfauld ;
Into your enemies hand this night,
　　I fairly hae you sauld."

"If that be true ye tell to me,
　　Do ye repent it sair ? "
"Oh, that I do, dear Wallace,
　　And will do evermair.

"The English did surround my house,
　　And forcit me theretill ;
But for your sake, my dear Wallace,
　　I could burn on a hill."

Then he gae her a loving kiss,
　　The tear drapt frae his e'e
Says, "Fare-ye-weel for evermair,
　　Your face nae mair I'll see."

She dress'd him in her ain claithing,
　　And frae her house he came ;
Which made the Englishman admire
　　To see sic a stalwart dame.

Now Wallace to the Hielands went,
　　Where meat nor drink had he ;
Said, "Fa' me life, or fa' me death,
　　To some town I maun drie."

He steppit ower the river Tay—
　　On the North Inch steppit he ;
And there he saw a weel-faur'd May,
　　Was washing aneath a tree.

"What news, what news, ye weel-faur'd May ?
　　What news hae ye to me ?
What news, what news, ye weel-faur'd May,
　　What news in the South countrie ? "

"O see ye, sir, yon hostler-house,
    That stands on yonder plain,
This very day have landed in it
    Full fifteen Englishmen,

"In search of Wallace, our champion,
    Intending he should dee!"
"Then, by my sooth," says Wallace wicht,
    "These Englishmen I'se see.

"If I had but in my pocket
    The worth of a single pennie,
It's I wad to the hostler-house
    These gentlemen to see."

She put her hand in her pocket,
    And pull'd out half a-cronn,
Says, "Tak ye that, ye belted knicht,
    And pay your lawin' doun."

As he went frae the weel-faur'd May
    A beggar bold met he,
Was cover'd wi' a clouted cloak,
    In his hand a trustie tree.

"What news, what news, ye silly auld man?
    What news hae ye to gie?"
"Nae news, nae news, ye belted knicht,
    Nae news hae I to thee;
But fifteen lords in the hostler-house,
    Waiting Wallace for to see."

"Ye'll lend to me your clouted cloak,
    That covers ye frae heid to shie;
And I'll go to the hostler-house,
    To ask for some supplie."

Now he's gane to the West-muir wood,
    And pull'd a trustie tree;
And then he's to the hostler-house,
    Asking there for charitie.

Doun the stair the captain comes,
　　The puir man for to see,
"If ye be captain as gude's you look,
　　Ye'll gie me some supplie."

"Where were ye born, ye cruikit carle?
　　Where, and in what countrie?"
"In fair Scotland, sir, was I born,
　　Cruikit carle as ye ca' me."

"O I wad give ye fifty pounds
　　Of gold and white monie;
O I wad give ye fifty pounds,
　　If Wallace ye wad let me see."

"Tell doun your money," quo' the cruikit carle,
　　"Tell doun your money good;
I'm sure I have it in my pouir,
　　And ne'er had a better bode."

The money was told upon the table,
　　Of silver pounds fiftie;
"Now here I stand!" quo' the gude Wallace,
　　And his cloak frae him gar'd flee.

He slew the captain where he stood;
　　The rest they did quake and rair;
He slew the rest around the room,
　　Syne ask'd were there ony mair.

"Get up, get up, gudewife," he says,
　　"And get me some dinner in haste,
For it soon will be three lang days' time,
　　Sin' a bit o' meat I did taste."

The dinner was na well readie,
　　Nor yet on the table set,
When other fifteen Englishmen
　　Were lichtit at the yett.

"Come out, come out, thou traitor Wallace,
    For this day ye maun dee!"
"I lippen nae sae little to God," he says,
    "Though I be but ill wordie."

The gudewife had an auld gudeman,
    By gude Wallace he stiffly stude,
Till ten o' the fifteen Englishmen
    Lay weltering in their blood.

The other five he took alive,
    To the greenwood as they ran;
And he has hang'd them, but mercie,
    Up heich upon a grain.

Now he is on the North Inch gane,
    Where the May wash'd tenderlie;
And "By my sooth," said the gude Wallace,
    "It's been a sair day's wark to me."

He's put his hand in his pocket,
    And pull'd out twenty pounds;
Says, "Tak' ye that, ye weel-faur'd May,
    For the gude luck o' your half-cronn."

Full five-and-twenty men he slew,
    Five hang'd upon a grain;
On the morn he sat wi' his merry men a',
    In Lochmaben toun at dine.

                              ANONYMOUS.

THE WEARY COBLE O' CARGILL.[*]

DAVID DRUMMOND'S destinie,
    Gude man o' appearance o' Cargill,
I wat this bluid rins in the flude
    Sae sair against his parents' will.

---

[*] This fine old ballad was first printed by William Motherwell in his *Minstrelsy, Ancient and Modern*, who had it from the recitation of an old woman then residing in the neighbourhood of Cambus

She was the lass o' Ballathy toun,
   And he the butler o' Stobhall,
And mony a time she wauked late
   To bore the Coble o' Cargill.

His bed was made in Kercock ha',
   O' gude clean sheets and o' the hay,
He wadna rest a'e nicht therein,
   But on the proud waters he wad gae.

Michael, in the parish of St. Martins. In Motherwell's opinion it possesses the elements of good poetry, and he adds that, had it fallen into the hands of those who make no scruple of interpolating and corrupting the text of oral song, it might have been made, with little trouble, a very interesting and pathetic composition. According to tradition, the ill-fated hero of the ballad, who was a butler to Chancellor Drummond of Stobhall, had a leman, or sweetheart, in each of the two villages of Kercock and Ballathy, on the opposite side of the Tay, and it was on the occasion of his paying a visit to his Kercock love that she of Ballathie, in a frenzy of jealousy and revenge, scuttled the boat in which he was to recross the Tay to Stobhall. There are two versions of the ballad ; the original, recovered by Motherwell, and a modern improved version which has been seldom printed. A serious defect of the older copy is seen in the fact that it gives no reason *why* "the lass o' Ballathy toun" should have scuttled the boat in which her lover was to recross the river. It says "his bed was made in Kercock ha', o' gude clean sheets and o' the hay ;" but that can scarcely be regarded as sufficient cause for jealousy when it is immediately followed by the assurance that "he wadna rest a'e nicht therein, but on the proud waters he wad gae." The modern version wisely provides a *casus belli*.

David Drummond, the hero of the ballad, was, tradition says, the son of a certain John Drummond in Kercock, and that the heroine was named Jeanie Low, or Gow, and was daughter of the joiner of the *then* laird of Ballathy—hence her acquaintance with the fatal angur. Tradition further tells that the "lass of Ballathy toun" had no sooner "bored the coble in seven parts" than she relented the cruel deed, and hastened to fashion seven pins wherewith to plug the fatal holes ; but before her return with these her fickle lover had "put his feet into the boat" and left the shore, and she reached the bank of the river just in time to hear his cries for help, and witness the coble sinking in mid waters. She went out of her reason ; and the terrible cause of her mental derangement continued to pull at the tangled ends of her ravelled memory, she persistently made pins to the end of her days. Since her demise her patient ghost has "kept on the business ;" and there are people living who aver that "when winter nights are dark and drear" the ghost of "Pinnie" may still be heard on the banks of the Tay.

His bed was made in Ballathy toun,
 O' gude clean sheets and o' the strae,
But I wat it was far better made
 Into the bottom o' bonnie Tay.

She bored the Coble in seven parts,
 I wat her heart micht hae been sair,
For there she got the bonnie lad lost,
 Wi' the curly locks and the yellow hair.

He put his foot into the boat,
 He little thocht o' ony ill;
But before that he was mid waters,
 The weary Coble began to fill.

"Wae be to the lass o' Ballathy toun,
 I wat an ill death may she dee,
For she bored the Coble in seven parts,
 And let the waters perish me!

"Help! oh help! I can get nane,
 Nae help o' man can to me come,"
This was about his dying words,
 When he was chok'd up to the chin.

"Gae tell my father and my mother,
 It was naebody did me this ill,
I was a-going my ain errands
 Lost at the Coble o' bonnie Cargill."

She bored the boat in seven parts,
 I wat she bored it wi' gude will,
And there they got the bonnie lad's corpse
 In the kirk shot * o' bonnie Cargill.

Oh, a' the keys o' bonnie Stobhall,
 I wat they at his belt did hing;
But a' the keys o' bonnie Stobhall
 They now lie low into the stream.

---

* The fishing station almost opposite Ballathy House is still known as the Kirk Shot, and the inference here is that the salmon fishers brought the hero's body from the river in their net.

A braver page unto his age
   Ne'er set a foot upon the plain;
His father to his mother said,
   "Oh, sae sune's we've wanted him!"

I wat they had mair love than this
   When they were young and at the schule,
But for his sake she wauked late
   And bored the Coble o' bonnie Cargill.

"There's ne'er a clean sark gae on my back,
   Nor yet a kame gae in my hair;
There's neither coal nor candle licht
   Shine in my bower for evermair.

"At kirk or market I'se ne'er be at,
   Nor yet a blythe blink in my e'e;
There's ne'er a ane shall say to anither,
   That's the lassie gar'd the young man dee.

"Between the yetts o' bonnie Stobball
   And the Kirkstyle o' bonnie Cargill,
There is mony a man and mother's son,
   That was at my luve's burial."

ANONYMOUS.

THE WEARY COBLE O' CARGILL.

(MODERN VERSION.)

THE course o' true love ne'er runs smooth,
   So say the sages o' langsyne,
My waefu' tale upbears the truth—
   This weary, waefu' tale o' mine.

A youthfu' pair wha offer'd fair
   O' nuptial joy to drink their fill,
But ither drink for them was brewed
   Within the Coble o' Cargill.

The lad was Chanc'llor Drummond's page,
    When gude Earl James was wi' the King,
And a' the keys o' bonnie Stobha',
    I wat they at his belt did hing.

She was the belle o' Ballathie toun,
    O' lovers she had wile and will;
But sad her fate—she waukit late,
    And bor'd the Coble o' Cargill.

She bor'd the Coble in seven parts,
    Na doot her heart was sick and sair,
When there she sealed the laddie's fate,
    Wi' the curly locks and the yellow hair.

His bed was made in Kercock ha',
    O' gude clean sheets and o' the strae,
But he wadna' sleep a'e nicht therein,
    For a' a mither's lips could say.

He would across the flooded Tay,
    He wadna bruik o' ony ill,
And wi' wary step he bent his gaet,
    To the weary Coble o' Cargill.

Wi' youthfu' airm he grasped the oar,
    I trow he grasp'd it wi' gude will,
But e'er he was mid waters through
    The weary Coble began to fill.

He baled the boat wi' baith his hands,
    Forsooth he baled it heartily,
But augur's skaith soon stopped his breath,
    And gart the bonnie laddie dee.

"Oh, help, oh, help, I can get nane,
    Nae help o' man can come to me,
For the rollin' flow o' the burden'd stream
    Is hastenin' on my destiny.

"My bed was made in Kercock ha',
    O' gude clean sheets and o' the hay,
But gentler hands hae smooth'd the sands,
    And I maun sleep beneath the Tay.

"Gae hame and tell my parents baith
    I blame mysel' for a' this ill;
When waukin' late I met my fate
    By the weary Coble o' Cargill."

Deceitfu' barge, thy helpless charge,
    Is laid behind yon sacred fane,
Where vesper bell and native song
    Shall ne'er be heard by him again.

And a' within the barony
    Were present at his funeral,
And bore him from his master's ha'
    To the lonely kirkyard o' Cargill.

Alas, for Jean! when a' was dune,
    Her conscience work'd and wadna still,
Confessed the fate that drove her late
    To bore the Coble o' Cargill.

"On Beltane e'en upon the Green
    He danced wi' Bess o' Bishopha',
Her witchin' glance and winnin' een
    I thocht had wiled his heart awa'.

"A fearfu' frame crept o'er me then,
    And held o' me the mastery,
And my wither'd heart was blawn in flame
    By that dread demon, jealousy.

"Our early vows made fause by him,
    The very thocht my heart did kill,
And spell-bound, driven by that dream,
    I bor'd the Coble o' Cargill.

"Oh, wha could guess 'twad come to this
    When we were young and at the schule,
And pu'd the slaes on Ballathie Braes,
    And broke the weirdly cake at Yule.

"There's ne'er a sark gae on my back,
    Nor yet a kame gae in my hair,
Nor will there coal or candle licht
    Shine in my bower for evermair.

"At kirk or fair I'se ne'er be seen,
    Nor yet a blythe blink in my e'e,
Nae finger's end shall point to Jean
    And say I gart my laddie dee.

"Yon ruin'd walls shall be my hame,
    Where ghaists and howlets nightly cry;
And the sadd'nin' sound o' the rollin' stream
    Shall nichtly sing my lullaby.

"This bracken bush shall be my bower,
    Where aften by the moon I see
Yon spectre boat wi' my love afloat,
    Wha wags his windin'-sheet at me."

ANONYMOUS.

THE BONNIE BANKS O' FORDIE.*

THERE were three ladies lived in a bower,
    Ech, wow, bonnie!
An' they went forth to pu' a flower
    On the bonnie banks o' Fordie.

---

* This old ballad was long a popular favourite in the southern parishes of Perthshire; and, I believe, is still occasionally heard by the cottage and bothy inglesides. Its historical bearing (if any) and exact locality have never been clearly defined. Sometimes it is found under the title of "Baby-Lon," sometimes "The Duke of Perth's Three Daughters." But there is no tradition in the Perth ducal family corresponding with the story. There is, of course, the burn of Ordie in Perthshire—about equi-distant between Perth and Dunkeld—and no stream in Scotland of the name of *Fordie*; and since editors

They hadna pu'd a flower but ane,
       Ech, wow, bonnie!
When up their started a banish'd man
       On the bonnie banks o' Fordie.

He's taen the first sister by the hand,
       Ech, wow, bonnie!
An' he's turned her round and made her stand
       On the bonnie banks o' Fordie.

"Now, whether will ye be a rank robber's wife,"
       Ech, wow, bonnie!
"Or will ye dee by my wee penknife
       On the bonnie banks o' Fordie?"

"It's I'll no' be a rank robber's wife,"
       Ech, wow, bonnie!
"But I'll rather dee by your wee penknife
       On the bonnie banks o' Fordie."

He's killed this May, an' he's laid her by,
       Ech, wow, bonnie!
For to bear the red rose companie
       On the bonnie banks o' Fordie.

He has ta'en the second ane by the hand,
       Ech, wow, bonnie!
An' he's turned her round and made her stand
       On the bonnie banks o' Fordie.

"It's whether will ye be a rank robber's wife,"
       Ech, wow, bonnie!
"Or will ye dee by my wee penknife
       On the bonnie banks o' Fordie?"

---

generally name Perthshire as the native locality of the ballad, may the original phraseology of the oft repeated refrain not have been "The bonnie banks of Ordie"? From that to "the bonnie banks o' Fordie" would be a simple and likely transition—probably is a clerical error.

    The name of the hero, "Baby-Lon," is presumably a corruption by the reciters of "Burd-alane," signifying "The Solitary."

"It's I'll no' be a rank robber's wife,"
    Ech, wow, bonnie!
"But I'll rather dee by your wee penknife
    On the bonnie banks o' Fordie."

He's kill'd this May, an' he's laid her by,
    Ech, wow, bonnie!
For to bear the red rose companie
    On the bonnie banks o' Fordie.

Then he's ta'en the youngest by the hand,
    Ech, wow, bonnie!
An' he's turned her round and made her stand
    On the bonnie banks o' Fordie.

Says "Will ye be a rank robber's wife,"
    Ech, wow, bonnie!
"Or will ye dee by my wee penknife
    On the bonnie banks o' Fordie?"

"It's I'll no' be a rank robber's wife,"
    Ech, wow, bonnie!
"Nor will I dee by your wee penknife
    On the bonnie banks o' Fordie.

"For I hae a brither in this wood,"
    Ech, wow, bonnie!
"An' gin ye kill me, it's he'll kill thee
    On the bonnie banks o' Fordie."

"Now, tell me what is thy brother's name?"
    Ech, wow, bonnie!
"My brother's name is Baby-Lon,
    On the bonnie banks o' Fordie."

"O, sister, sister, wae be to me,"
    Ech, wow, bonnie!
"O, have I done this ill to thee
    On the bonnie banks o' Fordie?

"The lift shall lie on yonder green,"
  Ech, wow, bonnie!
"Or ever I shall again be seen
  On the bonnie banks o' Fordie."

So he's ta'en out his wee penknife,
  Ech, wow, bonnie!
An' he's twyned himsel' o' his ain sweet life
  On the bonnie banks o' Fordie.
ANONYMOUS.

CROMLET"S LILT.*

SINCE all thy vows, false maid,
  Are blown to air,
And my poor heart betrayed
  To sad despair,
Into some wilderness
My grief I will express,
And thy hard-heartedness,
  O cruel fair!

Have I not graven our loves
  On every tree
In yonder spreading groves,
  Though false thou be?

---

* Robert Burns, in his notes to Johnson's *Museum*, says:—"The following interesting account of this plaintive dirge was communicated to Mr. Riddel by Alexander Tytler, Esq. of Woodhouselee:—' In the latter end of the 16th Century, the Chisholms were proprietors of the estate of Cromleck (now possessed by the Drummonds). The eldest son of that family was very much attached to the daughter of Stirling of Ardoch, commonly known by the name of Fair Helen of Ardoch. At that time the opportunities of meeting between the sexes were more rare, consequently more sought after than now; and the Scottish ladies, far from priding themselves in extensive literature, were thought sufficiently book-learned if they could make out the Scriptures in their mother tongue. Writing was entirely out of the line of female education. At that period the most of our young men of family sought a fortune or found a grave in France. Cromleck, when he went abroad to the war, was obliged to leave the management of his correspondence with his mistress to a lay-brother of the monastery of Dunblane, in

Was not a solemn oath
Plighted betwixt us both—
Thou thy faith, I my troth—
Constant to be?

Some gloomy place I'll find,
Some doleful shade,
Where neither sun nor wind
E'er entrance had;
Into that hollow cave,
There will I sigh and rave,
Because thou dost behave
So faithlessly.

---

the immediate neighbourhood of Cromleck, and near Ardoch. This man, unfortunately, was deeply sensible of Helen's charms. He artfully prepossessed her with stories to the disadvantage of Cromleck; and, by misinterpreting, or keeping up the letters and messages entrusted to his care, he entirely irritated both. All connexion was broken off betwixt them. Helen was inconsolable; and Cromleck has left behind him, in the ballad "Cromleck's Lilt," a proof of the elegance of his genius, as well as the steadiness of his love. When the artful monk thought time had sufficiently softened Helen's sorrow, he proposed himself as a lover. Helen was obdurate; but at last, overcome by the persuasions of her brother, with whom she lived, and who, having a family of thirty-one children, was probably very well pleased to get her off his hands, she submitted rather than consented to the ceremony. But there her compliance ended; and, when forcibly put into bed, she started quite frantic from it, screaming out that, after three gentle raps on the wainscot at the bed-head, she heard Cromleck's voice crying "O! Helen, Helen, mind me!" Cromleck soon after coming home, the treachery of the confidant was discovered, her marriage annulled, and Helen became Lady Cromleck.' N.B.— Margaret Murray, mother to these thirty-one children, was daughter to Murray of Strewan, one of the seventeen sons of Tullybardine, and whose youngest son, commonly called the Tutor of Ardoch, died in the year 1715, aged 111 years."

Burns, Riddel of Glenriddel, and Tytler of Woodhouselee, one or other, or all, had been misinformed on an important point here. Helen Stirling was not the daughter of Stirling of Ardoch, but the daughter of William, a younger brother of the laird's, whose name was Henry. William Stirling's house was in Dunblane, and it was to it that Sir James Chisholm came on the occasion of Helen's reluctant marriage. The hero and heroine were united in the bonds of holy wedlock in 1591, and their immediate descendants were the last Chisholm lairds of Cromlix.

The song or dirge is given in Ramsay's *Tea-Table Miscellany*, with the signature X., signifying that the author is unknown. It is also given, with the music, in the *Orpheus Caledonius* (1725). The tune is the well-known one of "Robin Adair."

Wild fruit shall be my meat,
    I'll drink the spring,
Cold earth shall be my seat;
    For covering
I'll have the starry sky
My head to canopy,
Until my soul on high
    Shall spread its wing.

I'll have no funeral fire,
    Nor tears nor sighs,
No grave do I desire,
    Nor obsequies;
The courteous redbreast, he
With leaves will cover me,
And sing my elegy
    With doleful voice.

And when a ghost I am
    I'll visit thee,
O thou deceitful dame,
    Whose cruelty
Has killed the fondest heart
That e'er felt Cupid's dart,
And never can desert
    From loving thee."

HER REPLY.[*]

HE whom I most affect
    Doth me disdain;
His causeless disrespect
    Makes me complain;
Wherefore I'll me address
Into some wilderness,
Where instead I'll express
    My anxious pain.

---

[*] This has been seldom printed. It was given from an old broadside, by James Maidment, in his *Scottish Songs and Ballads* in 1859.

Did we not both conjure
    By Stygian lake,
That sacred oath most pure
    The gods did take,
That we should both prove true;
You to me, I to you,
By that most solemn vow
    We both did make?

But thou perfidiously
    Didst violate
Thy promise made to me,
    To my regret;
For all the great respect
Wherewith I thee affect,
Is paid with such neglect,
    Love's turned to hate.

What tyrant e'er could hatch,
    Though inhumane,
A torturing rack, and match
    To this my pain?
O, barbarous cruelty,
That I, for loving thee,
Should basely murdered be
    By thy disdain.

I'll go find out a cell,
    Where light ne'er shined;
There I'll resolve to dwell
    And be confined,
Until it pleaseth thee
With love to pity me,
Forsake thy cruelty,
    And prove more kind.

In that dark vault I'll call
    For bats and owls;
The starth-owl, worst of all
    Prodigious fowls,

Shall be my mate by day,
By night with her I'll stay,
In dark and uncouth way,
    'Mongst wandering souls.

And in that strange exile
    I'll thee arrest
Amongst those monsters vile,
    To be my guest
Until that thou relent,
And thy hard heart repent,
Freely to give consent
    To my request.

No cloth shall deck my skin,
    No raiment soft,
But haircloth rough and thin,
    That's comely wrought;
No bed will I lie on,
My pillow shall be a stone,
Each accent prove a groan
    Repeated oft.

No dainty dish I'll eat,
    Composed by art,
No sauces for my meat,
    Sweet, sour, or tart;
My food shall be wild fruits,
Green herbs and unboiled roots,
Such as poor hermits eat
    In wild deserts.

All solace, mirth, and game
    I will despise;
A doleful mourning then,
    With watery eyes,
Shall be my music sound,
Till all the hills resound,
And fill the valleys round
    With piteous cries.

Yet for all this I'll not
    Abandon thee,
Nor alter in a jot
    My first decree;
But in despite of fate,
Thy griefs to aggravate,
I'll love thee, though thou hate,
    Until I dee.

ANONYMOUS.

THE DUKE O' ATHOL'S NURSE.

As I gaed in by the Duke o' Athol's yett,
  I heard a fair maid singing;
Her voice was sweet, she sang sae complete,
  That all the woods were ringing.

"O it's I am the Duke o' Athol's nurse,
  And I wat it weel does set me;
But I wad gie a' my half-year's fee,
  For a'e sicht o' my Johnie."

"Keep weel, keep weel your half-year's fee,
  Ye'll sune get a sicht o' your Johnie;"
"O here is my hand, but anither has my heart,
  And I daurna mair come near ye."

"Ohon, and alace, if anither has your heart,
  These words ha'e fair undone me;
But let us set a tryst to meet again,
  Then in gude friends ye will twine me."

"Ye will do' ye doun to yon change-house,
  And drink till the day be dawing,
And as sure as I ance had a love for you,
  I'll come there and clear your lawing.

"Ye'll spare not the wine, altho' it be fine,
  Nor Malago, tho' it be rarely,
But ye'll aye drink the bonnie lassie's health,
  That's to clear your lawing fairly."

Then he's done him down to yon change-house,
  And drank till the day was dawing,
And aye he drank the bonnie lassie's health,
  That was coming to clear his lawing.

And aye as he birled, and aye as he drank,
  The gude beer and the brandy,
He spared not the wine, altho' it was fine—
  The sack nor the sugar-candy.

"It's a wonder to me," the knight he did say,
  "My bonnie lassie's sae delaying;
She promis'd as sure as she loved me ance,
  She would be here by the dawing."

He's dune him to the shot-window,
  To see gin she were coming;
And there he spy'd her nine brithers bauld,
  That ower the hill cam' running.

"Where sall I rin, O where sall I gang,
  Or where now sall I lay me?
For she that ance was my ain true-love,
  Has sent nine men to slay me!"

He's gane to the landlady o' the house,
  Says, "O can ye supply me:
For she that was to meet me in friendship this day
  Has sent nine men to slay me?"

She ga'e him a suit o' her ain female claes:
  "Your life sall no be taken;"
The bird ne'er sang mair sweet on the bush,
  Nor the knight sang at the baking.

Sae loudlie as they rappit at the yett,
   Sae loudlie as they were ca'ing;
"Had ye a young man here yestreen?
   We'll shortly clear his lawing."

"I had nae stranger here last night
   That drank till the day was dawing,
But ane that took a pint and paid it ere he went,
   And there's naething to clear o' his lawing."

They stabbed the house baith but and ben,
   The curtains they spared nae riving;
But for a' that they did search and ca',
   For a kiss o' the knight they were striving.

A'e lad amang the rest being o' a merry mood,
   To the young knight fell a talking;
The wife took her foot and ga'e him a kick,
   Says, "Be busy, ye jilt, at your baking."

They searched the house a' round and round,
   And they spared nae the curtains to tear them;
But little they wist it was him they socht
   That was baking the bread sae near them.

So they gaed as they cam', and left a' undone,
   Though the bonnie lad's heart was quaking,
While the landlady stude upo' the stair-head
   Crying, "Maid, be busy at your baking."
                                  ANONYMOUS.

SIR JAMES THE ROSE.*

O HEARD ye o' Sir James the Rose,
   The young heir o' Baleichan?
For he has killed a gallant squire,
   Whase friends are out to take him.

---

* This pathetic and beautifully simple old Perthshire ballad is well known all over Scotland, there being one ancient (the present), and

Now he is gane to the house o' Mar,
   Whaur nane might seek to find him,
To seek his dear he did repair,
   Weening she would befriend him.

"Whaur are ye gaun, Sir James," she said,
   "Or whaur awa' are ye riding?"
"O I am bound to a foreign land,
   And now I'm under hiding;

"Whaur shall I gae, whaur shall I run,
   Whaur shall I hie to stay me?
For I hae kill'd a gallant squire,
   And his friends they seek to slay me."

"O gae ye doun to yon laigh house,
   And I'll pay there your lawing;
And as I am your leman true,
   I'll meet ye at the dawing."

"I'll no gae doun to yon laigh house,
   For you to pay my lawing,
But I'll lie doun upon the bent,
   And bide there till the dawing."

He's turned him richt and round about,
   And rowed him in his brechan,
And he has gane to take a sleep,
   In the lawlands o' Baleichan.

He wasna weel gane out o' sight,
   Nor was he past Millstrethen,
When four-and-twenty belted knights
   Cam' riding owre the Lethan.

---

two modern versions of it; one of the latter—perhaps the most popular of the three—being from the pen of Michael Bruce, the author of the immortal "Ode to the Cuckoo." The ballad has been claimed for other parts of Scotland, but the mention of "the Heights o' Lundie," together with "Baleichan," and other slightly-disguised names in the district, point to Ballechan, near Ballinluig, as very clearly being the scene of the tragedy.

"O hae ye seen Sir James the Rose,
    The young heir o' Baleichan?
For he has kill'd a gallant squire,
    And we're sent out to take him."

"O I ha'e seen Sir James," she said,
    "He pass'd by here on Monday,
Gin the steed be swift that he rides on,
    He's past the Heights o' Lundie."

But as wi' speed they rode awa',
    She loudly cried behind them,
"Gin ye'll gie me a worthy meed,
    I'll tell ye whaur to find him."

"O tell, fair maid, and on our band,
    Ye'se get his purse and brechan."
"He's in the bank aboon the mill,
    In the lawlands o' Baleichan."

They sought the bank aboon the mill,
    In the lawlands o' Baleichan,
And there they found Sir James the Rose,
    Lying sleeping in his brechan.

Then out and spak' Sir John the Græme,
    Who had the charge in keeping,
"It's ne'er be said, my stalwart feres,
    We kill'd a man when sleeping."

They seized his braid sword and his targe,
    And closely him surrounded;
And when he waked out o' his sleep,
    His senses were confounded.

"Rise up, rise up, Sir James," he said,
    "Rise up, since now we've found ye,
We've ta'en the broadsword frae your side,
    And angry men are round ye."

"O pardon, pardon, gentlemen,
    Ha'e mercy now upon me!"

"Such as you gave, such shall you have,
    And so we fall upon thee."

"Donald, my man, wait till I fa'
    And ye sall get my brechan,
Ye'll get my purse, though fu' o' gowd,
    To tak' me to Loch Lagan."

Syne they took out his bleeding heart,
    And set it on a spear;
They took it to the house o' Mar,
    And showed it to his dear.

"We couldna gi'e ye Sir James's purse,
    Nor yet could we his brechan,
But ye sall ha'e his bleeding heart,
    But and his bloody tartan."

"Sir James the Rose, oh! for thy sake
    My heart is now a-breaking;
Cursed be the day I wrought thy wae,
    Thou brave heir o' Baleichin."

Then up she raise, and forth she gaes,
    And in that hour o' tein,
She wander'd to the dowie glen,
    And never mair was seen.

ANONYMOUS.

THE BONNIE EARL OF MORAY.[*]

YE Highlands, and ye Lowlands,
    Oh! where hae ye been?
They hae slain the Earl of Moray,
    And hae lain him on the green.

---

[*] James Stuart, celebrated in song and history as "The Bonnie Earl of Moray," was the elder son of Lord Doune, who died in 1590. He acquired the title of Moray by marrying Elizabeth, eldest daughter of the "Good Regent," on whose death, without male issue, the earldom had reverted to the Crown. He was singularly handsome in person,

Now, wae be to thee, Huntly!
    And wherefore did ye sae?
I bade ye bring him wi' you,
    But forbade you him to slay.

He was a braw gallant,
    And he rade at the ring;
And the bonnie Earl of Moray,
    Oh! he might hae been a King.

He was a braw gallant,
    And he played at the ba';
And the bonnie Earl of Moray
    Was the flower amang them a'.

He was a braw gallant,
    And he played at the glove;
And the bonnie Earl of Moray,
    Oh! he was the Queen's love.

---

and beautiful in countenance. Queen Anne regarded him with much favour, which fact stirred the jealousy of King James, who commissioned his deadly enemy, the Earl of Huntly, to bring the Earl of Moray into his presence, on the pretence of his having harboured the turbulent Earl of Bothwell. Huntly surrounded the castle of Donibristle, whence the Earl had gone on a visit to his mother, and summoned him to surrender. He refused, whereupon the castle was set on fire. Dunbar, Sheriff of Moray, who was with the Earl at the time, said to him, with self-sacrificing generosity, "Let us not stay to be burned in the flaming house. I will go out first, and the Gordons, taking me for your Lordship, will kill me, while you may escape in the confusion." The noble sacrifice was unavailing. Dunbar rushed out, and met instant death. Moray followed, but the silken tassels of his skull-cap or helmet having caught fire as he passed through the flames, betrayed him to his enemies, who pursued and killed him. Huntly himself, as one account bears, stabbed him in the face, to whom he said with his last breath, "You have spoiled a better face than your own."

    The Countess Dowager of Moray carried to Edinburgh on litters the bodies of her son and the Sheriff, and had them buried in the aisle of St. Giles' Church. She appealed to the King for justice on their murderers, and sought in vain to move his heart by presenting to him a picture of her son's mangled corpse.

    There are three versions of the ballad extant; two with the above title, and one usually printed under the heading of "Young Waters."

>   Oh! lang will his lady
>   Look ower the Castle Doune,
>   Ere she see the Earl of Moray
>   Come sounding through the toun.
>   ANONYMOUS.

GILDEROY.*

> O GILDEROY was a bonny boy;
>   Had roses till his shoon;
> His stockings were of silken soy,
>   Wi' garters hanging doon,
> It was, I ween, a comely sight,
>   To see sae trim a boy;
> He was my joy, my heart's delight,
>   My handsome Gilderoy.

---

* This old song has yet a certain popularity in most country districts in Scotland. The subject of it was a man named Patrick Macgregor, but more familiarly Gillieroy (the red-haired lad), whose life and morals were, like those of his more illustrious namesake, framed on

> " The good old rule, the simple plan,
>   That they should take who have the power,
>   And they should keep who can."

Gilderoy was, in fact, a notorious freebooter, or cattle-lifter, who flourished in the early part of the seventeenth century, and was the leader of a numerous gang of caterans, who practised stouthrief and robbery with violence far and wide, but chiefly in the Highlands of Perthshire and Aberdeenshire. In February, 1636, seven of his accomplices were taken, tried, condemned, and executed at Edinburgh. They were apprehended, chiefly through the exertions of the Stewarts of Athole, and in revenge Gilderoy burned several houses belonging to the Stewarts, which act proved his speedy ruin. A reward of a thousand pounds was offered for his apprehension; and he was soon taken, along with five more accomplices (some accounts say ten), and the whole gang were executed at the Cross of Edinburgh on the 27th July, 1636, the leader, as a mark of unenviable distinction, receiving a higher gibbet than the others—a circumstance which is alluded to in the ballad. Some wonderful stories are told of this wild cateran, such as his having picked the pocket of Cardinal Richelieu while he was celebrating high mass in the church of St. Dennis, Paris; his having carried off with consummate assurance a trunk of plate from the house of the Duke Medina-Celi at Madrid; and his having attacked Oliver Cromwell and two servants while travelling from Portpatrick to Glas-

O, sic twa charming een he had;
   His breath as sweet's a rose;
He never wore a Highland plaid,
   But costly silken clothes;
He gained the love of ladies gay,
   Nane e'er to him was coy;
Ah, wae's me! I mourn the day,
   For my dear Gilderoy.

My Gilderoy and I were born
   Baith in a'e toun thegither:
We scant were seven years before,
   We 'gan to love each other,
Our daddies and our mammies, they
   Were fill'd with meikle joy,
To think upon the bridal day
   'Twixt me and Gilderoy.

For Gilderoy, that love of mine,
   Gude faith, I freely bought
A wedding sark of holland fine,
   Wi' silken flowers wrought,
And he gied me a wedding ring,
   Which I received with joy;
Nae lad and lassie e'er could sing
   Like me and Gilderoy.

Wi' meikle joy we spent our prime,
   Till we were baith sixteen;
And aft we pass'd the langsome time
   Amang the leaves sae green;

---

gow, and shooting the Protector's horse, which fell upon him and broke his leg, whereupon he placed Oliver on an ass, tied his legs under its belly, and dismissed the pair to seek their fortune. The ballad itself is said to have been originally composed by the hero's mistress, a young woman belonging to the higher ranks of life, who had become attached to the noted cateran, and was induced to live with him. It is to be found in black letter broadsides as far back as 1650. The present improved version was first printed in Durfey's *Pills to Purge Melancholy*, volume v., 1719, and is said to have been re-set by Lady Wardlaw, authoress of the well-known ballad of "Hardyknute." The original, according to Percy, contained "some indecent luxuriances that required the pruning hook."

Aft on the banks we'd sit us there,
   And sweetly kiss and toy;
Wi' garlands gay wad deck my hair,
   My handsome Gilderoy.

O, that he still had been content
   Wi' me to lead his life;
But ah, his manfu' heart was bent
   To stir in feats of strife;
And he in many a venturous deed
   His courage bauld wad try,
And now this gars my heart to bleed
   For my dear Gilderoy.

And when of me his leave he took,
   The tears they wat mine e'e,
I gave him a love-parting look,
   "My benison gang wi' thee!
God speed thee weel, mine ain dear heart,
   For gane is all my joy;
My heart is rent sith we maun part,
   My handsome Gilderoy."

My Gilderoy baith far an near
   Was fear'd in ilka toun,
And bauldly bear away the gear
   Of mony a lowland loun;
Nane e'er durst meet him hand to hand,
   He was sae brave a boy;
At length wi' numbers he was ta'en
   My handsome Gilderoy.

The Queen of Scots possessit nought,
   That my love lat me want;
For cow and ewe he to me brought,
   And e'en when they were scant;
All those did honestly possess,
   He never did annoy,
Who never failed to pay their cess
   To my love Gilderoy.

Wae worth the loun that made the laws
    To hang a man for gear!
To reave of life, for ox or ass,
    For sheep, or horse, or mear.
Had not their laws been made so strict
    I ne'er had lost my joy;
Wi' sorrow ne'er had wat my cheek,
    For my dear Gilderoy.

Gif Gilderoy had done amiss,
    He might have banish'd been;
Ah, what sair cruelty is this,
    To hang sic handsome men!
To hang the flower o' Scottish land,
    Sae sweet and fair a boy!
Nae lady had sae white a hand
    As thee, my Gilderoy!

Of Gilderoy sae fear'd they were,
    They bound him meikle strong;
Till Edinburgh they led him there,
    And on a gallows hung;
They hung him high abune the rest,
    He was sae trim a boy;
There died the youth whom I loved best,
    My handsome Gilderoy.

Thus having yielded up his breath,
    I bore his corpse away;
Wi' tears that trickled for his death,
    I washed his comely clay;
And siccar in a grave sae deep,
    I laid the dear loved boy;
And now for ever maun I weep
    For winsome Gilderoy.

ANONYMOUS.

BESSIE BELL AND MARY GRAY.*

O BESSIE BELL and Mary Gray,
They were twa bonnie lasses,
They biggit a bower on yon burn-brae,
And theekit it o'er wi' rashes.

---

*The story on which this popular ballad is founded has been often told, and is so charged with tender pathos that it never fails to command attentive hearing. It belongs to the time of the great plague, or pestilence, which, down to the year 1665, was the terror of Scotland, and which at one time reduced the city of Perth of about one-sixth of its population. The common tradition is that Bessie Bell and Mary Gray were the daughters of two country gentlemen in the neighbourhood of Perth, and an intimate friendship subsisted between them. Bessie Bell, daughter of the laird of Kinvaid, was on a visit to Mary Gray, at her father's house of Lednock, now called Lynedoch, when the plague of 1666 broke out in the country. To avoid the infection, the two young ladies built themselves a bower in a very retired and romantic spot known as the Burn-braes, on the side of the Brachie Burn, situated about three-quarters of a mile west from Lynedoch House. Here they lived for some time; but the plague raging with great fury, they caught the infection from a young gentleman of Perth who, it is said, was in love with the one or the other, or with them both; and who, having discovered their rural habitation and the scanty fare it afforded, had made it his daily duty to supply them with provisions from the "Borough toun." According to a traditionary story which I have received at various times from the lips of old persons in Perthshire, the provisions were not the vehicle by which the pestilence was conveyed. But the young gentleman on one of his visits having brought with him, among other presents for their gratification, a rare necklace which he had purchased of a Jew, and which had unhappily been originally the property of one who had died of the plague, the infection was in this way communicated to the young ladies, and proved fatal to them both. According to custom in cases of the plague, they were not buried in the ordinary place of sepulture, but in a secluded spot called the Dronach-haugh, at the foot of the brae of the same name, and near to the bank of the river Almond. The young man having also died of the plague, was laid at their feet. Dranoch, or Dronoch, in the Gaelic means sorrowful, therefore the likelihood is that this piece of ground takes its name from the fact of these hapless young persons being buried in it.

The earliest authentic information concerning the grave of Bessie Bell and Mary Gray is found contained in a letter dated 21st June, 1781, written by Major Barry of Lednock, and published in the Transactions of the Society of Antiquaries of Scotland, Vol. II., 1822. This gentleman explains that when he came first to Lednock he was shown in a part of the grounds called the Dronach-haugh, a heap of stones almost covered with briers, thorn, and fern, and which he was assured was the burial place of the hapless ladies whose names are immortalised in the fragment of ballad poetry bearing their names as

> They theekit it o'er wi' rashes green,
>   They theekit it o'er wi' heather;
> But the pest cam' frae the Borough's toun,
>   And slew them baith thegither.

---

its title. Major Barry caused all the rubbish to be removed from the little spot of classic ground, and inclosed it with a wall, planted it round with flowering shrubs, made up the grave double, and fixed a stone in the wall, on which were engraved the names of Bessie Bell and Mary Gray.

In 1787 Lynedoch estate passed into the possession of Mr. Thomas Graham of Balgowan, afterwards Lord Lynedoch, and the wall erected round the graves in the Dronach-haugh by Major Barry half a century before, being discovered by this later proprietor, on his return from a lengthened pilgrimage abroad, to have fallen into a dilapidated state, he had the remains of the wall removed and a neat stone parapet and iron railings five feet high placed round the spot. He also covered the graves with a stone slab, on which were inscribed the words, "They lived, they loved, they died." This railing still stands; but the stone slab within the railing is not visible to the eye, being covered with stones heaped up cairn-wise, brought hither by the many visitors who have made pilgrimages to this famous Scottish shrine.

The verses were first printed by Charles Kirkpatrick Sharpe, under the title of "The Twa Lasses."

Starting with the first four lines of the original, Allan Ramsay produced a song which is frequently printed in the collections. It is a performance not without merit, but as the author has dared to transform the burden of the verses from tender pathos to lively humour, we give him credit for it with a grudge, for the good reason that in so far as his version gains popularity a sweetly-pathetic historic romance loses its hold on the public mind.

Here are Ramsay's verses:—

> O, Bessie Bell and Mary Gray,
>   They were twa bonnie lasses,
> They biggit a bow'r on yon burn brae,
>   And theekit it ower wi' rashes.
> Fair Bessie Bell I lo'ed yestreen,
>   And thocht I ne'er could alter;
> But Mary Gray's twa pawkie een
>   Gar'd a' my fancy falter.
>
> Bessie's hair's like a lint-tap,
>   She smiles like a May mornin',
> When Phœbus starts frae Thetis' lap,
>   The hills wi' rays adornin';
> White is her neck, saft is her hand,
>   Her waist and feet fu' genty,
> Wi' ilka grace she can command
>   Her lips, Oh, now, they're dainty.

They thocht to lie in Methven kirkyard,
   Amang their noble kin;
But they maun lie in Dronach haugh,
   And beik fornenst the sun.

And Bessie Bell and Mary Gray,
   They were twa bonnie lasses,
They biggit a bower on yon burn-brae,
   And theekit it o'er wi' rashes.

ANONYMOUS.

THE WHEEL OF LIFE.

A Song.

THE wheel of life turns whimsically round,
And nothing in this world of constancy is found;
No principle, no tie, in either Church or State,
But int'rest overrules; such is the will of fate.

    Mary's locks are like the craw,
      Her een like diamonds glances;
    She's aye sae clean, redd-up, and braw,
      She kills whene'er she dances.
    Blythe as a kid, wi' wit at will,
      She blooming, tight, and tall is,
    And guides her airs sae gracefu' still—
      Oh, Jove, she's like thy Pallas!

    Young Bessie Bell and Mary Gray,
      Ye unco sair oppress us;
    Our fancies jee between ye twa,
      Ye are sic bonnie lasses.
    Wae's me! for baith I canna get,
      To ane by law we're stintit;
    Then I'll draw cuts and tak' my fate,
      And be wi' ane contentit.

One of the only two poems which Robert Nicoll allowed to drift into print before the publication of his *Poems and Lyrics* dealt with the fate of "Bessie Bell and Mary Gray." And a long but somewhat flabby ballad on the subject was written by James Duff, "the Methven poet," and appears in the volume of his poems published in Perth in 1816; also in *Auld Scots Ballants* (Paisley: Alex. Gardner, 1889).

The Churchman, who in faith should be refined,
The weathercock does blame that wheels with ev'ry wind;
Yet touch him with your coin, and you shall quickly see
The needle to the pole wheels not so fast as he.

The Lawyer swears he's sure your case is just,
And bids you, with a smile, on him repose your trust;
But if a greater fee into his hand they slide,
He straight begins to doubt, and wheels to the other side.

The Soldier, who with honour is replete,
By solemn oath is bound to serve the King and State;
But if contending two Pretenders come in play,
He wheels about to him that gives the greater pay.

The Courtier turns to gain his private ends,
Till he's so giddy grown he quite forgets his friends;
Prosperity of time deceives the proud and vain,
It wheels them in so fast, it wheels them out again.

Thus all mankind on Fortune's wheel do go,
And, as some mount on high, some others tumble low;
From whence we all agree, though many think it strange,
No sublunary thing can live without a change.

Then fill about a bumper to the brim,
Till all repeat it round, and every noddle swim;
How pleasing is the charm that makes our table reel,
And all around it laugh at Fortune and her wheel.
    ALEXANDER ROBERTSON *of Struan*.

SINCE LOYALTY IS STILL THE SAME.

SINCE loyalty is still the same,
Whether to win or lose the game,
To flinch it were a burning shame,
  Since Mar has gained a battle;

Let each brave, true-hearted Scot
Improve the victory he has got,
Resolving all shall go to pot,
    Or James the Eighth to settle.

Let those unmanly men of fears,
With downcast looks and hanging ears,
Who think each shadow that appears
    An enemy pursuing:
Let such faint-hearted souls begone!
The dangers of the field to shun,
We'll make Argyll once more to run,
    And think on what he's doing.

Can poor, low-country water-rats
Withstand our furious mountain-cats
The dint of whose well-armed pats
    So fatally confoundeth,
When many hundred warlike men
Were so well cut and so well slain,
That they can scarce get up again [*]
    When the last trumpet soundeth?

Come, here's to the victorious Mar,
Who bravely first conceived the war,
And to all those who went so far
    To shake off Union's slavery;
Whose fighting for so good a cause,
As king, and liberty, and laws,
Must from their foes e'en force applause,
    In spite of their own knavery.
        ALEXANDER ROBERTSON *of Struan.*

---

[*] They must be regarded as very effectually put to death whose chance of future awaking is doubtful.

THE FATE OF THE LOOKING-GLASS.

Poor Strephon's aspect and his air,
When young, could captivate the fair,
And, easily gazing in his glass,
Narcissus-like, he loved his face;
The glass was true, which made him glad,
For Strephon was a comely lad.

Now Strephon's fifty years and more,
Declining swiftly to three score;
And at that age the bloom's decayed,
When wrinkles and grey hairs invade:
The glass, still true, sincerely told,
To Strephon's grief, that he was old.

Quoth he, "My darling looking-glass,
With transitory things must pass:
The faithful with the faithless go,
The gods and I will have it so;
And yet thy doom is most undue,
Pronounced alone for being true."

Thus having said, he lifted high
The glass, in which he fixed his eye,
And, still displeased the change to see,
'Twixt twenty-one and fifty-three,
"Adieu," said he, "Old friends at length must part,
And if I break not thee, thou'lt break my heart!"
   Alexander Robertson *of Struan.*

KILLIECRANKIE. *

Claverse and his Highlandmen
 Came down upon the raw, man;
Who, being stout, gave mony a shout;
 The lads began to claw, then.

---

* The Battle of Killiecrankie, which decided the fate of the Jacobite insurrection in 1689, is a subject of familiar history. The insurrection

Wi' sword and targe into their hand,
  Wi' which they werena slaw, man,
Wi' mony a fearfu' heavy sigh
  The lads began to claw, then.

---

was headed by Viscount Dundee, the "Bloody Claverse," and the object of it was to overturn the Revolution settlement, and to restore the exiled Stuarts to the throne. To effect this daring design, Dundee, after he had been denounced an outlaw and a rebel, retired to the Highlands, and raised and organised the clans. In the middle of July he left Moy, in Inverness-shire, and made a rapid march to the south. General Mackay was sent north by the Government, at the head of a superior force, to oppose him. The rival forces met in the Pass of Killiecrankie, and the result, as everybody knows, was complete victory to the clans. And surely never was a fiercer conflict witnessed beneath the sun. "I dare be bold to say," says the writer of the *Memoirs of Viscount Dundee*, "there were scarce ever such strokes given in Europe as were given that day by the Highlanders. Many of General Mackay's officers and soldiers were cut down through the skull and neck to the breasts; others had their skulls cut above their ears like nightcaps; some soldiers had both their bodies and cross-belts cut through at one blow; pikes and small swords were cut like willows, and whoever doubts this may consult the witnesses of the tragedy." About two thousand of the Royalists were killed, and five hundred of them made prisoners, while their baggage, cannon, and stores fell into the hands of the conquerors. But the victory was purchased at a cost which was the ruin of the cause of the victors. Claverhouse himself was among the slain. At the beginning of the action, says Macaulay, Dundee had taken his place in front of his little band of cavalry. He bade them follow him, and rode onward. But it seemed to be decreed on that day the Lowland Scotch should appear to disadvantage in both armies. The horse hesitated. Dundee turned round, stood up in his stirrups, and waving his hat invited them to come on. As he lifted his arm his cuirass rose and exposed the lower part of his left side. A musket ball struck him, his horse sprang forward, and plunged into a cloud of smoke and dust, which hid from both armies the face of the victorious General. As he fell from his horse he asked "How goes the day" of the man who caught him. "Well for the King, but I am sorry for your Lordship," was the answer. "Since the day goes well for my master," was the reply, "It matters little for me." He never spoke again.

The Viscount was buried in the church of Blair Athole, and, as has been strikingly and truly said, "With him was buried the cause of King James in Scotland."

Various poets, including Burns and Aytoun, have found in Killiecrankie a theme of immortal song. In the oldest and best known ballad—the one here quoted—the chief attention is directed to the mode of fighting, and the sentiments and expressions of the mountaineer soldiery.

Ower bush, ower bank, ower ditch, ower stank,
    She flang amang them a', man;
The butter-box gat mony knocks;
    Their riggings paid for a', then.
They gat their paiks wi' sudden straiks,
    While, to their grief, they saw, man,
Wi' clinkum-clankum ower their crowns,
    The lads began to fa', then.

Her leap'd about, her skipp'd about,
    And flang amang them a', man;
The English blades gat broken heads,
    Their crowns were cleaved in twa, then;
The durk and dour made their last hour,
    And proved their final fa', man;
They thocht the devil had been there
    That played them sic a paw, man.

The Solemn League and Covenant
    Cam' whigging up the hill, man;
Thocht Highland trews durst not refuse
    For to subscribe their bill, then;
In Willie's name they thocht nae ane
    Durst stop their course at a', man;
But Her-nain-sel', wi' mony a knock,
    Cried, Eurich, Whigs, awa', man.

Sir Evan Dhu and his men true
    Cam' linking up the brink, man;
The Hoggan Dutch, they feared such,
    They bred a horrid stink, then.
The true MacLean and his fierie men
    Cam' in amang them a', man;
Nane durst withstand his heavy hand,
    A' fled and ran awa', then.

Och on a righ! och on a righ!
    Why should she lose King Shames, man?
Och rig in di! och rig in di!
    She shall break a' her banes, then;

With furichiuich, and stay a while,
   And speak a word or twa, man;
She's gie ye a straik out ower the neck,
   Before ye win awa', then.

Oh, fie for shame, ye're three for ane!
   Her-nain-sel's won the day, man,
King Shames' redcoats should be hung up,
   Because they ran awa', then.
Had they bent their bows like Highland trews,
   And made as lang a stay, man,
They'd saved their King, that sacred thing,
   And Willie'd run awa', then.
ANONYMOUS.

THE BATTLE OF SHERIFFMUIR. *

THERE'S some say that we wan, and some say that they wan,
   And some say that nane wan at a', man;
But a'e thing I'm sure, that at Sheriffmuir
   A battle there was, that I saw, man.
      And we ran, and they ran; and they ran and we ran,
      And we ran, and they ran awa', man.

---

* There are no fewer than four songs—all more or less popular—descriptive of the famous Battle of Sheriffmuir, in each of which its wavering proceedings and uncertain issue, together with the particular behaviour of many of the chief persons engaged on both sides, are humorously and cleverly hit off. The battle was fought on the 13th November, 1715, and took place at Sheriffmuir, situated in the parish of Dunblane. The struggle was between the clans under the Earl of Mar and the royal forces under John, Duke of Argyll. The principal feature in the battle—the one to which it owes its popular repute, as also the attention of the humorous poets—was that both parties were partially successful and partially defeated—the right wings of both armies being triumphant, and the left wings routed. Briefly, there had been running on both sides, and on that circumstance most of the humorous sarcasm of the songs is formed. Of the four songs on the subject I give first the oldest—in many respects the best—said by Burns to have been written by the Rev. Murdoch M'Lennan, minister of Crathie, on

Brave Argyll and Belhaven,[1] not like frighted Leven,[2]
  Which Rothes[3] and Haddington[4] saw, man;
For they all, with Wightman,[5] advanced to the right,
    man,
  While others took flight, being raw, man.

Lord Roxburgh[6] was there, in order to share
  With Douglas,[7] who stood not in awe, man,
Volunteerly to ramble with Lord Loudoun Campbell;[8]
  Brave Islay[9] did suffer for a', man.

Sir John Shaw,[10] that great knight, with broadsword
    most bright,
  On horseback he briskly did charge, man,
A hero that's bold, none could him withhold,
  He stoutly encountered the targemen.

Deeside, who died in 1783. Whether the reverend author witnessed in person the semi-farce of Sheriffmuir, as is indicated in the opening verse of the song, there is no means of knowing; and, indeed, the knowledge of such a circumstance is of little consequence. Living contemporaneous with the event he would have the fullest knowledge of the particulars, and this granted, it must be said to his credit that his description is most appreciably impartial. With respect to the reference to Rob Roy in the song as having " stood watch on a hill, for to catch the booty," it has been explained, in extenuation, that that redoubted hero was prevented, by mixed motives, from joining either party; he could not fight against the Earl of Mar consistently with his conscience, nor could he oppose the Duke of Argyll without forfeiting the protection of a powerful friend.

    1, 2, 3, 4. Lord Belhaven, the Earl of Leven, and the Earls of Rothes and Haddington, all of whom bore arms as volunteers in the royal army.

    5. Major-General Joseph Wightman, who commanded the centre of the royal army.

    6. John, first Duke of Roxburgh, a loyal volunteer.

    7. Archibald, Duke of Douglas, who commanded a body of his vassals in the royal army.

    8. Hugh Campbell, third Earl of Loudoun, of the royal army.

    9. The Earl of Islay, brother to the Duke of Argyll. He came up to the field only a few hours before the battle, and had the misfortune to get wounded.

    10. Sir John Shaw of Greenock, an officer in the troop of volunteers, noted for his keen Whiggish spirit.

For the cowardly Whittam,[11] for fear they should cut him,
   Seeing glittering broadswords will apa', man,
And that in such thrang, made Baird *aide-de-camp*,
   And from the brave clans ran awa', man.

The great Colonel Dow gaed foremost, I trow,
   When Whittam's dragoons ran awa', man;
Except Sandy Baird and Naughton, the laird,
   Their horse showed their heels to them a', man.

Brave Mar and Panmure[12] were firm I am sure,
   The latter was kidnapped awa', man;
But with brisk men about brave Harry[13] retook
   His brother, and laughed at them a', man.

Grave Marshall,[14] and Lithgow,[15] and Glengarry's[16] pith too,
   Assisted by brave Logie A'mon',[17]
And Gordons, the bright, sae boldly did fight,
   The redcoats took flight and awa', man.

Strathmore[18] and Clanronald[19] cried still "Advance, Donald!"
   Till both of these heroes did fa', man;
For there was sic hashing, and broadsword a-clashing,
   Brave Forfar[20] himsel' got a claw, man.

---

11. Major-General Whitham, who commanded the left wing of the King's army.
12. James, Earl of Panmure.
13. The Honourable Harry Maule of Kellie, brother to the foregoing, whom he recaptured after the engagement.
14, 15. The Earls of Marischal and Linlithgow.
16. The Chief of Glengarry.
17. Thomas Drummond of Logie-Almond.
18. The Earl of Strathmore, killed in the battle.
19. The Chief of Clanranald.
20. The Earl of Forfar—on the King's side—wounded in the engagement.

Lord Perth[21] stood the storm, Seaforth,[22] but lukewarm,
    Kilsyth[23] and Strathallan[24] not slaw, man;
And Hamilton[25] pled the men were not bred,
    For he had no fancy to fa', man.

Brave, generous Southesk,[26] Tullibardine[27] was brisk,
    Whose father, indeed, would not draw, man,
Into the same yoke, which served for a cloak,
    To keep the estate 'twixt them twa, man.

Lord Rollo,[28] not feared, Kintore[29] and his beard,
    Pitsligo[30] and Ogilvie[31] a', man,
And brothers Balfours, they stood the first stours;
    Clackmannan[32] and Burleigh[33] did claw, man.

But Cleppan[34] acted pretty, and Strowan,[35] the witty,
    A poet that pleases us a', man,
For mine is but rhyme, in respect o' what's fine,
    Or what he is able to draw, man.

For Huntly[36] and Sinclair,[37] they baith played the tinkler,
    With conscience black like a craw, man;

---

21. James, Lord Drummond, eldest son of the Earl of Perth, was Lieutenant-General of Horse under Mar, and behaved with great gallantry.
22. William Mackenzie, fifth Earl of Seaforth.
23. The Viscount Kilsyth.
24. The Viscount Strathallan.
25. Lieutenant-General George Hamilton, commanding under the Earl of Mar.
26. James, fifth Earl of Southesk.
27. The Marquis of Tullibardine, eldest son of the Duke of Athole.
28. Lord Rollo.
29. The Earl of Kintore.
30. Lord Pitsligo.
31. Lord Ogilvie, son of the Earl of Airlie.
32. Bruce, Laird of Clackmannan.
33. A relation of Lord Burleigh, an excitable person, almost a madman.
34. Major William Clephane.
35. Alexander Robertson of Struan, the chief of the Robertsons, a poet, noticed in this work, who died in 1749.
36. Alexander, Marquis of Huntly, afterwards Duke of Gordon.
37. The master of Sinclair.

Some Angus and Fife men, they ran for their life, man,
    And ne'er a Lot's wife there at a' man.

Then Lawrie,[38] the traitor, wha betrayed his master,
    His King, and his country and a', man,
Pretending Mar might give orders to fight,
    To the right of the army awa', man.

Then Lawrie, for fear of what he might hear,
    Took Drummond's best horse and awa', man;
'Stead of going to Perth, he crossed the Forth,
    Alongst Stirling Bridge and awa', man.

To London he pressed, and there he addressed,
    That he behaved best o' them a' man;
And there, without strife, got settled for life,
    A hundred a year to his fa', man.

In Borrowstounness, he rides with disgrace,
    Till his neck stands in need o' a draw, man;
And then in a tether, he'll swing from a ladder,
    And go off the stage with a pa', man.

Rob Roy[39] stood watch on a hill, for to catch
    The booty, for aught that I saw, man;
For he never advanced from the place he was stanced,
    Till no more to do there at a', man.

So we all took the flight, and Mowbray, the wright,
    But Letham, the smith, was a braw man,
For he took the gout, which truly was wit,
    By judging it time to withdraw, man.

---

38. A person who left the Duke of Argyll and joined the Earl of Mar before the battle, intending to act as a spy; and being employed by Mar to inform the left wing that the right was victorious, gave a contrary statement, and, after seeing them retire, went back to the royal army.
39. The celebrated Rob Roy.
40. An honorary popular title of the Duke of Gordon.
41. Carnegie of Finhaven.

And trumpet M'Lean, whose breeks were not clean,
  Through misfortune he happened to fa', man;
By saving his neck, his trumpet did break,
  Came off without music at a', man.

So there such a race was, as ne'er in that place was,
  And as little chase was at a', man;
From other they ran, without took of drum,
  They did not make use of a paw, man.

Whether we ran, or they ran, or we wan, or they wan,
  Or if there was winning at a', man,
There's no man can tell, save our brave generall,
  Wha first began running awa', man.

Wi' the Earl o' Seaforth, and the Cock o' the North:[40]
  But Florence ran fastest ava', man,
Save the Laird of Finhaven,[41] wha swore to be even,
  Wi' ony general or peer o' them a', man.
      And we ran, and they ran; and they ran, and we ran,
      And we ran, and they ran awa', man.
          Rev. MURDOCH M'LENNAN.

A DIALOGUE BETWEEN WILL LICKLADLE AND TOM CLEANCOGUE, TWA SHEPHERDS WHA WERE FEEDING THEIR FLOCKS ON THE OCHIL HILLS ON THE DAY THE BATTLE OF SHERRA-MUIR WAS FOUGHT.*

AIR—"THE CAMERON'S MARCH."

W.—Pray came you here the fight to shun,
  Or keep the sheep wi' me, man?
Or was you at the Sherra-muir,
  And did the battle see, man?

---

* Burns wrote an improved version of this song for Johnson's *Museum.*

Pray tell whilk o' the parties won,
For weel I wat I saw them run,
Baith north and south when they begun
  To pell and mell, and kill and fell,
  With muskets snell, and pistol's knell,
    And some to hell did flee, man.

    Hooch! hey dum dirrum hey dum dan,
    Hooch! hey dum dirrum dey dan,
    Hooch! hey dum dirrum hey dum dandy,
    Hey dum dirrum dey dan.

T.—But, my dear, Will, I kenna still
  Whilk o' twa did lose, man;
For weel I wat they had gude skill
  To set upo' their foes, man.
The redcoats they were train'd, you see,
The clans always disdain to flee:
Wha then should gain the victory?
  But the Highland race, all in a brace,
  With a swift pace to the Whigs' disgrace,
    Did put to chase their foes, man.

    Hooch! hey dum dirrum, etc.

W.—Now, how deil, Tam, can this be true?
  I saw the chase gae north, man;
T.—But weel I wat they did pursue
  Them even unto Forth, man.
Frae Dumblane they ran in my ain sight,
And gat o'er the bridge wi' a' their might,
And those at Stirling took their flight;
  Gif only ye had been wi' me,
  You had seen them flee of each degree,
    For fear to dee wi' sloth, man.

    Hooch! hey dum dirrum, etc.

W.—My sister Kate came o'er the hill,
  Wi' crowdie unto me, man,
She swore she saw them running still
  Frae Perth unto Dundee, man.

The left wing general had nae skill,
The Angus lads had nae gude-will
That day their neighbours' blood to spill:
  For fear, by foes, that they should lose
  Their cogues o' brose, all crying woes—
    Yonder them goes, d'ye see, man?

    Hooch! hey dum dirrum, etc.

T.—I see but few like gentlemen
  Among yon frighted crew, man,
I fear my Lord Panmure be slain,
  Or that he's ta'en just noo, man.
For though his officers obey,
His cowardly commons run away,
For fear the redcoats should them slay:
  The sodgers' hail made their hearts fail,
  See how they skail, and turn their tail
    And run to flail and plough, man.

    Hooch! hey dum dirrum, etc.

W.—But now brave Angus comes again
  Into the second fight, man;
They swear they'll either die or gain,
  No foes shall them afright, man;
Argyll's best forces they'll withstand,
And boldly fight them sword in hand,
Give them a general to command,
  A man of might, that will but fight,
  And take delight to lead them right,
    And ne'er desire the flight, man.

    Hooch! hey dum dirrum, etc.

But Flanderkins they have nae skill
  To lead a Scottish force, man;
Their motions do our courage spill,
  And put us to a loss, man.
You'll hear of us far better news,
When we attack wi' Highland trews,
To hash, and smash, and slash, and bruise,

                Till the field, though braid, be all o'erspread,
                But coat or plaid, wi' corpses dead,
                    In their cauld bed, that's moss, man.

                    Hooch! hey dum dirrum, etc.

T.—Twa generals frae the field did run,
            Lords Huntly and Seaforth, man:
        They cried, and run, grim death to shun,
            Those heroes of the North, man.
        They're fitter far for book or pen,
        Than under Mar to lead on men;
        Ere they came there they might weel ken
            That female hands could ne'er gain lands,
            'Tis Highland brands that countermands,
                Argathlean bands frae Forth, man.

                Hooch! hey dum dirrum, etc.

W.—The Camerons scour'd as they were mad,
            Lifting their neighbours' cows, man.
        M'Kenzie and the Stewart fled,
            But philebeg or trews, man,
        Had they behav'd like Donald's core,
        And killed all those came them before,
        Their king had gone to France no more;
            Then each Whig saint wad soon repent
            And straight recant his covenant,
                And rent it at the news, man.

                Hooch! hey dum dirrum, etc.

T.—M'Gregors they far off did stand,
            Badenoch and Athol, too, man;
        I hear they wanted the command,
            For I believe them true, man.
        Perth, Fife, and Angus, wi' their horse,
        Stood motionless, and some did worse,
        For though the redcoats went them cross,
            They did conspire for to admire
            Clans run and fire, left wings retire,
                While rights entire pursue, man.

                Hooch! hey dum dirrum, etc.

W.—But Scotland has not much to say
 For such a fight as this is,
Where baith did fight, baith ran away :
 The devil take the miss is,
That every officer was not slain,
That run that day and was not ta'en,
Either flying to or from Dumblane :
 When Whig and Tory, in their fury,
 Shore for glory, to our sorrow
  This sad story hush is.

  Hooch ! hey dum dirrum, etc.
     Rev. John Barclay.

WILL YE GO TO SHERIFFMUIR.*

Will ye go to Sheriffmuir,
Bauld John o' Innisture,
There to see the noble Mar,
 And his Highland laddies ;
A' the true men o' the north,
Angus, Huntly, and Seaforth,
Scouring on to cross the Forth,
 Wi' their white cockadies ?

There you'll see the banners flare,
There you'll hear the bagpipes rair,
And the trumpets deadly blare,
 Wi' the cannon's rattle ;

---

*This song was first published by Hogg in the *Jacobite Relics.* "Had I only rescued six such pieces as this from oblivion," he says, "I conceive posterity should be obliged to me ; not on account of the intrinsic merit of the songs, but for the specimens left them of the music and poetry of the age, so ingeniously adapted to one another. I have no conception who 'bauld John o' Innisture' was. The other four noblemen mentioned in the first verse were among the principal leaders of the Highland army. It is likely, from the second stanza, where only three of the clans are mentioned, that some verses have been lost."

"Bauld John o' Innisture" is evidently a corruption of "Bauld John o' Inchture."

There you'll see the bauld M'Craws,
Cameron's and Clanranald's raws,
And a' the clans, wi' loud huzzas,
    Rushing to the battle.

There you'll see the noble Whigs,
A' the heroes o' the brigs,
Raw hides and wither'd wigs,
    Riding in array, man.
Riven hose and raggit hools,
Sour milk, and girnin' gools,
Psalm-beuks, and cutty-stools,
    We'll see never mair, man.

Will ye go to Sheriffmuir,
Bauld John o' Innisture?
Sic a day and sic an hour,
    Ne'er was in the north, man.
Siccan sichts will there be seen,
And, gin some be nae mista'en,
Fragrant gales will come bedeen,
    Frae the water o' Forth, man.

ANONYMOUS.

LADY KEITH'S LILT. *

I MAY sit in my wee croo house,
  At the rock and the reel to toil fu' dreary;
I may think on the day that's gane,
  And sigh and sab till I grow weary,

---

* Lady Mary Drummond, who, it is alleged, wrote this song for the purpose of encouraging her two sons in their action in the cause of the Pretender, was the daughter of John, fourth Earl of Perth, commonly called "The Chancellor." She married William, ninth Earl Marischal, and bore him two sons—George and James. On the death of his father George succeeded to the title and estates—the which, for his action in the rebellion of 1715, he forfeited to the Crown. The circumstances are thus detailed in Sharpe's Peerage :—"The extensive property of the family having been dilapidated during the civil wars, it was reduced to the three estates of Dunottar, Fetteresso, and Inveru-

I ne'er could brook, I ne'er could brook,
    A foreign loon to own or flatter;
But I will sing a rantin' sang,
    That day our King comes ower the water.

O, gin I live to see the day,
    That I hae begg'd and begg'd frae heaven,
I'll fling my rock and reel away,
    And dance and sing frae morn till even;
For there is ane I winna name,
    That comes the reignin' byke to scatter;
And I'll put on the bridal-gown,
    That day our King comes ower the water.

I hae seen the gude auld day,
    The day o' pride and chieftain glory,
When Royal Stuarts bare the sway,
    And ne'er heard tell o' Whig or Tory,
Though lyart be my locks and grey,
    And eild has crooked me down—what matter?
I'll dance and sing a'e ither day,
    The day our King comes ower the water.

---

gie; and the Earl preferring a military life, was by favour of Queen Anne, constituted in February, 1714, captain of the Scotch troop of horse grenadier guards. He signed the proclamation of King George the First, but being unacceptable to John, Duke of Argyll, was deprived of his command at the same time that his cousin, the Earl of Mar, was dismissed from office as Secretary of State. The Earl Marischal set out for Scotland in disgust, and meeting his brother James at York, on his way to town in pursuit of military promotion, they returned home under strong feelings of irritation together, where they were easily instigated by their mother, who was strongly attached to the abdicated family, to enter into the Rebellion of 1715." Ruin of course followed, and "the office of Marischal, which had been seven centuries in the family, was with his titles and estates forfeited to the Crown."

    The song appears in Hogg's collection, without any indication of its origin, and its rare beauty as a pathetic effusion provokes in Dr. Chambers' mind a suspicion of its genuineness; indeed, he says it bears all the marks of having proceeded from the Shepherd's own pen. Hogg's known love of the mysterious gives force to this or any such suspicion. Still, until there is positive proof to the contrary, we prefer to regard the song as the production of Lady Mary Keith. The air to which it is sung is a variety of "The Boyne Water."

A curse on dull and drawling Whig,
    The whining, ranting, low deceiver,
Wi' heart sae black, and look sae big,
    And canting tongue o' clish-ma-claver!
My father was a gude lord's son,
    My mother was an earl's daughter;
And I'll be Lady Keith again,
    The day our King comes ower the water.

                      LADY MARY DRUMMOND.

THE GATHERING OF THE HAYS.*

GATHERING.

MACGARADH! MacGaradh! red race of the Tay,
Ho! gather! ho! gather! like hawks to the prey.
MacGaradh, MacGaradh, MacGaradh, come fast,
The flame's on the beacon, the horn's on the blast;
The standard of Errol unfolds its white breast,
And the falcon of Luncarty stirs in her nest.
Come away, come away, come to the tryst,
Come in MacGaradh, from east and from west.

MacGaradh! MacGaradh! MacGaradh! come forth,
Come from your bowers, from south and from north,
Come in all Gowrie, Kinnoul, and Tweeddale,
Drumelzier and Naughton come locked in your mail,
Come Stuart, come Stuart, set up thy white rose,
Killour and Buccleugh, bring thy bills and thy bows,
Come in MacGaradh, come armed for the fray,
Wide is the war cry, and dark is the day.

---

* This was first published in 1822 from a copy found pasted into an old MS. History of the family by John Hay Allan. The first stanza, he says, is of considerable antiquity, the second belongs to the period after 1646, and the rest is traditionally ascribed to Captain James Hay about the time that the Earl of Erroll joined the Pretender's standard at the Braes o' Mar. "Holleu MacGaradh" was the slogan of the Hays of Erroll.

QUICK MARCH.

The Hay! the Hay! the Hay! the Hay!
MacGaradh is coming, give way! give way!
The Hay! the Hay! the Hay! the Hay!
MacGaradh is coming, give way,
MacGaradh is coming, clear the way,
MacGaradh is coming, hurra! hurra!
MacGaradh is coming, clear the way,
MacGaradh is coming, hurra!

MacGaradh is coming, like beam of war:
The blood-red shields are glinting far;
The Stuart is up, his banner white
Is flung to the breeze like a flake of light.
Dark as the mountain's heather wave
The rose and the misle are coming brave.
Bright as the sun which gilds its thread,
King James's tartan is flashing red,
Upon them, MacGaradh, bill and bow,
Cry, holleu! MacGaradh! holleu! holleu!

CHARGE.

MacGaradh is coming! like stream from the hill,
MacGaradh is coming, lance, claymore, and bill,
  Like thunder's wild rattle
  Is mingled the battle,
With cry of the falling, and shout of the charge.
  The lances are flashing,
  The claymores are clashing,
And ringing the arrows on buckle and targe.

BATTLE.

MacGaradh is coming! the banners are shaking,
The war-tide is turning, the phalanx is breaking.
  The Southrons are flying,
  "Saint George!" vainly crying,
And Brunswick's white horse on the field is borne down.
  The red cross is shattered,
  The red roses scattered,
And bloody and torn the white plume in its crown.

PURSUIT.

Far shows the dark field the streams of Cairn Gorm,
Wild, broken, and red, in the skirt of the storm:
    Give the spur to the steed,
      Give the war-cry its holleu,
    Cast loose to wild speed,
      Shake the bridle, and follow;
The rout's in the battle,
    Like blast in the cloud,
The flight's mingled rattle
    Peals thickly and loud.
Then holleu! MacGaradh! hollen, MacGaradh!
Holleu! holleu! holleu! MacGaradh!

                        ANONYMOUS.

THE ATHOL GATHERING.*

WHA will ride wi' gallant Murray?
    Wha will ride wi' Geordie's sel'?
He's the flow'r o' a' Glenisla,
    And the darling o' Dunkel'.
See the white rose in his bonnet!
    See his banner o'er the Tay!
His gude sword he now has drawn it,
    And has flung the sheath away.

---

* This song, says Hogg, seems to have been taken from an anonymous Jacobite poem of some merit, evidently written at the very time the clans were rising in 1745. Lord George Murray, fifth son of the first Duke of Athole, joined Prince Charles' standard at Perth in September, 1745. He was appointed Lieutenant-General of the Prince's forces, and acted as such at the battles of Prestonpans, Falkirk, and Culloden, marched into England with them, and brought up the rear in their retreat from thence. He was attainted of high treason by Act of Parliament, but escaped to the Continent, and arrived at Rome on 21st March, 1747, where he was received with great distinction by Prince Charles, who fitted up an apartment for him in his palace, and introduced him to the Pope. He died at Medenblinck, in Holland, 11th October, 1760.

Every faithful Murray follows,
  First of heroes! best of men!
Every true and trusty Stewart
  Blythely leaves his native glen.
Athol lads are lads of honour,
  Westland rogues are rebels a';
When we come within their border,
  We may gar the Campbells claw.

Menzies he's our friend and brother;
  Gask and Strowan are nae slack;
Noble Perth has ta'en the field,
  And a' the Drummonds at his back.
Let us ride wi' gallant Murray,
  Let us fight for Charlie's crown;
From the right we'll never sinder,
  Till we bring the tyrants down.

Mackintosh, the gallant soldier,
  Wi' the Grahams and Gordons gay,
They hae ta'en the field of honour,
  Spite of all their chiefs could say.
Bend the musket, point the rapier,
  Shift the brog for Lowland shoe,
Scour the dirk, and face the danger—
  Mackintosh has all to do.

ANONYMOUS.

THE BIRKS OF INVERMAY.*

THE smiling morn, the breathing spring,
Invite the tuneful birds to sing;
And while they warble from each spray,
Love melts the universal lay.

---

* To these verses by Mallet, the original title and refrain of which found expression in "The Shades of Endermay," the following stanzas composed by the Rev. Alexander Bryce of Kirknewton, have been frequently added in the collections. They are distinctly inferior both

Let us, Amanda, timely wise,
Like them improve the hour that flies ;
And in soft raptures spend the day,
Among the birks of Invermay.

For soon the winter of the year,
And Age, Life's winter, will appear,
At this thy living bloom must fade,
As that will strip the vernal shade.
Our taste of pleasure then is o'er,
The feathered songsters love no more ;
And when they droop, and we decay,
Adieu the birks of Invermay.

DAVID MALLET.

---

in sentiment and execution, and for that reason, primarily, are here cut adrift from the original song :—

> The laverocks, now, and lintwhites sing,
> The rocks around with echoes ring ;
> The mavis and the blackbird vie,
> In tuneful strains, to glad the day.
> The woods now wear their summer suits :
> To mirth all nature now invites ;
> Let us be blythesome, then, and gay,
> Among the birks of Invermay.
>
> Behold the hills and vales around
> With lowing herds and flocks abound ;
> The wanton kids and frisking lambs
> Gambol and dance around their dams ;
> The busy bees, with humming noise,
> And all the reptile kind rejoice :
> Let us, like them, then, sing and play,
> About the birks of Invermay.
>
> Hark, how the waters, as they fall,
> Loudly my love to gladness call ;
> The wanton waves sport in the beams,
> And fishes play throughout the streams.
> The circling sun does now advance,
> And all the planets round him dance :
> Let us as jovial be as they,
> Among the birks of Invermay.

THE BIRKS O' INVERMAY.

Modern Version.

The e'enin' sun was glintin' bricht,
  On Invermay's sweet glen and stream,
The rocks and woods, in ruddy licht,
  Were kythin' like a fairy dream.
In lovin' fear I took my gate,
  To seek the tryst that happy day,
Wi' bonnie Mary, young and blate,
  Amang the birks o' Invermay.

It wasna till the sklent moon's shine
  Was glancin' deep in Mary's e'e,
That, a' in tears, she said, "I'm thine,
  And ever will be true to thee!"
A'e kiss, the lover's pledge, and then,
  We spak' o' a' that lovers say,
Syne lingered hameward through the glen,
  Amang the birks o' Invermay.

ANONYMOUS.

WILLIAM AND MARGARET.*

'Twas at the silent solemn hour,
  When night and morning meet;
In glided Margaret's grimly ghost
  And stood at William's feet.

---

* This beautiful and much admired ballad was first printed in a London periodical entitled *The Plain Dealer*, in the year 1724, while the author of it was yet a very young man. In a letter addressed to the editor of the journal, Mallet vouchsafed the information that the poem was founded on a fact which had shortly before occurred under his own observation. A young lady of an agreeable person, and possessed of many intellectual accomplishments, was courted and seduced by a vain, presuming. unprincipled, young man, whom her unsuspecting heart had too credulously trusted. When she could no longer conceal her imprudence and dishonour, her father, formerly unacquainted with her situation, now applied to the deceitful lover, and generously offered him the half of his fortune provided he would marry

His face was like an April morn,
  Clad in a wintry cloud;
And clay-cold was her lily hand,
  That held her sable shroud.

So shall the fairest face appear,
  When youth and years are flown:
Such is the robe that kings must wear,
  When death has reft their throne.

Her bloom was like the springing flower,
  That sips the silver dew;
The rose was budded in his cheek,
  Just opening to the view.

But love had, like the canker-worm,
  Consumed her early prime;
The rose grew pale, and left her cheek;
  She died before her time.

---

his daughter. This offer the perfidious wretch indignantly rejected, notwithstanding the entreaties and tears by which it was urged, and even proceeded so far as to accuse, with the most injurious and public indecency, the innocence of her whom he had thus villainously betrayed. The news of this treatment so deeply affected the young lady that a fever ensued, which, bringing on premature labour, quickly put an end to her life and sufferings, when both she and her child were buried in one grave.

The ballad immediately won for its author a place among the poets of the day, and soon numbered him among the friends of Pope and Young, and other eminent men of letters. It has been greatly praised by some. Ritson calls it one of the finest ballads that was ever written. Scott, on the other hand, says, "The ballad, though the best of Mallet's writing, is certainly inferior to its original, which I presume to be the very fine and even terrific old Scottish tale beginning—

'There came a ghost to Margaret's door.'"

Mallet himself had admitted that the opening lines of an old ballad, which he supposed to be lost, were the stimulating means of his own, and this is quite likely. The editor of the first series of *The Harp of Renfrewshire* makes an elaborate but unsuccessful attempt to deprive Mallet of the authorship of the ballad altogether. Another editor claims it for Andrew Marvell. There can be no doubt that David Mallet was the author of "William and Margaret," even although it is true that he never wrote anything else in the same line nearly so good.

"Awake!" she cried, "thy true love calls,
    Come from her midnight grave;
Now let thy pity hear the maid
    Thy love refused to save.

"This is the dark and dreary hour,
    When injur'd ghosts complain;
Now yawning graves give up their dead,
    To haunt the faithless swain.

"Bethink thee, William, of thy fault,
    Thy pledge, and broken oath;
And give me back my maiden vow,
    And give me back my troth.

"Why did you promise love to me,
    And not that promise keep?
Why did you swear mine eyes were bright,
    Yet leave those eyes to weep?

"How could you say my face was fair,
    And yet that face forsake?
How could you win my virgin heart,
    Yet leave that heart to break?

"Why did you say my lip was sweet,
    And made the scarlet pale?
And why did I, young, witless maid,
    Believe the flattering tale?

"That face, alas! no more is fair,
    Those lips no longer red;
Dark are my eyes, now closed in death,
    And every charm has fled.

"The hungry worm my sister is;
    This winding-sheet I wear;
And cold and weary lasts our night,
    Till that last morn appear.

"But hark! the cock has warned me hence;
    A long and last adieu!

Come see, false man, how low she lies,
   Who died for love of you."

The lark sung loud, the morning smiled
   With beams of rosy red;
Pale William shook in ev'ry limb,
   And raving left his bed.

He hied him to the fatal place
   Where Margaret's body lay,
And stretch'd him on the grass-green turf,
   And wrapped her breathless clay.

And thrice he called on Margaret's name,
   And thrice he wept full sore;
Then laid his cheek to her cold grave,
   And word spake never more.

                              DAVID MALLET.

FOR LACK OF GOLD.*

FOR lack of gold she has left me, O,
And of all that's dear she's bereft me, O;
She me forsook for Athole's Duke,
   And to endless woe she has left me, O.

---

* "This song," says Burns, "was written by the late Dr. Austin, physician at Edinburgh. He had courted a lady, to whom he was shortly to have been married; but the Duke of Athole, having seen her, became so much in love with her, that he made proposals of marriage, which were accepted of, and she jilted the doctor." The lady in question was Jean, daughter of John Drummond, Esq., of Megginch. Her cousin, Adam Austin, M.D., Edinburgh, a native of Kilspindie, who had been brought up from childhood within the radius of her charms, had been paying his addresses to Miss Jean, if he was not actually her accepted lover, when at an assembly held at Perth in October, 1748, she met James, Duke of Athole. Duke James at this time was a man above middle life, and a widower. He was smitten with the charms of Jean Drummond, proposed and was accepted by her, the marriage being solemnized in May, 1749. Surviving his Grace, by whom she had no issue, she married, as her second husband, Lord Adam Gordon, fourth son of Alexander, second Duke of Gordon,

A star and garter have more art
Than youth, a true and faithful heart;
For empty titles we must part—
　For glittering show she has left me, O.

No cruel fair shall ever move
My injured heart again to love,
Through distant climates I must rove,
　Since Jeanie she has left me, O.

Ye powers above, I to your care
Resign my faithless, lovely fair;
Your choicest blessings on her share,
　Though she's for ever left me, O.
　　　　　　　　　ADAM AUSTIN, M.D.

FAREWELL TO ABERFOYLE.

To thee my filial bosom beats,
　On thee may heaven indulgent smile,
And glad thy innocent retreats,
　And bless thee, lovely Aberfoyle.
How pleasing to my pensive mind
　The memory of thy bold cascade,
Thy green woods waving in the wind,
　And streams in every vocal glade!

---

and commander of the forces in Scotland. She died in 1795. Although Dr. Austin says—

"No cruel fair shall ever move
My injured heart again to love,"

he did not keep his vow of eternal celebacy, but in 1754 married Anne Sempill, sister of the Right Honourable Lord Sempill, by whom he had a large family. The song, which appeared first in *The Charmer*, published in 1751, has taken a place among the popular ballads of Scotland.

The simple church, the schoolhouse green,
   The gambols of the schoolboy crew,
Meadows and pools that gleam between,
   Rush on my retrospective view;
Shades, too, and lanes by old age sought,
   To wander in at close of day,
To ruminate the pious thought
   And pray for children far away.

Timely descend, ye fostering showers!
   With plenty bliss that humble vale;
And fair arise, ye fragrant flowers,
   And healthful blow, thou western gale.
And there, meand'ring, Avendow,
   By no invidious fen defiled;
Clear may thy youthful current flow,
   And love to linger in the wild!
                WILLIAM RICHARDSON.

THE ROSE.

AN IDYLLION.

SAID INO, "I prefer the Rose
To every vernal ffower that blows;
For when the smiling seasons fly,
And winds and rain deform the sky,
And Roses lose their vivid bloom,
Their leaves retain a sweet perfume.
Emblem of Virtue! Virtue stays
When Beauty's transient hue decays;
Nor Age, nor Fortune's frown efface
Or injure her inherent grace."
"True," answered DAPHNIS; "but observe,
Unless some careful hand preserve
The leaves before their tints decay,
They fall neglected; blown away
By wintry winds and beating rains,
No vestige of perfume remains.

Some kindly hand must interpose,
For sore the wintry tempest blows,
And weak and delicate the Rose.
             WILLIAM RICHARDSON.

THE GARB OF OLD GAUL.*

IN the garb of old Gaul, with the fire of old Rome,
From the heath-covered mountains of Scotia we come;
Where the Romans endeavoured our country to gain,
But our ancestors fought, and they fought not in vain.

---

* Mr. Whitelaw says, this song, which appears in *The Lark* (1765), and also in Herd's Collection (1769), was written by Lieutenant-General Sir Harry Erskine, Bart. and M.P., who succeeded his uncle, the Hon. General St. Clair, in the command of the Royal Scots in 1762, and died at York in 1765. And Mr. W. Anderson, in *The Scottish Nation* (1870), and Mr. Ogle in *The Songs of Scotland* (1871), and other collectors, give the same authorship, with almost similar *notanda*. Notwithstanding, the authorship is disputed. Colonel David Stewart of Garth, in his *Sketches of the Highlanders* (1820), says:—" The words to 'The Garb of Old Gaul' were originally composed in Gaelic, and the officers had all assisted at the translation; the names of these officers are recorded, but I am unwilling to mention one in preference to another. Mr. Maclagan, the chaplain, who was himself a poet, composed words of his own in Gaelic to the same music; also to the quick march of 'The Highland Laddie.'" Colonel Stewart joined the 42nd in 1789, while the traditions of the regimental song were necessarily quite fresh. To bear himself out in the above statement he goes on to say:—"An intelligent officer who nearly sixty years ago (1762) commenced a service in the 42nd Regiment relates—'I cannot at this distance of time recollect the name of the man who composed "The Garb of Old Gaul," but he was from Perthshire, as also John Du Cameron, who was drum-major when I joined, and who sang and repeated several of the man's poems, and says that he thought his manner of speaking the Gaelic words of "The Garb of Old Gaul" preferable to the English. Before my time there were many poets and bards among the soldiers. Their original compositions were generally in praise of their officers and comrades who had fallen in battle, and many of them beautiful.'" The late Mr. P. R. Drummond, of Perth, says there is nothing in the song characteristic of a man in Sir Harry Erskine's position, " but it is precisely the language of the ranks—clever, but full of Highland gasconade." The same writer, supporting the claim of his native shire, further adds—" In a trial for murder, it is absolutely necessary to have a *corpus delicti*, and here it will be found in the fourth verse of the song—

Such is our love of liberty, our country, and our laws,
That, like our ancestors of old, we'll stand in freedom's cause,
We'll bravely fight like heroes bold, for honour and applause,
And defy the French, with all their art, to alter our laws.

' Quebec and Cape Breton, the pride of old France,
   .   .   .   sued for a truce,'

and at Paris, on the 11th of February, 1763, Cape Breton was finally ceded to the British nation and the conquest of Canada sustained. Here was ground for exultation—here was a subject for celebration in song; and a soldier of the 42nd composed one, and the Major set it to music. This must have been done between February, 1763 (date of the armistice), and October, 1765 (date of *The Lark*). Now, where was Captain Erskine during these two years? Such an absurd vision as his presence here never rose before men. There had been no Captain Erskine for very many years. It took Reid twenty years to creep up from Lieutenant-General to Major (two steps). How long would it take Erskine to mount from Captain to Lieutenant-General (four steps) in the same time?—possibly not forty years, nor thirty, nor twenty, but certainly ten years. Thus, a Lieutenant-General of 1762 suggests a Captain of 1752, seven years before Cape Breton was disturbed by the British. We are not only asked to believe that Captain Erskine wrote this song in 1773, but we are left to imagine how a man who had been, to our knowledge, six years a Lieutenant-General in command of a brigade, a Baronet, and a Member of Parliament, could become a Captain and the author of a regimental lyric like this." After all that is said above, it seems to have entirely escaped the knowledge of Mr. Drummond, and the various song-collectors previously mentioned as well—whose finding Mr. Drummond so strenuously and—on the line taken—successfully combats—that there are two English versions of "The Garb of Old Gaul," and this being so, there may be facts on both sides. Sir Harry Erskine may have written a version of the song. Whether the original or the improved one, it were hazardous to say—yea, even somewhat hazardous to say which is the original and which not. Time and chance may have "mixed those babies up" as well as have "mixed" their authors, I don't, of course, affirm that there has been any "mixing" in the matter; only, there are two songs and two claimants for authorship, and I simply place these before you, my reader, make my bow, and leave you to make your own arrangement. The tune—"The Highland or 42nd Regiment's March"—unquestionably, was composed to General John Reid, who bequeathed a sum of money for establishing a professorship of music in Edinburgh College. In connection with this latter, in terms of the testator's will, an annual concert is given in Edinburgh at which "The Garb of Old Gaul" must be sung.

No effeminate customs our sinews embrace,
No luxurious tables enervate our race,
Our loud-sounding pipe breathes the true martial strain,
And our hearts still the old Scottish valour retain.

   Such is our love of liberty, etc.

We're tall as the oak on the mount of the vale,
And swift as the roe which the hounds doth assail;
As the full moon in autumn our shields do appear,
Ev'n Minerva would dread to encounter our spear.

   Such is our love of liberty, etc.

As a storm in the ocean when Boreas blows,
So are we enraged when we rush on our foes;
We sons of the mountains, tremendous as rocks,
Dash the force of our foes with our thundering strokes.

   Such is our love of liberty, etc.

Quebec and Cape Breton, the pride of old France,
In their numbers fondly boasted till we did advance,
But when our claymores they saw us produce,
Their courage did fail, and they sued for a truce.

   Such is our love of liberty, etc.

In our realm may the fury of faction long cease,
May our councils be wise, and our commerce increase;
And in Scotia's cold clime may each of us find
That our friends still prove true, and our beauties prove kind.

   Then we'll defend our liberty, our country, and our laws,
   And teach our late posterity to fight in freedom's cause,
   That they, like their ancestors bold, for honour and applause
   May defy the French, with all their art, to alter our laws.

SIR HARRY ERSKINE (?)

THE GARB OF OLD GAUL.*

In the garb of old Gaul, and the fire of old Rome,
From the heath-covered mountains of Scotia we come;
On those mountains the Romans attempted to reign,
But our ancestors fought, and they fought not in vain.
Though no city nor Court of our garment approve,
'Twas presented by Mars at the senate to Jove,
And when Pallas observed at a ball 'twould look odd,
Mars received from his Venus a smile and a nod.

No intemperate tables our sinews unbrace,
Nor French faith nor French Popery our country disgrace;
Still the hoarse-sounding pipe breathes the true martial strain,
And our hearts still the true Scottish valour retain.
'Twas with anguish and woe that of late we beheld
Rebel forces rush down from the hills to the field;
For our hearts are devoted to George and the laws,
And we'll fight like true Britons in liberty's cause.

But still at a distance from Briton's lov'd shore
May her foes in confusion her mercy implore!
May her coasts ne'er with foreign invasions be spread!
Nor detested rebellion again raise its head!
May the fury of party and faction long cease!
May our councils be wise and our commerce increase!
And in Scotia's cold climate may each of us find
That our friends still prove true, and our beauties prove kind!

Anonymous.

---

* Copied from *The Edinburgh Musical Miscellany* (1792.)

THE SKULL.*

As I sat by the grave, at the brink of its cave,
    Lo! a featureless skull on the ground;
The symbol I clasp, and detain in my grasp,
    While I turn it around and around.

Without beauty or grace, or a glance to express
    Of the by-stander nigh a thought;
Its jaw and its mouth are tenantless both,
    Nor passes emotion its throat.

No glow on its face, no ringlets to grace
    Its brow, and no ear for my song;
Hush'd the caves of its breath, and the finger of death
    The raised features hath flattened along.

The eyes' wonted beam, and the eyelids' quick gleam—
    The intelligent sight, are no more;
But the worms of the soil, as they wriggle and coil,
    Come hither their dwellings to bore.

No lineament here is left to declare
    If monarch or chief wert thou:
Alexander the Brave, as the portionless slave
    That on dunghill expires, is as low.

Thou delver of death, in my ear let thy breath
    Who tenants my hand unfold,
That my voice may not die without a reply
    Though the ear it addresses is cold.

Say, wert thou a may, of beauty a ray,
    And flatter'd thine eye with a smile?
Thy meshes didst set, like the links of a net,
    The hearts of the youth to wile?

---

* This poem is strongly suggestive of—what its author had almost certainly never read—Hamlet's moralizings by Ophelia's grave.

Alas! every charm that a bosom could warm
   Is changed to the grain of disgust!
Oh! fie on the spoiler for daring to soil her
   Gracefulness all in the dust!

Say, wise in the law, did the people with awe
   Acknowledge thy rule o'er them—
A magistrate true, to all dealing their due.
   And just to redress or condemn?

Or was righteousness sold for handfuls of gold
   In the scales of thy partial decree;
While the poor were unheard when their suit they preferr'd,
   And appeal'd their distresses to thee?

Say, once in thine hour, was thy medicine of power
   To extinguish the fever of ail;
And seem'd, as the pride of thy leech-craft e'en tried,
   O'er omnipotent death to prevail?

Alas! that thine aid should have ever betray'd
   Thy hope when the need was thine own;
What salve or annealing sufficed for thy healing
   When the hours of thy portion were flown?

Or, wert thou a hero, a leader to glory,
   While armies thy trencheon obey'd;
To victory cheering, as thy foemen careering
   In flight, left their mountains of dead?

Was thy valiancy laid, or unhilted thy blade,
   When came onwards in battle array
The sepulchre-swarms, ensheathed in their arms,
   To sack and to rifle their prey?

How they joy in their spoil, as thy body the while
   Besieging, the reptile is vain,
And her beetle-mate blind hums his gladness to find
   His defence in the lodge of thy brain!

Some dig where the sheen of the ivory has been,
  Some, the organ where music repair'd ;
In rabble and rout they came in and came out
  At the gashes their fangs have bared.

· · · · ·

Do I hold in my hand a whole lordship of land,
  Represented by nakedness here ?
Perhaps not unkind to the helpless thy mind,
  Nor all unimparted thy gear ;

Perhaps stern of brow to thy tenantry thou !
  To leanness their countenances grew—
'Gainst their crave for respite, when thy clamour for
    right
  Required, to a moment, its due ;

While the frown of thy pride to the aged denied
  To cover their head from the chill,
And humbly they stand, with their bonnet in hand,
  As cold blows the blast of the hill.

Thy serfs may look on, unheeding thy frown,
  Thy rents and thy mailings unpaid ;
All praise to the stroke their bondage that broke !
  While but claims their obeisance the dead.

· · · · ·

Or a head do I clutch whose devices were such
  That death must have lent them his sting—
So daring they were, so reckless of fear,
  As Heaven had wanted a king ?

Did the tongue of the lie, while it couch'd like a spy
  In the haunt of thy venomous jaws,
Its slander display, as poisons its prey
  The devilish snake in the grass ?

That member unchained by strong bands is restrain'd,
  The inflexible shackles of death ;
And its emblem, the trail of the worm, shall prevail
  Where its slaves once harbour'd beneath.

And, oh! if thy scorn went down to thine urn,
   And expired with impenitent groan;
To repose where thou art is of peace all thy part,
   And then to appear—at the throne!

Like a frog, from the lake that leapeth, to take
   To the Judge of thy actions the way,
And to hear from His lips, amid nature's eclipse,
   Thy sentence of termless dismay.

. . . . .

The hardness thy bones shall environ,
   To brass-links the veins of thy frame
Shall stiffen, and the glow of thy manhood shall grow
   Like the anvil that melts not in flame.

But wert thou the mould of a champion bold
   For God and His truth and His law;
Oh! then, though the fence of each limb and each sense
   Is broken—each gem with a flaw—

Be comforted thou! For rising in air
   Thy flight shall the clarion obey;
And the shell of thy dust thou shalt leave to be crush'd,
   If they will, by the creatures of prey.
DUGALD BUCHANAN.

THE LAST ADIEU TO THE HILLS.*

YESTREEN I stood on Ben Dorain, and paced its dark grey path,
Was there a hill I did not know—a glen, or grassy strath?

---

* Donacha Ban was seventy-eight years old when, in September, 1802, on a visit to his native wilds, he wandered a whole day among the scenes he loved so well, and then and there composed his "Last Adieu to the Hills," which, every competent critic maintains, is the most beautiful of all his poems.

Oh! gladly in the times of old I trod that glorious ground,
And the white dawn melted in the sun, and the red-deer cried around.

How finely swept the noble deer across the morning hill,
While fearless played the fawn and doe beside the running rill;
I heard the black and red cock crow, and the bellowing of the deer—
I think those are the sweetest sounds that man at dawn may hear.

Oh! wildly, as the bright day gleamed, I climbed the mountain's breast,
And when I to my home returned, the sun was in the west;
'Twas health and strength, 'twas life and joy, to wander freely there,
To drink at the fresh mountain stream, to breathe the mountain air.

And oft I'd shelter for a time within some shieling low,
And gladly sport in woman's smile, and woman's kindness know;
Ah, 'twas not likely one could feel for long a joy so gay,
The hour of parting came full soon—I sighed, and went away.

And now the cankered, withering wind has struck my limbs at last;
My teeth are rotten and decayed, my sight is failing fast;
If hither now the chase should come, 'tis little I could do;
Though I were hungering for food, I could not now pursue.

But though my locks are hoar and thin, my beard and
  whiskers white,
How often have I chased the stag with dogs full swift
  of flight!
And yet, although I could not join the chase if here it
  came,
The thought of it is charming still, and sets my heart on
  flame.

Ah! much as I have done of old, how ill could I wend
  now,
By glen and strath, and rocky path, up to the moun-
  tain's brow;
How ill could I the merry cup quaff deep in social cheer!
How ill now could I sing a song in the gloaming of the
  year!

Those were the merry days of spring, the thoughtless
  times of youth;
'Tis fortune watches over us, and helps our need,
  forsooth;
Believing that, though poor enough, contentedly I live,
For George's daughter † every day my meat and drink
  doth give.

Yestreen I wandered in the glen; what thoughts were
  in my head!
There had I walked with friends of yore—where are
  those dear ones fled?
I looked and looked; where'er I looked was nought but
  sheep! sheep! sheep!
A woeful change was in the hill! World, thy deceit was
  deep!

From side to side I turned mine eyes—alas! my soul
  was sore—
The mountain bloom, the forest's pride, the old men
  were no more—

---

† "George's Daughter" was the musket carried by the author as a member of the City Guard of Edinburgh, and a servant of King George.

Nay, not one antler'd stag was there, nor doe so soft and slight;
No bird to fill the hunter's bag—all, all were fled from sight!

Farewell, ye forests of the heath! hills where the bright day gleams!
Farewell, ye grassy dells! farewell, ye springs and leaping streams!
Farewell, ye mighty solitudes, where once I loved to dwell—
Scenes of my spring-time and its joys—for ever fare-you-well!

Duncan Macintyre.

CHARMING PHILLIS.

As charming Phillis, all alone,
   Walk'd on the banks of Isla water,
The fish up to the surface came,
   The birds on ev'ry tree did chatter.
All joined so in the harmony,
   As if it was by them concerted,
How to engage her to the place,
   Or how she should be there diverted.

So slowly flow'd the gentle stream,
   As if it meant she should discover,
By its aversion to depart,
   How much it also was her lover.
But when press'd on by the next wave
   Which also made all haste to have her,
It mourn'd, and murmur'd all along,
   That it should be constrain'd to leave her.

Then Phœbus lifted up his head
   To see this much admired creature,
He blush'd that she should him exceed,
   And spread his rays o'er ev'ry feature.

Thinking that, by his scorching heat,
　　He should have made those eyes to cover,
That him of light and life defeat,
　　And made each creature her fond lover.

But whilst she then did him attack,
　　The nimble deer came out to meet her,
And to their silent shades and groves,
　　With all their art they did invite her.
With armed heads and winged heels,
　　So cheerfully they tripp'd before her;
And when she stood they stop'd and gaz'd
　　As if they humbly would adore her.

By accident I passed by,
　　While thus each creature she alarms;
None was more captivate than I,
　　Nor more engaged to her charms.
I fix'd mine eyes on ev'ry part,
　　And them I turn'd up to heav'n,
Wishing the gods might send relief
　　To cure the wound that she had giv'n.

　　　　　　　　　Alexander Nicol.

EPITAPH ON ALEXANDER ROBERTSON OF STRUAN.

Poor Struan's eyes are closed, he lies
　　Now in death's darksome shade;
His cheerful voice and mirthful joys
　　Are all in silence laid;
In this he err'd, that he preferr'd
　　The man he hated most
To be his heir, and took not care
　　Till his estate was lost.
He in his life had not a wife
　　Among the human race;
But the nine lasses of Parnassus
　　By turns he did embrace;

No children did from him proceed
    Of the terrestrial kind,
But thousands stand in well-ranged bands,
    The produce of his mind;
These will show forth his fame and worth
    Through ages to ensue;
No time can waste, nor envy blast
    A character so true.
What he desired he ne'er acquired,
    And that was once to see
Each ancient lord to's own restored
    And James supreme to be;
But all may know that here below
    None can be satisfied;
For all men wish some certain bliss
    That is by heaven denied.
But now his shade is from us fled,
    And joined the seraphs blest,
There to complete the numbèrs sweet
    That here he oft express'd.
Let Scotsmen all, both great and small,
    Lament the death of Struan,
And every thing that seems to bring
    About their country's ruin.

ALEXANDER NICOL.

SONG OF THE ROYAL HIGHLAND REGIMENT.

FOR success a prayer, with a farewell, bear
    To the warriors dear of the muir and the valley—
The lads that convene in their plaiding of green,
    With the curtal coat and the sweeping *eil-e*.
In their belts array'd, where the dark blue blade
    Is hung, with the dirk at the side;
When the sword is at large, and uplifted the targe,
    Ha! not a foe the boys will abide.

The followers in peril of Ian the Earl,
  The race of the wight of hand;
Sink the eyes of the foe, of the friend's mounts the
    glow,
  When the Murdoch's high blood takes command.
With Loudon to lead ye, the wise and the steady,
  The daring in fight and the glorious,
Like the lightning ye'll rush, with the sword's bright
    flash,
  And return to your mountain victorious.

Oh, sons of the lion! your watch is the wildlands,
  The garb of the Highlands is mingled with blue,
Though the target and bosses are bright in the High-
    lands,
  The axe in your hands might be blunted well, too.
Then forward—and see ye be huntsmen true,
  And, as erst the red-deer felling,
So fell ye the Gaul, and so strike ye all
  The tribes in the backwoods dwelling.

Where ocean is roaring, let top-sails be towering,
  And sails to the motion of helm be flying;
Though high as the mountain, or smooth as the foun-
    tain,
  Or fierce as the boiling floods angrily crying;
Though the tide with a stroke be assailing the rock,
  Oh, once let the pibroch's wild signal be heard,
Then the waves will come bending in dimples befriend-
    ing,
  And beckoning the friends of their country on board.
The ocean-tide's swelling, its fury is quelling,
  In salute of thunder proclaiming your due;
And methinks that the hum of a welcome is come,
  And is warbling the Jorram to you.

When your levy is landed, oh, bright as the pearls
  Shall the strangers who welcome you, gladly, and
    greeting

Speak beautiful thoughts; aye, the beautiful girls
  From their eyes shall the tears o'er the ruby be
    meeting,
And encounter ye, praying, from the storm and the
    slaying,
  "From the stranger, the enemy, save us, oh, save!
From rapine and plunder, oh, tear us asunder,
  Our noble defenders are ever the brave!"

"If the fondest ye of true lovers be,"
  So cries each trembling beauty,
"Be bold in the fight, and give transport's delight
  To your friends and the fair, by your duty."
"Oh, yes!" shall the beautiful hastily cry:
  "Oh, yes!" in a word, shall the valiant reply;
"By our womanly faith we pledge you for both,
For where'er we contract, and where'er we betroth,
  We vow with the daring to die!"

Faithful to trust is the lion-like host,
  Whom the dawn of their youth doth inure
To hunger's worst ire, and to action's bold fire,
  And to ranging the wastes of the moor.
Accustom'd so well to each enterprise snell,
  Be the chase or the warfare their quarry;
Aye ever they fight the best for the right,
  To the strike of the swords when they hurry.
                    JAMES MACLAGGAN.

CORUNNA'S LONE SHORE.*

Do you weep for the woes of poor wandering Nelly?
  I love you for that, but I love now no more;
All I had long ago lies entomb'd with my Billy,
  Whose grave rises green on Corunna's lone shore.

---

  * Mr. P. R. Drummond, in *Perthshire in Byegone Days*, says:—
"The chain of unfortunate circumstances which suggested to the mind
of Andrew Sharpe the composition of the ode, 'Corunna's Lone

Oh! they tell me my Billy looked noble when dying,
That round him the noblest in battle stood crying,
While from his deep wound life's red floods were drying,
   At evening's pale close on Corunna's lone shore.

That night Billy died, as I lay on my pillow,
   I thrice was alarmed by a knock at my door;
Thrice my name it was called in a voice soft and mellow,
   And thrice did I dream of Corunna's lone shore.

Shore,' was shortly this. In the year 1808, William Herdman, a handsome and well-conducted young tradesman, lived in a land of houses facing the river, which has been lately removed to make way for Tay Street, and on the opposite side dwelt Ellen Rankine, whose father was gardener at Bellwood. Frequently passing and repassing across the river, the two formed a fond mutual attachment, which was about to resolve itself into their becoming man and wife, when a misunderstanding of a very trivial nature arose between Herdman and Ellen's father, which became aggravated into a quarrel, and the young man, being too proud to submit, took revenge on all by enlisting in the 92nd Regiment, then under orders for foreign service. Within a few months he was carrying a musket and knapsack across the trodden and hungry orange groves of Old Castile, and under Sir David Baird, eventually joined Sir John Moore's retreat upon Corunna. The same evening, the 16th of January, 1809, that they buried Sir John Moore in the centre of the battery at Corunna, they buried William Herdman under the green turf on the outside of the battery walls, and within a few feet of the ebbing and flowing waters of the Bay of Biscay.

The first news William Herdman's father and mother heard of him, after his enlistment, were the news of his death—terribly distracting news to them, accompanied as they were with full details of his last moments on the field of battle.

Andrew Sharpe had observed that, since Herdman's departure, Ellen Rankine was greatly changed. Her passionate blue eyes had begun to fade, and her luxuriant brown hair, the pride of better days, to get tangled and dry; but when the news of his death came she sank into helpless idiocy, and, despite the careful watchings of her distressed parents, she stole from them in a luckless moment, and, taking the back of the hill, went crooning and singing for a whole week away through the howe of Strathmore, the burden of her song taken no doubt from Sharpe—

   Oh! Corunna's lone shore.

The interest taken in the beautiful but crazed maiden, and the kindness shown to her wherever she went, have been the theme of many a story. She has been described by those who had seen her as walking at a rapid pace, bare-headed and bare-footed, waving a red handkerchief in her right hand, and under her white, naked left arm carrying her masses of brown hair tied up in an inextricable bundle."

Methought Billy stood on the beach where the billow
Boom'd over his head, breaking loud, long, and hollow,
In his hand he held waving a flag of green willow,
   "Save me, God!" he exclaimed on Corunna's lone shore.

And now when I mind on't, my dear Billy told me,
   While tears wet his eyes, but those tears are no more,
At our parting, he never again would behold me,
   'Twas strange, then I thought on Corunna's lone shore.
But shall I ne'er see him when drowsy-eyed night falls,
When through the dark arch Luna's tremulous light falls,
As o'er his new grave slow the glow-worm of night crawls,
   And ghosts of the slain trip Corunna's lone shore?

Yes, yes, on this spot shall these arms enfold him,
   For here hath he kissed me a thousand times o'er;
How bewildered's my brain, now methinks I behold him,
   All bloody and pale on Corunna's lone shore.
Come away, my sweetheart, come in haste, my dear Billy,
On the wind's wafting wing to thy languishing Nelly;
I've got kisses in store, I've got secrets to tell thee,
   Come, ghost of my Bill, from Corunna's lone shore.

Oh! I'm told that my blue eyes have lost all their splendour,
   That my locks, once so yellow, now wave thin and hoar;
'Tis, they tell me, because I'm so restless to wander,
   And from thinking so much on Corunna's lone shore.
But, God help me, where shall I go to forget him,
If to father's, at home in each corner I meet him,
The arbour, alas! where he used aye to seat him,
   Says, "Think, Nellie, think on Corunna's lone shore."

And here as I travel all tattered and torn,
  By bramble and briar, over mountain and moor,
Ne'er a bird bounds aloft to salute the new morn,
  But warbles aloud, "Oh! Corunna's lone shore."
It is heard in the blast when the tempest is blowing,
It is heard in the white broken waterfall flowing,
It is heard in the songs of the reaping and mowing,
  Oh, my poor bleeding heart! Oh, Corunna's lone shore!

ANDREW SHARPE.

ROW WEEL, MY BOATIE.*

Row weel, my boatie, row weel,
  Row weel, my merry men, a',
For there's dool and there's wae in Glenflorich's bowers,
  And there's grief in my father's ha'.

And the skiff it danced light on the merry wee waves,
  And it flew o'er the water sae blue,
And the wind it blew light, and the moon it shone bright,
  But the boatie ne'er reached Allandhu.

Ohon! for fair Ellen, ohon!
  Ohon! for the pride of Strathcoe,—
In the deep, deep sea, in the salt, salt bree,
  Lord Reoch, thy Ellen lies low.

ALEXANDER CAMPBELL.

NOW WINTER'S WIND SWEEPS.

Now Winter's wind sweeps o'er the mountains,
  Deeply clad in drifting snow;

---

* This beautiful song was set to music by the author's friend, Mr. R. A. Smith, and was long a concert favourite throughout Scotland.

Soundly sleep the frozen fountains,
   Ice-bound streams forget to flow :
The piercing blast howls loud and long,
The leafless forest oaks among.

Down the glen, lo ! comes a stranger,
   Wayworn, drooping, all alone :—
Haply, 'tis the deer-haunt ranger!
   But alas ! his strength is gone !
He stoops, he totters on with pain,—
The hill he'll never climb again.

Age is being's winter season,
   Fitful, gloomy, piercing cold ;
Passion, weaken'd, yields to reason,
   Man feels *then* himself grown old ;
His senses one by one have fled,
His very soul seems almost dead.

                ALEXANDER CAMPBELL.

THE DEIL AND M'OMMIE.

A'E nicht when I ga'e owre my wark,
An' took a range doun thro' the park,
It was na late, but yet was dark
           Thro' a' the nation,
For nox had spread his sable sark
           Owre the creation.

Syne just as I gaed owre the hicht,
Doun in the howe there was a licht,
That put me in an eerie fricht—
           I maist did swoon,
Yet I gaed on to see the sicht,
           An' sat me doun.

Syne Hornie did present himsel';
I didna like his seety smell,

Nor yet could I his likeness tell,
                It was sae queer,
He looked as he had been in hell
                For mony a year.

"Auld lad," quo' I, "ye are na' blate,
To pitch your tent on our estate,
I redd you gae some ither gate
                Before the morn;
Than you, I'm sure, a greater cheat
                Was never born."

"Young man," quo' he, "gin that be a
For whilk you do me sae misca',
Your reasons are na' worth a flaw;
                I winna lee,
Amo' yoursel's there's hunders twa,
                Waur cheats than me.

"Witness M'Ommie o' Newmill,
I wish that he may burn his kiln,
For mony a time he's dune me ill,
                An' I'm afraid
My cheatin' trade he'll fairly spill,
                An' brak' my bread.

"He rides an' rins to ilka airth,
He squeezes a' the shire o' Perth,
He's the first man that rises dearth
                Amo' the meal;
There's not a rub like him on earth,
                Nor yet in hell.

"Just here upon St. John's-day fair,
He to Perth Borough did repair,
Among meal-sellers raised a steer,
                That greedy snake;
He gar'd them hicht their costly ware
                Two-pence a peck.

"It's but of late that he did tell
The honest fouks about Dunkel',
Had he a sharper till himsel'
   They dung should eat,
An' gar them their ain bairns fell,
   To be their meat.

"Guid corn he buys up for meal,
An' manufactures them for sale,
But micht as weel your siller steal
   Out o' your hand;
To mix them up he does na fail
   Wi' dust an' sand."

"Ay, ay," quoth I, "you're fairly out,
Your bread is broken here, I doubt,
But micht na ye tak' him a clowt,
   An' drive him blae?
There's no a puir man hereabout
   That wad be wae."

Quo' he, "I had him ance on wing,
An' ready for to tak' his swing,
He wad hae danced his hin'most spring
   Upo' the gallows,
But his vile servants lowsed the string—
   Shame fa' the fellows.

"But I've been thinkin' o' a plot,
Whilk aiblins yet will be his lot;
My bastard son will gie'm a shot
   Thro' head an' brains,
Or draw a whittle owre his throat,
   To mak' amends.

"Syne I'll provide for him a lodgin',
Where he maun gae spite o' his grudgin';
For a' his wiles, an' his hudgemudgin',
   He'll be nae fainer;
I'll pluck his wings, like ony pigeon
   Fit for a dinner.

"The worm within his soul shall gnaw,
An' I without will gie'm the law,
While nane will say for him 'fu's a'?'
    Nor for him care;
I'll place him in the squeezer raw,
    An' haud him there."
JAMES SIM.

A SOLILOQUY.

AND must I die, and leave this earth?
 Must I my soul resign
To that great God who gave me birth,
 Infinite and divine?

Must I before the judgment-seat
 Of my Creator come,
Where everyone, both small and great,
 Receive their final doom?

Is heaven prepared for God's elect?
 Are sinners sent to hell?
In one of these must I expect
 For evermore to dwell?

Yes, true it is that I must die,
 And at God's bar appear,
Nor from his presence can I fly—
 He's present everywhere.

If I to Heaven be doomed to go,
 His presence fills the Throne,
Where countless millions, bending low,
 Adore the great Three-One.

If I in hell be doomed to spend,
 Mine endless years in pain,
There sovereign mercy's at an end,
 Strict justice then remains.

A fiery deluge God maintains,
    From vials of His rage,
That swell through all those dire domains,
    And never will assuage.

O thou, my soul, when wilt thou fly
    To shun those scenes of horror?
When God Himself's thine enemy,
    And every object terror.

Fly to the Saviour, and confess
    Thy sins, which many be,
Pray that His spotless righteousness
    He may impute to thee.

Lord, bring me to that happy place,
    Where doth Thine honour dwell;
Make me a trophy of Thy grace,
    Triumphant over hell!

And tune my heart, that I may sing
    That sweet celestial song,
Which will cause heaven's wide arches ring
    Eternity along.

JAMES SIM.

THE LAND O' THE LEAL.*

AIR.—"*Hey tutti taiti.*"

I'M wearin' awa', John,
Like snaw-wreaths in thaw, John,
I'm wearin' awa'
    To the land o' the leal.

---

* By reason of the delicate beauty of this lyric, and the fact that it appeared first of all anonymously, and only a short time after Burns's death, whilst unknown poems and songs of his were still frequently being discovered, it was, in its still well-known tinkered form—"Jean" being substituted for "John"—made to appear as Burns's last song to his wife. As this, too, it was long popularly accepted,

> There's nae sorrow there, John,
> There's neither cauld nor care, John,
> The day is aye fair
> In the land o' the leal.

---

although no editor of Burns, happily, was led to incorporate it in his collected works. For nearly half a century the most ingenious and indefatigable collectors and editors of Scottish songs endeavoured to penetrate the secret of the authorship without success. In his *Songs of Scotland*, published at Edinburgh in 1848, Mr. G. Farquhar Graham includes "The Land o' the Leal," with the following note :—" The excellent verses here given were published about the year 1800 ; the author is still unknown. The words were originally 'I'm wearin' awa', John ;' they seem to have been altered with the intention of making the song appear to be the parting address of Burns to his wife. The fifth and seventh stanzas have generally been omitted, and it is doubtful whether the latter is not an interpolation by a different hand." In Mr. Graham's version the following stanzas have been interpolated :—

> " Ye've been leal and true, Jean,
> Your task is ended noo, Jean,
> And I'll welcome you
> To the land o' the leal.
>
> " A' our friends are gane, Jean,
> We've lang been left alane, Jean,
> We'll a' meet again
> In the land o' the leal."

After an extensive correspondence, it was the privilege of the late Dr. Charles Rogers to make known to the world who was the author of the song, and to relate the affecting circumstances under which it was produced. Briefly stated, the facts are as follows :—In the course of the year 1798, whilst Carolina Oliphant (afterwards Baroness Nairne) was staying with her brother's family in the North of England, Mrs. Campbell Colquhoun, of Killermont, an early and attached friend of the poetess, had to mourn the death of her first-born child, which had died when scarcely a year old. When tidings of her friend's bereavement reached her, Carolina despatched to her a letter of condolence, accompanied by the verses which have since become so dear to every Scottish heart. Mrs. Colquhoun was entreated not to divulge the authorship, and she strictly fulfilled her friend's request, for she did not entrust any one with the secret. "Many years after," says Dr. Rogers, "when Lady Nairne was verging on old age, she wrote concerning the origin of 'The Land o' the Leal' in these words— '"The Land o' the Leal" is a happy rest for the mind in this dark pilgrimage. . . . O, yes ! I was young then. I wrote it merely because I liked the air so much, and I put these words to it, never fearing questions as to the authorship. However, a lady would know, and took it down, and I had not Sir Walter's art of denying. I was present when it was asserted that Burns composed it on his death-bed, and that he had it *Jean* instead of *John*, but the parties could not

UNIV. OF
CALIFORNIA

I'm wearin awa John
Like snow when it's thaw John
I'm wearin awa to the land o the

There's nae sorrow there John
There's neither cauld nor care John
The day's aye fair in the land o't
Our bonny bairn's there John
She was baith gude & fair John
And O we grudged her sair
To the land o the leal

But sorrow's zeel wears past John
And joy is comin fast John
The joy that's aye to last
In the land o the leal.
Now had ye leal & true John
Your day it's weel near thro John
And I'll welcome you
To the land o the leal

O dry your glistenin ee John
My soul langs to be free John
And angels beckon me
To the land o the leal.
Now fare ye weel my ain John
This world's cares are vain John
We'll meet & we'll be fain
In the land o the leal

Our bonnie bairn's there, John,
She was baith gude and fair, John,
And oh! we grudged her sair
    To the land o' the leal.

But sorrow's sel' wears past, John,
And joy's a-comin' fast, John,
The joy that's aye to last
    In the land o' the leal.

Sae dear's that joy was bought, John,
Sae free the battle fought, John,
That sinfu' man e'er brought
    To the land o' the leal.

Oh! dry your glist'ning e'e, John,
My saul langs to be free, John,
And angels beckon me
    To the land o' the leal.

Oh! haud ye leal and true, John,
Your day it's wearin' through, John,
And I'll welcome you
    To the land o' the leal.

---

decide why it never appeared in his works, as his last song should have done. I never answered.'"

In its original form, it may be remarked, the song consisted of seven four-line verses. At a subsequent period, when the writer became more enlightened respecting the Gospel scheme, she incorporated these lines:—

> "Sae dear's that joy was bought, John,
> Sae free the battle fought, John,
> That sinfu' man e'er brought
>   To the land o' the leal."

Three double stanzas, as a rule, only are sung, or printed even in the collections, the third being omitted. Altogether, "The Land o' the Leal" is a song of the purest womanly affection, the sex of the writer being made conspicuously evident in the verse beginning—

> "Our bonnie bairn's there, John."

It is a mother's thought that Heaven will be more dear and desirable because her child is there. And why the tinkered version has maintained a greater popularity than the original must be a puzzle to people of the finest taste. Henceforth, by all means, let the word be "John," and not "Jean."

Now fare-ye-weel, my ain John,
This warld's cares are vain, John,
We'll meet, and we'll be fain,
 In the land o' the leal.
                    BARONESS NAIRNE.

THE LAIRD O' COCKPEN. *

THE Laird o' Cockpen, he's proud and he's great;
His mind is ta'en up wi' affairs o' the state;
He wanted a wife his braw house to keep;
But favour wi' wooin' was fashious to seek.

---

* The authorship of "The Laird o' Cockpen" has been variously attributed to Sir Alexander Boswell, the son of the famous biographer of Johnson, and himself the undisputed author of several popular songs, including "Jenny Dang the Weaver," "Jenny's Bawbee," and others; to Miss Ferrier, the authoress of *Marriage* and *Destiny*, and other novels of distinguished merit; and to Baroness Nairne, the authoress of "The Land o' the Leal." Nowadays, and with good reason, it is universally ascribed to the last-named writer. Lady Nairne composed the song in the Auld House of Gask, while she was still young, and the name M'Clish, contained in the second verse, may have been suggested to her by that of the parish minister of Gask, who, in 1746, refused to pray for the family, and rode to Perth to bring on them the vengeance of the Duke of Cumberland. Old Mr. Oliphant of Gask wrote—"May God forgive the minister, as I do;" and the authoress must often have heard her father deprecate the conduct of the heartless ecclesiastic. The song was written by Lady Nairne with a view to supersede an older set of words which were connected with the air, "When she cam' ben she bobbit," and which were much in vogue on account of the excellence of the melody. The older version, entitled "Cockpen," and believed to belong to the reign of Charles II., was exceptional on the score of refinement. Burns purged it of its indecencies, but left a poor enough song when that was done. Let us see:—

" O, when she cam' ben she bobbit fu' law,
 O, when she cam' ben she bobbit fu' law;
 And when she cam' ben she kissed Cockpen,
 And syne she denied that she did it at a'.

 And wasna Cockpen richt saucy witha',
 And wasna Cockpen richt saucy witha',
 In leaving the dochter of a lord,
 And kissing a collier lassie an' a'?

Down by the dyke-side a lady did dwell,
At his table-head he thought she'd look well;
M'Clish's a'e daughter o' Clavers-ha' Lee,
A penniless lass wi' a lang pedigree.

> O, never look down, my lassie, at a',
> O, never look down, my lassie, at a',
> Thy lips are as sweet, and thy figure complete,
> As the finest dame in castle or ha'.
>
> Though thou hae nae silk and holland sae sma',
> Though thou hae nae silk and holland sae sma',
> Thy coat and thy sark are thy ain handywark,
> And Lady Jean was never sae braw."

How much Lady Nairne here improved on Burns does not require to be pointed out. The song as it left her ladyship's hands forms a lyrical character sketch unexcelled in British literature. Some persons, however, will *not* let well alone; and Miss Ferrier, the novelist, or some one else, added two verses which have followed the song like an ill-conditioned ghost, and bring ruin on the splendid conception on every occasion where they are allowed to intrude. They are these:—

> " And now that the Laird his exit had made,
> Mrs. Jean she reflected on what she had said—
> 'Oh, for ane I'll get better, it's waur I'll get ten;
> I was daft to refuse the Laird o' Cockpen.'
>
> Neist time that the Laird and the lady were seen,
> They were gaun arm-in-arm to the kirk on the green.
> Now she sits in the ha' like a weel-tappit hen,
> But as yet there's nae chickens appeared at Cockpen."

It is a gross violation of artistic taste, and utterly at variance with the character of the Laird of Cockpen, as expressed in the original song, to insinuate even that the woman who once refused the offer of his hand should ever receive another opportunity. Why, look at the man! "He was proud, he was great." His mind was absorbed in State affairs. He wanted a wife to adorn the head of his table—not to love. He condescended to ask Miss M'Clish of Clavers-ha'Lee. Was "dumfoundered" when she refused him. But not heart-broken, mark you; for "nae sigh did he gie." He went off in a rage, indeed,

> " And aften he thought, as he rade through the glen,
> She's *daft* to refuse the Laird o' Cockpen."

Miss M'Clish's answer, too—so coolly decisive, and so creditable to her—left no hope for further advances. She never hesitated a second, but coldly said

> " 'Na,'
> And wi' a laich curtsey she turned awa'."

There was an end to the wooing at that point at once and for ever, and there the song should end.

His wig was weel pouther'd, as gude as when new,
His waistcoat was white, his coat it was blue;
He put on a ring, a sword, and cock'd hat,—
And wha could refuse the Laird wi' a' that?

He took the gray mare and rade cannilie,
And rapped at the yett o' Clavers-ha' Lee;
"Gae tell Mistress Jean to come speedily ben;
She's wanted to speak wi' the Laird o' Cockpen."

Mistress Jean she was makin' the elder-flower wine;
"And what brings the Laird at sic a like time?"
She put aff her apron, and on her silk gown,
Her mutch wi' red ribbons, and gaed awa' down.

As to the real Laird of Cockpen—the hero of the old song of the same name—an anecdote has been preserved which affords some idea of his odd character. He is represented as having been the attached friend of his Sovereign. And having been engaged with his countrymen at the battle of Worcester in the cause of Charles, he accompanied the Monarch to Holland, and forming one of the little Court at the Hague, amused his royal master by his humour, and especially by his skill in Scottish music. In playing the tune "Brose and Butter" he particularly excelled. And it became a request of the King that he should be lulled to sleep every night and wakened every morning by this enchanting air. At the Restoration, Cockpen found his estate confiscated for his attachment to the royal cause, and had the mortification to discover that he had suffered on behalf of an ungrateful Prince, who gave no response to his many petitions for the restoration of his inheritance. Visiting London, he was denied an audience, but he still entertained the hope that, by securing a personal conference with the King, he might attain his object. To accomplish this, he had recourse to the following artifice. He formed an intimacy with the organist of the Chapel-Royal, and obtained permission to officiate as his substitute when the King came to service. All going as he had wished, at the dismissal he struck up His Majesty's old favourite, "Brose and Butter." The artifice succeeded. The King proceeded to the organ-gallery, where he found Cockpen, whom he saluted familiarly, declaring he had "almost made him dance." "I could dance, too," said Cockpen, "if I had my lands again." The request to which every other entreaty could gain no response, was yielded to the power of music. Cockpen was restored to his possessions. The estate, it may be worth noting, which is situated in the parish of Cockpen, in Edinburghshire, is now the property of the Earl of Dalhousie.

And when she cam ben, he bowed fu' low;
And what was his errand he soon let her know;
Amazed was the Laird when the lady said, "Na,"
And wi' a laich curtsey she turned awa'.

Dumfoundered he stood, but nae sigh did he gie;
He mounted his mare, and he rade cannilie;
And aften he thought as he rade through the glen,
"She's daft to refuse the Laird o' Cockpen."

BARONESS NAIRNE.

THE AULD HOUSE. *

OH, the auld house, the auld house,
   What tho' the rooms were wee!
Oh! kind hearts were dwelling there,
   And bairnies fu' o' glee;
The wild rose and the jessamine
   Still hang upon the wa',
How many cherish'd memories
   Do they, sweet flowers, reca'!

Oh, the auld laird, the auld laird,
   Sae canty, kind, and crouse,
How many did he welcome to
   His ain wee dear auld house!
And the leddy too, sae genty,
   There shelter'd Scotland's heir,
And clipt a lock wi' her ain hand †
   Frae his lang yellow hair.

---

* The old house of Gask in which Lady Nairne was born. It stood on a hill, overlooking the Earn, about fifty yards below the present mansion, which was commenced in 1801. Being much infested by rats, which on one occasion assailed the baby heir in his cradle, it was pulled down, with the exception of a small portion left to mark the site.

† In this description the poetess afterwards acknowledged she had indulged a poetic license. The lock was acquired under circumstances less romantic. "I enclose," she writes to an Edinburgh friend, "a

The mavis still doth sweetly sing,
    The bluebells sweetly blaw,
The bonny Earn's clear winding still,
    But the auld house is awa'.
The auld house, the auld house,
    Deserted tho' ye be,
There ne'er can be a new house
    Will seem sae fair to me.

Still flourishing the auld pear tree *
    The bairnies liked to see,
And oh, how often did they speir
    When ripe they a' wad be!
The voices sweet, the wee bit feet
    Aye rinnin' here and there,
The merry shout—oh! whiles we greet
    To think we'll hear nae mair.

For they are a' wide scattered now,
    Some to the Indies gane,
And ane, alas! to her lang hame;
    Not here we'll meet again.
The kirkyard, the kirkyard!
    Wi' flowers o' every hue,
Shelter'd by the holly's shade
    And the dark sombre yew.

The setting sun, the setting sun,
    How glorious it gaed doon!
The cloudy splendour raised our hearts
    To cloudless skies aboon!

---

few of *Charlie's hairs* which were given to my grandmother, Strowan, the day they were cut, by the man who cut them, one John Stewart, an attendant of the Prince. This is marked on the paper in her own handwriting. I have heard her mention this John Stewart, who dressed the Prince's hair. The writing had been done in James's lifetime, for an outer paper is marked 'The King's hair,' to correct the inner, which is inscribed 'The Prince's hair.'"

* "I have heard," writes Mr. Kington Oliphant, "one of the bairnies of the song, then an old woman, reproach herself for having cribbed pears from the auld pear tree."

The auld dial, the auld dial,
It tauld how time did pass;
The wintry winds hae dung it doon,
Noo hid 'mang weeds and grass.

BARONESS NAIRNE.

YE'LL MOUNT, GUDEMAN.*

Leddy.

"YE'LL mount, gudeman; ye'll mount and ride;
Ye'll cross the burn, syne doun the loch side,
Then up 'mang the hills, thro' the muir and the heather
And join great Argyle where loyal men gather."

---

* In a note appended to this song in *Lays from Strathearn*, the heroine is described as one of the Homes of Wedderburn. This seems to be an error. Margaret Blair Carnegie and John, twelfth Lord Gray, were married in 1741, when, as the result of said union, the estate of Kinfauns passed to the noble House of Gray, which still retains it. The anecdote of the kettle is historical. Lord Gray had, as Lord-Lieutenant of Perthshire, waited on the Duke of Cumberland at Dundee, when his Royal Highness was there on his way to the North to quench the Rebellion of 1745 in the blood of Culloden. He was coldly received by the haughty Hanoverian, and felt so insulted that he rode home hastily to Kinfauns determined to immediately join the standard of Prince Charlie. His lady knew too well his lordship's obstinate temper to appear to oppose him in his determination, but, as he complained of fatigue, she recommended him to have his feet bathed before retiring to rest. She lovingly herself undertook the bathing process, and when his lordship's unclothed limbs were placed in the bath, she, through an apparent awkward blunder, spilled a kettle of boiling water on them, and exclaimed, "Let them join the Prince that may, ye'll stay at hame and be Laird o' Kinfauns." The Baron was so scalded that he was not able to leave his room for several weeks; and in the meantime, the public career of Prince Charlie had closed on Drummossie Moor.

Exercising the poet's license, the authoress has made it appear that it was not in feet-bathing, but in making a "dish" for his lordship, before he should leave, that the kettle was "coupit;" as also that there was an argument between the couple which led up to the leg-scalding *denouement*.

Laird.

"Indeed, honest luckie, I think ye're no blate,
To bid loyal men gang ony sic gate;
For I'm gaun to fecht for true loyaltie,
Had the Prince ne'er anither, he still will ha'e me."

Leddy.

"About Charlie Stuart we ne'er could agree;
But dearie, for ance, be counsell'd by me;
Tak' nae pairt at a'; bide quietly at hame,
And ne'er heed a Campbell, M'Donald, or Graham."

Laird.

"Na, na, gudewife, for that winna do,
My Prince is in need, his friends they are few;
I aye lo'ed the Stuarts: I'll join them the day:
Sae gi'e me my boots, for my boots I will ha'e."

Leddy.

"Oh! saftly, gudeman, I think ye're gane mad;
I ha'e na the heart to preen on your cockaud;
The Prince, as ye ca' him, will never succeed;
Ye'll lose your estate, and maybe your head."

Laird.

"Come, cheer ye, my dear, and dry up your tears!
I ha'e my hopes, and I ha'e my fears;
But I'll raise my men, and a' that is given,
To aid the gude cause—then leave it to Heaven.

"But, haste ye now, haste ye, for I maun be gaun,
The mare's at the yett, the bugle is blawn,
Gie me my bonnet, it's far in the day,
I'm no for a dish, there's nae time to stay."

Leddy.

"Oh, dear! tak' but ane, it may do ye gude!"
But what ails the woman? she surely is mad!
She's lifted the kettle, but somehow it coup'd
On the legs o' the laird, wha roar'd and wha loup'd.

Laird.

"I'm brint! I'm brint! how cam' it this way?
I fear I'll no ride for mony a day!
Send aff the men, and to Prince Charlie say,
My heart is wi' him, but I'm tied by the tae."

The wily wife fleech'd, and the laird didna see,
The smile on her cheek thro' the tear in her e'e—
"Had I kent the gudeman wad ha'e had siccan pain,
The kettle, for me, sud hae coupit its lane."

BARONESS NAIRNE.

KITTY REID'S HOUSE.*

HECH! hey! the mirth that was there,
 The mirth that was there,
 The mirth that was there;
Hech! how! the mirth that was there,
 In Kitty Reid's house on the green, jo.

---

* A short way east of the Cross, on the South side of the High Street of Perth, is a house, in the front of which a marble stone is inserted, bearing the arms of the Mercers of Aldie and Meikleour, and with this inscription, "Here stood the House of the Green." It was on this spot, according to the legend, that the British temple dedicated to Mars stood, in which Agricola is said to have worshipped, and which had been built by the son of Regan, who governed Britain long before the birth of the Saviour. The house raised by the Mercers on this site early in the fifteenth century, after having been long their town residence, was demolished in the seventeenth century; and was succeeded by that which was called "The House of the Green." This latter was a famous hostelry, and the favourite resort of the country lairds. Its hostess, when it was in the height of its popularity, was one Kitty

There was laughin' an' singin', an' dancin' an' glee,
In Kitty Reid's house, in Kitty Reid's house;
There was laughin' an' singin', an' dancin' an' glee,
  In Kitty Reid's house on the green, jo.

Hech! hey! the fright that was there,
  The fright that was there,
  The fright that was there,
Hech! how! the fright that was there,
  In Kitty Reid's house on the green, jo.
The light glimmer'd in thro' a crack i' the wa',
An' a' body thought the lift it wad fa',
An' lads an' lasses they sune ran awa',
  Frae Kitty Reid's house on the green, jo.

Hech! hey! the dule that was there,
  The dule that was there,
  The dule that was there,
The birds an' beasts it wauken'd them a',
  In Kitty Reid's house on the green, jo.

Reid, whence it was also called "Kitty Reid's House." An old song of which it was the subject names many of the guests who were in the habit of frequenting it :—

"Kirkpottie, Kintullo, Pitcur, an' Laird Rollo,
  Cam' a' to this house, to Kitty Reid's house;
Invermay, Monivaird, Balbeggie, Kinnaird,
  Cam' a' to the house on the green, jo.
    Hech, hey, the mirth that was there, etc.,

Gan' tell Tullylum, that he's wanted to come,
  To Kitty Reid's house, to Kitty Reid's house;
Tell Bousie, an' Kerr, an' Ruthven the peer,
  To come to the house on the green, jo.
    Hech, hey, the mirth that was there, etc.,

Most of these would be familiar names to Lady Nairne, but that fact alone did not lead her to the composition of her own version of the song, as Dr. Rogers infers. The verses themselves afford the clearest evidence that they were written to hit off the serio-comic terror and confusion which had been caused to a social party by the collapse of a part, or the whole, of the ramshackle building.

The wa' gie'd a hurly an' scattered them a',
The piper, the fiddler, an' Kitty an' a',
The kye fell a-routin', the cocks they did craw,
  In Kitty Reid's house on the green, jo.

BARONESS NAIRNE.

CALLER HERRIN'.*

WHA'LL buy my caller herrin'?
They're bonnie fish and halesome farin';
Wha'll buy my caller herrin',
  New drawn frae the Forth?

When ye were sleepin' on your pillows,
Dreamed ye aught of our puir fellows,
Darkling as they faced the billows,
A' to fill the woven willows?
  Buy my caller herrin',
  New drawn frae the Forth.

Wha'll buy my caller herrin'?
They're no brought here without great darin';
Buy my caller herrin',
Haul'd through wind and rain.
  Wha'll buy my caller herrin'? etc.

Wha'll buy my caller herrin'?
Oh, ye may ca' them vulgar farin',
Wives and mithers, maist despairin',
Ca' them lives o' men.
  Wha'll buy my caller herrin'? etc.

---

* This song was written for the benefit of Nathaniel Gow, musical composer, son of the more celebrated Niel Gow. The MS., written in a borrowed hand, was conveyed to Gow by an Edinburgh gentlewoman, to whom Lady Nairne had confided her great secret. In the letter which enclosed the song to her friend, the Authoress wrote :— "If it is to be any use to Nathaniel, perhaps it should be dedicated to the Duchess of Athole." The advice was followed, and the words together with Gow's music have often been printed.

When the creel o' herrin' passes,
Ladies clad in silk and laces,
Gather in their braw pelisses,
Cast their heads and screw their faces.

    Wha'll buy my caller herrin'? etc.

Caller herrin's no' got lightly,
He can trip the spring fu' tightly,
Spite o' tauntin', flauntin', flingin',
Gow has set you a' a-singin'.

    Wha'll buy my caller herrin'? etc.

Neebour wives, now tent my tellin';
When the bonnie fish ye're sellin',
At a'e word be in your dealin'—
Truth will stand when a' thing's failin'.

    Wha'll buy my caller herrin'? etc.
          BARONESS NAIRNE.

HEY THE RANTIN' MURRAY'S HA'.[*]

Hey the rantin' Murray's Ha'!
  Mirth and glee amang them a'!
The courtly laird, the leddy braw,
  They'll welcome ye to Murray's Ha'.
Come ye hungry, come ye dry,
  Nane had ever need to wait;
Come ye brisk, or come ye shy,
  They'll meet ye or ye're at the yett.

---

[*] At the hospitable residence of Mr. John Graeme Murray, Carolina Oliphant and her sisters spent many happy days during the period of their youth. The "General" whose valour is commended in the song is the celebrated Thomas Graham of Balgowan, the hero of Barossa, afterwards Lord Lyndoch, who was a near relation of the Laird of Murray's Hall. The details of the story of the ghaist that haunted the Ha' have not come down to the present day; but if it be true that the apparition was frightsome enough to send terror to the soul of the gallant Graham he may be considered to have quit the district for the district's good.

Some were feastin' in the ha',
    Some at sports upon the green;
Peggie, flower amang them a',
    Dancin' like a Fairy Queen.
Blythest o' my blythesome days
    I ha'e spent at Murray's Ha',
But oh, my heart was like to break
    When I saw Peggie gang awa'.

Whan she gaed, or why gaed she,
    Few were there that weel could tell;
I thought it was to lightlie me—
    She maybe scarcely kenn'd hersel'.
They said a ghaist was in the wa',
    Sometimes aneath, sometimes aboon;
A' body heard—naebody saw,
    But a' were sure they'd see it soon.

Some say the General, honest man,
    That fear'd na bullets, great or sma',
Wad rather face the *Mons Meg* gun
    Than meet the ghaist o' Murray's Ha'.
'Tis no the gate I think ava,
    To lay a ghaist wi' mirth and glee,
Scholar'd lads and lasses braw
    Need nae ghaist nor goblin dree.

                    BARONESS NAIRNE.

THE ROWAN TREE.

OH! rowan tree, oh! rowan tree, thou'lt aye be dear to me;
Entwin'd thou art wi' mony ties o' hame and infancy.
Thy leaves were aye the first o' spring, thy flow'rs the simmer's pride;
There was na sic a bonnie tree in a' the country side.
                    Oh! rowan tree.

How fair wert thou in simmer time, wi' a' thy clusters white,
How rich and gay thy Autumn dress, wi' berries red and bright!
On thy fair stem were mony names, which now nae mair I see,
But they're engraven on my heart—forgot they ne'er can be.
        Oh! rowan tree.

We sat aneath thy spreading shade, the bairnies round thee ran,
They pu'd thy bonnie berries red, and necklaces they strang;
My mither! oh! I see her still, she smiled our sports to see,
Wi' little Jeanie on her lap, and Jamie at her knee.
        Oh! rowan tree.

Oh! there arose my father's prayer, in holy evening's calm,
How sweet was then my mother's voice, singing the Martyr's psalm!
Now a' are gane! we meet nae mair aneath the rowan tree,
But hallowed thoughts around thee twine o' hame and infancy.
        Oh! rowan tree.
       BARONESS NAIRNE.

THE HUNDRED PIPERS.*

Wi' a hundred pipers, an' a', an' a',
Wi' a hundred pipers, an' a' an' a';
We'll up an' gie them a blaw, a blaw,
Wi' a hundred pipers, an' a' an' a'.

---

* On receiving the submission of the civic authorities and the surrender of the castle, Prince Charles Edward entered Carlisle, on

Oh, it's ower the Border awa', awa',
It's ower the Border awa', awa';
We'll on an' we'll march to Carlisle Ha',
Wi' it's yetts, it's castle, an' a' an' a'.

Oh, our sodger lads looked braw, looked braw,
Wi' their tartan kilts, an' a', an' a',
Wi' their bonnets, and feathers, and glittering gear,
And pibrochs sounding sweet and clear.
Will they a' return to their ain dear glen?
Will they a' return, our Highland men?
Second-sichted Sandy looked fu' wae,
And mithers grat when they marched away.
    Wi' a hundred pipers, etc.

Oh, wha is foremost o' a', o' a'?
Oh, wha does follow the blaw, the blaw?
Bonnie Charlie, the king o' us a', hurra!
Wi' his hundred pipers an' a', an' a',
His bonnet an' feather, he's wavin' high,
His prancin' steed maist seems to fly,
The nor' wind plays wi' his curly hair,
While the pipers blaw in an unco flare.
    Wi' a hundred pipers, etc.,

The Esk was swollen, sae red and sae deep,
But shouther to shouther the brave lads keep,
Twa thousand swam ower to fell English ground,
And danced themselves dry to the pibroch's sound.

Monday, the 18th November, 1745, preceded by one hundred pipers. So far our poetess has sung truly. But she is historically at fault with reference to the "two thousand." So many Highlanders of the Chevalier's army did indeed wade across the Esk; but it was in flight, not in triumph. They waded the Esk on their return to Scotland from an expedition which boded disaster. That they "danced themselves dry to the pibroch's sound" is literally correct. Mr. George G. Mounsey, Author of "Authentic Accounts of the Occupation of Carlisle," remarks of the Highlanders, that "the moment they reached the opposite side the pipers, struck up, and they danced reels until they were dry again." Probably Lady Nairne's father witnessed the scene.—CHARLES ROGERS.

Dumfounder'd, the English saw, they saw—
Dumfounder'd, they heard the blaw, the blaw;
Dumfounder'd they a' ran awa', awa',
Frae the hundred pipers an' a', an' a'.
  Wi' a hundred pipers, etc.

BARONESS NAIRNE.

THE LASS O' GOWRIE.*

'TWAS on a summer's afternoon,
A wee before the sun gaed doon,
A lassie wi' a braw new gown
  Cam' ower the hills to Gowrie.
The rosebud wet wi' morning shower
Blooms fresh within the sunny bower,
But Katie was the fairest flower
  That ever bloomed in Gowrie.

There are no fewer than four versions of this song extant. The above—perhaps the best of them all, and the one to which public opinion has given the stamp of its approval—being of unknown authorship. One is ascribed to Colonel James Ramsay of Stirling Castle, which was revised from an old stall copy by Dr. Thomas Lyle; one is by Baroness Nairne; and one—"Kate o' Gowrie"—by William Reid of Glasgow, an inveterate song-tinker, who tried his hand on Burns's "O' a' the airts the wind can blaw," "John Anderson, my Jo," and other well-known songs. Whether the heroine was a real or an imaginary "lass," no one seems to know. Whitelaw, in *The Book of Scottish Song*, introduces two additional verses, between the second and third of the above, which are clearly out of harmony with the rest of the song, and tend to a confusion of the sense of it. They are never sung. Here they are:—

"A silken gown o' siller grey
My mither coft last New Year's Day,
And buskit me frae tap to tae,
  To keep me oot o' Gowrie.
Daft Will, short syne, cam' coortin' Nell,
And wan the lass, but what befel,
Or whare she's gane; she kens hersel';
  She staid na lang in Gowrie."

Sic thoughts, dear Katie, ill combine
Wi' beauty rare, and wit like thine;

I praised her beauty loud and lang;
Around her waist my arms I flang,
And said, "My dearie, will ye gang
   To see the carse o' Gowrie?
I'll tak' ye to my father's ha'
In yon green field beside the shaw;
I'll mak' ye lady o' them a'—
   The brawest wife in Gowrie."

Saft kisses on her lips I laid;
The blush upon her cheek soon spread:
She whispered modestly and said—
   "I'll gang wi' you to Gowrie."
The auld fouks soon gae their consent;
Syne to Mess John we quickly went,
Wha tied us to our hearts' content;
   And now she's Lady Gowrie.
                ANONYMOUS.

THE LASS O' GOWRIE.

A WEE bit north frae yon green wood,
   Whare draps the sunny showerie,
The lofty elm trees spread their boughs
   To shade the braes o' Gowrie.
An' by yon burn you scarce can see
   There stands a rustic bowerie,
Whar lives a lass mair dear to me
   Than a' the maids in Gowrie.

Nae gentle bard e'er sang her praise,
   'Cause fortune ne'er left dowrie;
The rose blaws sweetest in the shade,
   So does the flower o' Gowrie.

Except yoursel', my bonnie quean,
   I care for nought in Gowrie.
Since first I saw you in the shiel,
To you my heart's been true and leal;
The darkest night I fear nae de'il,
   Warlock, or witch, in Gowrie."

When April strews her garlands roun'
   Her bare feet treads the flowerie;
Her sang gars a' the woodlands ring
   That shade the braes o' Gowrie.

Her modest blush and downcast e'e
   A flame sent beating through me;
For she surpasses a' I've seen
   This peerless flower o' Gowrie.
I've lain upon the dewy green
   Until the evening hourie,
An' thought gin e'er I durst ca' mine
   The bonnie lass o' Gowrie.

The bushes that o'erhang the burn,
   Sae verdant, and sae flowerie,
Can witness that I lo'e alane
   The bonny lass o' Gowrie.
Let ithers dream, an' sigh for wealth,
   And fashion fleet and flowerie;
Gi'e me that heav'nly innocence
   Upon the braes o' Gowrie.
      ASCRIBED TO COLONEL JAMES RAMSAY.

THE LASS O' GOWRIE.

'TWAS on a summer's afternoon,
A wee afore the sun gaed doon,
A lassie wi' a braw new goun
   Cam' ower the hills to Gowrie.
The rosebud wash'd in summer's shower,
Bloom'd fresh within the sunny bower;
But Kitty was the fairest flower
   That e'er was seen in Gowrie.

To see her cousin she came there,
An' oh! the scene was passing fair;
For what in Scotland can compare
   Wi' the Carse o' Gowrie?

The sun was setting on the Tay,
The blue hills melting into grey,
The mavis and the blackbird's lay
   Were sweetly heard in Gowrie.

Oh, lang the lassie I had woo'd,
An' truth an' constancy had vow'd,
But cam' nae speed wi' her I lo'ed,
   Until she saw fair Gowrie.
I pointed to my faither's ha',
Yon bonnie bield ayont the shaw,
Sae lown that there nae blast could blaw,—
   Wad she no bide in Gowrie?

Her faither was baith glad an' wae;
Her mither she wad naething say;
The bairnies thocht they wad get play,
   If Kitty gaed to Gowrie.
She whiles did smile, she whiles did greet;
The blush an' tear were on her cheek—
She naething said, an' hung her head,
   But now she's Leddy Gowrie.

               BARONESS NAIRNE.

KATE O' GOWRIE.

When Katie was scarce out nineteen,
Oh, but she had twa coal-black een!
A bonnier lass ye wadna seen
   In a' the Carse o' Gowrie.
Quite tired o' livin' a' his lane,
Pate did to her his love explain,
And swore he'd be, were she his ain,
   The happiest lad in Gowrie.

Quo' she, "I winna marry thee,
For a' the gear that ye can gi'e;
Nor will I gang a step ajee,
   For a' the gowd in Gowrie.

My father will gi'e me twa kye;
My mother's gaun some yarn to dye;
I'll get a gown just like the sky,
   Gif I'll no gang to Gowrie."

"Oh, my dear Katie, say nae sae!
Ye little ken a heart that's wae;
Hae! there's my hand: hear me, I pray
   Sin' thou'lt no gang to Gowrie?
Since first I met thee at the shiel,
My saul to thee's been true and leal;
The darkest night I fear nae deil,
   Warlock, or witch, in Gowrie.

"I fear nae want o' claes, nor aught;
Sic silly things my mind ne'er taught.
I dream a' nicht, and start about,
   And wish for thee in Gowrie.
I lo'e thee better, Kate, my dear,
Than a' my rigs and out-gaun gear;
Sit down by me till ance I swear,
   Thou'rt worth the Carse o' Gowrie.'

Syne on her mou' sweet kisses laid,
Till blushes a' her cheeks o'erspread;
She sigh'd, and in soft whispers said,
   "Oh, Pate, tak' me to Gowrie!"
Quo' he, "Let's to the auld folk gang;
Say what they like, I'll bide their bang,
And bide a' nicht, though beds be thrang;
   But I'll hae thee to Gowrie."

The auld folk sune baith gi'ed consent;
The priest was ca'd—a' were content;
And Katie never did repent
   That she gaed hame to Gowrie.
For routh o' bonnie bairns had she;
Mair strappin' lads ye wadna see;
And her braw lasses bore the gree
   Frae a' the rest o' Gowrie.

WILLIAM REID.

WHEN YE GANG AWA, JAMIE.*

She—WHEN ye gang awa, Jamie,
  Far across the sea, laddie ;
When ye gang to Germanie,
  What will ye send to me, laddie ?

He—I'll send ye a braw new gown, Jeanie,
  I'll send ye a braw new gown, lassie ;
And it shall be o' silk and gowd,
  Wi' Valenciennes set round, lassie.

---

* The original of this popular song, under the title of "The Duke of Athol," was first printed in Mr. Kinloch's collection, where it is said to have been taken from the recitation of an idiot boy in Wishaw. It runs as follows :—

" I am gaing awa', Jeanie,
  I am gaing awa',
I am gaing ayont the saut seas,
  I am gaing sae far awa'."

" Whan will ye marry me, Jamie ?
  Whan will ye marry me ?
Will ye tak' me to your countrie,
  Or will ye marry me ? "

" How can I marry thee, Jeanie,
  How can I marry thee ?
When I've a wife and bairns three,
  Twa wad na weill agree."

" Wae be to your fause tongue, Jamie,
  Wae be to your fause tongue ;
Ye promised for to marry me,
  And has a wife at hame."

" If my wife wad dee, Jeanie,
  And sae my bairns three,
I wad tak' ye to my ain countrie,
  And married we wad be."

" O, an' your head war sair, Jamie,
  O, an' your head war sair,
I'd tak' the napkin frae my neck,
  And tie doun your yellow hair."

" I hae nae wife at a', Jeanie,
  I hae nae wife at a',
I hae neither wife nor bairns three,
  I said it to try thee.

She—That's nae gift ava, Jamie,
  That's nae gift ava, laddie;
 There's ne'er a gown in a' the toun,
  I'd like, when ye're awa', laddie.

He—When I come back again, Jeanie,
  When I come back, lassie,
 I'll bring wi' me a gallant gay,
  To be your ain gudeman, lassie.

She—Be my gudeman yoursel', Jamie,
  Be my gudeman yoursel', laddie,
 An' tak' me ower to Germanie,
  Wi' you at hame to dwell, laddie.

He—I ken na how that would do, Jeanie,
  I ken na how that can be, lassie,
 For I've a wife and bairnies three,
  An' I'm feart ye wadna gree, lassie,

She—You should tell'd me that in time, Jamie,
  You should tell'd me that in time, laddie,
 For had I kent o' your fause heart,
  You ne'er had gotten mine, laddie.

He—Your een were like a spell, Jeanie,
  Your een were like a spell, lassie;
 That ilka day bewitch'd me sae,
  I couldna help mysel', lassie.

She—Gae back to your wife and hame, Jamie,
  Gae back to your bairnies three, laddie,
 And I will pray they ne'er may thole,
  A broken heart like me, laddie.

  " Blair in Athol is mine, Jeanie,
   Blair in Athol is mine;
  Bonnie Dunkeld is whare I dwell,
   And the boats o' Garry's mine."

Whether the narrative had any origin in fact no one appears to know. There is a rendering of the song by the Baroness Nairne, but the above version, the author of which is unknown, is the one of universal favour.

He—Dry that tearfu' e'e, Jeanie,
  My story's a' a lee, lassie,
I've neither wife nor bairnies three,
  And I'll wed nane but thee, lassie.

She—Think weel for fear ye rue, Jamie,
  Think weel for fear ye rue, laddie,
For I hae neither gowd nor lands,
  To be a match for you, laddie.

He—Blair in Athole's mine, Jeanie,
  Little Dunkeld is mine, lassie,
St. Johnston's bower, and Hunting-tower,
  An' a' that's mine is thine, lassie.
ANONYMOUS.

ANSWER TO "I'M WEARIN' AWA', JOHN."

OH! you are happy now, jo,
Your care is a' through, jo,
Nae pain reaches you
  In the land o' the leal.

Our lassie wan awa, jo,
Nor muckle sorrow saw, jo:
Now I mourn twa
  In the land o' the leal.

But a' is gude and weel, jo,
Though nature it maun feel, jo,
Ilk pain will he heal
  In the land o' the leal.

My locks are thin and grey, jo,
My powers fast decay, jo,
I'm laith lang to stay
  Frae the land o' the leal.

But my tears drap in vain, jo,
Alane I maun remain, jo,
Till we meet again
    In the land o' the leal.

Though trouble here us tries, jo,
'Tis blessing in disguise, jo,
To mak' us mair prize
    The land o' the leal.
              CHRISTIAN GRAY.

THE FAITHFUL SWAIN.

KEEN blaws the blast on the high hill o' Gaston,
    And thick through the Shandy wood drives the cauld snaw;
Yon boughs, bending heavy wi' bonny green ivy,
    The pitiless tempest is tearing awa'.
The shepherds, affrighted, their flocks leave benighted,
    All hungry and heartless they lag on the lea;
        But caulder the blast shall blaw,
        Thicker shall drive the snaw,
        Ere it keep me awa',
           Nanny, frae thee.

The broad moon arising the eastlands illuming,
    The wast was in saft starry beauty arrayed,
When we parted in tears where the heather was blooming,
    And the craik's thrilling note sounded far o'er the mead.
My first love was true love, I'll ne'er cherish new love,
    Though richer and fairer than her I may see;
        And caulder the blast shall blaw,
        Thicker shall drive the snaw,
        Ere it keep me awa',
           Nanny, frae thee.

By Annat's young wood, where the beech tree now
    withers,
Beneath the green pines, where the wild birds repose,
And round the Raith hill, where the sunny wreath
    gathers,
Wi' her I hae pu'd the sweet gowan and rose.
Daylight is departing, my speed of foot thwarting,
  Far wrang I may wander while drift blinds my e'e;
    But caulder the blast shall blaw,
    Thicker shall drive the snaw,
    Ere it keep me awa',
      Nanny, frae thee.
CHARLES SPENCE.

PURSUIT OF PRINCE CHARLIE.

BIRD of the budding bush,
  Sing soft and sparely,
See how the redcoats rush,
  Hunting Prince Charlie,
Beating the broomy fells
  Over and over;
Shaking the heather bells,
  Scaring the plover.

See by yon lonely cave,
  Wistfully weeping,
Over our Prince, the brave
  Flora watch keeping!
Lichen and liver grass,
  And the moss willow,
Curtain the narrow pass,
  And her stone pillow.

Bird of the budding spray,
  Sing not so clearly,
Lest your shrill notes betray,
  Him we lo'e dearly.

> Sing not so late at night,
>   Sing not so early,
> Till they have ta'en their flight,
>   Flora and Charlie.
>
> CHARLES SPENCE.

THE TWA BUMBEES.

THERE were twa bumbees met on a twig,
  Fim-fam, fiddle-faddle, fum, fizz!
Said "Whaur will we gang our byke to big?"
  Tig-a-leery, twig-a-leery, bum, bizz!
The modest Miss, bein' rather shy,
Twigg'd round her head and look'd awry
And ga'e her Dandy nae reply,
  But "Tig-a-leery, twig-a-leery, bum, bizz!"

  O! we will gang to yon sunny bank,
  Fim-fam, fiddle-faddle, fum, fizz!
Whaur the flowers bloom fair, and the fog grows rank,
  Tig-a-leery, twig-a-leery, bum, bizz!"
They sought the bank frae side to side,
In every hole baith straucht and wide,
But nane they saw could please the Bride,
  Tig-a-leery, twig-a-leery, bum, bizz!

---

* This song appeared in print for the first time, at my instigation, in the *Dundee Weekly News* some time ago, and will be welcomed here by not a few local literary antiquaries, and others, who have been in quest of it for a number of years back. The song owes its existence to the late Mr. George Porter, schoolmaster of Moneydie, an excellent and esteemed man, who was equal in many respects as a poet to Charles Spence himself, and far surpassed him, indeed, in the tender and graceful—the natural reflex of his own lovable character. George Porter and Charles Spence were bosom friends from their youth time upwards, and two more genial and kindly spirits never sat knee to knee. Porter, though possessing very little of a voice, was always ready in company to take his turn at a song. But sometimes, by reason of this shortcoming, the effect of his effort was not all that could be desired; so, in course of time, he asked Spence to compose a song for him, such that its wit and humour would make it tell, irrespective of musical execution. The result was "The Twa Bumbees," well known in these parts as *Mr. Porter's own special song.*

When they had sought frae noon till six,
  Fim-fam, fiddle-faddle, fum, fizz!
And on nae place their choice could fix,
  Tig-a-leery, twig-a-leery, bum, bizz!
They saw a hole beneath a tree,
"O! this our dwelling place shall be,"
They said, and entered cheerfully,
  Tig-a-leery, twig-a-leery, bum, bizz!

Jenny Wren cam' hame at night,
  Fim-fam, fiddle-faddle, fum, fizz!
And, O, but she got an unco fright,
  Tig-a-leery, twig-a-leery, bum, bizz!
She entered in, ne'er dreading harm,
When in her chamber snug and warm,
The roving pair rang the alarm,
  Tig-a-leery, twig-a-leery, bum, bizz!

Jenny Wren bein' smit with fear,
  Fim-fam, fiddle-faddle, fum, fizz!
Flew aff and ne'er again cam' near,
  Tig-a-leery, twig-a-leery, bum, bizz!
Quoth the gudewife to the gudeman,
"When night her mantle has withdrawn,
And Phœbus shines upon the lawn,
  Tig-a-leery, twig-a-leery, bum, bizz!

"We'll gather honey from each flower,
  Fim-fam, fiddle-faddle, fum, fizz!
And when the day begins to lower,
  Tig-a-leery, twig-a leery, bum, bizz!
We'll hither hie, and here we'll meet,
All shielded from the wind and weet,
And a' night lang enjoy the sweet,
  Tig-a-leery, twig-a-leery, bum, bizz!"

They hadna been lang beneath the tree,
  Fim-fam, fiddle-faddle, fum, fizz!
When out cam' bumbees, ane, twa, three,
  Tig-a-leery, twig-a-leery, bum, bizz!

Quoth Mr. Bum to Mrs. Bee,
"O! had ye a' these bees by me?"
Whilst jealousy lurk'd in his e'e,
   Tig-a-leery, twig-a-leery, bum, bizz!

Quoth Mrs. Bee to Mr. Bum,
  "Fim-fam, fiddle-faddle, fum, fizz!
They're a' as like you's mum's like mum,
   Tig-a-leery, twig-a-leery, bum, bizz!
I cowed the horns frae aff your brow!"
Quoth Mr. Bum, "O, wow, wow, wow!
And had I horns then to cowe?
   Tig-a-leery, twig-a-leery, bum, bizz!

"O! a' ye bumbees whaur'er you be,
  Fim-fam, fiddle-faddle, fum, fizz!
I pray a warning tak' by me,
   Tig-a-leery, twig-a-leery, bum, bizz!
Far rather lead a single life
Than wed a wayward wanton wife
Wha'll cause you meikle dule and strife,
   Tig-a-leery, twig-a-leery, bum, bizz!"

CHARLES SPENCE.

LINN-MA-GRAY.*

LINN-MA-GRAY I long to see
Thy heathy heights and broomy lea;
Whaur linnets lilt, and leverets play
Around the roar of Linn-ma-Gray.

---

* Linn-ma-Gray—or in its true Gaelic rendering, *Linne-mo-Ghraidh* — meaning the linn of my darling, or the dell of the devoted lover, is, though a small, yet a beautiful and romantic waterfall, situated on the south side of the Sidlaw Hills, about a mile and a half west from the village of Kinnaird, in the Carse of Gowrie. Its wild and rugged depth, overshadowed by the tall ash trees which spring from its bottom, and the foaming of its troubled waters as they dash headlong down the precipitous rocks, give a hallowed and awe-striking impression to the lonely spectator as he winds his way up the sylvan glade, and is withal, a spot well suited to impress the author with the deep sense of poetic

Linn-ma-Gray, when to the street
Crowds follow crowds, in crowds to meet,
I wend my solitary way,
An' climb the cliffs of Linn-ma-Gray.

Linn-ma-Gray, each mountain spring
From age to age doth tribute bring,
And rushing onward to the Tay,
Augment the stream of Linn-ma-Gray.

Linn-ma-Gray, round Baron hill
I've aften gane wi' richt gude will,
An' sat an' seen the dashing spray
Lash the dark rocks of Linn-ma-Gray.

Linn-ma-Gray, when in yon ha'
The merry wassailers gather a',
In vain their weel-trained bands essay
The minstrelsy of Linn-ma-Gray.

---

feeling here displayed in verse. The heroine of the song was, I believe, a Jeanie Bruce, a young woman who lived at Evelick, and with whom Spence fell deeply in love. They were to have been married, but the girl's mother forbade the banns. "What!" said she, "would you marry a *poet*?" Spence retalliated with :—

"Wow! Jeanie, wow! what ails you now?
To lichtly me, and a' that,
Although I choose to court the muse,
Am I the worse for a' that?"

Nay verily, but the truth is, this poetic shaft from Spence was blunted by the fact that, through his intense love of poetry and nature, that to which he owed his bread and butter was often allotted a secondary place in his arduous life-struggle. Poor Jeanie died, and Spence eventually married one Anne Bissett.

An engraved picture of Spence and his Jean, by Alexander Carse, finds a place at page 49 of Knox's *Topography of the Basin of the Tay*. It represents the loving pair contemplating the beautiful waterfall, and has the following verse-motto printed below :—

"Up the heights of Baron Hill
I've led my Jean with right goodwill,
And sat and seen the foamy spray
Lash the dark rocks of Linn-ma-Gray."

Linn-ma-Gray, an' ye were mine
Wi' birk an' beech, an' yew an' pine,
An' ash an aik, I would pourtray
The loveliness of Linn-ma-Gray.

Linn-ma-Gray, high on thy crest
The wag-tail builds her felty nest,
And down amid the misty spray
The snipe finds hame at Linn-ma-Gray.

Linn-ma-Gray, the cushats cool
Their pinions, fluttering in thy pool,
Where sunbeam never found its way
Far ben the glack of Linn-ma-Gray.

Linn-ma-Gray, thy hazels green
Lodge the thrush an' finch at e'en,
Lodge me too at close o' day—
I tune my harp at Linn-ma-Gray.

Linn-ma-Gray, another linn,
May hac its beauties, hearts to win;
But never can they wile away,
My wish to muse at Linn-ma-Gray.

Linn-ma-Gray the time has been
When I, unchallenged, here was seen
By those who now may come and say—
"Hence, vagrant, hence from Linn-ma-Gray."

Linn-ma-Gray, thy cliffs and streams,
What though an earthly lordling claims?
I only recognise the sway
Of *Nature's God* at Linn-ma-Gray.

Linn-ma-Gray, the holy sound
Of music in thy gorge profound
Might well the tyrant challenge stay
For those who muse at Linn-ma-Gray.

Linn-ma-Gray, if I might have
A wish—some friend would dig a grave,
Where they my cauld remains might lay
Beside the fall of Linn-ma-Gray.

My coronach would be its cry—
No stream the lack of tears supply;
And soundly till the *rising day*
I would sleep on at Linn-ma-Gray,

Linn-ma-Gray, a long farewell—
Nae mair thy solitary dell
Shall listen to my roundelay—
Nae mair I visit Linn-ma-Gray.
CHARLES SPENCE.

LASSIE WI' THE YELLOW COATIE.

LASSIE wi' the yellow coatie,
 Will ye wed a muirlan' Jockie?
Lassie wi' the yellow coatie,
  Will ye busk an' gang wi' me?
I hae meal an' milk in plenty,
I hae kail an' cakes fu' dainty,
I've a but an' ben fu' genty,
  But I want a wife like thee.

  Lassie wi' the yellow coatie, etc.

Although my mailin' be but sma',
An' little gowd I hae to shaw,
I hae a heart without a flaw,
  An' I will gie it a' to thee.

  Lassie wi' the yellow coatie, etc.

Wi' my lassie an' my doggie,
Ower the lea an' through the boggie,

Nane on earth was e'er sae vogie
   Or sae blythe as we will be.

   Lassie wi' the yellow coatie, etc.

Haste ye, lassie, to my bosom,
While the roses are in blossom,
Time is precious, dinna lose them ;
   Flowers will fade, an' sae will we.
Lassie wi' the yellow coatie,
Ah ! tak' pity on your Jockie ;
Lassie wi' the yellow coatie,
   I'm in haste, an' sae should ye !

JAMES DUFF.

THE HERO OF BAROSSA. *

ASSIST me ye muses of dear native Scotia,
   While thus in the praise o' your hero I sing,
Wha lately displayed on the heights of Barossa,
   Sic zeal for his kintry, an' love to his king.
'Twas there he despis'd ev'ry danger an' peril ;
   'Twas there he resolv'd British valour to shew ;
And there our brave vet'ran was crown'd wi' fresh laurels,
   For there he encounter'd an' vanquish'd the foe.

The cause o' his country first call'd him to arms,
   And soon were the proofs o' his valour display'd :
Sweet rural retirement could yield him no charms,
   Compar'd to what drums an' the trumpet convey'd.
At *Toulon* an' *Malta*, no valour was wantin',
   And mournful *Corunna*, where Moore met his fall,
The fate o' his friend could the Graham never dauntin',
   But that of Barossa surpasses them all.

---

* The battle of Barossa was fought and won by our gallant countryman, General Sir Thomas Graham, on the 5th March, 1811. On that day the British arms were victorious, over nearly three times their number.—*Author's Note.*

No wonder the French were soon all in confusion,
   And fled frae their Eagles wi' terror and shame.
To rally again were the height o' delusion,
   Or cope with an army led on by the Graham ;
A name sae lang famed in the history of Scotia,
   For sake o' that chieftain at Falkirk wha fell, *
And now made immortal so late at Barossa,
   Which Frenchmen for ages wi' sorrow may tell.

The bluid o' that hero still seems to pervade him,
   His name and his valour, his lineage proclaim.
La Pena † may blush, that he basely betrayed him,
   Or flinch'd frae the side o' a sodger like Graham.
That day he was deaf to the cries o' his nation,
   Regardless what shame his misconduct might bring,
While Graham, as a hero, stood true to his station,
   And fought like a lion for kintra an' king.

This feat of Barossa, oh ! could I explain it,
   But language would fail to express what I feel,
To tell how brave Graham, by the point o' the bay'net,
   Taught Frenchmen that Britons had plenty o' steel.
Then fill an' we'll drink to this son of auld Scotia,
   His name an' his country wi' transport we own,
For know that the hero, wha shone at Barossa,
   Was our honour'd chief, gallant Graham of Balgow'n.

JAMES DUFF.

THE BONNIE LASS O' LEVENSIDE.*

How sweet are Leven's silver streams,
   Around her banks the wild flowers blooming ;
     On every bush the warblers vie,
     In strains of bosom-soothing joy.

---

    * Sir John the Graeme.   † A Spanish General.
    * This song was written by Drummond while a clerk in Kirkland Works, near Leven, previous to his embarkation for India, and was inspired by the charms of a Miss Wilson, daughter of the proprietor

But Leven's banks that bloom sae braw,
 And Leven's streams that glide sae saucy,
Sic joy and beauty couldna shaw,
 An' 'twerna for my darling lassie ;
  Her presence fills them a' wi' pride,
  The bonnie lass o' Levenside.

When sober eve begins her reign,
The little birds to cease their singing,
 The flowers their beauty to renew
 Their bosoms bathe in diamond dew ;
When far behind the Lomonds high
 The wheels of day are downwards rowing,
And a' the western closing sky
 Wi' varied tints of glory lowing.
  'Tis then my eager steps I guide
  To meet the lass o' Levenside.

The solemn sweetness Nature spreads,
The kindly hour to bliss inviting,
 Within our happy bosoms move
 The softest sigh of purest love ;
Reclined upon the velvet grass,
 Beneath the balmy birky blossom,
What words could a' my joys express,
 When claspèd to her beating bosom !
  How swells my heart with rapture's tide,
  When wi' the lass o' Levenside !

---

of Pirnie, near Leven. The lady, it appears, subsequently became engaged to be married to the author, and for the consummation of the mutual agreement sailed for India in 1816. On her arrival she was kindly received by her affianced lover, but, in the interval, she became desirous of withdrawing from her engagement and returning home. Observing her coldness Drummond acceded to the request, and offered to pay the expense of her passage back to Scotland. Presently she was seized with fever, and died. Report alleged that her lover had been unfaithful, and that she had died of a broken heart, and thus the memory of Drummond has been unjustly aspersed.

 The song was first printed with the author's consent, though without acknowledgment, in a small volume of poems by William Rankin, Leven, published in 1812. Subsequently it has been claimed by William Glass, a painter-rhymster of Edinburgh, who gave it as his own in a volume of poems entitled *Scenes of Gloamin'*, published in 1814. Drummond is certainly the Author.

She never saw the splendid ball,
She never gazed on courtly grandeur;
  But, like her native lily's bloom,
  She cheerfu' gilds her humble home;
The pert reply, the modish air,
  To soothe the soul were never granted,
When modest sense and love are there
  The guise o' art may weel be wanted;
    O, Fate! gi'e me to be my bride
    The bonnie lass o' Levenside!
              DAVID DRUMMOND.

MARY OF SWEET ABERFOYLE.*

THE sun hadna peep'd frae behind the dark billow,
  The slow-sinking moon half illumined the scene,
As I lifted my head frae my care-haunted pillow,
  And wander'd to muse on the days that were gane.
Sweet hope seem'd to smile o'er ideas romantic,
  And gay were the dreams that my soul would beguile;
But my eyes filled wi' tears as I viewed the Atlantic,
  An' thought on my Mary of sweet Aberfoyle.

Though far frae my hame in a tropical wildwood,
  Yet the fields o' my forefathers rose on my view:
An' I wept when I thought on the days of my childhood,
  An' the vision was painful the brighter it grew.

---

* William Glen, author of "Wae's me for Prince Charlie," though a native of Glasgow, was intimately connected with Perthshire. He married a MacFarlane of Aberfoyle, whom he wooed and won on the banks of the lovely Loch Ard, where he also composed many of his sweetest songs; and here he spent, on the farm of Rainagour, the last eight years of his brief career. His widow, who, with their only daughter, had the management of the Orphan Institution at Aberfoyle, survived him by thirty-two years. She died at Craigie Cottage only a few years ago. Glen for some time resided in the West India Islands, where his commercial enterprises led him; and it was while sojourning there that he celebrated his betrothed in the present beautiful song.

Sweet days when my bosom with rapture was swelling,
  Though I knew it not then, it was love made me smile;
Oh! the snaw-wreath is pure where the moonbeams are dwelling,
  Yet as pure is my Mary of sweet Aberfoyle.

Now far in the east the sun slowly rising,
  Brightly gilded the top of the tall cabbage tree;
An' sweet was the scene such wild beauties comprising,
  As might have filled the sad mourner with rapture and glee.
But my heart felt nae rapture—nae pleasant emotion,
  The saft springs o' pleasure had lang, lang been seal'd;
I thought on my home 'cross the wide stormy ocean,
  And wept for my Mary of sweet Aberfoyle.

The orange was bathed in the dews of the morning,
  An' the bright drops bespangled the clustering vine;
White were the blossoms the lime-tree adorning,
  An' brown was the apple that grew on the pine.
Were I as free as an Indian chieftain,
  Sic beautiful scenes might gi'e pleasure the while;
But the joy o' a slave is aye waverin' an' shiftin',
  An' a slave I'm to Mary of sweet Aberfoyle.

When the mirk cloud o' fortune aboon my head gathers,
  An' the golden shower fa's where it ne'er fell before;
Oh! then I'll revisit the land o' my fathers,
  An' clasp to this bosom the lass I adore.
Hear me, ye angels, who watch o'er my maiden,
  Like ane o' yoursel's she is free frae a' guile,
Pure as was love in the garden o' Eden,
  Sae pure is my Mary of sweet Aberfoyle.
WILLIAM GLEN.

ST. JOHNSTOUN'S BELLS.

AIR.—"*Dumbarton drums beat bonny, O!*"

St. Johnstoun's bells ring bonny, O!
And awaken echoes mony, O!

  But I'll never think them sweet
  Since again I canna meet
  On the banks o' the Tay
  Wi' my Johnny, O!

When the day had passed, and the gloamin', O!
Brought the hour for careless roaming, O!
How glad I stole away
For a summer hour to stray,
On the bonny banks o' Tay,
Wi' my Johnny, O!
  Chorus—St. Johnstoun's bells, etc.

I'll aye mind the hour when he left me, O!
And of every joy bereft me, O!
When my head lay on a breast
That was very ill at rest,
Yet to soothe me his best
Did my Johnny, O!
  Chorus—St. Johnstoun's bells, etc.

But my laddie sighed for glory, O!
And too soon he graced a story, O!
He bartered love for fame,
His hame left for a name,
And he fought where gallant Graham
Led my Johnny, O!

Chorus—St. Johnstoun's bells ring bonny, O!
  And awaken echoes mony, O!
  But I'll never think them sweet
  Since again we canna meet,
  For Barossa's turf
  Covers Johnny, O!
      WILLIAM CLYDE.

CRAIGIE HILL.

THE praise of Yarrow, Teviot, Tweed,
 Ben Lomond's height, Gleniffer's dell;
Of Lugar, Irvine, Ayr, and Doon,
 Our woodland echoes often tell.

'Mid matchless grandeur, rich and gay,
   Muse of the North! then say, why still
Unsung the glorious banks of Tay,
   And sunny slopes of Craigie Hill?

Tay's "combinations of bright scenes
   Breathe music"—then no more be mute,
Whilst thousand rhymes on meaner floods
   Aid shepherd's pipe or lover's lute.
Sons of our mountains, ever brave—
   Maids of our glens, though chaste not chill—
These be thy theme, with banks of Tay,
   And sunny slopes of Craigie Hill.

The Romans, following from afar
   Agricola to northern wars,
In Tay and its fair banks beheld
   Their Tiber and their Field of Mars.
That landscape stopped the veterans' march
   Till admiration gazed its fill;
Their shouts resound along the Tay,
   And up the slopes of Craigie Hill.

Those shouts soon roused, o'er many a glen,
   The Caledonians in their pride—
"If worthy conquest, then our land
   Is worth defence!" they fiercely cried.
Italia's soldiers bit the dust,
   Their red blood died the mountain rill;
A thinn'd, desponding band recross'd
   The sunny slopes of Craigie Hill.

Are not yon fair fields Luncarty?
   Is not St. Johnstoun at our feet?
Where Dane and Southron our bold sires
   In the death struggle dared to meet;
Whence Charlie march'd his scanty band—
   For kingdoms three struck with a will;
They failed, although with gallant hearts
   They left the slopes of Craigie Hill.

And in our time, when Britain stood
    Against a banded world alone,
From the Unconquerable Isle
    The noblest of her youth were gone;
Lads of crisp locks and bearing free
    Tay sent, resolved their blood to spill,
Ere alien flag should float above
    The sunny slopes of Craigie Hill.

Roll on, proud Tay, by tower and town,
    Amid thy gorgeous scenery;
Aye be thy Strath unequalled for
    Luxuriant fertility.
The dwellers on thy banks the Muse
    Has sung. One part awaits her skill—
To chant thy beauties as they lie
    View'd from the slopes of Craigie Hill.
                      WILLIAM CLYDE.

TAK' IT, MAN, TAK' IT.*

WHEN I was a miller in Fife,
    Losh! I thought that the sound o' the happer
Said, Tak' hame a wee flow to your wife,
    To help to be brose to your supper.
Then my conscience was narrow and pure,
    But someway by random it rackit;
For I lifted twa neivefu' or mair,
    While the happer said, Tak' it, man, tak' it.
      Hey for the mill and the kill,
        The garland and gear for my cogie;
      Hey for the whisky and yill,
        That washes the dust frae my craigie.

Although it's been lang in repute
    For rogues to mak' rich by deceiving,

---

* This happily conceived and cleverly executed song was popular in the country districts of Perthshire from forty to fifty years ago, and may still occasionally be heard resounding from the bothy, the village inn, and the cottage ingle-nook in these parts. The more popular and effective way of delivering it is for the singer to be seated on a chair and to beat a mill-clapper-like accompaniment with his elbows and lists on a table before him.

Yet I see that it doesna' weel suit
   Honest men to begin to the thieving;
For my heart it gaed dunt upon dunt,
   Oh! I thought ilka dunt it would crackit;
Sae I flang frae my neive what was in't,
   Still the happer said, Tak' it, man, tak' it.
      Hey for the mill, etc.

A man that's been bred to the plough,
   Might be deaved wi' its clamorous clapper;
Yet there's few but would suffer the sough,
   After kenning what's said by the happer.
I whiles thought it scoff'd me to scorn,
   Saying, Shame, is your conscience no chackit?
But when I grew dry for a horn,
   It changed aye to, Tak' it, man, tak' it.
      Hey for the mill, etc.

The smugglers whiles cam' wi' their pocks,
   'Cause they kent that I liket a bicker;
Sae I bartered whiles wi' the gowks,
   Ga'e them grain for a soup o' their liquor.
I had lang been accustomed to drink,
   And aye when I purposed to quat it,
That thing wi' its clappertie clink,
   Said aye to me, Tak' it man, tak' it.
      Hey for the mill, etc.

But the warst thing I did in my life,
   Nae doubt but you'll think I was wrang o't,
O'd! I tauld a bit bodie in Fife
   A' my tale, and he made a bit sang o't;
I have aye had a voice a' my days,
   But for singing I ne'er got the knack o't;
Yet I try whiles, just thinking to please
   The greedy wi', Tak' it, man, tak' it.
      Hey for the mill, etc.

Now, miller and a' as I am,
   This far I can see through the matter,
There's men mair notorious to fame,
   Mair greedy than me or the muter!

For 'twad seem that the hale race o' men,
  Or wi' safety, the hauf we may mak' it,
Had some speaking happer within,
  That said to them, Tak' it, man, tak' it.
    Hey for the mill and the kill,
      The garland and gear for my cogie,
    Hey for the whisky and yill,
      That washes the dust frae my craigie.

DAVID WEBSTER.

DONALD GUNN.*

HEARD ye e'er o' Donald Gunn,
  Ance sae duddy, douf, and needy,
Now a laird in yonder toon,
  Callous-hearted, proud, and greedy?

Up the glen aboon the linn
  Donald met wi' Maggie Millar,
Wooed the lass amang the whins
  Because she had the word o' siller;
Meg was neither trig nor braw,
  Had mae fauts than ane laid till her;
Donald lookit ower them a',
  A' his thought was on the siller.
                Heard ye e'er, etc.

---

* "The ballad of 'Donald Gunn,'" says Mr. P. R. Drummond, "is founded on circumstances which occurred in the parish of Kilpatrick, in Dumbartonshire. A farmer's daughter had an only brother who had long been in Demerara, and, dying, had left her a large fortune. During the time the news was on the way, she committed herself to a working man in the neighbourhood, and unfortunately when the news came she was not in a position to resile, so that in the matter of choice her money did no service. However, the husband-elect kept his position, and a marriage ensued, which turned out a happy one. The amusing part of the story is that as soon as the news of the great legacy broke out, the poor girl was haunted by all the fortune-seeking sparks about Glasgow, until the *denouement* changed the boast into a query, 'When were you at Duntocher?' Webster's treatment of the married life of the husband is very highly coloured, and he was a good deal found fault with for it." Might we venture the hint that it was probably a case of "sour grapes," for, tell it not on Parnassus, "e'en poets they ha'e been ken'd" to "dearly lo'e the penny siller.'

Donald grew baith braid and braw,
　　Ceased to bore the whinstone quarry,
Maggie's siller pays for a',
　　Breeks instead o' duddy barrie :
Tho' he's ignorant as a stirk,
　　Tho' he's doure as ony donkey;
Yet, by accidental jirk,
　　Donald rides before a flunkey.
　　　　　　　　Heard ye e'er, etc.

Clachan bairnies roar wi' fright,
　　Clachan dogs tak' to their trotters;
Clachan wives the pathway dicht
　　To tranquillise his thraward features :
Gangrel bodies in the street
　　Beck and bow to mak' him civil,
Tenant bodies in his debt,
　　Shun him as they'd shun the devil.
　　　　　　　　Heard ye e'er, etc.

Few gangs trigger to the fair,
　　Few gangs to the kirk sae gaucie—
Few wi' Donald can compare
　　To keep the cantel o' the causie :
In his breast a bladd o' stane,
　　'Neath his hat a box o' brochan,
In his neive a wally cane,
　　Thus the tyrant rules the clachan.
　　　　　　　　Heard ye e'er, etc.
　　　　　　　　DAVID WEBSTER.

THE BONNIE WEE ROSEBUD.

A BONNIE wee rosebud grows down by yon burnie,
　　A bonnie wee rosebud as e'er you did see,
Wi' soft silken leaves underneath a green thornie,
　　O spare the wee rosebud, O spare it for me!

The redbreast sings wanton around the sweet blossom,
　　Sae fond to make love doth this wee birdie be,
But wha'd be as cruel as steal frae my bosom
　　This bonnie wee rosebud, O spare it for me!

Now, fain would I change for the wee birdie's station,
　　Now blythe would I chirp 'neath the green thorn tree,
Enraptured to muse and transported to gaze on
　　This bonnie wee rosebud, O spare it for me!

O hasten the moment, blest moment o' pleasure,
　　When locked to my breast the sweet rosebud shall be,
United for ever, my soul's dearest treasure,
　　O spare the wee rosebud, O spare it for me!
　　　　　　　　　　　　　　　　PETER AGNEW.

THE SPRING LARK.

In the purple of heaven, on the pinions of light,
The spring lark ascends, and her bosom is bright;
With glory and joy, from the sun's burning brim,
Lo! she sings and she soars like the young cherubim.
Far, far from her nest, and the dwellings of men,
Will she ever revisit the green earth again?
She ascends and she sings in the blue fields of ether,
Leaving danger and death in the low world beneath her;
Rejoicing in fulness and freeness of spirit
That the ocean of air is her own to inherit.
On the amber edged clouds she is resting her wings,
In a shrine of magnificent glory she sings.
The gush of her praises like incense ascends,
Refreshing men's hearts to the earth's utmost ends.
Thou seemest a link in the chain yet unriven,
Might draw a stray sheep to the pasture of heaven.
Thou art welcome, for ever, to sing in our skies,
If thou bring with thee flowers in their manifold dyes;
If thou bring with thee sunshine, and summer perfumes,
And all the rich radiance of ripe living blooms.

Oh! welcome to sing in the regions above,
And cherish our hearts with an anthem of love.
But winter will come, and thy music will cease,
And the tempest will roar in the desolate place;
The flow'rs that o'ershadow'd thy nest shall be gone,
And thou shalt be houseless, and weary, and lone.
The blue skies of beautiful summer are fled,
And the rose of the wilderness leafless and dead;
Yet the days of reviving in visions are come,
The spring of refreshing in beauty and bloom.
Oh! then shall the place where the tempest hath swept,
In the gold and the amber of morning be dipt;
Lo! the bright bow of mercy shall bend o'er the glen;
And the flow'rs shall look up fair and lovely again.
Ye have sung o'er the living, sweet bird of the morn;
And ye sing o'er the dead in your daily sojourn:
Oh, yes, ye will sing, when we all shall be gone,
When the green grass grows o'er us, and moss on our stone;
Thou wilt bathe thy grey breast in the day's chrystal urn,
Ere it shines on the dewdrops that spangle the thorn.
O'er the deep shady glens of the North, as ye soar,
The hymns of the morning, how sweetly ye pour;
On the day that is holy, thy notes are the sweetest,
On the day that is lovely, thy wings are the fleetest,
And thy soul-stirring song, more rich and more sweet,
While you spurn the wide earth, as it were, from your feet,
Most refreshing to him who is up and abroad,
And rejoiceth like thee in the light of his God.
He hears thee on high, in the far upper air,
And thinks on the time he will follow thee there;
He thinks on the hour when, his spirit set free,
He shall soar up rejoicing and gladsome as thee.
No frosts of the winter, no cold dropping rain,
No trouble, no toil, shall molest him again.
JAMES BEATTIE.

THE GOLDFINCH'S NEST.

FAR in the west, there is a nest,
   Wrought like a pearly shell;
The burn below, runs clear and slow,
   Pure as a mountain well.

The wee bird sits and sings, by fits,
   A bless'd and bonnie tune,
Five eggs are there, like blobs of air,
   From blue, blue heaven abune.

Oh! in this nest by Nature dress'd,
   Love's banners are unfurled;
True joy and peace are in this place,
   If they're in all the world.

On that green bough, there's music now—
   The ancient chestnut tree;
That wee bird sings, with fluttering wings,
   Like birds beyond the sea.

Through leafy boughs, the sunlight glows—
   The setting sun of gold;
And shadows still the waters fill,
   Deep, deep, and manifold.

Oh! pilgrim, come to this sweet home,
   At morning, noon, or even,
For here are wings and holy things,
   That tell of earthly heaven.

                   JAMES BEATTIE.

THE RAINBOW.

WE stood within a green alcove,
   And saw the bow of heaven,
Bending most gloriously above
   The golden gates of even;
Then fell a soft and quiet shower,
Feeding, with beauty, leaf, and flower.

A glorious spirit dwells on high,
   That lovely arch he threw;
He spreads the clouds along the sky,
   He sends the rain and dew;
And from the rainbow's purple crown
He sheds the ancient promise down.

Green earth, and all her flow'rs look up
   And smile to heaven again;
Red life is in the rose's cup,
   The spirit of the rain.
Heaven hath her rainbow and her showers,
And earth her beauty and her flowers.

Hope shines as fair, and builds as high,
   As ever rainbows were,
How can the splendid vision die
   That promiseth so fair?
All earthly hopes must fade away,
With man, the tenant of a day;
Yet shall he, like yon star, arise,
His heaven-born hope to realise.
                  JAMES BEATTIE.

THE LASS O' GLENSHEE.

A'E braw summer day, when the heather was blooming
   And the silent hills hummed wi' the honey-lade bee,
I met a fair maid as I homeward was roaming,
   A-herdin' her sheep on the hills o' Glenshee.

The rose on her cheek, it was gem'd wi' a dimple,
   And blythe was the blink o' her bonnie blue e'e;
Her face was enchantin', sae sweet and sae simple,
   My heart soon belanged to the lass o' Glenshee.

I kiss'd and caress'd her, and said, "My dear lassie,
   If you will but gang to St. Johnstone wi' me,
There's nane o' the fair shall set foot on the causeway,
   Wi' clothing mair fine than the lass o' Glenshee.

"A carriage o' pleasure ye shall ha'e to ride in,
  And folks shall say 'madam' when they speak to thee;
An' servants ye'll ha'e for to beck at your biddin';
  I'll make you my lady, sweet lass o' Glenshee."

"Oh! mock na' me, sir, wi' your carriage to ride in,
  Nor think that your grandeur I value a flee;
I would think mysel' blessed in a coatie o' plaidin',
  Wi' an innocent herd on the hills o' Glenshee."

"Believe me, dear lass, Caledonia's clear waters
  May alter their course and run back frae the sea—
Her brave hardy sons may submit to the fetters,
  But alter what will I'll be constant to thee.

"The lark may forget his sweet sang in the mornin',
  The spring may forget to revive on the lea,
But never will I, while my senses do govern,
  Forget to be kind to the lass o' Glenshee."

"Oh, leave me, sweet lad, for I'm sure I would blunder,
  And set a' the gentry a-laughin' at me;
They are book-taught in manners baith auld and young yonder,
  A thing we ken nocht o' up here in Glenshee.

"They would say, look at him wi' his dull Highland lady,
  Set up for a show in a window sae hie,
Roll'd up like a witch in a hameit-spun plaidie,
  And, pointing, they'd jeer at the lass o' Glenshee.'

"Dinna think o' sic stories, but come up behind me,
  Ere Phœbus gae round my sweet bride you shall be—
This night, in my arms, I'll dote on you kindly;"
  She smiled, she consented, I took her wi' me.

Now years ha'e gane by since we buskit thegither,
  And seasons ha'e changed, but nae change is wi' me,
She's ever as gay as the fine summer weather,
  When the sun's at it's height on the hills o' Glenshee.

To meet wi' my Jenny my life I would venture,
　　She's sweet as the echo that rings on the lea ;
She's spotless and pure as the snaw-robe o' winter,
　　When laid out to bleach on the hills o' Glenshee.

ANONYMOUS.

MY FIRST SAUMON.

When first I gaed to live on Tweed,
　　To spend a month's vacation,
I had to share in what is there
　　The common recreation.
Sae I coft a rod wi' brass weel shod,
　　The heicht o' Peebles Steeple ;
And bulky books wi' braw busked hooks,
　　That stunned the Tweeddale people.
For fishin' gear I didna spare—
　　Creels, boots, and gaff, an' a' man ;
For I had fairly set my mind
　　On grippin' nocht but saumon.

I thrashed a week, through pool and creek,
　　Till I was clean dumfounder'd ;
For fient a fin I e'er brocht in,
　　And wife and bairnies wonder'd.
The neibours roun', and folks frae toun,
　　In mockery lamented ;
And poachers sly, as they passed by,
　　Glower'd at me as demented.
While I, with keen and eident look,
　　Sae cunnin' and sae slaw, man,
Endeavour'd wi' my patent hook,
　　To wile out my first saumon.

I thocht, indeed, o' leavin' Tweed—
　　I cudna thole sic scornin'—
Till frae my bed, by instinct led,
　　I bang'd up a'e grey mornin',

Resolved ance mair that stream to dare
    When nane wad be observin';
For the evil eye of passers-by
    Aye kept my fingers swervin',
And doon wad thud my ravelled snood,
    Creatin' sic a jaw, man,
That little prospect e'er had I
    O' ocht but frichtin' saumon.

When I gaed oot, cam' fear and doubt,
    For o'er the water porin'
Twa Tweeddale clods wi' rusty rods
    The streams were sly explorin'.
They looked on me wi' scornfu' e'e,
    As ane wi' little gumption,
But wha, intent on sic a scent,
    Show'd plenty o' presumption.
"For wha," they mutter'd, "ever heard
    O' sic a want o' awe, man,
As for a fisher a'e week auld
    To think o' catchin' saumon?"

But luck at last ga'e me a cast—
    My stars they noo were brichtenin'—
My licht-thrown snood scarce touched the flood
    When doun it flew like lichtenin'.
My heart resiled, my een grew wild,
    The landscape round gaed whirlin';
But, quick as licht, I wanken'd bricht,
    To my pirn wildly skirlin',
Which noo I held to like a helm,
    And sae tentily did thraw, man,
That I had noo a nearer view
    O' grippin' my first saumon.

The Tweeddale loons they heard the soun's,
    And saw the fierce contention;
Sae doun they ran to lend a han'
    Wi' traitorous pretension.
I cried "Haud aff—let go the gaff!"
    And spite o' their persuasion,

I spurn'd their help, for noo I felt
   I rose to the occasion;
Sae gi'ein' line, and fishin' fine,
   I let him gently draw, man;
And when he took a sulky fit,
   I tickled my first saumon.

Hoo can I tell a' that befel?
   I fished like inspiration;
And mason lads frae dykes in squads,
   Look'd on wi' admiration.
Frae neebour hills ran shepherd chiels,
   Wi' collies mad careerin',
While by the flood in envious mood
   The Tweeddale lads stood jeerin',
Expectin' still, wi' richt ill-will,
   That something micht befa', man,
Which yet a novice might deprive
   O' grippin' his first saumon.

At last cleek'd fair wi' cannie care,
   In silver sheen sae splendid,
A saumon sound, o' thirty pound,
   Lay on the bank extended,
Nae tasteless dish o' lying fish,
   But ane run fresh frae ocean;
The first that year in Peeblesshire—
   Was ever sic commotion?
Sae fresh was he run frae the sea
   The lice stood in a raw, man;
And laced like beads the sonsy sides
   Of this, my maiden saumon.

The news flew aff like telegraph,
   And reached the toun before me,
And auld and young their wark doun flung
   To stare at and adore me.
My eldest loun, wi' parritch spoon,
   Hauf naked, ran to meet me,
While at the door, wi' smiles in store,
   The gudewife stood to greet me—

Protestin' loud before the crowd
   That she ne'er heard or saw, man,
O' sic a monster o' the deep
   As this, the gudeman's saumon.

"What wad ye wish done wi' the fish?"
   My wife began inquirin';
"The minister maun ha'e a share—
   His kindness is untirin'."
Sae doon it went, and up was sent
   A dinner invitation;
Syne to a party, saumon-pang'd,
   I gave a lang narration,
O' hoo I wrought, and hoo I fought,
   And still held by the maw, man,
This leviathan o' the Tweed—
   My first—my champion saumon.

Noo, far and wide, through a' Tweedside,
   I'm looked on as perfection,
In manse and ha', I crousely craw—
   I've formed a wide connection—
The *Scotsman*, scanned through a' the land,
   Announced the feat astoundin';
Next in the *Field* it was revealed,
   And in *Bell's Life* in London—
A' tellin' o' an Embro' chiel',
   A sportsman, fresh and raw, man,
Wha had sic luck, and showed sic pluck,
   In grippin' his first saumon.

WILLIAM GRAHAM, LL.D.

OUR LITTLE JOCK.

He's hallicut an' wild, he's gane ower his mither's thoomb,
He's like a sunny summer day owercome by winter's gloom,
Lanchin' like to split his sides, or greetin' like to choke,
Sae fu' o' fun an' devilry is our little Jock.

His towsy head is seldom kaim'd, he claws't for ever mair,
His een, I ken, are skellie baith, an' glower—I kenna where!
His mou' is like a mill-door, his nose is *on the cock*,
How beautiful—Oh! beautiful, is our little Jock.

He winna bide within doors, nor gang to kirk nor skule,
He wore a suit o' claes to rags, frae Lammas day to Yule;
He ran through winter's frost an' snaw, without a shoe or sock,
A hardy, stumpy, dumpy loon, is our little Jock.

His pouches, like a broker's shop, are crammed wi' orra things,
Buttons, bools, an' bits o' cawk, wi' peeries, taps, an' strings;
A broken file, a roosty knife, an' siclike laddie troke,
Wi' dawds o' crumpy aiten cake—the life o' little Jock.

If he behaud a herrin' cairt, or see a sweetie stand,
Be sure he's herryin' craw's nests, if he's no close at hand:
Barkin' like a tinkler's dog, or crawin' like a cock,
There ne'er was sick a funny loon as our little Jock.

An' Jock's a drummer in his way—he rattles on a pan,
An' fifer likewise to himsel'—he whistles just aff han';
How quickly a' his sodgers fire when he cries "Prime an' cock!"
The Queen has not a general like our little Jock.

Whaure'er there is a dog-fecht, he's there withouten fail,
Whaure'er an empty sugar-cask, he's at it tooth an' nail;
Whaure'er there is a wanton ploy, amo' the youthy fock,
The foremost aye amo' them a' is our little Jock,

JAMES STEWART.

FOUSCANHAUD.*

ARE you be climb the hielant hill,
  To shoot the bonnie moorcock ?
Are you be sneeshan in a mull,
  To gie a sneesh to poor folk ?
Here's your good health, sir, by the nose;
That be good snuff, sir, me suppose—
A bonnie box, too—hoo her close ?
  You'll no be faund a box so grand
  In ony hielant shentlam's hand—
The sass'nach's braw be our folk.

---

* The term *Fouscanhaud*,—*i.e.*, *fou's can haud*, signifying dead drunk,—is generally applied in Western Perthshire to Celtic keepers of low tippling-houses. The song here given with that word as its title was first sung at a concert in Crieff, and originated from the following circumstances. "An acquaintance of mine," says the author in a letter addressed to one of the editors of the posthumous volume of his poems, "a teacher of music, who at the close of his *season*, resolved as is usual with the 'profession,' to have a grand concert, beseechingly requested me to write a comic song for him." The song of "Fouscanhaud" was composed immediately, and being sung at the concert, was received with the greatest enthusiasm. Next morning it was the talk of the town, and an innkeeper there conceiving himself the hero of the piece, seems to have resolved upon the personal chastisement of the daring satirist. "Next day," continues Stewart, "a villanous trick was played me. Three fellows who had been bribed with the promise of a *fill*-fou, if by any possibility they could entice me into the house, came to me, and professing great friendship, asked if I would take a share of a dram with them. This offer, of course, in the 'half-fou' state I was, met with a ready acceptance. But, mark! —no house with them was more preferable than that of——. I demured to going there. But, said they—what was I afraid of?—were not they with me—and would they not prevent any collision?—and would not all of us get a glorious laugh on seeing the impotent rage of mine host and hostess? It was soon settled. My courage, I thought, must not be doubted; and so I accompanied them. I had scarcely crossed the threshold, however, when the hostess knocked me down with the poker. The three scoundrels bolted off, as if afraid, but took very good care to lock the door on the outside, the key having been left purposely for this act of treachery. I was struck down upon the floor, and mine host, threw heavily above me, with an open pen-knife in his hand, with which I believe, he would have cut my throat, had I not like Roderick Dhu, hit him in the left hand while he was clearing the way to get at my jugular. I forced myself to my feet, but in the struggle his knife grazed one of my eyebrows. I bear the mark yet. I

Did you'll be heard o' Fou's-can-haud?
   Her nainsel' just be me, man;
Are you be weary, dull, or sad?—
   Just come her drink an' prie, man.
The better drink no cross your mouth—
The better drink no kill your drouth—
As fack's the death me tells the truth,
   So you just micht come in this nicht
   To her nain house to see the sicht,
Get famous funs an' glee, man.

Mo chaileag laghach *—hoots, that be Earse:
   But what she'll gone to mean, man,
Her nainsel's wife he comes from Perse,
   Hims name they calls him Shean, man.
Hims be the bonnie lassie braw—
Hims skin be white's Ben-Vorlich's snaw—
Hims ee be black as hielant craw—
   An' she be crouse in her nain house,
   Wi' Shean her wife, the clever mouse;
Hooch! likes o' him's no seen, man

And Sheanie mak' the braxy kail,
   And Sheanie brew the tea, man;
Her nainsel fill the drams an' ale,
   And gather the bawbee, man.
That's Alster Faysac 'wa oot noo,
Within her house there's Pharig Dhu,

---

soon squeezed the knife out of his hand, but a blow from the wife on my right shoulder-blade with the poker, instantly made me relinquish the weapon. I had now disarmed mine host; but I had still to disarm his tigress. In a twinkling I snatched the poker, and—you may believe me!—they both got an abundant tasting of it, and gave audible demonstrations of the hearty punishment they were receiving. All this took place in a few minutes; and before anybody had notice of the row, I was out upon the street victorious, with the poker flourishing in my hand,—having smashed the window for an egress, after the door had baffled all my attempts to open it." It is not surprizing to learn that after this tragi-comic incident, the author found it necessary for his own comfort and peace of mind to quit the confines of Crieff, never to return.

        * My pretty girl.

And Shemus Beg—cod man, they're fou',
   They'll drank by more than stoups a score,
   And plenty siller till the fore;
Hooch! they're the man's for me, man.

They say should must a sangs be made
   On her and Sheans her lamb, man;
But what me cares? she'll plenty trade,
   In selling whisky dram, man.
Be mony shentlams her good freen',
That drinks wi' her and spokes wi' Shean,
So you'll be ken she's no to mean:
     And as me said, she's plenty trade,—
     Be thousand sangs about her made,
She dinna gie a *tam*, man!

Now, what you'll thocht to took a dram,
   This moment's very time, man?
Maybe you'll took a collop ham?
   Her Sheanie mak' her prime, man;
Come 'wa', no stand on stapping stones,
A dram will strong your very bones;
When me be sair, and cry *Och hones!*
     Me seldom long, till she's among
     The bottle wi' the double strong—
Best doctor for the wame, man.

JAMES STEWART.

THE TAILOR O' MONZIE.*

OUR gudeman's breeks were riven sair,
The tailor cam' to mak' a pair;
When gloamin' fell assembl'd were
   O's a' 'bout thretty three, man:
On stools an' auld tree roots we sat,
An' O, sae muckle fun's we gat,
Frae funny Patie Whip-the-cat,
   The tailor o' Monzie, man.

O, he's a curiosity,
A curious curiosity,
A perfect curiosity,
　　The tailor o' Monzie, man.

The lasses' spindles hadna space
To whirl an' bob their circlin' race,
For head an' thrawart, back an' face,
　　We sat promiscouslie, man,
"Like midges i' the motty sun,
Or corbie craws on tawtie grun'!"
Sae thick were we to hear the fun
　　Frae Patie o' Monzie, man.

　　　　O, he's a curiosity, etc.

A lang dispute anent the State,
Gley'd Andro Toshack held wi' Pate,
Wha drawin' a steek wi' nettled heat,
　　Drobb'd Andro's ringle e'e, man.
Andro' roar'd, grew pale an' faint,
"My feth," quo' the gudeman, "I kent,
He'd gi'e ye piercing argument,
　　Our tailor o' Monzie, man."

　　　　O, he's a curiosity, etc.

Wee Gibbie Bryce was greetin' vext,
That he had made the Kirk his text,
For Patie gat him jamm'd an' fixt
　　In Patronage's plea, man.

---

* The genuine old travelling tailor, or *whip-the-cat*, as he was generally termed throughout Scotland, is now extinct. To our forefathers the arrival of the tailor in the way of his *calling* was an advent long remembered. He very often united in his person the talent of wit with an accurate knowledge of mankind; being likewise a chronicle of all the gossip in his rounds, few people received such a hearty welcome within the *hallan* as the tailor. The author of the following sketch has seen in his younger years something akin to what he attempts to describe.—*Author's Note.*

He rave poor Gibbie's sense to rags,
Made him a lauchin'-stock to wags,
The hale house waved their arms like flags,
   "Hurrah for Pate Monzie, man!"
       O, he's a curiosity, etc.

Wi' canty tale an' funny joke,
Wi' lauchin' when the tailor spoke,
The nicht wore by till twal' o'clock,
   In loud guffaw an' glee, man;
The gudewife reavilt a' her yarn,
She tint the thread-end o' her pirn,
Lauchin' like her youngest bairn,
   At Patie o' Monzie, man.
       O, he's a curiosity, etc.

'Twad tak' a tale as lang's an ell,
'Twad tak' an hour that tale to tell,
O' what I heard an' saw mysel',
   That nicht o' nicht's to me, man.
If there's a man that we should dawt,
Wham Nature's made without a faut,
He's surely Patie Whip-the-cat,
   The tailor o' Monzie, man.
       O, he's a curiosity, etc.
              JAMES STEWART.

ALLAN MAC ALLAN DHU.

A HIGHLAND SHEARER.

WAUKEN, O wauken, Allan Mac Allan Dhu,
   High Cairn Gower gleams red in the sun,
Wauken, O wauken, Allan Mac Allan Dhu,
   The hairst's in the south, whaur a fee can be won.

Tak' a wee pickle meal on the road to mak' sturroch,
    Tie your brogues, Allan Dhu, hasten and run;
Allan Mac Allan Dhu, why do ye furroch ?
    The hairst's in the south, whaur a fee can be won.

Fear na but Allan has donn'd his blue bonnet,
    There's haste in his looks, there's dew on his shoon;
Eager yet kindly he cheers on his Shonat,
    While Shonat, poor lassie, mair fain wad sit doon.

The mists o' Ben Vrackie nae langer enfauld him,
    He rins wi' the Tummel, he marches wi' Tay,
The steep crags o' Birnam canna withhauld him—
    He hails the braw Lowlands wi' Highland "Good-day."

Far, far he wanders for Sassenach siller,
    Sair, sair he labours that siller to gain;
A pairt's for the laird, an' pairt for the miller—
    Allan Dhu's honest—they'll baith get their ain.

Say na poor Allan is beggarly greedy,
    Say that he's provident—naething's mair true;
Allan has wants, but amang a' the needy,
    Charity hasna beheld Allan Dhu.

What though the Lowlander jeer honest Allan ?
    Allan has virtues a king might revere;
Wha that has stappit within his clay hallan
    Faund unproffer'd welcome, or unproffer'd cheer ?

Be that Lowlander famish'd 'mid fulness and plenty,
    Unhoused when the north winds shall raise their haloo,
Unheard in his wailings, uncheer'd by his dainty,
    Wha winna show kindness to Mac Allan Dhu.

JAMES STEWART.

DUNCAN KER.*

The Atholl Paganini.

Hark the *tweedle-dum !*
   That bow-hand hath fleetness,
Gusts o' music come,
   Rich in Highland sweetness.
Hearts an' heels bestir—
   Rise my bonny hinny—
Dance to Duncan Ker,
   The Atholl Paganini.

The bridal ha' is lit,
   Bickers round are foamin',
Licht the dancers flit,
   As the wind o' gloamin';
Bobbin' through the reel,
   Like a water-waggie,
"Play," cries ilka chiel',
   "Tullochgorum, Pagie."

A bonnet meets his broo,
   Thrissle-badged, an' cockit,
Round him a surtout,
   I' the fashion—dockit;
Short's a plant o' fir,
   Onything but scraggie;
Such is Duncan Ker,
   Atholl's famous Pagie.

---

* The late Duncan M'Kerracher of Dunkeld, better known as "Atholl's Paganini," was widely esteemed from thirty to fifty years ago as one of the foremost reel and Strathspey fiddlers in Scotland. The author of these verses, of course, knew him well. I have myself seen "Pagie" and heard him play, and whether it be true or not, as has been stated, that he was displeased with the portraiture, I can vouch that, in its personal and other aspects as well, the description is to the very life.

A civil body, Pag,
   Pleasant as his fiddle,
Whistle, cry, or wag,
   At your beck he'll triddle ;
Seat him on a firm,
   Near a whisky kaggie,
The mavis canna chirm
   Sweeter notes than Pagie.

Bridals, balls, an' ploys,
   Haud the bottle clunkin' ;
They wha there rejoice,
   Need the aid o' Duncan ;
Dull wad be the stir,
   To Highland Jock an' Maggie,
Wantin' Dhonnach Ker,
   Atholl's famous Pagie.

Fastly flee the clouds,
   Driven by the storm,
Faster sorrow howds,
   Ilka gait before 'im.
Weel may we infer,
   A' his days are sunny ;
Wha's like Duncan Ker,
   The Atholl Paganini ?

               JAMES STEWART.

MARY ROSE.*

WE a' hae fond remembrances ;
   Our early anes how dear !
They shine like stars in Mem'ry's sky—
   Bright, mystical, and clear.

---

* Mary Rose, or rather Ross, used to visit my father's fireside when I was a "wee raggit laddie." She was of the old school, and a very kind-creature to boot. Well do I remember her barm-bannocks. She was an adept at baking, and many a piece I had of them, spread o'er

They glint a gladness round our hearts,
    Where'er our footsteps stray;
How dear are the remembrances
    O' boyhood's cloudless day!

Around my faither's ingle-lowe
    What happy beings there
At gloamin' met—their toils forgot—
    In social cracks to share!—
The pawky sutor fu' o' wit,
    The tailor sae jocose,
An' mony mair, and wi' them there
    Was canty Mary Rose.

O Mary was my mither's friend:
    An' when they were alane,
I drew my creepie by their side
    Upo' the warm hearth-stane,
An' heard their thoughts o' by-gane days—
    O' ploys when they were young;
An' whiles methought in Mary's e'e
    A tear o' sorrow hung.

The blinks o' fifty summer suns
    Had bleached her silken hair;
Whaur ance a dimple gemm'd her cheek,
    A wrinkle furrowed there.
Yet still she would in blythesome mood
    Count owre an' owre her joes;
Though ane by ane cool'd in his love,
    An' slighted Mary Rose.

Poor Mary had a woman's heart—
    O' gentleness 'twas fou';

---

with butter till not a blister raised by the *girdle* could be seen. Her death was a melancholy one, poor body. When age crept on her, and she could not win her ybread, her Scottish pride would not accept a morsel if she was given to understand it in the light of charity. The consequence was that poor Mary, unattended by a friend, was found dead in bed one day. Alas! poor Mary!—*Author's Note.*

Although it met wi' cauldrife love,
  It withered not, I trew.
A spirit whispered in her dreams
  Sweet words that fley'd her woes,
An' time ere lang brought happiness
  To slighted Mary Rose.

In Mary's dwelling mony a day,
  Atween the hours o' schule,
I've sat wi' neebor youngster loons
  Upon her buffet stule,—
An' as her spinnin' wheel birr'd round,
  Wild legends she'd disclose,
Till we believed that Fairyland
  Was kent to Mary Rose.

O, sweetly, sweetly, Mary sang
  The cradle *balaloo*
To mony a mither's waukrife bairn,
  Till sleep had smooth'd its broo.
Nane kent the bairnies frets an' ails,
  Nane mixed the healing doze,
Nor band their bruises, cuts, an' scars,
  Like gentle Mary Rose.

In after years I left my hame,
  'Mang strangers to sojourn;
If sorrow miss'd me when awa',
  It waited my return:—
I fand my faither 'neth the yird,
  My mither bowed wi' woes;
An' death—oh, death!—had stown awa'
  Kind, couthy Mary Rose.

                        JAMES STEWART.

JEAN LINN.

OH, haud na' your noddle sae hie, ma doo!
  Oh, haud na' your noddle sae hie!

The days that ha'e been may be yet again seen,
  Sae, look na' sae lightly on me, ma doo!
  Sae, look na' sae lightly on me!

Oh, geck na' at hame hodden grey, Jean Linn!
  Oh, geck na' at hame hodden grey!
Yer gutcher an' mine wad thocht themsel's fine
  In cleidin' sae bien, bonnie May, bonnie May,
  In cleidin' sae bien, bonnie May.

Ye mind when we wou'd in Whinglen, Jean Linn,
  Ye mind when we won'd in Whinglen;
Your daddie, douse carle, was cotter to mine,
  An' our herd was yer bonnie sel', then, Jean Linn!
  An' our herd was yer bonnie sel', then!

Oh, then ye were a'thing to me, Jean Linn!
  Oh, then ye were a'thing to me!
An' the moments flew by like birds through the sky,
  When tendin' the ousen wi' thee, Jean Linn,
  When tendin' the ousen wi' thee.

I twined ye a bower by the burn, Jean Linn,
  I twined ye a bower by the burn;
But dreamt na' that hour as we sat in the bower
  That fortune wad tak' sic a turn, Jean Linn,
  That fortune wad tak' sic a turn.

Ye busk noo in satins fu' braw, Jean Linn,
  Ye busk noo in satins fu' braw;
Yer daddy's a laird, mine's i' the kirkyaird,
  An' I'm yer puir ploughman, Jock Law, Jean Linn,
  An' I'm yer puir ploughman, Jock Law.

                      WILLIAM WILSON.

AULD JOHNNY GRAHAM.

DEAR Aunty, what think ye o' auld Johnny Graham?
  The carle sae pawkie and glee!
He wants a bit wifie to tend his bien hame,
  And the bodie has ettled at me.

Wi' bonnet sae vaunty, an' owerlay sae clean,
   An' ribbon that waved 'boon his bree,
He cam' doun the cleugh at the gloamin' yestreen,
   An' rappit, an' sune speir't for me.

I bade him come ben whaur my Minnie sae thrang
   Was birlin' her wheel eidentlie,
An', foul fa' the carle, he wasna that lang
   Ere he tauld out his errand to me.

"Hech, Tibby, lass! a' yon braid acres o' land,
   Wi' ripe craps that wave bonnilie,
An' meikle mair gear shall be at yer command,
   Gin ye will look kindly on me.

"Yon herd o' fat owsen that rout i' the glen,
   Sax naigies that nibble the lea;
The kye i' the sheugh, an' the sheep i' the pen,
   I'se gi'e a', dear Tibby, to thee.

"An' lassie, I've gowpens o' gowd in a stockin',
   An' pearlin's wad dazzle yer e'e;
A mettled, but canny young yaud for the yokin',
   When ye wad gae jauntin' wi' me.

"I'll hap ye an' fend ye, an' busk ye an' tend ye,
   An' mak' ye the licht o' my e'e;
I'll comfort an' cheer ye, an' daut ye an' dear ye,
   As couthy as couthy can be.

"I've lo'ed ye, dear lassie, sin' first, a bit bairn,
   Ye ran up the knowe to meet me;
An' deckit my bonnet wi' blue-bells an' fern,
   Wi' meikle glad laughin' an' glee.

"An' noo, woman grown, an' mensefu' an' fair,
   An' gracefu' as gracefu' can be;
Will ye tak' an' auld carle wha ne'er had a care
   For woman, dear Tibby, but thee?"

Sae, Auntie, ye see, I'm a' in a swither,
   What answer the bodie to gie,
But aften I wish he wad tak' my auld mither,
   An' let puir young Tibby abee.

                    WILLIAM WILSON.

MARY MORRISON.

Fareweel for aye to bonnie Tay,
    Fareweel to Craigie Lea,
Fareweel my native Highland hame,
    And fareweel aye to thee, Mary Morrison,
    And fareweel aye to thee.

The lily blooms in Logie bowers,
    The rose in Logie Shaw;
But I maun broken-hearted lea'
    The fairest flower o' a', Mary Morrison,
    The fairest flower o' a'.

Oh, hadst thou been a cottage maid,
    And I a cottar swain,
I might hae ta'en thee to the kirk,
    And made thee a' my ain, Mary Morrison,
    And made thee a' my ain.

But wae on fickle woman's love,
    And wae on warld's gear,
And wae be on the fause, fause loon
    That wiled awa my dear, Mary Morrison,
    That wiled awa my dear.

I'll trust nae mair to woman's faith,
    I'll woo nae mair her smile,
I'll lean nae mair on woman's love;
    'Tis a' a cheating wile, Mary Morrison,
    'Tis a' a cheating wile.

Adieu to bonnie, blythe Dundee,
    And Mary, fare thee weel;
Fause as thou art, yet near my heart
    I'll wear thy image leal, Mary Morrison,
    I'll wear thy image leal.
                      WILLIAM WILSON.

THE TOUN WHERE I WAS BORN.

The loch where first the stream doth rise
  Is bonniest to my e'e;
An' yon auld-warld hame o' youth
  Is dearest aye to me.
My heart wi' joy may up be heez'd,
  Or doun wi' sorrow worn,
But O! it never can forget
  The toun where I was born!

The lowly hames beside the burn,
  Where happy hearts were growin';
The peasant huts where, purely bright,
  The light o' love was flowin';
The wee bit glebes, where honest men
  Were toilin' e'en an' morn,
Are a' before me, when I mind
  The toun where I was born.

O! there were bonnie faces there,
  An' hearts baith high an' warm,
That neebors loved, an' strained fu' sair
  To keep a freend frae harm.
Nae wealth had they; but something still
  They spared when ane forlorn,
The puir auld beggar bodie, ca'd,
  The toun where I was born.

The gray auld man was honour'd there,
  The matron's words were cherish'd;
An' honesty in youthfu' hearts
  By age's words was nourished;
An' though e'en there we couldna get
  The rose without the thorn,
It was a happy, happy place,
  The toun where I was born.

Yon heather-theekit hames were blithe,
  When winter nights were lang,
Wi' spinnin' wheels, an' jokin' lads,
  An' ilka lassie's sang.

At Hansel-Monday we had mirth,
    An' when the hairst was shorn,
The maidens cam'—'twas cheerfu' aye
    The toun where I was born.

I maist could greet, I am sae wae—
    The very wa's are gane—
The autumn shilfa sits an' chirps
    Upon ilk cauld hearthstane;
Ae auld aik tree, or maybe twa,
    Amang the wavin' corn,
Is a' the mark that time has left
    O' the toun where I was born.

                                      ROBERT NICOLL.

BONNIE BESSIE LEE.

BONNIE Bessie Lee had a face fu' o' smiles,
    And mirth round her ripe lips was aye dancing slee;
And light was the footfa', an' winsome the wiles,
    O' the flower o' the parochin, our ain Bessie Lee.
Wi' the bairns she would rin, and the school laddies paik,
    And o'er the broomy braes like a fairy would flee,
Till auld hearts grew young again wi' love for her sake:—
    There was life in the blythe blink o' bonnie Bessie Lee.

She grat wi' the waefu', and laughed wi' the glad,
    And light as the wind 'mang the dancers was she;
And a tongue that could jeer, too, the little limmer had,
    Whilk keepit aye her ain side for bonnie Bessie Lee!
She could sing like the lintwhite that sports 'mang the whins,
    And sweet was her note as the bloom to the bee—
It has aft thrilled my heart whaur yon wee burnie rins,
    Whaur a'thing grew fairer wi' bonnie Bessie Lee.*

---

* The last four lines of this verse were introduced by Mr. Alexander Wilson, of Perth, to prevent the occurrence of an odd half stanza which had hitherto interfered with the effective singing of the song.

And she whiles had a sweetheart, and sometimes had
    twa—
  A limmer o' a lassie!—but, a'tween you and me,
Her warm wee bit heartie she ne'er threw awa'
  Though mony a ane had sought it frae bonnie Bessie
    Lee!
But ten years had gane since I gazed on her last—
  For ten years had parted my auld hame and me;
And I said to mysel', as her mither's door I passed,
  Will I ever get anither kiss frae bonnie Bessie Lee?

But Time changes a'thing—the ill-natured loon!
  Were it ever sae rightly, he'll no let it be;
And I rubbit at my een, and I thought I would swoon;
  How the carle had come roun' about our ain Bessie
    Lee!
The wee laughing lassie was a gudewife grown auld,
  Twa weans at her apron, and ane on her knee,
She was douce, too, and wise-like—and wisdom's sae
    cauld;
  I would rather hae the ither ane than this Bessie Lee.

ROBERT NICOLL.

THE FOLK O' OCHTERGAEN.

HAPPY, happy be their dwallin's,
  By the burn an' in the glen—
Cheerie lassies, cantie callans,
  Are they a' in Ochtergaen.

Happy was my youth among them—
  Rantin' was my boyhood's hour;
A' the winsome ways about them,
  Now when gane, I number o'er.

Weel I mind ilk wood an' burnie,
  Couthie hame and muirland fauld,—
Ilka sonsie, cheerfu' mither,
  An' ilka father douce an' auld!

Weel I mind the ploys an' jokin'
    Lads an' lasses used to ha'e—
Moonlight trysts and Sabbath wanders
    O'er the haughs an' on the brae.

Truer lads an' bonnier lasses
    Never danced beneath the moon;
Love and friendship dwalt amang them,
    An' their daffin' ne'er was dune—

I ha'e left them now for ever;
    But, to greet wad bairnly be;
Better sing, an' wish kind Heaven
    Frae a' dule may keep them free.

Where'er the path o' life may lead me,
    Ae thing's sure—I winna mane
If I meet wi' hands an' hearts
    Like those o' cantie Ochtergaen.
    Happy, happy be their dwallins,
        By the burn an' in the glen—
Cheerie lassies, cantie callans,
    Are they a' in Ochtergaen.
                  ROBERT NICOLL.

THE MUIR O' GORSE AND BROOM.

I WINNA bide in your castle ha's,
    Nor yet in your lofty towers,—
My heart is sick o' your gloomy hame,
    An' sick o' your darksome bowers;
An' O! I wish I were far awa'
    Frae their grandeur an' their gloom,
Where the freeborn lintie sings its sang
    On the muir o' gorse and broom.

Sae weel as I like the healthfu' gale
    That blads fu' kindly there,

An' the heather brown, an' the wild blue-bell,
  That wave on the muirland bare;
An' the singing birds, an' the humming bees,
  And the little lochs that toom
Their gushin' burns to the distant sea,
  O'er the muir o' gorse an' broom.

O! if I had a dwallin' there,
  Biggit laich by a burnie's side,
Where a'e aik-tree, in the simmer-time,
  Wi' its leaves that hame might hide,—
O! I wad rejoice frae day to day,
  As blythe as a young bridegroom;
For dearer than palaces to me
  Is the muir o' gorse and broom.

In a lanely cot on a muirland wild,
  My mither nurtured me:
O' the meek wild-flowers I playmates made,
  An' my hame wi' the wandering bee:
An' O,! if I were far awa',
  Frae your grandeur an' your gloom,
Wi' them again, an' the bladdin' gale,
  On the muir o' gorse an' broom!

ROBERT NICOLL.

THE FORSAKEN.

THE rowing waves, the ocean tides,
  Are changefu' baith at e'en and morn,—
Like sunshine and its following shade
  Upon the dew-wet, yellow corn;
The burn sings saftly o'er the lea,
  Where ance it like a torrent ran;
But a' are steadfastness itsel'
  When liken'd to the heart o' man.

Ane sought my love, when in my teens,
  A thoughtless lassie, I was gay!

I trusted, as a woman trusts,
   And made his love my bosom's stay;
And when, to gather gowd, he gaed
   To some far land ayont the main,
I lang'd at e'en, I lang'd at morn,
   To see my loved one back again.

I ne'er gaed near the youngsters' dance;
   But when the light o' day grew dim,
I sought the broomy trysting knowe,
   Where quietness dwelt, to think on him.
Years cam' and gaed; but hame to me
   He hied na, as he should ha'e dune;
But, O! I ne'er mistrusted him—
   His name I cherish'd late and sune.

My father and my mother baith
   Were laid aneath the cauldrife yird,
And I was left alane, alane,
   A mourning and a mateless bird.
He came at length,—and O! my heart
   Was glad as heart can ever be,—
He came wi' a' his treasured love,
   He came to gi'e it a' to me.

I heard his foot on my door-stane—
   He stood upon my lanely floor—
I gazed upon the manly form
   That did my lassie's heart allure;
And bitter thoughts came in my breast;
   For pride was dancing in the e'e
Whence love should ha'e been smiling sweet,
   To bless, and glad, and comfort me.

I saw his glance o' meikle scorn
   Upon my lanely maiden hame;
And O! I thought my heart wad break
   Where laigh I murmur'd forth his name.
He gazed upon my alter'd form,—
   I kent what in his e'e did gleam;
He thought na, in his cruelty,
   The change was wrought by waiting him.

He cauldly spake o' youthfu' days;
   And o' his plighted faith spake he;
And syne I scorned the world's slave,
   And proudly told him he was free.
He turn'd him wi' a mocking smile,
   And offer'd gowd and offer'd gear;
And *then* I sought in vain to dee,—
   For *this* I couldna, couldna bear.

Truth, love, and woman's faith, in youth,
   A dwellin' place had biggit me,—
A hame where joy upon my heart
   Had blinkit sunshine wondrouslie;
But falsehood came, and to the earth
   That palace o' the soul did fa';
For woman's trustin' faith was gane,
   And truth and love were far awa'.

I bared my breast beneath a ray
   Sent frae love's bonnie summer sun;
But, ere I wist, cauld winter cam',
   And hope and joy gaed one by one.
I maybe loved a thing o' earth
   Ower weel, and Heaven burst the chain;
I ken na; but my heart is sair,
   And age is comin' cauld and lane!

ROBERT NICOLL.

THE LAMENT OF BENEDICT THE MARRIED MAN.

I ANCE was a wanter, as happy 's a bee;
I meddled wi' nane, and nane meddled wi' me;
I whiles had a crack o'er a cog o' gude yill,
Whiles a bicker o' swats—whiles a heart-heezin gill.
And I aye had a groat if I hadna a pound,
On the earth there were nane meikle happier found.
   But my auld mither died in the year auchty-nine,
   And I ne'er hae had peace in this warld sin syne.

Fu' sound may she sleep! a douce woman was she,
Wi' her wheel, and her pipe, and her cuppie o' tea;
My ingle she keepit as neat as a preen,
And never speered questions as "Whaur 'hae ye been?"
Or "What were you doin'?" an' "Wha was ye wi'?"—
We were happy thegither my mither and me.

    But the puir bodie died in the year auchty-nine,
    An' I ne'er hae had peace in the warld sin syne.

When my mither was gane, for a while I was wae;
But a young chap was I, and a wife I wad hae—
A wife I sune gat, and I aye hae her yet,
And folks think thegither we unco weel fit.
But my ain mind hae I, tho' I maunna speak o't,
For mair than her gallop I like my ain trot.

    O! my auld mither died in the year auchty-nine,
    An' I ne'er hae had peace in the warld sin syne.

If I wi' a crony be takin' a drap,
She'll yammer and ca' me an auld drucken chap.
If an hour I bide out, loud she greets and she yowls,
And bans a' gude fellows, baith bodies and sowls.
And then sic a care she has o' her gudeman!
Ye wad think I were doited—I canna but ban!

    O! my auld mither died in the year auchty-nine,
    An' I ne'er hae had peace in the warld sin syne.

Our gilpie young dochters are lookin' for men,
An' I'll be a grandsire or ever I ken.
The laddies are thinkin' o' rulin' the roast,
Their faither, puir body, 's deaf as a post.
But he sees they're upsettin', sae crouse and sae bauld;
O! why did I marry, and wherefore grow auld?

    My auld mither died in the year auchty-nine,
    An' I ne'er hae had peace in the warld sin syne!

ROBERT NICOLL.

WE'LL MAK' THE WARLD BETTER YET.

THE braw folk crush the puir folk down,
    An' blood an' tears are rinnin'. het;
An' meikle ill an' meikle wae,
    We a' upon the earth have met.
An' Falsehood aft comes boldly forth,
    An' on the throne of Truth doth sit;
But true hearts a'—gae work awa'—
    We'll mak' the Warld better yet!

Though Superstition, hand in hand
    Wi' Prejudice—that gruesome hag—
Gangs linkin' still; though misers make
    Their heaven o' a siller bag;
Though Ignorance, wi' bloody hand,
    Is tryin' Slavery's bonds to knit—
Put knee to knee, ye bold an' free,
    We'll mak' the Warld better yet!

See yonder coof wha becks an' bows
    To yonder fool wha's ca'd a lord;
See yonder gowd-bedizzen'd wight—
    Yon fopling o' the bloodless sword.
Baith slave, an' lord, an' soldier too,
    Maun honest grow or quietly flit;
For freemen a', baith grit an' sma',—
    We'll mak' the Warld better yet!

Yon dreamer tells us o' a land
    He frae his airy brain hath made—
A land where Truth and Honesty
    Have crushed the serpent Falsehood's head.
But by the names o' Love and Joy,
    An' Commonsense, an' Lear an' Wit,
Put back to back,—and in a crack,
    We'll mak' *our* Warld better yet!

The Knaves an' Fools may rage and storm,
    The growling Bigot may deride—

The trembling Slave awa' may rin,
   An' in his Tyrant's dungeon hide;
But Free and Bold, and True and Good,
   Unto this oath their seal have set—
"Frae pole to pole we'll free ilk soul,—
   The Warld shall be better yet!"

ROBERT NICOLL.

THE POET'S GRAVE.*
(Written in North Leith Churchyard).

Is the poet's grave in some lonely spot,
Is his requiem sung by the wild-bird's throat,
Where the forest flowers are first in bloom,
Is this the place of the poet's tomb?

Do his bones repose on his native hills,
Is his spirit soothed by their dashing rills,
Where the heather waves and the free winds come,
Is this the place of the poet's tomb?

Is his last, long sleep made in hallowed mould,
Where the bones of his fathers rest of old,
Doth the same grey stone record his doom,
Is this the place of the poet's tomb?

No! alas, bright thoughts of a deathless name,
With o'ermastering power on his spirit came;
And his childhood's home, and his father's hearth,
He forsook for the busy haunts of earth!

---

* These remarkable elegaic verses give every indication of the possession of a poetical faculty of a high order, and they of themselves are sufficient, in my opinion, to place the writer in high rank among the poets of his time, although he had never written another line. The tale of his brother's life and death, and how he buckled on his helmet and went to battle against oppression and pain, is better told in these few stanzas than many men's lives have been in volumes. How any young man living on the very outer edge of the world of letters could, at one sitting, produce such a noble tribute to the memory of his deceased brother, and such a finished piece of versification, is difficult to understand.—*P. R. Drummond.*

He had dreamed a dream in the moorland glen,
Of oppression aud pain 'mongst his fellow men ;
He buckled his helmet with clasps of gold,
But fell ere half his tale was told.

Nor tree, nor flower o'er his lowly bed,
Their bright spring tears, or sere leaves, shed,
For, 'mid countless graves, and a city's gloom,
Sleeps Nature's child, in a nameless tomb.
WILLIAM NICOLL.

THE CITY PENT.

I WISH I were on a green hillside,
   With the breezes round me blowing,
While far beneath is the swelling tide,
   With murmurs onward flowing ;
To hold free converse with Nature there,
And heavenward mount on the wings of prayer.

Oh! would I were in the forest dim,—
   For true hearts still 'tis the holiest fane,—
When the gay lark carols his matin hymn,
   And the echoing woods return the strain,
No roof but God's blue sky above me ;
None nigh but one true heart to love me.

Oh! that I were in a cottage low
   In some far glen, aye there to bide,
With loved ones round me, that dearest grow
   Because unloved by all beside.
There wear out, in the joy of the dear caress,
All that life can give of happiness.

Oh! far would I live from the city's din,
   Its senseless noise and its sordid care,
Where outside glare hides a dusk within,
   And the hollow smile gilds dark despair,
And men barter that God sent-soul away
At the shrine of its image of dross and clay.
WILLIAM NICOLL.

FAREWELL.

Adieu! sweet maid, adieu for ever,
   Once how loved let Memory tell;
One fond kiss, and then we sever;
   One bitter pang, and then farewell.
Yet e'er we part, say will one thought,
   One kindly thought e'er turn on him,
Whose early love unstained, unbought,
   Made thee the goddess of his dream?

Wilt thou with interest view his path,
   Along of life the stormy wave,
Or should he sink beneath its wrath,
   One tear shed o'er his nameless grave?
Wilt thou when others loud condemn,
   In accents mild defend his name,
Whose heart to thee, if not to them,
   Once burned with friendship's purest flame?

E'en should the world's cankerous breath
   His name with blighting influence scar,
Wilt thou even in that worse than death,
   Remember that he once was dear,
And o'er his frailties draw a veil,
   And deem in secret he may mourn?
The heart from purity may fail,
   Then seek to hide regret in scorn.

And when another voice is sweet
   Unto thine ear, as once was mine—
When other eyes responsive meet
   With answering thought each glance of thine.
Oh! think not of me, then I'd be
   No rude intruder on thy joy:
But hours like these too quickly flee,
   And sorrows come, and cares annoy.

But should the hand of sorrow cloud
   In coming years that brow so fair,

Though newer scenes may memory shroud,
   That sorrow let my friendship share;
But now we part; alas! for ever;
   No tie, but that which memory brings
Remains for worldly cares to sever,
   And to that tie the heart still clings.

That midst the world's cares and sadness,
   I'll think of thee as what thou wert,
My early love, when joy and gladness
   Danced gaily through my youthful heart.
Again adieu! again endeavour
   To crush the thoughts my bosom swell,
And while this heart forgets thee never,
   With bursting sigh I say farewell!

WILLIAM NICOLL.

FAIR HELEN AND LORD WILLIAM.

THE village eyes for love and truth,
   Fair Helen fixed upon;
The joy of all the virtuous youth,
   The fair maid's paragon.

To parents she was dutiful,
   To everyone sincere;
To rivals she was beautiful,
   To all the village dear.

Lord William, in an evil hour,
   Espied the luckless fair,
Her fate—submission to his power;
   Her guerdon—sad despair.

Her father saw her altered form,
   Her visage pale and wan;
And though he felt a rising storm,
   Suppressed it as a man.

Apart her mother wiped the tear,
  Though smiles to her were shown;
For Helen was to her most dear,
  Of all her heart had known.

To soothe a father's rending care,
  Which time could ne'er remove,
A mother's tenderness to spare,
  And show her filial love.

Lord William, in his walk, she sought,
  The cause of her undoing.
Alas! poor Helen little thought
  She sought her final ruin!

"At eve," he said, "on yonder beach,
  You'll meet me at the tide,
And I'll save you from slander's reach,
  For you shall be my bride."

"Oh! spare my life, Lord William, spare!
  'Tis all your Helen craves!"
A ruthless pair the female bear,
  And dash her in the waves.

The two had rowed, for murder hired,
  Till out of reach of hearing,
Where Helen in the deep expired,
  And he no witness fearing.

"You've done your part full well," he said;
  "She can tease me no more.
Now, would you wish your hire well paid,
  Row quickly to the shore."

She was his bride; for he cried "Save!"
  As they to land were sailing.
The villains met a watery grave,
  And none to help their wailing.

JAMES C. SHAIN.

THE TAY.

An Extract.

I STAND upon a bridge that spans
   A gentle current far below;
No longer now the light breeze fans
   The lake's unruffled glow.
How peacefully it rests, with all
   Its mountains mirrowed on its bosom—
Field, crag, and cot, and waterfall,
   Green wavy branch, and wild flower's blossom!
How calm, how blest! . . .
   . . . Then stay thee, stay,
Nor leave thy parent lake to-day!

Yes, stay! But no; thou art onward still,
The happy dupe of thy playful will,
With thy dimpling smiles and thy merry song,
Swirling, eddying, glancing along;
By bush and bank, in sun and shade,
Peebles below and leaves o'erhead,
And well the listening muse could deem
Thy murmured thoughts, sweet froward stream;
For well could'st thou list her counsels sage,
And well can'st scorn the voice of age,
As youth ever does. If it were not a dream
Are these not thy murmurings, beautiful stream?—

"Oh, who would bide 'mid these mountains lone,
A lifeless thing, unnoticed, unknown?
When all around is cold and tame,
Changeless still, and ever the same?
Torrents unaltered from their birth,
What have they for a young heart's mirth?
An old oak bending over the face
Of a rifted rock from its rooted place,
Like a weeping ghost, by night and by day,
Ever the same, and never away!
The sombre swell of each mountain form,
Unvaried aye in calm or storm,

All grey with crag, or brown with heath,
Or swathed in fogs like shrouded death,
Where nothing new or pleasant appears,
But ever the same for a thousand years;
Crowding their images over my face,
And hugging me up in an iron embrace!
O, who would bide 'mid these lone hills, pray,
If able and free to bound away?

"I go, I go, with dance and song—
Sparkling, whirling, rushing along—
By bushy bank and flowery brae,
Sporting at will by night and by day.
Now gliding slow, without ripple or din,
Where arching boughs so closely entwine
That scarcely day dares enter in;
Now sparkling free in the broad sunlight,
Like a silver belt with diamonds dight;
Or dashing over the wild cascade,
White with foam, but never afraid!
Gliding, gushing, glancing on,
By ruin grey and warrior stone,
City proud and knightly hall,
Prized, and praised, and loved by all!
A thing of majesty and pride—
Old burly ocean's mountain bride!
Our tryst is by a lonely tower,
　　When the pale moon slants an eastern ray,
And there he has reared the bridal bower
　　Of his blue-eyed Highland Tay!"

The Tay! the Tay! pure placid stream!
　　Well do I know my native river—
My youthful muse's favourite theme,
The brightest wonder of her dream—
　　Yes, glide, and glide for ever!
My fathers loved thy sparkling flood—
　　And they are gone—and youth from me
Is parting like an autumn cloud—
　　Yet still thou'rt young and fair to see!

Age is not years—at least with thee.
  The forest monarch feels his prime,
And fades, all stubborn though he be :
  And mountains crumbling yield to time ;
But thou, though old, art ever young,
  Beginning still but to begin ;
Thy lullaby is yet unsung,
  Although thy lusty youth could win
An " Ecce, Ecce Tiber ! " from
  Rome's warriors in her warrior day ;
Yet there thou glidest sweetly on,
As if thy waters ne'er had shone,
  With sunlight till to-day.

DAVID MILLAR.

THE PRIEST O' KINFAUNS.

O, DID ye ne'er hear o' the Priest o' Kinfauns,
Wi' his black gown an' beads, an' his lang skleeny hauns—
His thin sallow face, and his big bricht e'en,
The whilk their marrows were never seen ?
Did ye never hear tell how he fastit an' prayed,
How mony ghostly visits he paid
To Elcho nuns, in their straits an' their stauns—
What a godly man was the Priest o' Kinfauns !

The Priest he fastit, the Priest he prayed,
Yet few kent weel what he did or said ;
He sleepit the day, an' he waukit the nicht,
An' he countit the stars till the morning licht.
But tho' he was holy as holy could be,
Nane likit the Priest wi' the big black e'e ;
Though clad like a saunt, an' tho' free wi' his aums,
What a fearfu' man aye was the Priest o' Kinfauns !

He gae to the puir, but he gae wi' a growl,
Or a look that gaed cauld to a puir body's soul ;

He prayed for the sick, an' he prayed for the sair,
Till the hale an' the thrivin' were trembling wi' fear.
Though his shrivin' was short an' the penance but sma',
Yet his shrive-days were sad days to ane an' to a';
But how they were sae still there's nane understauns—
What a terrible man was the Priest o' Kinfauns!

It was said through the country, an' a' thocht it true,
That the langer the Priest lived the better he grew:
For late an' for lang, baith at mornin' an' mirk,
He prayed to the Virgin for hours in the kirk.
An' often the wanderer, whan a' thing was still,
An' the last streak o' daylight had sunk o'er the hill,
Would hear in't strange soonds like the singin' o' saums—
What a marvellous man was the Priest o' Kinfauns!

That ook the fair Beatrice frae Elcho was missed—
Nae sister sae bonnie the rude ever kissed—
He prayed to the saunts baith the day an' the nicht
For the peace o' her soul, or the place o' her flicht,
Till its said that the Virgin, his faith to reward,
Cam' down in the e'en to that eerie kirkyard,
Nor left him till da'in was gray on the lawns—
What a high favoured man was the Priest o' Kinfauns!

But what she then tauld him there's nae ane can tell,
But strange were the soonds an' the sichts that befel!
Ae day, as the e'enin' gae place to the mirk,
Wild screamin' and lauchter were heard in the kirk;
And twice at the winnock, could fowk trust their e'en,
An' eerie licht blazed an' a lady was seen!
The trials o' the godly there's nane understauns—
What a sair wrastlin' man was the Priest o' Kinfauns!

It's strange! owre the parish nae e'e closed that nicht,
An' the dogs yaufft an' youl'd till the grey daylicht,
An' yet there was little on earth or in air,
O' sicht or o' soond, to breed terror or care;
The bairnies a' sabbit, an' kye at the sta'
Shuk wi' fear till the swyte ow'r their hurdies did fa',
An' horse quat the stake, spite o' bridle an' bauns:
There was ne'er sic a nicht near the kirk o' Kinfauns!

Neist mornin' the dew-draps glanced thick on the lea,
An' sweet sang the wee birds on ilka green tree;
A'thing luk't the same, but the kirkyard was gane,
An' priest, kirk, or kirkyard, were never mair seen,*
But a wee loch shone clear on the place whaur they stude,
An' a wull-duke already was soomin' its flude.
Fouk may say what they like, but for houses an' launs,
Few ere would coont kin wi' the Priest o' Kinfauns!

DAVID MILLAR.

OH, NEVER! NO, NEVER!

OH, never! no, never!
  Thou'lt meet me again!
My spirit for ever
  Has burst from its chain;
The links thou hast broken
  Are all that remain,
For never, oh! never,
  Thou'lt meet me again.

Like the sound of the viol,
  That dies on the blast;
Like the shade on the dial,
  Thy spirit has pass'd.

---

* The manse of Kinfauns, tradition avers, at one time stood about a furlong south from the present situation, and where there is now a pool of water called the Kaitress Loch. In the broad light of day it was observed to suddenly and mysteriously sink into the ground, and the loch referred to has ever since occupied the place. Many years afterward, upon a report arising that there was a golden cradle in this submarine manse, the people of Kirkstyle undertook to drain off the water, and had advanced so far with the work that they were in great expectation of obtaining the prize, when, looking round, they observed their houses all in flames. They at once ran home to save their goods and chattels, and, on coming back to the loch, to their great surprise it was as full of water as before. It is almost unnecessary to add that further search for the golden cradle was indefinitely postponed.

The breezes blow round me,
   But give back no strain;
The shade on the dial
   Returns not again.

Where roses enshrine thee,
   In light trellis'd shade,
Still hoping to find thee,
   How oft have I strayed!
Thy desolate dwelling
   I traverse in vain;—
The stillness has whisper'd
   Thou'lt ne'er come again.

I still haste to meet thee,
   When footsteps I hear;
And start when to greet me
   Thou dost not appear;
Then afresh o'er my spirit
   Steals mem'ry of pain,—
For never, oh! never,
   Thou'lt meet me again.

      CAROLINE OLIPHANT (*Younger*).

HOME IN HEAVEN.

A WIND-BOUND exile far from home,
   While standing near th' unfathomed main,
My eyes the far horizon roam,
   To see the land I long to gain.
Though dim with mists and faintly blue,
   The hills of bliss e'en now I view;
Oh! when will Heaven's soft breezes come
   And waft the weary exile home?

Let those who know no lovelier shore
   Their shells and sea-weed idly heap,
Then mourn to see their paltry store
   Dispersed and sinking in the deep.

My storehouse lies beyond the wave,
  My treasure fears no wat'ry grave.
And oh! I wish fair winds would come
  And waft me o'er to that blest home.

Already some I hold most dear,
  Have safe arrived on yonder strand;
Their backs afar like specks appear,
  The exiles now have gained the land.
Their parting signals wave no more,
  No signs of woe float from that shore!
And soon the skiff for me will come,
  And Heaven's own breath will waft me home.
                    CAROLINE OLIPHANT (*Younger*).

QUITTING THE MANSE.*

WE are leaving the scenes of our happiest hours,
So gay and so lovely with Spring's opening flowers;
Our children's last look to their homes has been given,
And faith's eye is fixed on her mansion in heaven.
  Now, Scotland, our task is accomplished for thee,
  And the Church of our country is faithful and free!

Last week in His house we united in prayer,
And we felt that the God of our father's was there;

---

* "When May, 1843, came," says her biographer, "Mrs. Stewart Sandeman joined the Free Church; and although she could not be in Edinburgh in person, her son and her daughter saw the whole proceedings of that memorable day. Early in the morning they were in St. Andrew's Church with the multitude, hearing the protest of ministers and elders read, seeing the Lord Commissioner withdraw overcome, and then they left the church along with the last outgoing men. Whilst the procession marched on towards Tanfield Hall, the crowd upon the pavements walked faster and arrived sooner. Thus they had a view of the entire procession, recognising many an honoured and well-known form. Thousands of young people received a life-long impulse from that scene." In her journal of date 26th May, 1843, Mrs. Sandeman has these verses, which give expression to a feeling then surging in many a tender heart.

Yet 'twas solemn and sad thus in parting to pray,
And the *last* song of praise on our lips died away.
  Now, Scotland, our task is accomplished for thee,
  And the Church of our country is faithful and free!

Yes, secured to thee now is the Gospel's sweet sound,
And our conscience is peaceful, our fetters unbound;
The shield of His truth He will over us fling,
And the shout that ye hear is the shout of a King!
The crown on His brow shall for ever endure,
His throne as eternity stedfast and sure.
  Now, Scotland, our task is accomplished for thee,
  And the Church of our fathers is faithful and free!
        MARGARET STEWART SANDEMAN.

THEN AND NOW.

FORTY-FIVE years have passed away
  Since the bells rang out for church, as now,
I sat alone, as I sit to-day,
  To take on the morrow the marriage vow.
This very hour they proclaimed me bride,
And his heart was full of joy and pride:

There was love, there was joy, in the bride's heart too,
  Yet clouds were floating across her sky;
For an earthly love was a light, 'tis true,
  But the other Sun she could scarce descry,
And fears *would* rise, and a tear would fall—
'Twas an earthly portion after all.

The morrow came, the loved were there,
  The bride and bridegroom's troth was plighted,
Loud acclamations rent the air,
  The gathered townsfolk cheered delighted.
A long, a prosperous wedded life,
Was waiting for the new-made wife.

The scene is changed. For that bride to-day
  The bells ring out to church e'en now.

I sit alone, with changed array,
   In his house who received my marriage vow;
But father and mother, and bridesmaids too,
And bridegroom, death hath hid from view:

Brothers and friends who formed the train,
   The patriarch who joined our hands,
Three noble sons and infants twain,
   Have followed them into the silent land.
I gaze on the flood whose ruthless sweep
Earth's hopes has buried in the deep.

But my hand is striking triumphal chords,
   And my voice is tuned to a deathless strain,
For the King of kings and Lord of lords
   Hath bidden my soul be glad again.
At this very hour He calls me bride
By a union that ever shall abide.

No clouds are floating before me now;
   Yon glorious Sun drives all away.
No sad foreboding shades my brow
   As I sit me down alone to-day.
Let joy's full tide my bosom swell,
With "Jesus only" all is well.

A morrow comes. All loved are there;
   Bride and Bridegroom are on the throne.
Loud acclamations rend the air;
An angel-voice cries, "It is done!"
Eternal bliss is ours to share:
The Lamb is all the glory there.

                MARGARET STEWART SANDEMAN.

WILLIE'S HAY STACK.

WE'VE haen a sair winter, likewise a cauld spring;
An' the gowk, though in May, has been scarce heard to sing;

O' cauld wintry weather we've haen a lang track,
Whilk has wroucht a great change on Willie's hay
  stack.
  An' wha hasna' heard o' Willie's hay stack!
  O' wha hasna' heard o' Willie's hay stack!
  'Twas squared like a soo on the road to your view,
  An' theekit wi' broom was Willie's hay stack.

It stood high an' dry for years half a score,
An' mony ane wonder'd to sce't to the fore;
Some gaed to Australia, got rich, an' cam back,
But aye there, untouched, stood Willie's hay stack.

There wasna' ane near him but wha's pickle hay,
Tho' e'er sae weel haen'd, wis dune lang ere May;
O' farmers an' cottars there wasna' ane slack
To covet an' grummil at Willie's hay stack.

The carters they tried it, but it widna' draw,
Sae hard an' sae dry, it aye brak' in twa;
They widna' been laith a good burden to tak',
If they could hae got it frae Willie's hay stack.

Ye ken that last summer the drouth was severe;
Mony ane o' their neeps cud scarce get a brier;
The little they had gaed dune in a crack,
Whilk made mair than Willie to try their hay stack.

When a' thing gaed dune, Willie seized the hay-knife;
His hand shook and trimmel'd like takin' a life;
There's nae muckle wonder suppose he did shak'
When a' his beas' meat was dune but the stack.

Noo a'body's lauchin' as by they do gang,
They see Willie's stack it canna last lang;
It's like an auld chair wi' a turned up back,
Ere lang they'll a' see an end to the stack.

Some young cummers giggle at nicht gaen hame,
As they pass the auld stethel they're like to think
  shame;

They mind o' the nicht when they got a bit smack,
While scoogin' a shower ahint Willie's hay stack.

ROBERT GAIRNS.

JENNY WHITELAW.

A BIT counsel I'll gi'e to you lasses,
   Wha young are, an' bonnie, an' braw ;
Try an' mak' hay i' the sunshine,
   An' no be like Jenny Whitelaw.

Jenny's a decent auld bodie,
   An' a' her wants are but sma'—
Nae fear for the time that is comin'—
   Contented is Jenny Whitelaw.

Last year, at the shearin' at Colen,
   There last the auld bodie I saw ;
Sair alter'd sin' she was in Gairdrum—
   Little buiket is Jenny Whitelaw.

She toil'd an' she swat for a mouthfu',
   Though a' she cou'd mak' was but sma' ;
She wants to ha'e something for winter—
   Richt thochtfu' is Jenny Whitelaw.

I mind weel, when I was a laddie,
   Her hair was as black as a craw ;
But three score o' summers ha'e whiten'd
   The locks o' puir Jenny Whitelaw.

Some neebours gang aften to see her,
   An' ithers they ne'er gang ava ;
I wish they wad a' mind an' gi'e her,
   For needfu' is Jenny Whitelaw.

Ah, lasses, though thrang at the courtin',
   Ye needna aboot yer lads blaw ;
In her youth she had nae lack o' sweethearts—
   Muckle thocht o' was Jenny Whitelaw.

ROBERT GAIRNS.

MORNING MUSINGS IN THE HIGHLANDS.

I GAZE on sunshine warm and bright,
Upon yon lofty pine-clad height;
  For down dark shadows creep;
The distant hills are towering high;
Their bold outlines against the sky
  In mazy grandeur sweep.

The golden rays have found their way
Through splinter'd rocks and boulders grey,
  And down the glen they stream;
See, glancing o'er the hoary peaks,
A sparkling flow of sunny streaks
  In dazzling radiance gleam.

From shelter'd depths have moved the sheep,
To bask upon each grassy steep,
  And welcome in the day;
Where the blithe morning minstrels sing,
The hawk darts down on hasty wing,
  In search of early prey.

A narrow stripe of waterfall
Pours down a dark and rocky wall,
  A mass of show'ry spray,
Till, lost in shady depths below,
Where stunted oaks and hazels grow,
  It urges on its way.

High perched upon a pointed peak,
A lonely raven opes his beak
  And croaks his warning notes;
Then spreads his wings and cleaves the air—
Ye timid fledgelings pray beware,
  For o'er ye now he floats.

'Tis something like our social plan,
When weaklings fear the stronger man,
  And might usurps the right;

Subjected to despotic rules,
The weak are treated just as tools,
   To toil, to slay, to fight.

Around me scenes sublime and grand—
The home once of a noble band,
   Brave heroes of high fame,
Missed in our brawny ranks of war;
They've gone to distant lands afar,
   That sportsmen may have game.

Well may we miss those gallant men,
Sons of the mountain and the glen—
   No braver ever bled.
What foe could stem the rushing charge
Of clansmen with claymore and targe,
   When by their chieftains led!

These hills have seen a noble sight
Of stalwart forms on every height,
   In tartan, proud array;
His sturdy ranks each Chieftain scans,
While wild "The Gathering of the Clans"
   The stately pipers play.

Ye foamy streams and whisp'ring rills!
Ye hoary craigs and rugged hills,
   Brake, bourne, and waterfall!
Ye weirdly wild and wooded glens,
And lonely lakes and boggy fens,
   I dearly love ye all!

WILLIAM ROBERTSON.

MATERNAL NIGHT.

MATERNAL Night came gently forth,
   As waned the setting sun,
And all the stars in heaven's roof,
   She lighted one by one.

And when her num'rous task was done,
    She bent her dewy head,
And lifted up her warning hand,
    And ope'd her mouth and said,—
"Now let no mirth or noise be made,
For I must put them all to bed."

She straightway shut the insect's wing,
    And stretched the beast to rest,
And stilled the fish in stream and sea,
    And bird in brake and nest,
And laid the babe on mother's breast,
    And labour's limbs composed,
And care surprised, and sickness soothed,
    And sorrow's eyelids closed.
"Now let there be no noise," she said,
"For I have put them all to bed."

And all night long she sat and watched
    Within that chamber vast,
And when the full-orbed moon arose,
    She clouds around her cast;
And called upon the piping winds,
    And warbling waves and streams,
To sing their softest lullabies,
    And give unbroken dreams.
And there she sat and vigil kept,
And mother's tears she o'er them wept,
And soothed and blessed them while they slept.
        REV. GEORGE JACQUE.

THE OLD HEARSE.

"THE hearse is coming!" shouted, as they ran,
A crowd of boys and girls. And maid and man
Flung windows up, or rushed into the street—
And some ran off the vehicle to meet;

For it was deemed a wonder to be seen,
And had for weeks the village topic been.
"The hearse is coming!"—on the tidings flew!
Down with a clang the smith his hammer threw.
Away went weaver's lay and delver's spade,
And forth from tub and wheel rushed wife and maid;
And age took up its staff and stuttered out,
To see what all the hubbub was about.
"The hearse is come! hurrah!" the children cried,
And noisy curs with bound and bark replied.
And there it was at last, with flaunting plume
And glossy sides, the chariot of the tomb!
"It was an honour to the town!" they said.
The old man mused, the widow shook her head.
Back to its wooden house, amidst the throng,
The idol of the day was borne along.
And all that day they feasted on the sight,
And spent in ale and gossip half the night.
And there it dwelt full forty years and more,
And child and mother, son and sire, it bore
Down to the silent tomb, until at last,
Of all who had in the forgotten past
Its advent hailed, but few remained to tell
What mirth and clamour on that day befell.
But earthly grandeur has its little day,
And must, like man, surrender to decay.
Year after year it old and crazy grew,
And through its chinks the winter tempests blew.
The worm was busy in its mouldering frame,
And foul reproach was heaped upon its name.
Until 'twas doomed to stand, inert, alone,
Its ancient prestige and employment gone.
Its wooden house, with tufts of moss bedeck'd,
No more its age from insult could protect.
By night the vagrant easy entrance found,
And slept within or 'neath it on the ground;
By day it was the favourite resort
Of boys from school, to ply their noisy sport.
Perched on its box, a mimic driver held
Fictitious reins, and fancied steeds impelled,

Whilst down below rose shout and fierce debate,
Where erst the dead had lain, in solemn state.
And as caprice evoked a different mood,
A ready target for their aim it stood;
And as a stone a rib or rafter split,
A loud huzza announced the happy hit.
And—worst of all—its plumes were reckless torn
From out their place, and in derision worn
In cap and bonnet, to be flung anon
Upon the dusty ground, and trod upon,
Or torn by dogs, and scattered here and there,
Which watchful sparrow picked up to repair
Its piebald nest; and winds would fragments pitch
Into the ash-pit foul or stagnant ditch.
And last of all, by piecemeal, plank and spoke,
It vanished from the earth in chimney-smoke.
" Sic transit "—but the moral is so stale,
That to repeat it were of small avail.
Rev. George Jacque.

AYE FEN' FOR YERSEL'.

There's heichts and there's howes
 On baith sides o' Life's brae,
Whaur Care aften meets
 Wi' her twin sister Wae;
But bear life's rebuffs
 Tho', nae doct, unco snell,
For still there's a way
 Aye to fen' for yersel'.

There's true mither wit
 I' the auld-fashion'd tale
" Let ilk' herrin' hang,
 By its ain siller tail ".
Frae this maxim learn,
 Self-control is the spell,
That opes Plenty's horn,
 When ye fen' for yersel'.

Let Truth be yer shield,
   And yer best coat o' mail ;
And Time your estate,
   Tho' nae lasting entail,
For pelf and for power
   Yer best birthright ne'er sell,
But keep the straucht gaet,
   And aye fen' for yersel'.

To press yer just claims,
   A moment ne'er swither,
The puir simple snool's
   The beggar's ain brither ;
When worth is sair chill'd
   Whiles in puirtith's cauld well,
E'en then be a man,
   And aye fen' for yersel'.

Ne'er miss a richt chance
   When it comes in yer way,
To hain yer spare gear
   For a cauld rainy day ;
In need it mak's freen's
   Wha, the plain truth to tell,
Will like ye the mair
   That ye fen' for yersel'.

Ne'er fawn nor despair,
   Though the wolf's at the door,
But aft bend the knee,
   And mair strength aye implore
Life's burdens to bear
   And Care's dark doubts repel :
For God helps the man
   Wha, in faith, helps himsel'.

                JOHN WHITE.

OUR LAST FLITTIN'.

Life's lease is unco short, John,
    And the term is comin' fast,
The flittin' day we'll min', John,
    Lest sorrow come at last.
A treasure we'll lay up, John,
    A' safe frae ilka fae,
Whaur ne'er a warnin's gien, John,
    A hame without a wae.

Come when the flittin' may, John,
    We'll e'en now do our best,
And aye look up for grace, John,
    To bring us peace and rest.
Wi' hearts sincere, we'll strive, John,
    To keep the narrow way,
And watch wi' jealous e'e, John,
    Our last, our flittin' day.

Ye ken we've flitted aft, John,
    And sair forfouchen been,
To keep our bairnies sax, John,
    And sticks a' ncat and clean;
But oh, it mak's me wae, John,
    (My only pride and stay)
To think that we might part, John,
    When comes the flittin' day.

Through a' our cares and toils, John,
    We've helpit ane anither,
And e'en when at the warst, John,
    We closer drew thegither.
Our bonnie bairnies few, John,
    Noo clad in white array,
We'll meet, if we hae faith, John,
    When comes the flittin' day.

We've warnin's had fu' aft, John,
    That filled our hearts wi' wae,

To tell us baith the truth, John,
   We're creepin' down the brae;
A' these were wisely sent, John,
   Sure inklin's o' decay,
That whisper'd aye, tak' tent, John,
   Ere comes the flittin' day.
JOHN WHITE.

THE KILTED HIELANDMEN.

I SAW a licht lowp ower the hill,
   I saw it glintin' through the glen;
It was the swift-winged fiery cross
   To rouse the kilted Hielandmen.
Auld Scotia's stalwart Hielandmen,
Her fearless, dauntless Hielandmen,
The swift-winged flickerin' fiery cross
   To rouse the kilted Hielandmen.

Whene'er the tide o' war has surged,
   Through city pent or open plain,
There, foremost 'mang the rushing brave,
   Are Scotland's kilted Hielandmen.
They shook the little Corsican,
   In Egypt, Belgium, and in Spain;
"The hero of a hundred fights"
   Was frighted at the Hielandmen.
At Scotland's kilted Hielandmen,
Her fearless, dauntless Hielandmen,
The eagle eye that erst ne'er quailed
   Was frighted at the Hielandmen.

On Balaclava's heights they stood
   When Russian horse like hurricane
Swept on to break the single line
   Of Scotland's brawny Hielandmen.
"O Colin, man, how dared you risk?
   You should hae triple lined your men,"

Quoth he, " Wi' ither troops I should,
   But no' wi' kilted Hielandmen.
Auld Scotland's darling Hielandmen,
Her fearless, dauntless Hielandmen,
I didna think it worth my while
   Wi' Scotland's kilted Hielandmen."

The savage Sepoys they did chase
   Through flood an' field, an' break an' fen,
The hero Havelock thwacked them sair
   Wi' fifteen hundred Hielandmen.
An' yet, ye heartless Hieland lairds,
You've stocked your every hill an' glen
Wi' moorcocks, hares, an' antler'd deer,
   An' harried out the Hielandmen.

When foemen on your borders press,
   When despots howl around ye; then,
When fightin' for your hames and hearths
   You'll maybe miss the Hielandmen.
Auld Scotland's brawny Hielandmen,
Her fearless, dauntless Hielandmen,
Your fine preserves of petted game
   Are puir exchange for Hielandmen.
        JOHN CAMPBELL ("*Will Harrow.*")

WEARIED AND WORN.

Written in Africa.

AULD and crazy, wearied and worn,
   I creep alang the shore;
I hirple ower the shining sand,
While my heart is awa' in a far off land,
   My land, alas! no more.

And I sadly muse on brighter days—
   Days now for ever flown;

For here I feebly creep an' cringe,
In every fibre feel a twinge,
  An ache in every bone.

When I was young, then on my brow
  Grief ventured not to trace
The sorrows that becloud it now,
When I am fading like a bough
  That's torn from its place.

Ah! what a mingled play we see
  Here on life's shifting stage,
Ever mingling life with death,
The coming with the parting breath—
  Bright youth with gloomy age.

"All flesh is grass," and o'er the field
  The mighty reaper goes;
And soon or late, no stalk is missed;
Yet o'er the world's perish'd dust
  Life's stream still gaily flows.

The number'd hour that's on the wing,
  'Tis well we do not know;
All that we know is only this—
Such ignorance is really bliss—
  When to the earth we go.

When comes my time, as come it will,
  Then my remains inhume
Within a verdant sunny slope,
Whereon the gladsome birdies hop,
  Among the golden broom.

Among the bonnie yellow broom,
  That breezes wanton wave,
The golden tassels wet "wi' dew"
(That every morning will renew),
  To gem my nameless grave,

On the wide uncultured moor,
   Far from the noisy town,
Where uncaged birdies blythely sing—
Where the untended wild flowers spring—
   There lay me gently down.
      JOHN CAMPBELL ("*Will Harrow.*")

EPISTLE TO TAMMAS BODKIN.

Written in Africa.

DEAR TAMMAS,
   I'm sittin' 'mang the burnin' sand,
     Elbow on knee and chin on loof,
   Musin' on life's ravelled web,
     Entangled warp an' woof;
   An' like to greet wi' bootless grievin'
   At the claith sae marred in weavin'.

Some folk hae talents nine or ten,
   Some only ane or twa;
The feck o' folk hae less or mair,
   But I had nane ava.
An' though you shak' the napkin oot
Ye'll no find ochtlins i' the cloot.

When folks wi' talents gathered gear—
   They wha had hands and harns—
I boost be goavin' i' the air
   An' glowering at the starns.
I hadna' talents—what was worse,
I had nae siller i' my purse.

An' sae the wolf began to howl,
   An' chased me far away;
Far frae the braes o' sweet Strathmore,
   An' flowery banks o' Tay;

Doon the Tay an' owre the Tyne,
An' far besouth earth's central line.

An' here I am 'mang burnin' sand,
  Whaur rude sou'-easters blow,
That lift the sand up bodily,
  An' drive it to an' fro;
An' whirl it through the blazin' lift,
Mair fierce than e'en Kingussie drift.

There's no a runnin' river here
  In a' this parched land;
They're maistly a' a string o' pools
  Slow sinkin' through the sand.
Or owre the scaurs, as at Lodore,
A gill a minute, less or more.

Musin' on my ain dear Tay,
  That fond remembered river,
That sweeps around my natal ground,
  Majestical as ever—
Musin' on that lovely stream
I fell asleep and dreamed a dream.

I dreamed I lay on Table Bay,
  The "sounding sea" before,
An' there I saw Poe's classic crow
  Hop, hopping on the shore.
Hopping, hopping ever hopping,
Hopping on the sandy shore.

Wi' quivering lips I cried, "O, raven,
  Will I ever see Kinclaven,
Or Strathmore, or ony place,
  On Scotia's classic shore?"
But the prophetic carrion crow—
The oracle of Edgar Poe—
  Sat croaking—"Nevermore."

      JOHN CAMPBELL ("*Will Harrow.*")

MY BAIRN.

OH! but the day was fair and bricht
    My bairn was ta'en awa';
The sun shed a' his gowden licht
    Ower mountains, vale an' ha'.
The fields were in their summer dress,
    The birds sang forth in glee,
But oh! they brocht nae gladness--
    Nae strains o' joy to me.

His faither press'd me to his breast,
    An' spak' o' promise given,
That tho' we sink in death's dark rest,
    We'll wauken a' in heaven;
And that we'd meet our laddie there,
    Frae a' earth's sorrow free,
A bricht and bonnie cherub fair—
    But oh! it sooth'd na me.

Oh! he was aye sae meek an' mild
    He seemed nae bairn o' earth;
An' at its pleasure aft he smiled—
    He joy'd na in its mirth;
An' yet I see his saddest smile
    Illume ilk' saft 'blue e'e,
An' oh! thae thochts forever wile
    The big saut tears frae me.

I see him by the ingle-cheek
    When the sun is at its hicht;
An' in my dreams for him I seek
    At the lane mid oor o' nicht.
Oh! wha can ken a mither's love
    Oh! wha her soul can see;
Or wha her anguish, can reprove!
    My bairn was dear to me!

                      DAVID IMRIE.

THE VALLEY OF THE EARN.

Scotland, wi' thy hills sae mony,
   Silent glens, and wimpling burns,
Scotland, wi' thy haughs sae bonnie,
   Still to thee fond memory turns.

Memories tipped wi' golden tints
   Ere I trod life's miry way,
Limpid streams and dewy lawns
   That glittered in life's morning ray.

I can see my native valley,
   As on Keltie's heights I stand,
Glowing in the summer sunset,
   Radiant as a fairy land.

There's not a knoll, nor pleasing hollow,
   Where my young feet were wont to rove,
But what's enshrined in mem'ry's landscape,
   Like a ne'er forgotten love.

And the green hills dance before me,
   Laughing in the month of June;
Flowers and heather gang thegither
   Wi' the wild bee's humming tune.

I can see my native Dunning
   Running o'er its stony bed,
Hastening on to join the Earn,
   Where in youth sweet sports I've had.

Every grassy bank's remembered,
   So is every weel kenn'd stane,
Where the speckled trout I grop'd for
   In the days sae lang syne gane.

And Dunruib, I love to linger
   Round thy auld walks and parks sae green,
And dream my boyish dreams again
   When love and hope endeared ilk scene.

And wander round thy streets O Dunning,
   And gambol o'er my auld play grounds,
Or view the church and auld grey tower
   Amang the graveyard's lowly mounds.

I enter now my father's cottage,
   I see my mither in her chair,
My brither and my sisters greet me,
   I hear my father's fervent prayer.

And now the evening shadows gather,
   I've seen the sun's departiug ray;
It burnish'd up auld Dupplin's towers,
   And shone on birks of Invermay.

It glinted on the braes of Gask,
   It purpled Earn's dark blue stream,
It shed a glory 'mang the groves
   Where Nairne wont to muse and dream.

O, pleasant land! O, fruitful vale!
   I see thy fields of waving corn;
The fragrance of thy summer flowers
   Upon the evening breeze is borne.

The blackbird sits upon the bough,
   And sings to Heaven his parting lay;
The craik and beetle bee unite,
   And saftest gloamin' shrouds the day.

O Nairne, Queen of Scottish Song!
   Thy "Land o' Leal" fa's on mine ear,
As if an angel's harp sent forth
   Its dulcet music, saft aud clear.

The poet's sang, the flowers and birds
   That wont to charm in youthful prime;
Your echoes float around me still,
   Sublimely o'er the sands of time.

I ken this land is fair and young,
    And kindly voices greet mine ears;
But Scotia, we have parted been
    By the wild waves for thirty years.

Yet still I love thee a' the same,
    And my last wish to Heaven shall be,
May choicest blessing still be poured,
    My country, upon thine and thee.

And on thy banks, my beauteous Earn,
    Thy sunny banks sae fair and high,
While calm descend life's evening shades,
    There let me live, there let me die.

Near the murmur of thy waters,
    By thy wavelets ever bright,
I could lay me down in peace,
    And calmly bid the world good-night.

                        JOHN NELSON.

A CRONIE O' MINE.

Air—"*The Days o' Langsyne.*"

YE'LL mount your bit naggie, an' ride your wa's doun,
'Bout a mile an' a half frae the neist borough toun,
There wons an auld blacksmith, wi' Janet his wife—
An' a queerer auld cock ye ne'er met i' your life
    As this cronie o' mine, this cronie o' mine;
    O! be sure that ya ca' on this cronie o' mine.

Ye'll find him, as I do, a trustworthy chiel',
Weel tempered wi' wit frae his head to his heel,
Wi' a saul in his body Auld Nick ne'er could clout,
An' a spark in his throat, richt ill to droon out—
    This cronie o' mine, this cronie o' mine,
    For a deil o' a drouth has this cronie o' mine.

His smiddie ye'll ken by the twa trough stanes
At the auld door-cheeks, an' the black battered panes—
By the three airn cleeks that he drave in the wa',
To tie up wild yad's when high customers ca' ;
   O ! this cronie o' mine, this cronie o' mine !
   Sure the hail country kens him, this cronie o' mine.

Up agen the auld gable 'tis like you may view
A tramless cart, or a couterless plough,
An auld teethless harrow, a brechem ring rent,
Wi' mae broken gear, that are meant to be men't
   By this cronie o' mine, this cronie o' mine ;
   He's a richt handy craftsman, this cronie o' mine.

There's an auld broken sign-board looks to the hie
   road,
Whilk tells ilka rider where his naig may be shod ;
There's twa or three wordies that ye'll hae to spell,
But ye needna find fault, for he wrote it himsel' ;
   This cronie o' mine, this cronie o' mine,
   He's an aul'-farrant carle this cronie o' mine.

When ye find this auld smiddie, ye'll like, there's nae
   doubt,
To see the inside o't as weel as the oot ;
Then stap ye in bauldly, altho' he be thrang,
Gif the pint-stoup but clatter, ye'll ken him ere lang,
   This cronie o' mine, this cronie o' mine,
   Baith wit, fun, and fire has this cronie o' mine.

Twa or three chiel's frae the toon-en' are sure to be
   there—
There's the bauld-headed butcher, wha tak's aye the
   chair,
'Mang the querest auld fallows, ae way an' anither,
That ere in this warld were clubbit thegither ;
   A' cronies o' mine, a' cronies o' mine,
   They'll a' mak' ye welcome, thae cronies o' mine.

There's Dominie Davie, sae glib i' the mou',
But it's like ye will fin' the auld carle blin' fou';
Wi' the wee barber bodie, an' his wig fu' o' news,
Wha wad shave ony chap a' the week for a booze;
    A' cronies o' mine, a' cronies o' mine,
    They'll a' mak' ye welcome, thae cronies o' mine.

There's our auld Town Clerk, wha has ta'en to the pack,
That is naething in bulk to the humph on his back;
His knees are sae bow'd, his splay feet sae thrawn,
Troth it's no easy tellin' the road whilk they're gaun,
    Tho' a cronie o' mine, a bauld cronie o' mine,
    They'll a' mak' ye welcome, thae cronies o' mine.

There's Robin the ploughman, wha's cram'd fu' o' fun;
Wee gamekeeper Davie, wi' bag, dog, an' gun;
An' the miller, wha blythely the pipes can play on,
So you're sure to fa' in wi' the "Miller o' Drone—"
    A' cronies o' mine, a' cronies o' mine,
    They'll a' mak' ye welcome, thae cronies o' mine.

Then wi' thumpin' o' hammers, an' tinklin' o' tangs,
Wi' auld-fashioned stories wrought into queer sangs,
Wi' this soun' and that, ye'll aiblins be deaved—
An' tak' care o' your breeks that they dinna get sieved—
    Wi' this cronie o' mine, this cronie o' mine,
    For an arm o' might has this cronie o' mine,

Then the Vulcan his greybeard is aye sure to draw
Frae a black sooty hole whilk ye'll see i' the wa',
An' lang ere its empty, frien', I meikle doubt,
Gif the tae chap kens weel what the tither's about.
    Wi' this cronie o' mine, this cronie o' mine,
    O! be sure that ye ca' on this cronie o' mine.

Come now, my gude frien', gie's a shak' o' yer haun',
The nicht's wearin' thro', an' ye maun be gaun;
The callan' will bring down your naig in a blink,
But before that ye mount, again let us drink—
    To this cronie o' mine, this cronie o' mine,
    Here's lang life an' pith to this cronie o' mine.

ALEXANDER MACLAGAN.

HURRAH FOR THE THISTLE.

Hurrah for the thistle! the brave Scottish thistle,
The evergreen thistle of Scotland for me!
A fig for the flowers in your lady-built bowers—
The strong-bearded, weel-guarded thistle for me!

'Tis the flower the proud eagle greets in his flight,
When he shadows the stars with the wings of his might;
'Tis the flower that laughs at the storm as it blows,
For the stronger the tempest the greener it grows!
  Hurrah for the thistle, etc.

Round the love-lighted hames o' our ain native land—
On the bonnetted brow, on the hilt of the brand—
On the face o' the shield, 'mid the shouts of the free,
May the thistle be seen where the thistle should be!
  Hurrah for the thistle, etc.

Hale hearts we ha'e yet to bleed in its cause;
Bold harps we ha'e yet to sound its applause;
How then can it fade, when sic chiels an' sic cheer,
And sae mony braw sprouts o' the thistle are there?

Then hurrah for the thistle, the brave Scottish thistle,
The evergreen thistle of Scotland for me!
A fig for the flowers in your lady-built bowers—
The strong-bearded, weel-guarded thistle for me!
    Alexander Maclagan.

MY AULD GRANNIE'S LEATHER POUCH.

Dear frien's, ye'll think me daft, nae doubt,
My wee bit blink o' wit blawn out,
To deave your learned lugs about
 My auld grannie's leather pouch!

I mind in life's sweet sunny springs,
When we were laughin', toddlin' things,
How blythe we were to loose the strings
  O' auld grannie's leather pouch!

Sae queer it's look—sae strange the shape,
Sae strongly bound wi' red silk tape,
Sae awfu' wide the mou' did gape,
  O' auld grannie's leather pouch!

There's preens, an' sweeties, raisins, rock,
There's A B abs, for Will and Jock,
There's ribbons for a braw wee frock,
  In auld grannie's leather pouch!

A pair o' specks, a pair o' shears,
A preen-cod, aged fifty years,
Aye danglin' at the side appears
  O' auld grannie's leather pouch!

There's bodkins, thummels, hanks o' thread,
There's awfu' whangs o' cheese an' bread,
The beggars' bairns an' hens to feed,
  In auld grannie's leather pouch!

There's sangs that sing o' Scotland's richt,
O' Wallace, wi' his arm o' micht,
O' Bruce's battle-axe sae bricht,
  In auld grannie's leather pouch!

Some ditties hae a favoured place,
Sir James the Rose, an' Chevy Chase,
An' some about the Stuart race,
  In auld grannie's leather pouch!

We kent to time her kind, kind look,
When she took up the Holy Book,
We kent the time when we micht pook
  At auld grannie's leather pouch!

But gif we broke decorum's laws,
We had to flee like frichtit craws,
A' tremblin', for the lang-taed tawse
   In auld grannie's leather pouch!

An' if we went to open strife,
When taunts an' blows were rather rife,
We fled before the "Butcher's knife,"
   In auld grannie's leather pouch!

We kent richt weel to wale ilk word,
We kent there was a "little bird,"
Whilk blabbit ilka thing it heard,
   In auld grannie's leather pouch!

E'en pussie durstna mak' a din,
When she sat doun to read or spin,
For fear it wad be stappit in
   To auld grannie's leather pouch!

Gif kames or buckles went astray,
When lads and lasses made the hay,
'Twas queer that a'thing faund its way
   To auld grannie's leather pouch!

I've kent o' pouches rather queer,
Some fou' o' wun', some fou' o' gear,
But never ane that e'er cam' near
   My auld grannie's leather pouch!

When ye want sermons, salves, or saws,
For mendin' heads, or hearts, or laws,
Mak' up your minds, an' gang your wa's
   To auld grannie's leather pouch!

ALEXANDER MACLAGAN.

TIBBY AND THE LAIRD.

Auld Robin, our laird, thocht o' changin' his life,
But he didna weel ken whaur to wale a gude wife.
A plump quean had he, wha had served him for years;
"Ho, Tibby!" he cried. Lo! douce Tibby appears.
"Sit doun," said the laird; "ye are wanted awee,"
"Very weel, sir," quo' Tibby, "sae let it be."

"Noo, Tibby," quo' he, "there's a queer rumour rins,
Through the hale country-side, that there's naebody
    spins,
Bakes, washes, or brews, wi' sic talents as you;
An' what a' body says, ye ken, maun be true,
Sae ye ought to be gratefu' for their courtesie;"
"Very weel, sir," quo' Tibby, "sae let it be."

"Noo, it seemeth but just, an' richt proper to me,
That ye milk your ain cow 'neath your ain fig-tree;
That a servant sae thrifty a gude wife will mak',
Is as clear as daylicht, sae a man ye maun tak',
Wha will haud ye as dear as the licht o' his e'e,"
"Very weel, sir," quo' Tibby, "sae let it be."

"The pearl may be pure, Tib, though rough be the
    shell—
Sae I'm determined to wed ye mysel'—
An' a' that a lovin' an' leal heart can grant
O' this warld's wealth, lass, troth, ye shall nae want;
Sae a kiss to the bargain ye maun gie to me,"
"Very weel, sir," quo' Tibby, "sae let it be."

The weddin'-day came, wi' bride-cake an' ban's,
Fand Tib i' the kitchen, 'mang tubs, pats, an' pans;
"Bless me," quo' the laird, "what on earth hauds you
    here?
Our frien's a' are met, in their braw bridal gear;
Ye maun busk in your best, lass, an' that speedilie,"
"Very weel, sir," quo' Tibby, "sae let it be."

When the blessin' was said, an' the feastin' was dune,
Tib crap to her bed i' the garret abune;
When she heard the laird's fit, an' his tap at her door,
She wonder'd—he ne'er took sic freedoms before.
"Come, Tibby, my lass, ye maun listen to me,"
"Very weel, sir," quo' Tibby, "sae let it be."

"Noo Tibby, ye ken, we were wedded this nicht,
An' that ye should be here, haith, I think is no richt.
It canna be richt; for, when women an' men
Are wedded, they ought to be bedded, ye ken;
Sae come doon the stair, Tib, an' e'en sleep wi' me,"
"Very weel, sir," quo' Tibby, "sae let it be!"

ALEXANDER MACLAGAN.

THE HILLS O' BREADALBANE.

HURRAH, for the Hills of Breadalbane!
   Hurrah, for the soul-stirring sight!
Hurrah, for the hopes of the patriot's soul,
   When he looks on their beauty and might!
Hurrah, for the lightnings that flash
   Their fires on the face of the lake!
Hurrah, for the thunders round lofty Ben Lawers!
   Hurrah, for the music they make!

      Then, here's to the Hills of Breadalbane—
         The snow-clad, the green, and the gray!
      Where the proud eagle mirrors the wings of his
         might,
         In the bright-beaming breast of Loch Tay!

Sing, hurrah, for the haunts of the deer,
   Down the glens where the wild rivers run!
Hurrah, for their joy when they leap o'er the hills,
   Like the beams of the morning sun!

Sing, Hurrah, for the fleet-footed roe!
  Hurrah for the life and the light
Of their glad-glowing eyes, when they break through
    the mist,
  Like stars through the shadows of night!
    Then, here's to the Hills of Breadalbane—
      The snow-clad, the green, and the gray!
    Where the proud eagle mirrors the wings of his
        might,
      In the bright-beaming breast of Loch Tay!
          ALEXANDER MACLAGAN.

GLENTULCHAN'S SWEET FLOWER.*

As oft as I roam by the Almond's clear water,
  Whether at skreigh of dawn or the soft gloaming
    hour;
My thoughts are absorb'd by the innkeeper's daughter,
  The charming young Jessie, Glentulchan's sweet
    flower.
If she only deigns a bright smile to cast on me,
  Neither sunshine nor moonlight have o'er me such
    power;
Her grace and her beauty have wholly undone me—
  The lovely young Jessie, Glentulchan's sweet flower.

I have lived two score years in this world, and I well
    know
  Every wile and each art that o'er beauty hath power;
And though they ne'er fail with the proud city belle, no
  Such arts can I try with Glentulchan's sweet flower.

---

* On the occasion many years ago of an Anglo-Indian gentleman paying a visit to Glentulchan House, he suddenly fell over head and ears in love with a rustic beauty of the neighbourhood, and Mr. Mercer having noticed his guest's penchant wrote the above verses and left a copy of them on the enamoured swain's dressing-table over night that they might meet his eye the first thing in the morning. What the effect was we cannot tell.

Oh! if she'd not scorn me, I care for no neighbour—
   Confiding in Jessie as in a strong tower—
I'd retire from this world and from life's eerie labour
     With my own darling Jessie, Glentulchan's sweet flower.

Yet 'tis humbling for one who has been such a rover,
   Who has killed his twelve elephants ere breakfast hour,
To be checked in his roaming and thus tumbled over
     By a well-planted shot from Glentulchan's sweet flower.
I never can think of the herds on their wooded-hills
   Roving free and unscath'd, but grief does me devour;
But, pshaw! I'm grown old and gray—love now my bosom fills,
     Ardent, strong, and most pure, for Glentulchan's sweet flower.

Oh! would she but wed me, I'd sell Kattaboolé,
   Kooroowakké I'd settle upon her as dower;
My evening of life I would relish most truly
     With her who was once of Glentulchan the flower.
Oh! how happy I'd be with my dear Mrs. Allway
   In the wilds of Glenbrain, in our heathery bower!
I would fish, shoot, and stalk, and make love in no small way
     With her who was once of Glentulchan the flower.

Should the gled of adversity round us e'er hover,
   Like a poor wounded bird to my bosom she'd cower;
There she'd nestle in safety till danger was over,
     And then be as gay as my Glentulchan flower.
And our dear darling babes we with kindness would smother!
   How they'd shield us in age should misfortune then lower!
How proud they would be of so faultless a mother
     As Jessie!—no longer Glentulchan's sweet flower.

And when grim old Death, of all terror divested,
   Should have lured us like dicky birds into his power,
All calmly we'll sleep, as if we from life rested,
   Or had faded, mown down like a Glentulchan flower.
No tablet we'd need, for our memory would cling fast
   To our dear children's hearts until their last hour ;
And when they went hence we should be as a thing past,
   Nor cared for so much as a Glentulchan flower.

                      GRÆME REID MERCER.

PIPER M'NEE.

I WINNA sing sorrows, I ha'e nane to sing,
Nor mope owre the evils to-morrow may bring,
I'll tune up my reed on a happier key,
An' gi'e ye a lilt aboot Piper M'Nee.

The piper is windy an' weel he can blaw,
A' gloomy distempers he frichtens awa',
A cure mair effectual than whisky or tea,
Leaps forth frae the chanter o' Piper M'Nee.

He lives in a hoose by the side o' a burn,
Whaur the jucks an' the puddocks wallop in turn,
Tho' hairy and Hielan', an' fond o' a spree,
A capital piper is Piper M'Nee.

When the grey o' the gloamin' begins to come doon,
He screws up his pipes an' he pits them in tune.
Then laddies an' lassies o' every degree
Come loupin' an' laughin' roon' Piper M'Nee.

When Katie an' Lizzie come in frae the kye,
An' synd their milk coggies an' lay them a' by ;
Then few are the gentry sae lichtsome as we,
Wha dance to the chanter o' Piper M'Nee.

Oor health is oor wealth, an' contentment oor store,
We always hae plenty, an' dainties galore;
We jump an' we thump, an' cry oot in oor glee,
"Success to the chanter o' Piper M'Nee."

Gran'faither is hoochin' an' crackin' his thooms,
An' granny's forgettin' her toothache an' rheums,
Their hearts are sae gladdened the young anes to see,
A' dance to the chanter o' Piper M'Nee.

The motties that trouble the too open eye,
They fash us but little, or never come nigh,
The dark spots o' the warl', if ony such be,
Are' scattered and brichtened by Piper M'Nee.

Oors are the pleasures that never breed pain,
That after-thochts sweeten an' seek for again,
Such pleasures as happy hearts ever shall pree,
That dance to the chanter o' Piper M'Nee.

If gout or rheumatics e'er trouble your banes,
Or the cares o' the warl' e'er jumble your brains,
Jist come to the Hielan's gin summer wi' me,
An' dance to the chanter o' Piper M'Nee.

If foemen should ever endeavour to land
Oor ticht little island, to brag or to brand,
The lads o' Balquhidder wad gie them their fee,
If led to the battle by Piper M'Nee.

Then health to the piper, an' blest be the feet
That trip it sae neatly to music sae sweet,
Lang may they be soople an' willin' an' free
To dance to the chanter o' Piper M'Nee.

FINLAY FARQUHARSON.

THE WISDOM O' MY GRANNY.

My granny wis a worthy dame,
   Her word wis seldom dootit,
The neebor wives aft to her came
   Wi' maitters sair disputit.
She brocht me up wi' meikle care,
   She ca'ed me guid an' bonnie,
An' saftly whispered in my ear
   " Be carfu' o' yer money."

I min' a'e day we were alane
   Whaur nane cud clashes carry,
I spak' richt up an' said " my gran',
   I think I'm gaun to mairry."
" Wow! wow!" quo' she, " remember that's
   A thorny path, my sonny,
Its joys are few, aweel I wat,
   Unless they're backed wi' money."

There's Mary White, an' Katie Black,
   Twa gay an' dashy lasses,
But a' their tocher's on their back,
   In useless, gaudy dresses.
An' puir he'll be whae'er will tak
   Sic like for bosom crony,
For gab an' chat he winna lack,
   But ne'er a plack o' money.

My laddie, whan ye need a wife
   I'll tell ye whaur to seek her,
'Mang decent fouk, whaur siller's rife,
   An' nae whaur else bespeak her.
Learn then an' tak example by
   Oor rulin' elder, Johnny!
For he's ta'en Parson Mammon's May
   Wha has a mint o' money.

Money is honour, trust, an' worth,
　　An' fules they are wha doot it,
The fairest face, the noblest birth,
　　Are bubbles a' withoot it.
The houp o' youth, the staff o' age
　　Mak's ilka day sae sunny,
If ye wad pass for saunt or sage,
　　Be carefu' o' yer money.

For money's a'thing that ye please,
　　It's faither, wife an' mither,
A frien' yer hardships will release
　　Mair faithfu' than a brither.
Money's the worth o' a' kent thing,
　　The bee, the flower, the honey,
The maiden's smile, the marriage ring,
　　The king o' life is—money.

FINLAY FARQUHARSON.

HYMN TO FIRE.

ANCIENT and eternal fire,
Unto thee I string my lyre,
　　And sing thy power supreme;
God within and over all,
Thee undoubtingly I call,
　　All else to thee is dream!
Rapid, restless in thy course,
Strong, resistless in thy force,
　　Wild panther of the sky;
Springing o'er black gulfs of night
In thy swift and furious might,
　　Without or term or tie;
Pressing forward in thy sweep,
Gaining ever on the deep,
　　Fearlessly plunging on,
Darkness before, and light behind,
　　Thou flashest, and art gone!

Still wave on wave, as from an eye,
Pour thy billows through the sky;
   Nor ever rest or pause;
Always changing, ne'er delaying,
They with tireless tongues are saying,
   "Ours are eternal laws!"
Foe tremendous! friend sincere!
Thou the cottage-hearth dost cheer,
   And the palace burnest!
In the mountain's entrails thou
Plantest pangs that scorch his brow,
   And him to Tophet turnest;
Dreadful art thou in thy course,
Mystic, distant in thy source,
   Yet fruitful, too, and kind.
Nursing nature with thy beam,
Pouring daylight on thy stream,
   Feeding all human kind.
Beauty on thy steps attendeth,
Love with thee her nature blendeth,
   With thee in hand she goes;
Thine the rainbow's starry arch,
Thine the season's ceaseless march,
   And thine the blushing rose;
The milk of motherhood is thine,
And the virgin's blush divine,
   And the young lover's rage;
Thine on the poet's brow the flush,
And thine the wild and fervent gush
   Of heart which fires his page:
Thou swim'st undrowned the blood of men,
Thou lurkest in the lions' den,
   And breathest in his breath;
Thou gleamest on the serpent's skin,
Thou edgest, too, the sabre keen,
   Barbest the shaft of death.
All precious stones through thee are bright,
Sitting in their central night,
   The wonders of the mine;
Thine, too, the sea's phosphoric waves,

And thine the deep and sparry caves,
　　Though shivering they shine;
The rich red clouds of morn and even,
Praise thee and the Autumn heaven,
　　The while the ripened grain
Sending back thy light and power
In an upward rushing shower,
　　Asserts thy golden reign.
Eternal snow itself from thee
Derives its stern divinity,
　　From thee its glitt'ring sheen,
As towering in the Andes high,
It seems to fret the blue-black sky
　　With thousand needles keen.
They say that these serene abodes
Are temples of the living gods
　　Exalted 'bove the earth,
Because at even and morn they shine
With the lustre half divine
　　To which, thou, Fire, giv'st birth!
The earth appears a dull, cold clod,
With scorn rejecting thee as God,
　　All save those faithful slaves,
Etna, Vesuvius, and the rest
Which love thee, worship thee the best,
　　With their labouring waves.
No! for within that cold, chill globe,
With mountain border, grassy robe,
　　There beats a burning heart,
Traitor to it, but true to thee,
And which, on opportunity,
　　Shall take its parent's part,
And burn, but burn not earth alone,
But all the works that are their own,
　　Man, Nature, in one pyre,
Proclaiming in a thunder strain
Once, and again, and yet again,
　　Thy glorious god-head, Fire!

REV. GEORGE GILFILLAN.

MOUNT PILATUS.

MIDNIGHT among the Alps! Pilatre* stern
Rises upon my vision, with the shade
Of Pilate washing in the " Infernal Lake,"
And thus let me essay to paint the scene :—

In the gloom Pilatus stands
Washing aye his gory hands,
Crying to himself alone,
Half a shriek, and half a moan—
"Shadow I, is *that* a shade ?
It has never yet decayed,
Since the hour when hopeless I,
Upon a spur of Calvary
(With those eyes so calm and meek,
With that pale and ghastly cheek,
With that brow so lofty, lone,
Rising like a silver throne,
Silver, not with years, but care,
Standing quiet before me there !)
In dreadful doubt and terror cried,
Like dying wretch, with thirst adried,
For 'water, water ;' it was brought,
And I washed my hands, methought,
In a wave which, bubbling up,
Of red blood became a cup,
While a voice rang in mine ear,
'Wash, and wash, for ever there ;
Wash thy hands, and wash thy head,
Wash thee till this man be dead ;
Yes, and after long years past,
Be this wave thy looking-glass,
Shadowing the hopeless woe

---

* In "Anne of Geierstein" Scott mentions the tradition of Pilate's ghost being sometimes seen washing his hands as if from the blood of Christ, in a lake called the Infernal Lake, where it is said he drowned himself; and at such times tempests are said to arise with great fury, and Mount Pilatre (or Pilatus) to get dark and lowering.

Which with thee shall onward go,
From Calvary to Alpine hills,
Where to end thine earthly ills—
Banish'd, tortured, lonely, left,
Thou shalt seek a sullen cleft,
Where a lake in wrath upcurled
From the first day of the world,
Waits for thee, and pants the while,
To give its first and latest smile,
As thy wrecked and wretched soul
To perdition down shall roll!'

"I laughed at it, and took no heed—
Fiend-driven, I went and did the deed;
And now for ages here I stand
On this dim and dreary strand,
Heaving up my lonely stone,*
Pouring out my weary moan,
Filling aye my riddled sieve;†
Seeking aye my soul's reprieve;.
But it stoops not from the monntains,
And it wells not up the fountains,
Down the wild blast comes with clouds,
Bringing demons all in crowds;
How they mock me at my task!
As with fiendish glee they ask,
'Pilatus, hath a single stain,
Yielded to wave, or wind, or rain?
Do thy fingers flush no more
With that pure and God-like gore?
Know that Christ's blood, when spilt in ire,
Is an everlasting fire,
And the worm that never dies
Round thy neck for ever lies!'
Then, and oh! how oft, alas!
Since here I stood, soft breezes pass;

---

* Alluding to Sisyphus.
† Alluding to the punishment of the Danaides in hell.

But they minister no calm,
And they drop no drop of balm,
Nay, they whisper words of fear,
'Who is this wretch? what doth he here?
Why, fiends, not burn him limb by limb?'
'BECAUSE HELL HATH REJECTED HIM.'

"Morning comes, no morn to me,
Evening smiles, I still must dree
My deep woe, and midnight dark
Hears me at my labour stark;
Stars look out and gaze at me,
Million eyes above I see,
Each like His at Calvary,
And with a dart in every beam,
And with a fire in every stream,
Till all scathed and shrunk I sink,
Down upon the water's brink,
Shading myself with bloody hands
From the stern heaven that o'er me stands.

"Sometimes, my wife beside me seems,
Her eye still laden with her dreams,
Her voice still moaning, 'Pilate, stay,
Beware of what thou dost to-day!
In vision I have seen the Man,
With bleeding brow and visage wan,
Surrendered by thy will to die
Upon the cross at Calvary.
And o'er that cross I saw a throne,
And the judge that sate thereon
Was the God of earth and heaven;
He into thy power is given
At whose bar thou, I, and all,
Must appear, to stand or fall.
Dream of dread! I shrieked to see,
Beware lest it be read by thee.'

"And now I see a ghostly form
Astride upon a sullen storm;

His brow it is a midnight cloud,
His dress it is a seamless shroud;
His eye it is the comet's glare,
Dabbled o'er with blood his hair,
A rope all scarlet winding there!
Blistered and black his lurid lips,
Like edges of the moon's eclipse,
Which erst the Master's mouth drew nigh,
Sealing the damnèd treachery.
Ever at his neck he touches,
O'er a bag he eager crouches—
A bag that rattles like the hail,
Or the shiver of struck mail,
He stands by me; the blast shrieks by,
And he looks me in the eye,
And cries, 'Pilatus, knowest thou me?
We are twins in infamy,
Judas I, this bag the price
Of my raging avarice,
This rope the badge of suicide.
Oh, that with me thy soul could ride,
Tied in torment to each other,
Like a demon and his brother.
In my endless misery,
'Twere relief to sail with thee;
But I leave thee to the hell
Thine own sin hath earned so well,
And if one devil rides with me,
Seven are left to wash with thee!'
I see him gain the blast before,
And am alone, I and this gore;
Gore eternal! Crucified!
Shall Thy wrath ne'er be satisfied?
Thy murderers thou didst forgive,
And saidst to dead and lost ones, live!
Me, me Thy murderer, set free,
Look on this blood and pity me!"

No answer from the midnight came—
None, or in words of lurid flame!

For, lo! a thunder-cloud in wrath
Lowered above the mountain path,
And on the " Infernal Lake ". there fell
A shadow like the frown of hell,
And wingèd lightnings cast a-glow
On all the woods and hills below,
And a furious hurricane
Rushed infatuate o'er the plain;
And through the gloom I marked afar
The secret shining of a Star,
Breaking 'mid a murky cloud,
Like a soft eye through a shroud,
And it looked upon the lake,
And it left on it a flake
Of widest splendour, like the beam
Of moonshine on a lonely stream;
And then I saw the lost one rise
With a glory in his eyes,
And a hope that pierced the skies!
Full the Star looked down on him,
Lighting up his visage dim,
And his hands, all barked with blood,
Shone out gold in that bright flood;
And then, like night, the landscape o'er,
Darkness fell—I saw no more.—*From " Night."*

REV. GEORGE GILFILLAN.

THE BONNIE BURNIE.

BONNIE runs the burnie down,
   Down the benty hill,
Darting, turning, glinting, spurning
   At its own sweet will.
Wandering 'mid the heather bells,
   Hiding in the fern,
A creeping, peeping, sweeping, leaping,
   Cantie little burn.

Weel I ken the sang it sings
   A' the day and night,
Wild and gladly, soft and sadly,
   In its fresh delight.
Making music as it flows,
   At each twist and turn,
A creeping, peeping, sweeping, leaping,
   Cantie little burn.

Would you know its secret thought!
   List, and I'll reveal;
Love's a bliss beyond a blessing,
   If the heart is leal.
Nothing in the world's so sweet
   As love that meets return,
Sings the peeping, creeping, leaping,
   Bonnie little burn!

CHARLES MACKAY.

THE WRAITH OF GARRY WATER.

"Go, Evan! go—the heart you swore
   In weal and woe alike to cherish,
You've broken by your cold deceit,
   And thrown upon the world to perish.

"A woman's curse is hard to bear—
   But may be turned, if love endeavour;
But the curse of a man with hoary hair,
   It weighs upon the soul for ever.

"And for the wrong that you have done,
   Upon your head all sorrow gather,
And in your soul, for evermore,
   Deep sink the curses of a father!"

The old man bared his grey, grey head,
   And clasp'd his wither'd hands together;
And Evan curl'd his lip in scorn,
   And rode his way across the heather.

" Why should I heed this dotard's words ?
　　The needle from the pole will vary—
And time will wear, and hearts will change ;—
　　I love no more his bonnie Mary !

" I trust that happy she may be,
　　Nor pine with sorrow overladen ;
And she may love another man,
　　And I will love another maiden."

The night was fair—the moon was up—
　　The wind blew low among the gowans ;
Or fitful rose o'er Athol woods,
　　And shook the berries from the rowans.

And Evan rode through Garry strath,
　　And quite forgot the old man's daughter ;
And when he came to Garry stream,
　　It ran a red and roaring water.

The summer rains had fallen fast,
　　The voice of streams made music merry ;
And brae-side burnies leap'd and danced,
　　And mingled in the tide of Garry.

And Bruar raised a joyful shout,
　　And Tilt to Ben-y-Gloe resounded ;
And Tummel in his pride of strength,
　　Down to his fall, rejoicing, bounded.

Green were the birks on Garry braes,
　　Soft through their leaves the moon was peeping ;
And 'mid the heather on the rock
　　There sat a bonnie maiden weeping.

Her kirtle seemed of velvet green ;
　　Her robes were azure, loosely flowing ;
Her eyes shone bright amid her tears ;
　　Her lips were fresh as gowans growing.

" What brings thee here, my lily-flower ?
　　High on the strath the storm-winds tarry ;

The night is chill, the hour is late—
   Why weep'st thou by the banks of Garry?"

The maiden raised her tearful eyes,
   And with her silvery voice replying,
Said, smoothing back her yellow locks,
   And speaking low and softly sighing;

" Though dark and swift the waters pour,
   Yet here I wait in dool and sorrow;
For bitter fate must I endure,
   Unless I pass the stream ere morrow.

"Oh! aid me in this deep distress,
   Nor seek its causes to unravel;
My strength, alas! is weak at best,
   And I am worn with toil and travel."

" Though swift," said Evan "is the flood,
   My good bay mare is strong and steady;
So trust thee, lassie, to my care,
   And quickly mount and make thee ready.

"For one glance of those eyes of blue
   Thy bonnie burden I will carry;
For one kiss of those honey lips
   I'll guide thee o'er the raging Garry,

" What is it ails my good bay mare?
   What is it makes her start and shiver?
She sees a kelpie in the stream,
   Or fears the rushing of the river!

" Ah, coward jade! but heed her not,
   For, maiden dear, we may not tarry;
The beast has swum a swifter flood—
   I'll see thee safely through the Garry."

He, mounted on the good bay mare—
   But vainly Evan strove to guide her;
Through all her frame a tremour crept—
   She trembled at her bonnie rider,

Then as she heard the maiden's voice,
   And felt her gentle fingers pat her,
She gave a neigh as loud and shrill
   As if an evil sprite had sat her.

And with a desperate bound she sprang
   High from the bank into the current,
While sounds of laughter seem'd to mix
   Amid the roaring of the torrent.

The waters rush'd in eddying whirls,
   And dash'd the foam-drops o'er the heather;
And winds that seem'd asleep till then,
   Let loose their fury all together.

Down—down—the awaken'd tempest blew—
   And faster down the flood came pouring—
And horse and riders, overwhelm'd,
   Sank 'mid the rush of waters roaring.

But on the surface of the flood,
   Her yellow locks with spray—fall dripping,
The maiden with the kirtle green,
   And azure robe, came lightly tripping.

And now she sank, now rose again,
   And dash'd the waves in rain-like shiver;
Then lay afloat, or tiptoe stood
   Upon the foam-bells of the river;—

And laugh'd the while, and clapp'd her hands,—
   Until at last the storm subsided,
When, like a gleam of parting light,
   Away upon the mist she glided.

And Evan's corpse at morn was found,
   Far down by Tummel, pale and mangled,
His features bruised by jutting rocks,
   His auburn locks with gore entangled.

Few were the mourners at his grave,
   But 'mid them two—a sire and daughter;

And loud she sobb'd, and loud she wept,
  Though tenderly her sire besought her.

"He loved me—and he did me wrong,"
  She said, "and darken'd all my morrow;
But in his grave Resentment sleeps,
  While Love survives to feed on Sorrow."

CHARLES MACKAY.

SCOTTISH SONG OF VICTORY.

THERE'S hope for servile England yet,
  Erin would fain be free;
But Scotland still the vanguard holds
  Of all the nations three.
    Hurrah for dear auld Scotland yet,
      Land of the brave and free;
    In Freedom's sacred cause to lead,
      Who else so fit as she?

When haughty Rome, in days of old,
  Aroused her patriot ire,
Even Rome's imperial legions quailed
  Before her martial fire.
    Hurrah, etc.

When Lochlin's vikings, daring, fierce,
  Infested every land,
Taught by defeat in many frays,
  They shunned the Scottish strand.
    Hurrah, etc.

When Saxon kings, with pomp and power,
  Sought Freedom to o'erturn,
The *coup* they met at Scotland's hand
  Was glorious Bannockburn.
    Hurrah, etc.

When Gallia fought by sea and land,
   Her conquests to enlarge,
Experience taught her warlike sons
   To fear the Scottish charge.
      Hurrah, etc.

To fetter Thought and dictate Faith,
   When kings and priests combined,
" The Solemn League and Covenant "
   Bespoke the Scottish mind.
      Hurrah, etc.

Despotic chiefs within her coasts
   Assailed her in their turn ;
But still within her children's breasts
   The fires of Freedom burn.
      Hurrah for dear auld Scotland yet,
         Land of the brave and free ;
      In Freedom's sacred cause to lead,
         Who else so fit could be ?
             PETER MACNAUGHTON.

THE BLIND EXILE'S RETURN.

" My eyes are dark," said a blind old man
   To his young and faithful guide,
" But methinks the breezes that fan my cheek
   Are those of the loved Tayside.
Then describe thou the skies, and the landscapes round,
   To the spot whereon we stand ;
That I may know, ere I breathe my last,
   If this be the Fatherland."

      Guide.

" The skies are not like our eastern skies,
   Lit up with a radiant glow,
Through the open rents in the drifting clouds
   A fainter azure they show,

Whence the sun at times looks fitfully out,
    With a gleam more cold and pale,
While shadows and light, alternately chased,
    Flit over the bosky vale."

Exile.

"They seem to be those of my own loved isle
    On a changeful April day,
Ere the summer assumes its sultry throne,
    Though tempests have passed away;
The shadows the same as in childhood I sought
    To grasp in my tiny hand,
Ere phantoms as shadowy lured me away
    From my dear old Fatherland."

Guide.

"The mountains are nought to the towering height
    Of the Himalayahs sublime;
Nor can they compare with the hoary Alps
    We saw in the Switzer's clime;
But one, to the west, hath a lofty crest,
    And wrapped in a mantle of snow,
While around the hills have a dusky shade
    With the heath descending low."

Exile.

"Ben Lawers! on whose rugged and giant form
    In boyhood I loved to gaze,
As with tremulous radiance, dazzling white,
    It shone in the sun's bright rays.
The scenes where in youth at the moss I toiled
    With the happy peasant band,
Oh! how they have haunted my waking dreams,
    When far from the Fatherland."

Guide.

"The knolls that rise on the slopes of the vale
    With a dark green shrub are clad,
While under their sheltering sunny sides
    The lambkins are sporting glad;

Away through meadows and fertile domains
    A bounteous river rolls,
Now placidly winding its sinuous course
    Then foaming o'er rocks and falls."

Exile.

"The broom, the broom! where we herded the kine,
    And kindled our Beltane fires,
And found in pastimes untrammelled by art
    Scope for our simple desires:
That river, I ween, is my native stream,
    With its brightly glistening sand;
Sweet in fancy's ear was its murmuring flow,
    When far from the Fatherland."

Guide.

"Before us a village in ruins lies,
    Its timbers and walls o'erthrown,
Its site, where the throbbings of life have been,
    With brambles and moss o'ergrown;
An old mill stands by the side of the burn
    With a sad forsaken air,
For no wheel revolves in the waterfall
    Nor sound of grinding is there."

Exile.

"Is my native village a ruined heap?
    Are its humble hearths all gone?
Is the children's glee on the common hushed?
    Are its brave and leal hearts flown?
Industrious in peace, in the muster for war
    Ever prompt at their king's command;
Failed worth so potent for them to secure
    A home in the Fatherland?"

    *   *   *   *   *

His soul's Polar star was that Fatherland,
    All bright it glowed in his dreams;
In fancy he traversed its heath-clad hills
    And roved by its winding streams.

Home-sick, and stricken with blindness at last,
   He hied to its sea-girt strand :
He came, alas ! but to grieve for its wrongs—
   He wept for the Fatherland !
                       PETER MACNAUGHTON

AULD JOHNNY SHAW.

AULD Johnny Shaw lived near by the Cross,
An' noo that he's gane we a' ken the loss ;
Ye micht seek for his match, an' seek a lang while,
For the equal o' Johnny doon by the kirk-stile.
Johnny Shaw was a soutar o' soutars the chief,
There wasna his equal in Muthill or Crieff,
Nor yet in Blackford, or the toon lang an' sma',
For a wonderfu' soutar was auld Johnny Shaw.

He could mak' ye dress boots, or mend yer auld shoes,
Could hone yer auld razor, or tell ye the news,
Could set yer watch richt wi' the ancient toon clock,
Or file an auld key doon to fit an auld lock ;
Put a valve in yer bellows or a foot to yer pat,
Or brush up like new an auld battered hat ;
He could box ye the compass or leather a ba',
For a versatile genius was auld Johnny Shaw.

A wonderfu' place was his warkshop, I ween ;
Sic marvels o' nick-nacks were there to be seen !
And the soutar—himsel' a mechanical riddle—
Micht be makin' a boot or mendin' a fiddle—
Thumpin' the lapstone, the glue-pot a-boiling,
Or bent owre a last, at an in-seam hard toiling ;
For a boot he could mak', or a fiddle fu' braw,
An' fit on the cat-gut could auld Johnny Shaw.

He had bottles on shelves fu' o' scorpions an' snakes,
An' queer-looking fish frae the rivers an' lakes ;
Had sharks' teeth an' spears frae the cannibal isles,
An' fragments o' pottery an' auld-warld tiles ;

An auld parritch-pat frae the days o' the Bruce,
An' lang rusty dirks that were ance o' some use;
A big shoe frae Lapland for trampin' owre snaw,
An' mony mair fairlies had auld Johnny Shaw.

He keepit a squirrel that turned roond a wheel,
An' a nest o' white mice in an auld tattie-creel;
A wonderfu' monkey, weel keen'd through the toon,
That folk ran to see, young an' auld, up and doon;
He had linties frae Dornock, an' starlings in cages,
He could tell ye their pedigrees, sexes, an' ages;
An' a droll gabbie parrot, besides a jackdaw,
For a student o' nature was auld Johnny Shaw.

He had beetles in boxes, and puddocks an' teads,
An' een for stuffed birds, just like strings o' glass beads;
He had stuffed birds an' butterflees, stuffed mice an' rats;
He had hedehogs an' wild cats, an' otters an' bats;
He could stuff ye a cat, or a pig, or a dog,
An eel frae the loch, or a snipe frae the bog;
He could stuff ony beast, frae a horse to a craw—
There ne'er was a stuffer like auld Johnny Shaw.

But his hammer nae langer is heard at the Cross,
An' aiblins his lapstane is covered wi' moss;
His birds an' his fiddles, that strangers gaed seein',
Hae lang, lang ere this time been "barkin' an' fleein'."
A rare hand was the soutar—the wonder o' Crieff,
Amang the bright natives auld Johnny was chief;
But noo he has gane to his lang hame awa',
An' nane fills the bannet o' auld Johnny Shaw.

JOHN MCCULLOCH.

WE'RE A' A'E MITHER'S BAIRNS.

THERE'S freedom on the auld grey hills,
    And joy amang the trees;
The woods, and rocks, and pebbly rills
    Are singin' wi' the breeze.

There's harmony in Nature's law,
   Tho' man nae muckle learns;
And love unbounded breathes thro' a'—
   We're a' a'e mither's bairns.

O, gin the warld frae Nature's book
   Wad only tak' a leaf;
A' men wad hae a blyther look,
   An' lichter loads o' grief;
And life wad hae less heichs and howes,
   And mair o' fruits than ferns;
A' hearts uphold what truth avows—
   We're a' a'e mither's bairns.

We want less greed o' gowd, and mair
   O' love for a' that's leal,
A lesser gap 'tween rich and puir,
   And mair o' hearts that feel.
That sune micht fa' foul wrang, and a'
   Oppressions deadly airns;
And men revere a'e richteous law—
   We're a' a'e mither's bairns.

A' born to do the best we can
   For ithers and oursel',
And leave the future warld o' man
   A better tale to tell.
O' friendly help we a' hae need
   To cheer life's crook and cairns;
Ne'er mind the kintry or the creed—
   We're a' a'e mither's bairns.

The child that's doun, oh! dinna scorn,
   But help him gin ye can,
Tho' aff the path o' virtue borne,
   He's aye a brither man.
Be't he wha pines in prison chains,
   Or he wha toils and earns,
Or lord, or king o' wide domains—
   We're a' a'e mither's bairns.

It's no oursel's that moulds us what
    We a' appear to be,
The pauper, prince, and beggar brat
    Were made like you and me.
Necessity's eternal law
    Our weal and wae concerns,
Tho' born in hovel, hut, or ha'—
    We're a' a'e mither's bairns.

Tho' poortith be a brither's lot,
    Owre toiled and starved by turns,
Yet aft beneath a raggit coat
    The noblest friendship burns;
And tho' we a' may frown or fret,
    We ha'ena got our ser'ns,
We'll a' be better brithers yet—
    We're a' a'e mither's bairns.

The stamp o' man is in the deed,
    And principle within,
And no the kintry, claes, or creed,
    Or colour o' the skin.
Humanity's great bond we claim,
    As glorious truth discerns,
Tho' differin' a' and no the same—
    We're a' a'e mither's bairns.
JOHN MACLEAY PEACOCK.

MY AULD SCOTTISH BONNET.

I ANCE had a bonnet, a bonnie blue bonnet,
Weel worthy a sermon, a sang, or a sonnet,
My young head it happit for mony a year,
Thro' poortith an' plenty, an' trouble, an' steer.
For mony cauld winters an' braw simmers gane,
Whan toilin', an' moilin', an' wanderin' my lane,
Owre mony strange kintries, an' far owre the sea,
A guid couthie hap was my bonnet to me.

Wi' braw tappie-toorie, my bonnet o' blue
Was wove in Auld Killie o' guid Hielan' woo',
An' proud I was o't aye, as gin it had been
The gowden love gift o' the bonniest queen.
It sat on my head, an' sae weel may I sing,
Mair blythe than the crown on the head o' a king.
A crown has its flaws that ane fashes awee,
But saft was the hap o' my bonnet to me.

At meetin', or market, the fast, or the fair,
'Mang gentle, or simple, the rich, or the puir,
It mattered nae whither that bonnet o' mine
Was doff'd ne'er to ane but the leal and the kin';
Nor left the lang locks that it sheltered sae weel,
Save aye in respect to some guid honest chiel',
Whan a' ither fouk in the fashion wad be,
My auld Scottish bonnet clang couthie to me.

Fu' aft in my wand'rings when dowie and dry,
I've boo'd to the burnie clear murmurin' by,
And drank o' its waters far sweeter than wine—
The croon o' my bonnet the cup that was mine.
An' whan I was weary wi' wand'ring, an' wae,
An' e'enin's grey curtain fell darkly owre day,
To sleep I hae gane 'neath the bonnie moon's e'e,
My bonnet a saft, soothin' pillow to me.

In mony queer places, baith hovels an' ha's,
'Mang lairdlin's an' leddies, an' baubles an' braws;
My bonnet has aye been wi' me, an' the same
As gin I was stappin' the threshold o' hame.
But ance it was lent to a mountebank chiel'—
To play Cuddy Headrig, or Robin the Deil—
Wha had it lang spontin', or pawned for the spree,
Till ance it cam' back like an auld freen to me.

A'e summer I swat like a slave in the sun,
My broo wi' my bonnet a' dappled an' dun;
It hadna been scoor'd sin' it fell in the Tyne,
Sae I doff'd it for ane o' a gentler kin'.

An' noo in the land o' the puir opprest Paddie
It haps the red head o' a wee Irish laddie,
Wha rugs raggit rack frae the rocks o' the sea,
An's blythe wi' the bonnet ance cosy to me.

JOHN MACLEAY PEACOCK.

RUTH.

THE golden smile of morning
   On the hills of Moab play'd,
When at the city's western gate
   Their steps three women stay'd.
One laden was with years and care,
   A gray and faded dame,
Of Judah's ancient lineage,
   And Naomi her name;
And two were daughters of the land,
   Fair Orpah and sweet Ruth.
Their faces wearing still the bloom,
   Their eyes the light of youth;
But all were childless widows
   And garb'd in weeds of woe,
And their hearts were full of sorrow,
   And fast their tears did flow,
For the Lord God from Naomi
   Her spouse and sons had taken,
And she and these that were their wives,
   Are widow'd and forsaken;
And wish or hope her bosom knows
   None other but to die,
And lay her bones in Bethlehem,
   Where all her kindred lie.
So gives she now upon the way
   To Jordan's western waters—
Her farewell kisses and her tears
   Unto her weeping daughters;
"Sweet daughters mine, now turn again
   Unto your homes," she said,

"And for the love ye bear to me,
    The love ye bear the dead,
The Lord with you deal kindly,
    And give you joy and rest,
And send to each a faithful mate
    To cheer her widow'd breast."

Then long and loud their weeping was,
    And sore was their lament,
And Orpah kiss'd sad Naomi,
    And back to Moab went;
But gentle Ruth to Naomi
    Did cleave with close embrace,
And earnest spake, with loving eyes
    Up-gazing in her face—
"Entreat me not to leave thee,
    Nor sever from thy side,
For where thou goest I will go,
    Where thou bidest I will bide;
Thy people still my people,
    Thy God my God shall be;
And where thou diest I will die,
    And make my grave with thee."

So Naomi, not loath, was won
    Unto her gentle will;
And thence with faces westward set,
    They fared o'er plain and hill;
The Lord their staff, till Bethlehem
    Rose fair upon their sight,
A rock-built town with towery crown,
    In evening's purple light,
'Midst slopes in vine and olive clad,
    And spread along the brook,
White fields with barley waving,
    That woo'd the reaper's hook.

    .   .   .   .   .

Now for the sunny harvest field
    Sweet Ruth her mother leaves,

And goes a-gleaning after
  The maids that bind the sheaves.
And the great lord of the harvest
  Is of her husband's race,
And looks upon the lovely one
  With gentleness and grace;
And he loves her for the brightness
  And freshness of her youth,
And for her unforgetting love,
  Her firm enduring truth—
The love and truth that guided Ruth
  The border mountains o'er,
Where her people and her own land
  She left for evermore;
So he took her to his home and heart,
  And years of soft repose
Did recompense her patient faith,
  Her meekly-suffered woes;
And she became the noblest dame
  Of palmy Palestine,
And the stranger was the mother
  Of that grand and glorious line
Whence sprung our royal David,
  In the tide of generations,
The anointed King of Israel,
  The terror of the nations;
Of whose pure seed hath God decreed
  Messiah shall be born,
When the day-spring from on high shall light
  The golden lands of morn;
Then heathen tongues shall tell the tale
  Of tenderness and truth—
Of the gentle deed of Boaz,
  And the tender love of Ruth.

    SIR WILLIAM STIRLING MAXWELL.

SHALLUM.

OH, waste not thy woe on the dead, nor bemoan him,
   Who finds with his fathers the grave of his rest;
Sweet slumber is his, who at night-fall hath thrown him
   Near bosoms that waking did love him the best.

But sorely bewail him, the weary world-ranger,
   Shall ne'er to the home of his people return;
His weeping worn eyes must be closed by the stranger,
   No tear of true sorrow shall hallow his urn.

And mourn for the monarch that went out of Zion,
   King Shallum, the son of Josiah the Just;
For he the cold bed of the captive shall die on,
   Afar from his land, nor return to its dust.

              SIR WILLIAM STIRLING MAXWELL.

ELEGIAC LINES.*

SISTER, these woods have seen ten summers fade,
Since thy dear dust in yonder church was laid.
A few more winters and this heart, the shrine
Of thy fair memory, shall be cold as thine.
Yet may some stranger, lingering in these ways,
Bestow a tear on grief of other days;
For if he, too, have wept o'er grace and youth,
Goodness and wisdom, faith, and love, and truth,
Untinged with worldly guile or selfish strain,
And ne'er hath looked upon thy like again,
Then imaged in his sorrow, he may see
All that I loved, and lost, and mourn in thee.

              SIR WILLIAM STIRLING MAXWELL.

---

* In the old burying-ground of Lecropt, within the home park of Keir, there is an ornamental stone cross, elaborately carved, which has a brass plate fixed on its base bearing these very beautiful elegiac lines, composed by Sir William to the memory of his sister Hannah Ann Stirling. Her body lies in the family vault below Lecropt Church.

"LOVE OF RIGHT, AND SCORN OF WRONG."

*"Fraudulent Bankruptcy of the old established firm of————,
etc., etc."*—DAILY PAPER.

MUST we wail in dirgeful numbers,
Over an apostate age;
And arraign a nation—faithless
To her noblest heritage?
Why these stoops to base intriguing?
Where has high-soul'd Honour fled?
Why the beauteous shrine so empty
Where she once was worshippèd?
What erewhile was Britain's glory
Chronicled in prose and song,
Reckoned an effete old story—
"*Love of right, and scorn of wrong.*"

Vain to boast, "her meteor-pennon
Braves the battle and the breeze;"
That her adamantine navies
Ride the champions of the seas:
Vain that on gigantic anvils
Hundred thousand hammers ring,
Wealth of brain and power of muscle
Cyclop trophies fashioning :—
If she suffer pelf and mammon,
Lording o'er her million throng,
To eclipse her yeoman motto—
"*Love of right, and scorn of wrong.*"

Owners of her fields of plenty,
Ye who reap the golden grain,
As ye store your harvest treasures,
Hold in scorn illicit gain.
As ye walk the marts of commerce,
As ye plant, or build, or sell,
Let all arts of over-reaching
Shunned be as the gates of hell.

Keep your conscience pure, untainted;
Be existence short or long,
Hold aloft the golden watchword—
"*Love of right, and scorn of wrong.*"
REV. J. R. MACDUFF, D.D.

"THE LORD IS MY SHEPHERD."

THE Lord is my Shepherd, nought else shall I need!
   Once far from His fold in my loneliness pining,
To His own verdant pastures He brought me to feed,
   And by the still waters I now am reclining.

Though darkness, at times, should be shrouding my sky,
   And I gaze on a wilderness blighted and dreary;
The meadows seem withered, the rivulets dry,
   I wander through thorny-brakes, footsore and weary:—

'Tis only in order my soul to restore,
   And for His Name's sake in a right path to guide me:
My Shepherd would teach me to seek for no more
   Save the pastures His wisdom sees meet to provide me.

Yea, though I should journey through Death's shadow'd vale,
   No evil I fear, for His arms will enfold me:
With His Presence vouchsafed, not a foe can assail,
   His rod and His staff through the gloom will uphold me.

The Keeper of Israel a table has spread
   Prepared in the presence of foes that surround me;
With oil, rare and precious, anointing my head,
   The wastes of the desert made fragrant around me.

Surely Goodness and Mercy, with blessings anew,
   Will follow me on to the brink of the river;
The rush of its waters conducting me through,
   To dwell in the house of Jehovah for ever!
REV. J. R. MACDUFF, D.D.

THE IRON HORSE.

Come Hieland man, come Lowland man, come every
 man on earth, man,
And I'll tell you how I got on atween Dundee and
 Perth, man;
I gaed upon an iron road, a rail they did her ca', man;
It was ruggit wi' an iron horse, an awfu' beast to draw,
 man.
        Sing fal lal la.

Then, first and foremost, near the door, there was a wee
 bit wicket,
It was there they gar'd me pay my ride, and they gi'ed
 me a ticket,
I gaed awa' up through the house, sat down upon a
 kist, man.
To tak' a look o' a' I saw on the great big iron beast,
 man.
        Sing fal lal la.

There was hooses in a lang straught raw, a' stannin' upon
 wheels, man;
And then the chiels that fed the horse were as black's a
 pair o' deils, man;
An' the ne'er a thing they ga'e the brute but only coals
 to eat, man—
He was the queerest beast that e'er I saw, for he had
 wheels for feet, man.
        Sing fal lal la.

A chap cam' up, an' round his cap he wore a yellow
 band, man;
He bad' me gang an' tak' my seat. Says I, "I'd rather
 stand, man."
He speer'd if I was gaun to Perth. Says I, "an' that I
 be, man;
But I'm weel enough just whaur I am, because I want to
 see, man."
        Sing fal lal la.

He said I was the greatest fule that e'er he saw on
    earth, man ;
For it was just the hooses on the wheels that gaed frae
    this to Perth, man.
An' then he laugh't an' wondered hoo I hadna mair dis-
    cernment,
Says I, "the ne'er a ken kent I ; I thought the hale
    concern went."
            Sing fal lal la.

The beast it roared, an' aff we gaed, through water,
    earth, and stanes, man ;
We ran at sic a fearfu' rate, I thought we'd brak our
    banes, man ;
Till by and by we stoppit at a place ca'd something
    Gowrie,
But ne'er a word had I to say, but only sit an' glower
    aye.
            Sing fal lal la.

Then after that we made a halt, an' in comes yellow
    band, man ;
He asked me for the ticket, an' I a' my pouches fand,
    man,
Bnt ne'er a ticket I cud get—I'd tint it on the road,
    man—
So he gar'd me pay for't ower again, or else gang aff to
    quod, man.
            Sing fal lal la.

Then after that we crossed the Tay, an' landit into
    Perth, man,
I vow it was the queerest place that e'er I saw on earth,
    man,
For the hooses an' the iron horse were far aboon the
    land, man,
And hoo they got them up the stair I canna understand,
    man.
            Sing fal lal la.

But noo I'm safely landit, an' my feet are on the sod, man;
When I gang to Dundee again I'll tak' anither road, man;
Though I should tramp upon my feet till I'm no fit to stand, man,
Catch me again when I'm ta'en in wi' a chap in a yellow band, man.
        Sing fal lal la.
                CHARLES BALFOUR.

THE BATTLE OF CORRIEMUCKLOCH.*

DECEMBER, on the twenty-first,
  A party o' our Scottish Greys,
Rode up amang the Highland hills,
  Some smuggled whisky for to seize;
Wi' sword and pistol by their side
  They thocht to mak' a grand attack,
But a' they wanted was to find
  Poor Donald wi' his smuggled drap.

  Dirrim dye, adoo, aday,
    Dirrim dye adoo a daddie,
  Dirrim dye adoo aday,
    Poor Donald wi' his smuggled drap.

---

* The authorship of this song, of which there are slightly varied readings, has given rise to considerable discussion, and does not yet appear to be settled with any certainty. Among others to whom it has been confidently attributed was James Stewart, author of "Sketches of Scottish Character," but Stewart did not go to Crieff until 1828, whereas the song was popular there in 1824, shortly after the battle; and, besides, it is far below his powers. A distinguished Crieff antiquary when reviewing Stewart's "Sketches," ascribed the song to "a kindred spirit, John Ritchie;" but subsequently, in the *Beauties of Upper Strathearn* he declared the piece to be "the joint production of a pair of local rhymsters," adding, "the poets were, of course, Crieff men, and enjoyed heartily, like all their townsmen, the discomfiture of the interloping excisemen," although the names of the poetic pair are, curiously, withheld. Duncan Campbell, well known locally by the cognomen of "Millochan," is by some believed to be the author.

The gauger he drew up his men
   And soon poor Donald did surround;
Said he, "your whisky I must seize,
   By virtue of the British Crown."
"Hoot, toot!" said Donald, "not so fast—
   You ken her whisky's a' her nain;
She fears not you, nor your grey horse,
   Nor yet your muckle bearded men."
      Dirrim dye, adoo, aday, etc.

Then Donald a' his men drew up,
   And Donald he did give command;
But a' the arms poor Donald had
   Was a gude oak stick in ilka hand.
And where poor Donald's men drew up,
   A gude stane dyke was at their back;
So, when their sticks to *proonach* went,
   Wi' stanes they made a bold attack.
      Dirrim dye, adoo, aday, etc.

When the action it was ower,
   A horseman lay upon the plain;
Says Donald unto Sandy syne,
   "We've killed ane o' the bearded men!"
But up he gat, and aff he ran,
   And straight to Aumulree he flew;
And left the rest to do their best,
   As they had done at Waterloo.
      Dirrim dye, adoo, aday, etc.

Then Donald he took speech in hand,
   And garr'd the beardies quit the field,
The gauger loon he thumpit weel,
   Afore his pride wad let him yield.
Says Donald—"O you gauger loon,
   If e'er you come this gaet again,
As fack as death, she tells you true,
   You'll no gang back wi' a'e hale bane!"
      Dirrim dye, adoo, aday, etc.

When the battle's din was o'er,
   And not a horseman to be seen,
Then Donald to his men did say,
   "Come sit ye doon upon the green.
And noo, my lads, ye just shall taste
   A drappie o' the thing we hae,
And troth" quo Donald, "they did get
   A filthy hurry doon the brae."
     Dirrim dye, adoo, aday, etc.

ANONYMOUS.

THE WITCH ON THE BRAE.

A' THE witches lang syne were humphbackit and auld,
Clad in their tattered rags that scarce kept out the cauld,
A' were bleer-e'ed and toothless, and wrinkled, and din,
Ilk ane had an ugly grey beard on her chin;
But fu' sweet is the smile, and like snaw the bit bosom,
   And black are the een—ay, black as the slae—
And as blooming the cheeks as the roses' white blossom,
   O' the bonnie young witch that wons on the brae.

They might travel at night in the shape o' a hare,
They might elfshoot a quey, they might lame a grey mare;
They might mak' the guidwife ca' in vain at her kirn,
Loose the loop o' her stocking, or ravel her pirn,
Put the milk frae her cow, and mae tricks as uncanny,
   As queer and as deil-like as ony o' thae;
But o' a' the auld witches e'er kent by your granny,
   I could wager there's nane like the witch on the brae

'Twere a sin to believe she colleagued wi' the deil;
Yet, for a' that, she casts her enchantments as weel;
And although she ne'er rode on a stick to the moon,
She has set the auld dominie twice aff the tune;

Ay, and even Mess John aince or twice ga'e a stammer,
   But brought himsel' right wi' a hum and a hae;
And a'body says it was just wi' some glamour
   Frae the twa pawkie een o' the witch on the brae.

No a lad i' the parish e'er gets a night's sleep,
There's nane mak's a tryste that he ever can keep,
Ilk lass far and near fears she'll dee an auld maid,
And the piper and fiddler complain o' dull trade.
For although tailor Rab night an' day has been busy,
   Yet there's nae been a waddin' this six months an' mae,
And they say it's a' for that winsome young hizzie,
   The bit bonnie young witch that wons on the brae.

She ne'er passes the mill but the dam aye rins out,
For the miller forgets what he should be about;
Neither mason nor sclater can e'en work a turn,
And whene'er the smith sees her some shoe's sure to burn.
And the sergeant ne'er speaks now o' war, fame, and glory,
And the droll drouthy shoemaker, Sandy M'Rae,
Ne'er sings a queer sang now, or tells a queer story,
   For they've a' felt the power o' the witch on the brae.

The thin student, puir chiel'! ower the linn lap yestreen,
And wad sure hae been drown'd, but by gude luck was seen;
And he says that the witch drove him thus to despair,
For she took his last poem to paper her hair.
Like the rest I was put in a gey eerie swither,
   I had nae peace at hame, and nae heart whaur to gae;
But to end baith my sang and her witchcraft thegither,
   I will soon be the warlock that wons on the brae.

                      WILLIAM STEWART.

THE HOLOCAUST OF THE WITCH OF MONZIE.*

An Extract.

FROM Fowlis and Logiealmond, even from Perth,
   The rabble-multitude poured thick and fast,
Until it seemed as if the conscious earth
   Believed this spectacle might be the last
Of Fire and Faggot she would e'er behold,
   Lighted by legal cruelty and crime,
For never did such hosts of young and old,
   Of tottering crones, and women in their prime,
Of high and low, of poor men and of rich,
Assemble at the burning of a witch.

---

* Sometime in the latter half of the seventeenth century, one of the servants in the family of the Græmes of Inchbrakie, was a female named Kate M'Niven, who was nurse to the laird's young son, Patrick, afterwards laird of Inchbrakie, who, from his sombre complexion, was honoured with the *soubriqnet* of "Black Pate." Kate's nursing of this sable youth seems to have been none of the kindliest : for, being impressed with a presentiment that one day or other he would prove the means of her death, she is said to have frequently attempted to destroy him by poison. In the meantime she was a witch, and gave conclusive proofs of it. One of these was memorable. The laird of Inchbrakie ("Pate's" father) rode over to Dunning to attend some public meeting, and according to the usage of the times, took his knife and fork in his pocket. While dining at that place, he was annoyed by a bee which buzzed about his ears ; he laid down his knife and fork for a moment to make use of his hands in getting rid of the intruder ; the bee soon left him and flew out by the window ; he returned to table ; but his knife and fork were gone, and, though all the company were strictly searched, the articles (at that time rare and precious) could not be found. When the laird returned to Inchbrakie he mentioned his misfortune, and immediately the old nurse produced his identical knife and fork.

Kate's gloomy presentiment was at last realized, and it happened in this wise. There was an aged thorn at Dunning, with which it would appear that her fate was mysteriously connected. This thorn was destroyed in some tumult, and, before it was possible that news of the event could have reached Inchbrakie, the witch suddenly exclaimed,— "alas, the thorn's felled, and I'm undone !" Her foster-son, who was present, and on whom the knife-and-fork affair had not been lost, was at once confirmed in his suspicions, and had Kate taken up for a witch. Tradition says there was much difficulty in seizing the accused, for that, besides being a witch, she was fleet of foot.—At length, however, she was lodged in "durance vile," and, in course of time, condemned. When brought to the stake, she appears to have been treated with no

And women's tongues were plying fast and loose,
  As the crowd moved along the slippery way;
And much they talked about the roasted goose,
  Which Satan would devour that blessed day;
And some opined that such a withered crone
  As Kate M'Niven was declared to be,
Would furnish little more than skin and bone
  To any of the black fraternity;
While others deemed, that, seasoned well with yew,
A living witch might make a savoury stew.

---

indulgence; the minister of Monzie and others being "bitter against her." The laird of Inchbrakie—the same, whose knife and fork she had purloined at Dunning—was the only influential person who dared, at the eleventh hour, to interpose in her behalf; and Kate, in the gratitude of her heart, bit off (for her hands were bound) a bead from her necklace, and spitting it towards her intercessor, declared, that so long as the house of Inchbrakie should preserve that *charm*, it would never fail of a direct heir, or lose the patrimonial property—adding, that out of the King's Craig would come what would do them all good. She likewise predicted, that so long as the Shaggie (a neighbouring stream) should continue to run in its present course there should not be a lineal descendant to the house of Monzie, nor should the ministers of that parish ever prosper; and the parish would never want a mad woman or a sot. Other accounts make no mention of the necklace, but merely affirm that she spat out of her mouth a precious stone. This stone, which is said to be an uncut sapphire, was set in a ring, which was long carefully preserved in the Inchbrakie family.

Whether the witch's prophecy had been false or the family of the "Gallant Graeme" had lost the charmed stone is uncertain, but it is an undoubted fact that the estate which for many generations belonged to the family was sold in 1882 to the adjoining laird of Abercairney, and a small mound of stones only is left to indicate the site of the ancient mansion-house of Inchbrakie. However, the prophecy about the King's Craig is said to have been fulfilled. At one time "the lands of Inchbrakie had been pledged in wadset"—the day was close at hand when either the money was to be paid or the lands to be lost—and the laird was in extremities. A friend advised him to apply to the Bank of Strathearn (meaning the Balgowan family, which was called so at that time). He did apply, and obtained the money; the servant who received it to carry home thrust it into a cloakbag, and placed it on his horse in one of the Balgowan stables. The low stable-door would hardly permit the horse and bag to get out; but the servant pushed the latter through, exclaiming when he had done so, that the witch's prophecy was now fulfilled, for the stable was built out of the King's Craig.

The place where Kate M'Niven expiated her witchcraft at the stake is situated on the south-eastern brow of the Knock, and is known to this day as M'Niven's Craig.

But some there were who differed from the rest,
    And thought, or seemed to think, the witch's fate
Deserved not thus the ribald-laugh and jest,
. But rather to be held in righteous hate;
And not a few among that motley throng
    Averred that witchery was all a lie,
And urged the controversy loud and long,
    Some in deep earnest, some in raillery;
Till short of patience, argument and breath,
All reached at length the destined place of death.

And now the radiant orb of heat and light
    Was fast approaching to his western goal,
Where woody Turlem rears his giant height,
    And Earn's streams in glittering currents roll;
And countless multitudes, from far and near,
    Covered the vale and lined the lofty rocks,
Which made the scene from neighbouring heights appear
    A gathering vast of cattle and of flocks;
For never in Monzie had living man
Seen such a multitude since time began.

And soon the crowd, which during many an hour
    In silent patience had been lingering there,
Began, like darkening thunderclouds, to lower,
    And with impatient shouts to rend the air;
And to and fro, as when the molten glass
    Of ocean's mirror is dispersed in spray,
An angry murmur swept the living mass,
    Rushed down the hill, and slowly died away;
And then again, still louder and more loud,
It burst into a shout from all the crowd.

At length a movement on the western side,
    Proclaimed the object of their rage at hand;
And like a vessel steering through the tide,
    A cart, surrounded by a martial band,
Was seen advancing by a winding route,
    To where the stake was planted in the ground;

And all the crowd began to hiss and hoot,
    And vie in horrid dissonance of sound—
When Kate M'Niven's laithely form was seen,
Attired in mock-habiliments of green.

She uttered not a word, while many a voice
    Was shouting imprecations fierce and loud ;
But when at length the clamour and the noise
    Had died away along the furious crowd—
" Ye hell-hounds," she exclaimed, " ye bring me here,
    To die a death which ye would spare a dog !
Beshrew-me, if ye do not pay full dear
    For all this waste of faggot and of log !
The time is near when ye shall rue this day,
And call to mind the words which now I say."

" Waeworth the witch ! " a thousand voices cried —
    " Down with the hag, and tear her limb from limb "—
" No, no," said others, " let the witch be fried ;
    Perhaps she will not burn, though she can swim."
" Light up the pile," a cruel voice exclaimed,
    And spit her on a pitch-fork for a time,
Until her valour is a little tamed,
    And then perchance she may confess her crime ;
For that's the only Christian plan, I guess,
To make a witch be honest and confess."

" I *am* a witch—if that be any crime—
    A witch I've lived, and as I've lived will die ;
But long and sadly ye shall rue the time
    That brought ye here to clamour and to cry ;
For even now I see a coming flood,
    Which ere this very year has passed away,
Shall drench the braes of Sherra'muir with blood,
    And many who are here in life this day
Shall think of me, when with their dying breath
They curse the hour they clamoured for my death."

" The torch, the torch ! " was now the general shout ;
    And forthwith she was fastened to the stake,

With pitchy logs encompassed all about,
  And many a broken door and shattered flake.
On these she stood as on a lofty mound,
  And soon the wreaths of smoke began to rise;
And then it was that, like the deafening sound
  Of fierce valcano darting to the skies,
A shout arose, which shook the solid earth,
And, some maintain, was even heard in Perth.

But while the sheets of mingled flame and smoke
  Began to thicken round her haggard form,
Old Kate again with imprecations spoke,
  Like the controlling spirit of the storm;
And looking round, as if she dared defy
  The utmost fury of the yelling mob,
"Ye cowards," she exclaimed, "I die—I die—
  And soon this heart of mine shall cease to throb.
Another hour and nought shall live of me,
Except that bitter curse which *you* must dree.

"A witch I am—and if a witch's curse
  Is fraught with mischief or with bale to man,
The parish of Monzie shall fare the worse
  And minister and flock shall dree the ban.
Yon bonnie manse shall ne'er a tenant see
  Who shall not yet this bitter day abye,
And never shall the parish of Monzie
  Forget the hour that I was doomed to die;
For either a mad woman or a sot
Shall vex the parish while my ashes rot.

"And Auchterarder too shall ashes see
  Ere yet the merry-making day of Yule;
And many who are here shall think of me,
  When but and ben shall glimmer mirk and gule;
And every house shall be a cinder-heap,
  Like that on which you see me stand this day;
While many a mother with her child shall sleep
  In wreaths of snow until it melt away;
And then, mayhap, the husband or the nurse
Will think of Kate M'Niven and her curse."

Scarce had the frantic woman ceased to speak,
   When the black pile burst out into a blaze;
And then arose a blended shout and shriek
   From the dense masses who had come to gaze—
To gaze, and yet to shudder—for the sight
   Was horrible to all whose hearts could feel;
And some who saw her in that woeful plight,
   Blackened with smoke and struggling to conceal
Her mortal agonies, did now bedene,
That ne'er again they'd come to such a scene.
REV. GEORGE BLAIR.

THE POWER OF LOVE.

THERE'S a glory in summer, a beauty in spring,
And the laverock the hymn of the morning will sing;
But the magic of Nature is lost upon me,
For the raven-haired Flora has pride in her e'e.

I'm restless by day, and I'm sleepless by night—
The stream has no music, the sunbeam no light;
I'm weary of life as a mortal can be,
For the raven-haired Flora has pride in her e'e.

I roam through the meadows at gloaming alone,
Musing sadly of pleasures all withered and gone;
Death, often I think, would be welcome to me,
Since the raven-haired Flora has pride in her e'e.

But now, what a change has come over my dream,
Each flower has a grace, and a music each stream;
All Nature is glory and beauty to me,
For my raven-haired lassie has love in her e'e.
REV. JOHN ANDERSON, D.D.

THE PAST.

When the long farewell is spoken,
   And the light of life has fled,—
How blest the simplest token
   That recalls the sleeping dead!
That gilds the dear departed
   With the olden smile they wore,—
The pure-souled, the sunny-hearted,
   Who gladden home no more.

When I walk the dewy meadows,
   Some common flower will cast
On my path the gliding shadows
   Of those who long have passed,—
Passed away from home's bright number,
   From earth and all its joys,
To the bed of dreamless slumber,
   To the crowd without a voice.

When, beside the glowing embers,
   I muse at close of day,
By that light I well remember
   The faces passed away.
Then Memory comes to greet me
   With some familiar tone,
And, though shadows only meet me,
   I feel not all alone.

And thus I love to wander
   Among the dewy flowers,
Or to sit and gently ponder
   Through Memory's vesper hours.
Oh! Wisdom, cold thy warning,—
   To me 'tis not in vain
To fancy back life's morning,
   And live it o'er again.

         Rev. John Anderson, D.D.

THE SUNDAY COUGH.

OR THE RIGHTS OF SCOTLAND.

Cough! cough! cough!
  Oh! but the weather is cold.
Cough! cough! cough!
  'Tis the right of the young and the old.
Cough! cough! cough!
  And now the weather is warm;
In vain may the parson plead or scold,
  For a Sunday cough has a wondrous charm.

Cough! from the tattered old man
  (A most unearthly note),
To Tommy, who seems to try if he can
  Make similar fun from his throat.
Cough! from the elder's pew,
  Guttural, steady, and deep;
The beadle would try the luxury too,
  If he were not so fast asleep.

What though the sermon prove
  The very best of the year,
A thing that the dullest fool might love
  With his heart and his soul to hear!
When the passage, so powerfully written,
  Is thrilling so touchingly off,
Some reckless throat, by the frenzy smitten,
  Goes cough! cough! cough!

What though a friend's devotion
  Is ruffled, or something worse,
Till I sadly fear, in the mind's commotion,
  His prayer is changed to a curse!
Who can stifle a cough?
  Have we not paid for our sitting?
And our neighbours are very well off
  If we ape not the Yankee in spitting.

You say 'tis a custom vile
    Which a gentleman might suppress;
But live we not in Liberty's Isle?
    With the freedom of Church and Press,
To speak and to write as we may?
    Our Cousins are scarce better off—
They may spit every hour of the day,
    And we have our Sunday Cough!

Weather warm or cold—
    Weather freezing or warm—
In vain has the druggist's pill been rolled,
    In vain is the parson's weekly scold;
For a Sunday cough to the young and old
    Has a most peculiar charm!

    Rev. John Anderson, D.D.

DEATH.

There's something noble in thy mien, O Death!
Ghastly indeed and cruel, overswift
To execute a sentence—honest still.
Thou speakest truth. Thy name is on thy brow,
And reading it, the proudest bows himself,
And straight prepares to go away with Thee.
The brigand of the cave, the warrior armed,
The ruler of the empire, bows to Thee!
Not like the stealthy steps of Time and Change
Are thine. Insidiously they creeping come
To sap and undermine, to melt and mar,
What we esteemed as proof against their power.
The Early Dead alone shall never know
What wreck and havoc Time and Change can work,—
Gnawing with cruel teeth the sweets we stored.—

With mouldy hands aye crumbling what in youth
We *lived* to build,—and then insulting us
By offering salve for wounds we wish to bleed
Until we find again what we have lost.
In the fast chariots of the dewy morn
The Early Dead go Home, leaving us to
The heat of noon, and evening chill. They take
Away with them the choicest flowers
All blooming in high summer's gorgeous tints,
Fit to replant within a heavenly bower.

Yes Death, we can forgive thee, thou sett'st free
The prison'd bird to fly in warmer skies.
Owning His power who wrench'd from thee thy sting,
Thou art His messenger to carry safe
Up to His glory those He longs for there.
For this it was His royal head He bowed
Upon the awful cross : Redeemer ! He
Of the saved millions paid their penalty,
And held thee thenceforth as His minister,
To open unto each the gate of life.
Yet what insignia of royalty
He left with Thee, and what a hush of fear
Spreads at thy coming; for the word is pledged,
That of all other foes thou'lt clear the field ;
THE LAST ENEMY THAT SHALL BE DESTROYED
  IS DEATH.

MRS. M. F. BARBOUR.

RECEIVE, RESIGN, RESTORE.

FREELY RECEIVE, is still His royal word,
  Once breathed on earth, now sounding from His throne,
Freely Thy gifts I take, ascended Lord !
  And with a fearless heart hail them mine own.
As one by one upon this throbbing breast,
  Freighted with Thine own love, they richly fall,
Why should I dread their loss, of Thee possessed
  They but Thy mirror'd love, and THOU my all.

So when the voice that lately said, RECEIVE,
   Shall whisper in love's deeper tones, RESIGN,
Trembling and fainting, back to Thee I'll give
   Whate'er Thou claimest back—the earth is Thine.
Thou and Thy heaven are mine, and shall I weep
   When Thy sweet gifts to my bright home take wing?
Distance and death do but more surely keep
   The treasures to which all my heartstrings cling.

Soon, soon the voice which all the worlds obey
   Shall sound throughout His vast domains, RESTORE!
And boundless spheres shall their glad tribute pay
   To Jesus and his church for evermore.
Then in heaven's wine-cup, given her running o'er,
   And in the weight of glory she shall wear,
Each long-past joy shall endless sweetness pour,
   And not a jewel lost, be missing there.

                MRS. M. F. BARBOUR.

MAGGIE LYLE.

My lassie sits by yonder burn,
   Singin' a' the while,
Saftly blaws the wastlan' wind
   Round sweet Maggie Lyle;
Oh, there's nane like Maggie,
   Winsome Maggie Lyle;
My love's the queen amang the flowers—
   Bonnie Maggie Lyle.

The gowan on the simmer mead—
   Whiter than the snaw—
Glints like yonder bonnie star
   That's sae far awa;
But it's no' like Maggie,
   Wi' her silvery smile—
My love's the queen amang the flowers—
   Modest Maggie Lyle.

My Maggie's fairer than the rose
  Enframed in vernal green;
Wot ye whaur my wild bud grows
  In the brake unseen;
Oh, list, ye slumbering flowers,
  Fairy notes beguile,
'Tis your queen that warbles there—
  Gentle Maggie Lyle.

The dewdrops glance in summer's morn
  Like my Maggie's een,
On the blaworts in the corn
  Brichter are na seen;
An' they droop to Maggie,
  Trippin' ower the style;
My love's the queen amang the flowers—
  Blythesome Maggie Lyle.

FRANCIS BUCHANAN.

KINNOULL CLIFF.

ROMANTIC scene! once more from thy proud steep,
  Kinnoull, I view the prospect far below;
Stirr'd with the memories of the past I weep,
  As in my fancy boyhood's pleasures grow;
  Even now I feel as I felt long ago.

Far down beneath me, in the vernal sun,
  Majestic Tay, impatient to be free,
Rolls his broad waters, sparkling as they run
  Thro' many a lovely spot, towards the sea;
  And at this height methinks I hear their minstrelsy.

Full many a happy hour I've roamed, I ween,
  On yonder dappled banks in days of yore,
Watching at even the silvery Lunar beam,
  And the crimp'd ripple plashing on the shore;
  But those gay hours are dead—the past returns no more.

Kinfauns, thy castle peers amid the trees,
  The turrets gilded as with burnished gold ;
The crimson standard waving in the breeze,
  As it was wont when Longueville the bold
  With his retainers fought the Southron 'neath its fold.

And thou, forlorn Elcho, famed in lore
  For gallant deeds of noble Wallace wight,
Whose patriot fame is known on every shore ;
  His mighty arm asserted Scotia's right,
  And led her hardy sons triumphant thro' the fight.

Now thy grey walls are crumbling fast away,
  And mould'ring ruin seizes thee amain.
These moss-grown gaps tell of Time's potent sway,
  And the green woodbine, with its creeping train,
  Seems to protect from waste thy tott'ring form in vain.

Dark Moredun, too, rears up his furrow'd head,
  Where, long ago, Rome's legions from afar
Swept o'er his craggy heights with thund'rous tread,
  Equipp'd in all the barbarous pomp of war—
  The spear, the sword and buckler, horse and rattling car.

Far as mine eye can reach the verdant plain
  Displays its gorgeous beauty, rich, serene.
There rears a noble mansion, here again
  A clump of lowly cottages is seen,
  With woods, green fields, and rivers interspersed between.

Oh, Scotland ! land of peace and happiness,
  Of all the climes of this old earth the best ;
Beneath thy soil, scenes of my early bliss,
  I pray to Heaven my weary bones may rest,
  Where oft in boyhood's day my foot the heath hath prest.

Farewell, ye rocky steeps! Sweet Tay, farewell!
 Ye woods, ye wilds, and solitudes, adieu!
I may not e'er again (ah, who can tell?)
    Thus feast mine eyes upon this matchless view,
    Life's but a flickering light—our days are number'd few.

FRANCIS BUCHANAN.

SING, LITTLE BIRD.

Sing, sing, little bird, sing!
    Sing to the morning star,
Ere it fade and die in the brightening sky
    With the light that cometh from far.

Sing, sing, happy bird, sing!
    Sing to the rising sun
For sweet is the light on valley and height,
    When the long dreary night is gone.

Sing, sing, merry bird, sing!
    For the day is wondrous fair,
And sweet is thy song the green leaves among
    With never a note of care.

Sing, sweet bird, to the dewy eve,
    A tranquil and soothing song,
Ere it pass into night in Time's ceaseless flight
    Let thy voice its beauty prolong.

Sing, O sing, till heavenward rise
    My soul with thy soaring song;
Till in the bright skies where all sorrow dies
    I shall dwell my loved ones among.

THOMAS STEVEN

HEREAFTER.

When mortal being ends,
And her pure soul ascends
Beyond our vision's range,
  Will her fair radiant face
Take on diviner change
  To more celestial grace ?

I wonder if her voice
Among a thousand, choice,
Sweet, soft, and musical,
  Will catch a sweeter strain
That shall no more recall
  Love's morning song again.

Shall splendour of her eyes
That life's dull skies,
A glory mid the gloom
  Of this dark atmosphere,
New radiance there assume,
  Effacing all things here ?

Her form of finest mould,
Refined like precious gold,
Fashioned and finely wrought
  In grace and symmetry,
To such perfection brought,
  Can it more perfect be ?

Her hand, whose lightest touch
To me doth mean so much
Of love's most tender grace ;
  Her lovely lily hand,
Formed for love's soft caress,
  Shall I no more command ?

My love! my heart's delight!
My dream by day and night,
What will she be to me?
   Will she be mine no more.
In love's sweet mystery,
   Upon that other shore?

I darkly understand,
To meet in some far land
The child I loved before
   In womanhood's ripe grace—
The sweet child's kiss no more;
No more the child's caress.

Sweet rose of womanhood,
So winsome in the bud,
I cannot shape my dream
   To form of fairer mould,
Nor in hereafter deem
   Diviner grace unfold.

                THOMAS STEVEN.

LUMBAGO.

Oh, dear, had you ever Lumbago?
It catches the back of the way-go,
   And shoots through the spine
   When yourself you incline
To sit down to relieve the Lumbago.

Oh, cruel, relentless Lumbago,
Beware every one of the plague, O!
   Rheumatics or gout
   May be soon physicked out
But it's hard to get rid of Lumbago

I'd as soon ride as far as Otago
Upon the bare back of a naig, O !
   Though tender my hide,
   And rough be the ride,
It could not be worse than Lumbago.

A colic is bad, but it may go.
This sticks like a gleg to a staig, O !
   And screws up the groins,
   And unhinges the loins—
Lay you flat on your back will Lumbago.

If by chance you forget for a while, O !
When addressing a friend with a smile, O !
   And turn round quick,
   Then something plays "nick,"
And you end in a cursing style, O !

However relentless, you find foe,
You respect him if he has a mind so
   To fight in fair tack ;
   But a stab in the back,
Oh, crickey ! it cuts at your wind so.

A treacherous fiend is Lumbago,
The advantage it takes is the plague, O !
   For it seizes your hip,
   And you cannot get up,
But must lie and submit to Lumbago.

Oh, banish the heartless Lumbago,
Consume it in flames like Chicago,
   No more to show face,
   Or lay hold of the place
Subjected so long to Lumbago.

JOHN YOUNG.

THE DARWINIAN THEORY.*

AIR—"*The King of the Cannibal Islands.*"

OH! have you heard the news of late,
About our great original state;
If you have not, I will here relate
    The grand Darwinian theory.
Take care as you saunter along the street,
How you tread on the dust beneath your feet;
You may crush a cherub in embryo sweet,
For each atom may hold a germ complete,
Which, by some mystical process slow
And selective power, to a monkey may grow,
And from that to a man—the truth to show
    Of the grand Darwinian theory.
    Oh! hokey-pokey, Kan-yu-wan,
    From nothing to something, from monkey to man,
    Oh! this is the great developing plan
        Of the grand Darwinian theory.

The beginning of all was a little cell,
Composed of what substance no one can tell;
Endowed with a power to develope and swell
    Into general life by this theory.
With a power to select what it wished to be,
A fungus or flower, a bush or a tree,
A fowl of the air, or a fish of the sea,
A cow or a sheep, a bug or a flea,
Or, if tired of these, it may change its plan,

---

* Darwin's theory of the origin of our species, immediately subsequent to its promulgation before the members of the British Association, provoked quite a number of poetical squibs—some of them from the pens of eminent poets—but than the present certainly no *jeu d'esprit* amongst them contained more argument in its nonsense, or more delightsome nonsense in its argument.

Be a cat or a dog, or O-rang-oo-tan,
But culminating at last in a man
    By this grand Darwinian theory.
  Oh! hokey-pokey, power of selection,
  Choose yourself your particular section
  A peasant or lord with a great connection,
    By the grand Darwinian theory.

Your attention, ladies—let me win it;
Just think of this theory for a minute;
Is there really not something distressing in it—
    To think that you sprung from a monkey?
That delicate hand was a monkey's paw,
Those lovely lips graced a monkey's jaw,
Those handsome ankles, so trim and neat,
One time surmounted a monkey's feet;
Those sparkling eyes a monkey did lend,
That graceful form from one did descend,
From a monkey you borrowed the Grecian bend,
    By this grand Darwinian theory.
  Oh! hokey-pokey, protoplasm,
  'Tween monkey and man there is no chasm;
  Why shouldn't you clasp them to your bosom,
    They are infant men by this theory.

Such murderers we—far worse than Cain—
For darker deeds our characters stain;
For thousands of brothers we've eaten and slain,
    By this grand Darwinian theory.
When sitting at breakfast, and picking the wing
Of a pigeon, or grouse, or some other thing;
Or dining on mutton, or lamb, if in spring,
Or on salmon, or trout, or on cod, or on ling;
Gaze into the future, and you can see
What horrible cannibals we must be,
Devouring the flesh which may yet become we,
    By the grand Darwinian theory.
  Oh! hokey-pokey, ringo-ging,
  The cannibal islands once had a king
  Who ate his own kin, but to us he's no thing
    When compared in the light of this theory

But why should the theory end with man?
If he has been less, surely more he can,
And should, by the great developing plan
    Of the grand Darwinian theory.
Why should he not on this earth yet be
    An angel, or god, like Mercury,
With a wing on each shoulder, each ankle and knee?
Oh, how delightful then it would be,
When sighing and wishing your sweetheart to see,
To wipe your beak, and just upwards flee,
Like birds, and meet your love on a tree,
    Or the top of a hill, by this theory.

    Oh! hokey-pokey, ringo-ging,
    The world then literally on the wing;
    No street cabs needed, or any such thing
        By the grand Darwinian theory.
                JOHN YOUNG.

BEWITCHED.

I DID a reckless deed yestreen,
    The brunt I'll bear for mony a day—
I tint baith wit and wealth, I ween,
    Through twa sweet een o' lovely grey.

I vowed their mystic light was blue
    (They winna change though I should pray),
I pledged my worth—would it were true—
    She proved me wrang, and I maun pay.

Sweet maiden, what is wealth to me,
    Could I possess? But nought I may
Than worship what is sweet in thee,
    But never own those een o' grey.

Yes! at a distance I must stand,
　　And envious gaze from day to day,
And see another take thy hand,
　　And claim those een o' matchless grey.

Blest be thy ignorance o' guile,
　　Ye little ken the pow'r they sway;
Unconscious thou, yet a' the while
　　Drivest Cupid's darts frae een o' grey.

Thy face sae fair, thy smile sae sweet,
　　Far harder hearts than mine would slay;
And doomed is he whose gaze should meet
　　Those winning een o' witching grey.

　　　　　　　　　　JOHN YOUNG.

THE QUEEN'S VISIT.

(A Condensed Extract.)

IN autumn, eighteen forty-two,
　　At Granton pier was seen,
That noble chief—the bold Buccleuch—
　　Give welcome to our Queen.

And up along the crowded quay,
　　He gaily led the way;
And Scotland felt through all its bounds,
　　O'erjoyed and proud that day.

Dun-Edin's tow'rs gave back again,
　　The welcome loud and long—
Which loyal hearts repeated oft,
　　A gay and joyous throng.

As up Dun-Edin's crowded streets
　　The Royal progress sped,
The deafening cheers were voic'd again,
　　The Castle guns o'erhead.

The bold Buccleuch has ta'en his way,
    All past the Castle gate,
And soon with quicken'd pace they reach
    His halls in royal state.

Dalkeith's proud towers a welcome fling
    Upon the autumn wind,
And here the Queen and Consort Prince
    Each Scottish comfort find.

But short their stay, though full of joy—
    Each Scottish heart was gay—
The Royal progress starts again
    Upon its northward way.

Dun-Edin—Fifian towns are pass'd—
    On by Kinross they speed;
Loch Leven's hoary pile looks grim,
    Regretting still that deed,

When Mary's royal hand was forc'd
    By caitiff, graceless men,
To abdicate her crown with heart
    Reluctant as her pen.

Still on the Royal progress speeds,
    By hill and dale they wind,
Till needed rest and welcome cheer,
    'Neath Dupplin's tow'rs they find.

Still on they press till Perth is reached,
    That ancient city fair,
Where royal lips in thousands join
    To cheer the Royal pair.

The good old town revives again
    Beneath the Royal tread;
Its ancient glories start to view,
    And courtly life long dead.

To Scone proud Scotland's honour'd Queen
   With joyous heart proceeds;
To Scone—historic Scone—grown old
   In brave and kingly deeds.

Its palace boasts historic fame;
   Its site is sacred ground;
For there for ages all our kings
   In solemn state were crowned.

The Royal chair, as aged bards
   Have dared to dream and sing
Is sacred still to Kenneth's line —
   That ancient Scottish King.

Though now its marble seat adorns
   Westminster's holy fane,*
'Tis still the coronation chair
   For Britain's wide domain.

And as the legend quaintly says—
   There still the Scots are found,
And we, rejoicing, bless the day
   Our darling Queen was crown'd.

At ancient Scone the Royal guests
   With Mansfield's lord abode
One passing eve—then hast'ning on,
   They took the Highland road.

Lord Mansfield rode the Queen beside,
   Imparting ancient lore,
And pointing out with patriot pride
   Those spots renown'd of yore.

---

* The poet here refers to the "Stone of Destiny," which Kenneth II., commonly known as Kenneth Mac-Alpine, brought from Dunstaffnage to Scone, and which was carried to Westminster Abbey by Edward I., in 1296. This remarkable stone is alleged to have been Jacob's pillow at Bethel—to have been carried from the East to Spain, from there to Ireland, from that to Iona, and from Iona to Dunstaffnage, from whence it was taken to Scone, and thence to Westminster Abbey.

The grand North Inch is pass'd, where knights
   In tourney oft have played—
There stood the lists—and here apart,
   The King the scene survey'd.

There too, at times, the battle notes
   Rang out with clarion tone,
And stalwart men rush'd down on death,
   In those dark ages gone.

The Royal progress, speeding on,
   Is viewed by joyous eyes;
At every turn, on every side,
   The shouts of welcome rise.

From prattling babe to aged sire
   The thrill of joy extends;
In rich and poor, a loyal throng,
   One noble feeling blends.

The Queen they love, admire, revere,
   With joyous heart hath come,
To smile her love on rich and poor,
   And gladden every home.

With loyal shouts they voice their love,
   And cheer her on her way;
The Grampian hills, now quite at hand,
   How proud they look to-day!

And Birnam Wood rejoicing moves
   To welcome Duncan's line;
Though 'neath Rohallion's grateful shade
   His halls in ruin pine.

The Royal progress nears Dunkeld,
   'Mid varied scenes sublime;

Here let us pause, while pause we may,
    And raise a hearty cheer,
God save and bless our noble Queen,
    God bless her Consort dear.

Be hers to know how full and deep
    Affection's current flows;
And may that eye which never sleep
    Preside where'er she goes.

                REV. SAMUEL FERGUSSON

A PRELUDE.

ONE linnet's note the more or less
    Within the wildwood's minstrelsy,
Can neither raise nor aught depress
    The sense of joyous revelry.

And yet each linnet from the spray
    His swelling note melodious flings,
And pipes his own sweet roundelay
    Heedless of how another sings.

He has a song 'tis his to sing,
    And that he sings right earnestly,
And waiteth not for anything
    To urge his heart to minstrelsy.

The skylark sings where bliss belongs,
    That song an ampler field be given;
Takes to the clouds his seraph songs—
    Throws half to earth and half to heaven.

And some sweet songster, near alight
    On thorny perch, amid the throng,
Gives to the passing heart delight,
    And cheers it with a joyous song.

So are the songs that poets sing
    Within secluded quiet retreat,
But single echoed notes, that bring
    Their quota for a choir complete.

Each pipes his own peculiar strain,
    On artful lute or simple reed,
And sings, and sings, and sings again,
    To satisfy his own heart's need.

Yet may some raptured thought out-reach
    Far, far the poet's dream above,
And some faint wavering heart beseech
    To deeds of grace, and hope, and love.

To sing has given one heart employ,
    And thus did end enough fulfil;
But if, resung, another's joy
    Is more enlarged, 'twere better still.

And so, self-pleased, I give the song
    That's kept my own past clear and bright,
If that, perchance, some other tongue
    May lift the lilt, and find delight.
                  ROBERT WHITTET.

A LEGEND OF THE DAISY.

LONG had sunk the light of day,
    When, prostrate on the cold, green sod,
Within Gethsemane, there lay,
    Disconsolate, the Son of God.

With bitter sighs His bosom heaved,
    In sorrow's voice He cried aloud,
Till, torn with grief, His heart relieved
    Itself with sweat of crimson blood.

Down from His quivering brow it fell,
   A dropping stream upon the ground;
And long that spot could passers tell,
   So bare amid the green around.

And autumn came, and spring-time's showers,
   And summer's zephyrs softly blew,
Yet on that spot no other flowers
   Save some sweet mountain daisies grew.

And as each raised its drooping head,
   Its serrate fringe was crimson dyed:
Memorial of the tears He shed,
   And of the hour to blood He sighed.

As in salvation's world-wide flow,
   The heaven-inspired apostle band,
First to God's chosen people go,
   And then abroad to every land;

So from that spot the daisy bears
   To all the world a message brief:
The crimson of its fringe declares
   The story of the Saviour's grief.

                            ROBERT WHITTET.

THE FROZEN BURN.

O WHERE is the wee brook that danced through the valley,
   Wha's murmur at gloamin' sae sweet was to me?
Or where are the gowans that decked a' the alley,
   And ga'e us, when bairnies, in summer sic glee?

O cauld cam' the rude blast that blew frae the wild hills,
   And keen bit the hoar-frost, and fierce drave the snaw,

And they've plucked a' the sweet flowers that buskit
   the wee rills,
And sealed up the burnie's wee wavelets an' a'.

But spring will soon come wi' its buds and its blossoms,
   The waving young leaflets will clead ilka tree,
The birdie's sweet love-notes will thrill frae their bosoms,
   And this snaw-covered desert an Eden will be.

The wee flowers will peep up their heads by the burnie,
   And its waters will dance in the sunbeams again;
Ilk thing that has life in't will flourish and charm ye,
   When the life now entombed shall have burst its ice
   chain.

Sae man, like the burnie when summer is glowing,
   Glides on in his rapture, free, lightsome, and gay;
But life has its winter, and towards us 'tis flowing,
   And soon will its rude breath freeze us in the clay.

But there is a summer the soul kens is comin',
   When life to these temples anew will be given;
Then fret nae, but cheer ye, and comfort yer gloamin'—
   The grave has but planted the flowerets for heaven.
                              ROBERT WHITTET.

KILBRYDE KIRKYARD.

O BONNIE grows the gowan in Kilbryde Kirkyard,
An' red-checkit is the rowan in Kilbryde Kirkyard,
      But the gowans fade awa'
      An' the rowan berries fa'
When winter haps the graves in Kilbryde Kirkyard.

O the stanes are auld an' gray in Kilbryde Kirkyard,
An' the banes are cauld as clay in Kilbryde Kirkyard,
      The moss is owre the stanes,
      An' the mould is on the banes,
That hae stood an' lain sae lang in Kilbryde Kirkyard.

O the brae is stey an' weary to Kilbryde Kirkyard,
An' the brig is auld an' eerie near Kilbryde Kirkyard,
    The howff where witches met
    Ere they forced the iron yett,
To keep their midnicht cantrips in Kilbryde Kirkyard.

O solemn is the Kirk in Kilbryde Kirkyard,
Shaded by a siller birk in Kilbryde Kirkyard,
    'Tis the Kirk o' auld Saint Bride,
    Within ance deck'd in pride,
But where owls an' bats noo bide, in Kilbryde Kirkyard

There the castle folks are sleepin', in Kilbryde Kirkyard,
An' Death his watch is keepin', in Kilbryde Kirkyard,
    In the vaults are knights and dames
    O' the Campbells, or the Grahames,
O' Kilbryde an' Aberuchil, in Kilbryde Kirkyard.

O' sweet's the laverock's sang in Kilbryde Kirkyard,
When the summer day is lang in Kilbryde Kirkyard,
    Frae the sky she sends us hope
    That the sleeper's eye shall ope
When the final trumpet clangs owre Kilbryde Kirkyard.

            REV. WILLIAM BLAIR, D.D.

GOLDEN GORSE.

GOLDEN gorse, whose stately plume
    Waves o'er moorland, crag, and fell,
Nods amid the yellow brume,
    Bramble-bank, and bracken-dell.
Where the hip and hawthorn spray
    Twine their arms across the brook;
Where the wild rose skirts the way
    There thou hast thy cosy nook.

Golden gorse, that gaily gleams
  O'er the upland and the dale,
As a royal banner streams
  In the freshening summer gale;
Heedless thou of winter's pang,
  When the timid snowdrops ope
Dost thy golden tassels hang,
  Tokens true of love and hope.

Golden gorse, that gems the wold,
  As with splendours of the mine,
Blazoned " floor of cloth of gold "—
  Such thy golden spangles shine;
" Burning bush, yet unconsumed,"
  Voice of God with tongue of fire,
Horeb's hill its light illumed,
  Baleful flame, a portent dire.

Golden gorse, in summer pride,
  Rolling like the billowy main,
When the golden even-tide
  Pours its flood athwart the plain.
Lo, the fabled gardens rise
  The Hesperides of old—
Golden fleece, the Argo's prize,
  Or Mida's touch that makes all gold.

Golden gorse, with prickly flower,
  Where the linnet makes her nest,
Sheltered in her sunny bower,
  Foe nor fear may her molest;
Happy bird, with bower so gay,
  Roofed with gold, and fenced with thorn,
Piping love-notes all the day,
  Fanned with fragrance till the morn.

                    REV. WILLIAM BLAIR, D.D.

THE LOFTY LOMONDS.

'Twas in my thoughtless boyhood,
   When all was bright and gay,
Like summer stole the rosy hours,
   And everywhere 'twas May;
We laughed, we sung; let what betide,
   We never cared to know,
When we clomb the lofty Lomonds,
   A long time ago.

Through rainbow-tints the earth gleamed fair,
   As 't ne'er knew fallen time;
For on young hearts the bloom of heaven
   Rests, as on Eden's prime;
Go where we may, these days will haunt
   Our souls, nor will they go,
Oh, the days we clomb the Lomonds,
   A long time ago!

And when the school at noontime
   Was free, we'd haste us down
On Leven's shore to wander—
   Sweet Leven of renown!
Or range the wild woods over,
   That on their steep sides grow,
In the days we clomb the Lomonds,
   A long time ago!

Now far apart from friendly ken
   Are many loved so well,
To them nor dirge nor song shall reach,
   Of griefs or joys to tell—
Some hushed in ocean beds repose,
   And scattered to and fro
Is that band which clomb the Lomonds
   A long time ago.

And some have gone to distant lands,
    Some fallen in battle's tide,
Others beneath ancestral trees
    Have lived, and toiled, and died;
But few remain. And never more,
    While rivers seaward flow,
Shall we meet to climb the Lomonds
    As long, long ago.

Again I've passed me o'er the scene
    Of life's romantic day;
How changed! The bounding heart, the dream,
    Those voices, where were they?
Farewell, ye spells to memory dear,
    Ye came and went like snow!
And farewell the lofty Lomonds
    Of long, long ago.

PETER NORVAL.

THE AULD CARLE'S COURTSHIP.

"COME, Kate, d'ye hear? bring my first waddin' coat,
    An' busk me richt gallant an' braw;
Syne pu' a red rose for the buttonhole o't,
    For I'm aff to the courtin' awa'!
    For I'm aff to the courtin' awa'!"

He gaed to the glass—to the keekin' he fell—
    An' he lauched till amaist like to fa';
Sae improved was his look that he kentna himsel'
    When aff to the courtin' awa',
    When aff to the courtin' awa'.

"O! wha is yon carle," quo he, "that's sae smirkie,
    An' looks sae weel-pleased ower me a'?
Is he really mysel', that cantie-like birkie,
    Wha's aff to the courtin' awa'?
    Wha's aff to the courtin' awa'."

He mountit auld Robin, an' bobbit fu' hie,
  Wi' siller spurs glancin' sae braw,
An' hat on's grey haffits set gayly agee,
  When aff to the courtin' awa',
    When aff to the courtin' awa'.

He rantit an' sang to himsel' the hale way,
  An' loud his ain trump he did blaw;
An' he swore by the rood he wad carry the day,
  Sin' aff to the courtin' awa'.
    Sin' aff to the courtin' awa',

"A wheen glaiket gipsies about me are gyte,
  Tho' my pow's bare, I'm loesome for't a',
An' at my first offer the hizzies wad bite,
  Fegs, catch me them courtin' ava!
    Fegs, catch me them courtin' ava!

"Let me see—there's Jean, Ann, and muckle gleyed Nan;
  An' Bess, wha's as black as a craw;
A' fechtin' like cats wha'll get Tam for gudeman,
  An' wad spean me frae courtin' ava'.
    An' wad spean me frae courtin' ava.

"They bind their fat bulks wi' their stays an' their lace,
  To mak' their waists jimpie an' sma';
An' they caper an' fling like cowtes i' the trace,
  Wi' sic nonsense I canna' awa'.
    Wi' sic nonsense I canna' awa'.

"Hech! But noo I'm near where my ain lass does bide—
  She's the queen an' the flower o' them a';
An' I'll aye bless the day when I made her my bride—
  That I gaed to the courtin' awa';
    That I gaed to the courtin' awa'."

PETER NORVAL.

THE ENGLISH KNIGHT.

THE night drove wild over Inkermann,
   As the Russian host was flying,
And the river red with the carnage ran
   Of the noble dead and dying.
Beneath the folds—lay an English Knight—
   Of his country's banner waving
That had streamed so fierce thro' the bloody fight,
   No foeman its terrors braving.

More and more faintly he grasped the brand,
   Which had many a death deliver'd,
As it flash'd—all the joy—in his martial hand,
   Now in countless fragments shiver'd.
"My once faithful steel, why fail," said he,
   "Thy lord in the hour of danger?
For I ne'er had, wer't not for thee,
   Died thus in the land of the stranger.

"Not so didst thou on the Alma's steep,
   Where thou sweptst down the boldest, strewing,
The earth with red heaps of the slaughter deep,
   Like the leaves, when wild winds are blowing.
Ne'er more shall the foe dread the lightning play
   Of thine edge its rich harvest reaping,
For run is the course of our short bright day,
   And with me thou'lt rest where sleeping."

Loud and clear rose an English "Hurrah!"
   O'er the din of the battle swelling,
And a smile o'er his dying face did play—
   'Twas the rout of the Muscove knelling.
He clapp'd his hands, shouted "Follow me!"
   While fast, fast was his life-blood streaming,
But ere kind hands came from all care was he,
   On his pale face victory beaming.

                        PETER NORVAL.

BONNIE OCHTERTYRE.

How sweet to roam the woods among,
    And wander on the hill,
Where heather bells bloom bonnilie
    Beside the mountain rill;
When from the West the golden hues
    The woods and vales attire,
How charming are the lovely braes
    Of bonnie Ochtertyre.

Among the knowes the lambkins play,
    In bowers the wild birds sing,
The scented flowers among the groves
    Around their fragrance fling;
But ah! I miss the kindest friend
    A leal heart could desire—
He loved and was beloved by all,
    The Chief of Ochtertyre.

I miss him when the evening star
    Is beaming in the sky;
I miss him when my soul is tuned
    For sweetest minstrelsy;
But come what will, go where I may,
    I'll strike the trembling lyre,
One song at least shall cheer my breast—
    I'll sing of Ochtertyre.

DUNCAN KIPPEN.

PIBROCH OF BONNIE STRATHEARN.

I FONDLY would linger in Bonnie Strathearn,
    In groves by the river's green banks I would roam;
And climb the proud steeps where the heather bells wave,
    And cull the wild flowers of my own Highland home,

The flowers bloom so fair round thy quiet rural cots,
   The birds sing their love-notes in woodland and dell;
Thy green sylvan paths and the scene from the hills
   Are treasured delights where fond memories dwell.

Though fierce storms sweep over mountain and moor,
   And cataracts foam like the wild raging sea,
Though ice binds the river and snow bars the way,
   The blithe hearts of home make it summer to me.
Thy daughters are fair as the fairest of flowers,
   True-hearted and brave are the sons of the glen,
And music's loved strains lend a pleasure to peace
   Or rouse up the spirit of heroes again.

Enshrined are thy glories in story and song,
   With tales of the old times by forest and lea;
The lays of the valley float over the land,
   And cheer hearts afar o'er the wide rolling sea.
The great in the land seek thy heathery braes,
   And breathe balmy zephyrs thy beauties among.
To see is to love thee. Oh, haste let us rove
   In bonnie Strathearn, the valley of song.
                             DUNCAN KIPPEN.

THE SCOTTISH PLAID.

THE plaid amang our auld forbears
Was lo'ed owre a' their precious wares,
Their dearest joys wad be but cares
   Without the plaid.

An' when the auld gudeman was deid,
'Twas aye by a' the house agreed,
That to his auldest son was fee'd
   His faither's plaid.

Ah! gin auld plaids cud speak or sing,
Our heids and hearts wad reel and ring
To hear the thrillin' tales that cling
   To Scotia's plaid.

To hear hoo Scottish men and maids
'Mang Scotland's hills and glens and glades,
Baith wrocht and focht wi' brains and blades
    In thae auld plaids.

The Star o' Scotland ne'er will set,
If we will only ne'er forget
The virtues in our sires, that met
    Aneath the plaid.

Amang the Scottish sichts I've seen
Was ane that touched baith heart and een;
A shepherd comin' owre the green
    Wi' crook and plaid,

And i' the plaid a limpin' lamb,
That on the hill had lost its dam,
And, like some trustfu' bairnie, cam',
    Row'd i' the plaid.

Anither sicht I think I see,
The saddest o' them a' to me—
The Scottish martyrs gaun to dee
    I' their auld plaids.

But let's rejoice, the times are changed,
The martyrs ha'e been a' avenged—
An English princess has arranged
    To wear the plaid.

                WILLIAM MURRAY.

MY FRIEND.

RESERVE for me on earth
    The man to call my friend:
In whom both mental worth
    And heavenly wisdom blend.

The man who has a heart
   To sympathize with grief,
And break misfortune's dart
   With counsel and relief.

The man whose voice will never
   Unrighteousness defend,
But scorneth to discover
   The weakness of a friend.

The man who stamps to dust
   Vile slander ere it grows,
And who is true and just
   Alike to friends and foes.

The man who worlds can trace,
   And yet in whom we find,
Combined with cultured grace,
   Humility of mind.

The man who's not ashamed,
   Though lord of every school,
However wise and famed,
   To own himself a fool.

Or, in a word, the man,
   Beneath affliction's rod,
Or, high in fortune's van,
   Who glorifies his God.

                        WILLIAM MURRAY.

DONALD MACINROY.[*]

SITTING by the great hall window,
    Gazing at the whirling snow,
Listening to the wind's hoarse moaning
    In the dark pine-wood below—

Dreaming of the buried summers,
    With their scent of faded flowers,
Hearing from the Past, faint echoes,
    As of bells in distant towers :

Echoes of the pleasant music
    Of young voices in their glee—
Voices that are hushed for ever,
    Do they whisper still to me?

Musing thus, the shadowy darkness
    Crept across the falling snow,
Till I heard a horse's footsteps
    Clatter in the court below.

"Norman Grant rides hither for thee"—
    Spake my sister, in surprise—
"Donald MacInroy is dying,
    And must see thee ere he dies."

In my plaid she warmly wrapped me;
    Through the drift we quickly rode;
Soon we reached the Highland sheiling,
    Donald MacInroy's abode.

---

[*] There is a tradition still existing in the Highlands of Perthshire of a Donald MacInroy, who was the son of a large sheep-farmer in that district, and who being, in the phrase of the North, a "pretty man," the heiress of the estate fell in love with him. In order to separate the lovers, Donald was sent to the wars, to serve under the young lady's father; whence he returned, after many years, to die. The ballad tells the rest.—AUTHOR'S NOTE.

"Sir," said Donald, "I am thankful
　　Thou hast come this night to me;
Ere my lips are sealed for ever,
　　I've a tale to tell to thee.

"When thy brother, the MacGregor,
　　Took me with him to the war,
'Twas to break a match for ever,
　　And a secret love to bar.

"For his lovely daughter Alice,
　　With her eyes of sunny blue—
Alice of the golden tresses—
　　Loved me tenderly and true.

"And her mother, high and haughty,
　　Sought that passion to destroy,
Hoping Alice, from me severed,
　　Would forget her MacInroy.

"O the dreary, dreary parting!
　　O the bitter tears we shed!—
But her angry mother knew not
　　That in secret we were wed.

"Then I followed her brave father
　　To that far and fatal shore
Where he fell, a hero worthy
　　Of the noble name he bore.

"But my Alice could not greet me
　　When I came back from the strife:
For the birth-hour of our Colin
　　Was the last hour of her life.

"Thou shalt find within my Bible
　　Proofs that we were duly wed,
That the honour's pure and stainless
　　Of my lovely Alice dead.

"And our Colin, whom thou lovest,
  And hast honoured with thy name,
Is the son of love and sorrow,
  But is not the child of shame.

"He is rightfully MacGregor—
  Blessings be upon the boy!
Let him stand among the proudest,
  Son of Donald MacInroy!

"Grandson of the Great MacGregor,
  Heir of Rannoch and Dunmore;
Come of soldiers true and gallant,
  Worthy those that went before.

"Brave and faithful, may he follow
  In the steps his fathers trod,
True to kindred and to honour,
  To his country and his God!"

And with faltering lip, still praying
  For a blessing on the boy,
To the strain of solemn pibroch,
  Passed the soul of MacInroy.

D. H. SAUNDERS.

CALEDONIA'S BLUE BELLS.

HAIL, bonnie Blue Bells! ye come hither to me
With a brother's warm love from far o'er the sea;
Fair flowerets! ye grew on a calm, sacred spot—
The ruins, alas! of my kind father's cot.
      Caledonia's Blue Bells, O bonnie Blue Bells!

What memories dear of that cot ye recall,
Though now there remains neither rooftree nor wall!

Alack-a-day ! lintel and threshold are gone,
While cold 'neath the weeds lies the hallowed hearth-
stone !
    Caledonia's Blue Bells, O bonnie Blue Bells !

'Twas a straw-roofed cottage, but love abode there,
And peace and contentment aye breathed in its air ;
With songs from the mother, and legends from sire,
How blithe were we all round the cheerie peat fire !
    Caledonia's Blue Bells, O bonnie Blue Bells !

Our sire long asleep, his fond mem'ry endeared ;
The mother still spared us, beloved and revered ;
Sweet Blue Bells with charmed recollections entwined
Of scenes in my childhood for ever enshrined.
    Caledonia's Blue Bells, O bonnie Blue Bells !
              DUNCAN MACGREGOR CRERAR.

THE EIRLIC WELL.*

O EIRLIC WELL ! dear Eirlic Well,
    Again I gaze on thee ;
What sacred mem'ries round thee cling,
    Fount of mine infancy.
Thy waters laugh and ripple now,
    As in the days of yore ;
'Mid changes thou art still unchanged,
    And ceaseless in thy store.

Long years have passed since last I kissed
    Thy gurgling wavelets sweet,
And oft I longed in climes afar
    To woo thy wild retreat.

---

* The Eirlic Well pours a rill into Girron Burn, at Amulree, situated in the south-eastern part of Breadalbane. Girron Burn is a tributary of the Fraochie, or Braan, which merges with the Tay at the foot of Birnam Hill.

Now that again I fondly hear
   The music of thy flow,
I sigh for those who with me shared
   Thy blessings long ago.

How joyously we bounded forth,
   When free from task and school,
To gather round thy mossy brink,
   And quaff thy waters cool.
Oh, youthful hearts and innocent,
   Pure as those sprays of thine,
Where are they now who clustered round
   Thy banks in auld lang syne?

Ah me! they all have gone, and here
   In pensive mood alone,
I meditate on bygone days
   Upon thy moss-clad stone.
Friends of my youth! the loved, the leal,
   I waft, where'er you dwell,
My warmest wishes; bless you all,
   Who drank from Eirlic well.

Loved Eirlic Well! flow ever on:
   Those cooling draughts of thine
The tired and weary aye shall cheer—
   Flow on, O boon Divine!
Farewell, charmed spot! I ne'er again
   Thy cheerie face may see;
But thou art graven in my heart,
   Scene of mine infancy.
                DUNCAN MACGREGOR CRERAR.

ALMA, COUNTESS OF BREADALBANE.

COUNTESS beloved! My warmest thanks to thee
   For thy most gracious gift—thine image dear—
I waft across the wide Atlantic sea,
   With gladdened heart and gratitude sincere.

Here beauteously and faithfully portrayed
    Thy graceful form and lovely classic face;
O noble lady, thou art winsome, fair,
    And genial, kind, and full of heaven-born grace.

Nor do I thank thee less for friendly words
    And warm regard for thine so far away;
No distance can undo the cords of love
    That bind us to the home of childhood's day.
Sweet as the fragrance of fresh heather bloom,
    The praises reach us of thine acts benign;
Thy charming courtesy and kindness rare
    We in our hearts will treasure and enshrine.

O wife devoted of Breadalbane's Lord!
    True Freedom's cause a friend has found in thee;
'Twas thine own hand that bravely raised the flag
    Which led our Perthshire on to victorie.
Heaven bless you both with peace, and spare you long
    To kindly rule your every strath and glen;
No land is richer in romance and song;
    No men are braver than Breadalbane men!

                        DUNCAN MACGREGOR CRERAR.

MY BONNIE ROWAN TREE.*

THRICE welcome, sweet green spray,
    Culled from my Rowan Tree,
By loved ones far away,
    In bonnie Amulree.

In boyhood's days thy root
    Was planted by my hand,
Just ere I left my dear,
    My Scottish fatherland!

---

* A spray of rowan, culled by my brother John (to whom I inscribe the verses) from a tree which I had planted in our mother's garden, thirty years ago.—AUTHOR'S NOTE.

Thou but a sapling then,
  Though now a shelt'ring tree,
While warblers in thy boughs
  Sing sweetest melodie.

Oh ! handsome Rowan Tree !
  I'm growing old and gray ;
But thou art fresh and green,
  Remote from all decay.

One boon for which I pray—
  A home in Amulree !
Where friends of yore I'd meet
  Beneath thee, Rowan Tree !

The Fraochie wimpling by,
  In cadence soft and slow—
Craig Thullich tow'ring high,
  The fragrant woods below.

The old Kirk on the knowe,
  The graveyard mossy green ;
Thy bosky birks, Lubchuil !
  Thy streamlet's silv'ry sheen.

With warm Breadalbane hearts,
  'Mong those romantic braes,
I happily could spend
  The gloaming of my days.

The mem'ries of langsyne—
  Bright days of gladsome glee—
We fondly could revive
  Beneath thee, Rowan Tree !

    Duncan MacGregor Crerar.

THE AULD CRAW'S LAMENT.

FAR up on the braes, in a sweet sunny spot,
    A bonnie green howe whaur a burnie rins by,
There stand the remains o' an auld Hielan' cot,
    Its flure is the grass, and its roof is the sky.
An' whiles I can fancy some auld-fashioned craw,
    Like a weary spirit, forsaken an' lane,
Sittin' croakin' a coronach there on the wa',
    Wi' a voice that soun's half 'twixt a sang an' a grane.
        Caw, caw, caw, caw;
          They've a' gane awa', they've a' gane awa';
        The auld an' the young, the stately an' strong,
        The hearty an' hopefu', the blythe an' the braw.

O! aften I think o' the days o' langsyne,
    The " gude auld times," as the by-word says;
They were glorious days wi' me an' mine,
    For peace an' plenty were on the braes.
Then cheery an' bricht was the licht frae the sky,
    An' the kind couthie folk made it cheerier still,
Wi' the ducks, an' the hens, an' the horse, an' the kye,
    An' the gentle, simple sheep on the hill.
        Caw, caw, caw, caw; etc.

How happy in sweet spring-time were we
    To follow the plough in the early morn;
How glad when the simmer cam' roun' to see
    The bonnie green fields o' wavin' corn.
An' in hairst the joy o' the folk we shared,
    When yellow an' ripe the crap they shore;
An' gathered it up in the auld stackyard,
    A' safe an' soun' for the winter's store.
        Caw, caw, caw, caw; etc.

There's the auld fir-tree whaur the bairnies played,
    An' the bourtree bush hingin' owre the burn;
An' through the pools whaur they used to wade,
    The water rins by wi' a waefu' murn.

O! mony's the joy an' sorrow I've seen,
   But few, few fauts o' the folk lived there;
And so in my heart is their memory green,
   And aye will be till it beats nae mair.

        Caw, caw, caw, caw; etc.

To a far better lan' they whiles spoke about gaun,
   Whaur they a' would be angels, as happy's could be,
For ever an' ever,—an', oh! in that lan',
   I wonder if there would be room for me.
I would like to be happy, an' bonnie, an' gude;
   I've a kind, warm heart, an' wish nae ill ava;
An' I've heard there is Ane that could mak', if He would,
   A white-wingit angel e'en out o' a craw.

        Caw, caw, caw, caw; etc.

                JOHN TAYLOR.

WI' THE PIPERS.

As the Volunteer Pipers were marchin' hame
Ae nicht frae a place that I needna name,
An auld man close by their side was seen,
Wi' a far-awa', wistfu'-like look in his een.

He lookit sae frail, an' his cheeks sae thin,
Ye could tell that the best o' his days were dune;
An' my heart seemed to warm to him there when I saw
Hoo he marched in the crood wi' his thochts far awa'.

The bagpipes were skirlin' up cheery an' bauld,
An' briskly an' blithely stepped young an' auld;
The roads micht be stourie, an' rough, an' hard,
But their step was as lichtsome as on the green sward.

"Were ye speakin', frien'? Did I hear ye richt?
Hard, stourie roads, an' a close sort o' nicht?
Man, my een seemed to look, an' my feet to fa'
On the saft heather hills that are far awa'.

"I felt na the roads, an' I saw na the nicht,
But I seemed in the glow of a glad sunny licht;
For memory had spread a sweet glamour owre a',
Frae the auld heather hills that are far, far awa'.

"The pipes, an' the kilt, an' the plaid, ye see,
Bring the days o' langsyne like a vision to me;
An' I canna tell hoo, but my heart jist fills
Wi' a flush o' the joy frae the auld heather hills.

"It needs but a glint o' the tartan, an' then
I'm a licht-fittit, licht-heartit laddie again;
My hair may be gray, an' my head may be bald,
But the heart an' the spirit 'll never grow auld.

"I've lived in the toon for this mony a year,
If ane may ca't livin', the way they dae here;
Nae wonder folk weary, sae rough is life's road,
An' whiles lose their faith baith in man and in God.

"But whatever the world may be turnin' to, noo,
And it looks rather dootfu', between me an' you;
There was honour, an' friendship, an' faith, an' truth,
'Mang the auld Hielan' hills in the days o' my youth.

"The leal-heartit trust o' the frien's that are gane,
In God an' His gudeness has strengthened my ain;
O, surely if e'er there was gude folk ava,
It was there 'mang the Hielan' hills far, far awa'.

"The thocht o' the auld Hielan' hame to mysel'
Has been just like a draucht frae the caller spring well;
It has kept me frae faintin', an' helped me alang,
When a'thing looked cheerless, an' houpless an' wrang.

"To mind the kind heart o' my mither sae dear,
Is better to me than a' worldly gear;
An' my faither's true spirit an' manly worth,
Than a' the houses an' lands on earth.

"I'm sure that the thocht o' their gudeness has been
The richest an' best o' a' legacies, frien';
An' I houp we'll live sae that our bairns may be
As prood when they mind o' their mither an' me.

"And so, though the roads micht be rough, ye see,
The soond o' the pipes made them smooth to me;
For saft an' licht seemed my feet to fa'
On the auld heather hills that are far awa'."

JOHN TAYLOR.

THE BRAES O' MOUNT BLAIR.

When lambkins were playing, and linties were singing,
And woodland and dell looked delightfully fair,
I carelessly wandered, a few hours beguiling,
'Mang beautiful scenes on the Braes o' Mount Blair.

The sun in his splendour, while calmly declining,
Shed brightly his beams on the landscape so rare;
The bee wi' his burden was hameward returning
Frae sipping the sweets on the Braes o' Mount Blair.

The cushat and mavis had there made their dwelling,
The leveret limp'd lightly, its heart free frae care;
And the deer and the roe frae afar were seen bounding
To drink frae the streams on the Braes o' Mount Blair.

While I stood beholding each scene so enchanting,
A maid, with whom Venus alone could compare,
Came tripping up to me—a goddess so blooming—
Eclipsing the scenes on the Braes o' Mount Blair.

Before me she stood wi' a smile sae bewitching—
In ringlets of gold hung her fair flowing hair,
And beauty and health in her cheeks were seen kissing—
The queen and the pride o' the Braes o' Mount Blair.

On the banks o' a burnie, where cowslips were blooming,
We baith sat us doon our fond thochts to declare ;
Enchanted wi' beauty sae modest and peerless,
Her hand I bespoke on the Braes o' Mount Blair.

She hung doon her head, while her saft cheeks were blushing,
And gied me a sign that I needna despair ;
I kissed her sweet dimples, and vowed ere the winter
To mak' her my ain on the Braes o' Mount Blair.

And now she's the pride and the joy o' my dwelling,
For poortith and sorrow we ne'er hae a care ;
While peace and contentment around us are smiling,
To crown a' our bliss on the Braes o' Mount Blair.

ALEXANDER FERGUSSON.

THE WIFIE O' CARGILL.

THERE was a wee wifie ance lived in Cargill ;
As cantie a wifie as e'er sell't a gill,
Wi' bandy bit leggies, and twa skelly een—
A queerer wee wifie there never was seen.

On the tap o' her chimla there flourish'd a broom,
As sign to the public she'd plenty o' room,
And plenty o' toddy, and wealth o' gude cheer,
Wi' naething frae warlocks or witches to fear.

When Grisel's gude neebours were a' sleepin' soun',
She mounted her broomstick and rade up and down,
In company wi' Maggie and Katie and Jean,
Three rantin' auld witches that lived at Broadgreen.

They sail'd ower the Tay in an auld washin' tub ;
They paidled in Isla as if 'twere a dub,
And Grisel ne'er wanted fresh salmon to fry—
Her beef-boat and girnal they never ran dry.

Ae nicht in her cantrips auld Grisel gat fou',
She fell aff her broomstick, I canna tell hoo,
But she gat sic an unco hard thump on the croon
That she lay till daylicht in a pitifu' swoon.

The de'il he heard tell o't, the deil he was croose,
He awa' to Cargill and he into her hoose;
An' he aff wi' the wife, wi' a laugh and a roar,
And noucht was e'er heard o' her Ladyship more.

ALEXANDER FERGUSSON.

THE MAID OF ISLA'S LAMENT.

I'LL be droon'd in Isla Water,
  I'll be found in Isla stream;
My feet they winna keep the gate,
  And oh! hoo will I win hame.

Willie he has gane and left me,
  Willie wi' the gowden hair;
Oh! my heart is sad and breaking,
  Ne'er will I see Willie mair.

Aft I wander'd wi' my Willie
  By yon bonnie birken shaw;
Aft I sat the lee-lang gloamin'
  Wi' my laddie that's awa'.

The mavis sweetly sang his matin
  'Mang the boughs o' yonder tree,
And the lintie caroll'd saftly
  To my Willie and to me.

Noo I wander sad and cheerless—
  Dowie looks the trysting tree,
Harshly murmurs flowing Isla,
  Naewhere Willie can I see.

Cruel the heart that banish'd Willie;
   Cruel my parents were to me;
They hae robb'd their only lassie
   O' the love they canna gie.

Broken-hearted, sad and weary,
   Lay me 'neath the trysting tree;
By the murmuring stream o' Isla,
   Till my Willie come to me.

I'll be lost in Isla water,
   I'll be found in Isla stream;
I'm broken-hearted, sad, and weary,
   I canna think o' gaen hame.

ALEXANDER FERGUSSON.

THE WOUNDED SOLDIER.

ON the banks of the Ganges, far, far from the shore,
That claims for her costume the tartans he wore,
A soldier, all bleeding, had sank on the ground,
Where many a comrade lay dying around.
Pale, pale was his cheek, but it was not from fear,
For deep in his side was the mark of a spear;
But the warrior, all wounded, forbore to complain,
Till he thought of the friends he might ne'er see again.

Is it thus! is it thus! Ah! my race is then run;
Farewell, thou green earth, and thou bright setting sun;
Farewell to each hope that my heart had in store;
The morning may come, but 'twill find me no more.
My father, farewell, and my mother, ah me!
Oh! mother, dear mother, I'm woeful for thee;
Fond hearts, but for ye I could die without pain,
But I ne'er shall see you, nor Balquhidder again.

Ye scenes of my childhood, Balquhidder, farewell;
Adieu to the mountain, adieu to the dell;

My blessing is yours,—all I can bequeath,
For no more, ah! no more shall I tread on your heath.
Farewell to the mist, the sunshine, the shade;
Farewell to the rock, to the lake and the glade;
They may send back their echoes to answer the strain
That I never shall hear in Balquhidder again.

Dear father and mother, Oh, weep not, nor sigh,
We will meet in a happier realm on high;
Yes, I'll meet you again in a region of bliss,
In a world that is brighter and better than this.
Farewell then, dear parents, I'll see you no more,
For my sufferings and sorrows will soon be all o'er
In a far distant land I shall sleep with the slain,
For I'll ne'er see my native Balquhidder again.

While thus musing he lay, he could hear from afar
The tumult and din of the unfinished war;
He raised himself up, for now swelled on his ear
The token of vict'ry, a loud British cheer;
"Victory, victory, hurrah!" thus in answer he cried,
Then o'erpowered by the effort, fell fainting, and died;
The sun went to rest, and the night cloud amain,
O'er the hero who'll ne'er see Balquhidder again.

JOHN J. S. STEWART.

THE WINDYGOWL.

'TIS wind fair or foul
At auld Windygowl,
Ahent Drumnacree on the knowe;
Frae Cathla it comes,
Alang a' the drums,
To shake up the trees o' the howe.

Round front, back, an' en',
Inside, but an' ben,
It rants an' it whistles wi' glee;

Sabbin' an' skirlin',
Twinin' an' twirlin',
Dingin' doon a' thing to get free.

A'e mament a hush,
Syne on wi' a rush,
Daddin', bladdin' windock an' door;
The sough or the yell,
O' breeze or o' gale,
Blaws ower Windygowl evermore.

Win's fierce, wild, an' lood,
The ha' has withstood;
It sits like a rock on the knowe,
An' taks in the range,
O' hill, dale, an' grange,
Aloof frae the reek o' the howe.

Fu' aft, weel I trow,
I ca'd up the knowe,
To hae a bit crack wi' the laird;
Oor freendship was true.
A' airts the wind blew,
The warld wagg'd awa', we ne'er cared.

We sat check by jowl
In auld Windygowl
Ower a'e tum'ler juist an' a snack;
Aye hearty an' hale,
Nae lull in oor tale,
An' laith to lave aff wi' oor crack.

Alake, the auld laird,
Lies in the kirkyard,
Nor hears the lood blast that still blaws—
Auld Windygowl peeps
Doon whaur he noo sleeps,
An' lane look the tenantless wa's.

Richt eerie at nicht
Was yon peekie o' licht,
Its waur an' waur noo, wi' nae lowe ;
Eldritch an' dreary,
Lanesome an' weary,
Looks auld Windygowl ower the howe.

JOHN SMITH.

WE'LL HUNKER DOON TO NANE !

WHILE Freedom's tartan cleids the clan,
  Oor land shall haud nae slave ;
Straucht in your shoon stan' up each man !
  Be honest, true, and brave :
What's line or lineage, birth or bluid,
  But mouldrin' dust an' bane ?
By love to man, an' a' that's guid,
  We'll hunker doon to nane—
    By throbbing pulse o' purple bluid,
    We'll hunker doon to nane.

You've seen the spider spread his web,
  An' on an insect prey ;
You've seen the bird seized by the hawk—
  Ilk beast has its ain day ;
But man, wi' mind unfetter'd, free,
  Shall stoop to stock nor stane ;
An' man to man by Heaven's decree,
  We'll hunker doon to nane :
    Man's love to man by Heaven's decree,
    We'll hunker doon to nane.

Nor tongue, nor sword, nor tyrant's grasp,
  Their selfish sway can hold,
For hand wi' heart we'll fondly clasp,—
  Love's stronger far than gold ;
It's banner bright o'er earth shall soar,
  Its power shall never wane ;

When men are men the warl' o'er,
  They'll hunker doon to nane—
    Then men, be men the warl' o'er,
    And hunker doon to nane.
JOHN SMITH.

SONG TO THE TAY.

BE'T Dee or Don, be't Clyde or Forth,
  The Tweed, or rapid Spey,
Or a' the rivers south or north,
  There's nane can match the Tay.
Thro' a' its length, in matchless strength
  It rushes wild and free;
And leaps along wi' swellin' song
  Frae Kenmore to Dundee.
    The rolling Tay, the rushing Tay,
      Let hills and valleys ring,
    Beneath a patriotic lay,
      To Scotland's river King.

The Forth may brag o' Stirling's keep,
  The Tweed the Border hold,
The Clyde may murmur in its sleep
  And dream of wealth untold.
The Dee and Spey their Highland lay
  May sing in accents strong;
But all must hush them when the Tay
  Uplifts its patriot song.

Stout John de Luce and kingly Bruce
  And Wallace wicht have stood
Beside its waves amid their braves
  And dyed them with their blood.
And Danish hordes and Roman swords
  Were broken on its shores;
And England's yeomen squires and lords
  Have felt our keen claymores.

In wintry might all foaming white
    It rises wild and grand;
In summer sheen a bonnier scene
    Is no in a' the land.
Then chaunt its praise in swelling lays
    Like rousing trumpet call;
Let Scotland sing unto the King
    Of Scotland's rivers all.

    The mighty Tay, the rushing Tay,
        Let hills and valleys ring,
    Beneath a patriotic lay,
        To Scotland's river King.

JAMES FERGUSON.

DUNSINANE.

O'ER the brow of Dunsinane the summer sun glows,
O'er the brow of Dunsinane the summer wind blows,
And fair is the landscape that's spreading beneath
The brow of Dunsinane, the hill of Macbeth.

To the eastward the ocean lies placid and still,
To the northward the Grampians rise hill upon hill,
To the southward and westward the Ochils uprise,
Till the heart of broad Scotland is bared to our eyes.

The past with its wonders is with us again,
And war has awaken'd and marshalled its men,
The war-pipes are sounding their summons of death,
O'er the brow of Dunsinane, the hill of Macbeth.

Roman legions before us go thundering past,
Now the yells of the horsemen arise on the blast,
And then like a tempest through valley and gorge,
The yeomen of England are shouting "St. George."

But spear-points are levelled and claymores flash bright,
Brave Scotland has girded herself for the fight,
And foeman on foeman she sweeps from her path,
'Neath the brow of Dunsinane, the hill of Macbeth.

How brightly the valleys are smiling below,
How brightly the fields in their summer garb glow,
How brightly the rivers are rolling along,
'Neath the splendour of summer with music and song.

And Peace like a queen on her emerald throne,
Is sitting to-day where war's trumpet hath blown,
And sweetness and beauty lie wedded beneath
The brow of Dunsinane, the hill of Macbeth.

Around us for ever heart-reaching and grand,
The strong voice of Freedom gives strength to our land,
And Liberty strides through each valley and glen,
On the feet of fair maidens and earnest-browed men.

From the brow of Dunsinane the proud boast is hurled
To match our broad Scotland we challenge the world;
For truth, worth and valour, and undying faith,
Surround grim Dunsinane, the hill of Macbeth.

JAMES FERGUSON.

TULLYMET.

FAIR Summer walks among the hills, and flowers rise up to greet
Her coming with a sunny smile, and kiss her jewelled feet;
The birds are tuned to song, and pour their orisons on high,
And beauty beams upon our gaze by land, and lake, and sky.
The woods, the mighty harps of earth, to solemn music bend;

High heavenwards to the throne of God the swelling
 strains ascend;
The listening earth looks up in love, and quivers like a
 gong
With ecstacy of bliss beneath the magic of the song.
The laughing burnies dance for joy beneath the passing
 breeze,
The waving corn-fields respond, and roll like silver seas;
The very shadows seem to smile in sunny Summer's face,
And softly creep to kiss her feet from out each hiding-
 place.
A fairer scene on all the earth I've never gazed on yet
Than this that greets my eyes upon the braes of Tully-
 met.

The spot is hallowed unto me; mayhap 'tis this that
 throws
Such glory o'er the spreading scene till all the prospect
 glows,
And brightens into beauty's best; for here, where now
 I stand,
Once stood my mother's baby feet. Here oft my
 mother's hand
Hath plucked the flowers from off the braes and gleaned
 among the corn;
In this thatched cottage by my side the sainted dead
 was born.
No wonder that it seems to me the fairest spot on earth,
No wonder that my heart awakes as if a newer birth
Had fallen on it as I tread the paths she must have trod,
Long e e her gentle soul had flown to walk above with
 God.
None knew the love I bore the dead, none now can ever
 know;
I feel her presence round me yet wherever I may go.
I would to God that she had lived to train my steps
 aright,
And teach me how to walk the world, and how to fight
 the fight;
A weed upon the sea of time I float about to-day,

The sport of all the waves of thought that o'er my feelings play;
She left me all too young—she died—I did not loudly rave;
How my struck heart was numbed that day they bore her to the grave.
The blow was far too deep. It stunned. Its deadening influence still
Weighs heavily on brain, and nerve, and heart, and soul, and will.
It made me what I am. Alas! Not what I might have been,
Had she but lived who loved me so. But let the false between
That spreads from that far time to this be buried where it lies.
Awake! my heart; from yon high heaven my mother's loving eyes
Look down on me. For her dear sake I'll make an effort yet,
And tune my life to better things; I swear it, Tullymet.

What stalwart men those braes have reared, my mother's kinsmen all,
Like sons of Anak trod the land, each buirdly breast a wall
That would have stemmed the tide of force when force was in its prime,
When Bruce and Wallace shook the hills with Freedom's battle rhyme.
Their hearts were of the hero stamp, their frames of hero mould!
True children of the hills they were, the dauntless and the bold.
We thought of battle as they sped on springing footsteps by,
And watched to see the beacons blaze, and list the slogan cry.
But thank the Ruler of the world, such sights and sounds have gone
Afar from Scotland's rugged side. From off her mountain throne

Sweet Peace looks down upon the land, and waves its wand on high,
Till flowers, and fruits, and spreading fields are smiling to the sky;
And birds, and bees, and waving winds move every hill and dell
To music, where in olden time hate's horrid discord fell;
And hillsmen test their muscles' strength at tossing stone and bar,
Instead of cleaving helms and heads filled with the lust of war.
To pruning hooks the spears are turned, the swords to scythes are set,
When golden harvest loads the lap of flow'ry Tullymet.

Yet battle's call hath reached them here, e'en in these times of rest,
And stirred the old fierce spirit up that slumbered in each breast:
And vine-clad Spain has heard the shout that foemen know so well,
And France has seen the claymores flash, and trembled as they fell
With death upon each dripping edge; and every land earth owns
Is dinted deep by Highland heels, and strewn with Highland bones.
O, who can dare the mountaineers when mountain blood is high?
And who can stem the tempest charge of Highland chivalry?
The Vikings of the sea went down beneath its force of yore,
And learnt to dread our land, and shun its thistle-guarded shore.
The masters of the world were braved when Rome was in her prime;
Their conquering march was stemmed and stayed in our unconquered clime,
And England's haughty heart was taught that north the Tweed we claim,

When Christendom in awe and fear, bent low before
    her name.
Untamed as ever still we rush, when battle gives the
    call,
O'er sea and shore, and sweep the plain, and storm the
    leaguered wall :
And where in all broad Scotland's length does Scotland's
    spirit start
So fiercely into force and fire as here within its heart;
Yea, here among the Athole hills, should Scotland's sun
    e'er set,
Its last bright rays will linger on the braes of Tullymet.

JAMES FERGUSON.

OOR HOOSE AT E'EN.

OH, what merry times we hae,
    In oor hoose at e'en ;
Ilk ane is blythe and gay,
    In oor hoose at e'en ;
Tho' the wintry win's may howl
And the storm-cluds darkly scowl,
And like hung'ry demons growl,
    Roun' oor hoose at e'en.

When oor gudeman comes in
    To oor hoose at e'en,
Tired o' fit, wi' drookit skin,
    To oor hoose at e'en.
See the willin' han's and feet,
To get in-ower their faither's seat,
And for dry claes change the weet,
    In oor hoose at e'en.

Syne the cheery cup o' tea
    In oor hoose at e'en
Mak's a' care and sorrow flee
    Frae oor hoose at e'en ;

Wi' the kindly jokes and smiles,
And the bairnies' winsome wiles,
Aye the langest nicht beguiles
  In oor hoose at e'en.

When, wi' hangin' sleepy head,
  In oor hoose at e'en,
Ane and a' prepare for bed,
  In oor hoose at e'en,
Oh, there's muckle love and bliss
In ilk wee bit darlin's kiss;
E'en their fauts we a' wad miss
  In oor hoose at e'en.

Then awa wi' sordid joys
  Frae oor hoose at e'en;
For there's pleasure that ne'er cloys
  In oor hoose at e'en;
Fain are we it sud be kent
That we're wi' oor lot content,
And the blessin' Heaven has sent
  To oor hoose at e'en.

              SARAH JANE STEWART.

THE SUNNY SIDE.

DRAW in your chair, my ain gudeman,
  And sit ye doon by me,
And a' the oors recount again
  We spent in youthfu' glee.

In fancy we'll gang roun' ance mair,
  Each auld familiar scene;
We'll walk thro' Bellfield's woods sae fair,
  Or rest us by the Dean.

In thocht we'll hear each croodlin' doo,
    Ilk merle and mavis sing;
And there, gudeman, we will renew
    Oor vows made in life's spring.

When wandrin' down by Fairy Hill,
    Whaur Irvine's stream rins wide,
Yer pawky whisper haunts me still,—
    "We'll tak' the sunny side."

That wordie cheer'd when grief and care
    Oor youthfu' looks did mar,
And smoothed oor broos when wrinkled sair
    Wi' mony an inlaid scar.

Tho' noo oor pows are whitenin' fast,
    Wi' warldly toil and strife,
We ha'e Hope's anchor aye to cast
    Thro' a' the storms o' life.

Oor hearts we'll free frae ilka clog,
    Tho' bluid rins thin and cauld;
And blythely to life's end we'll jog,
    Nor mind tho' we grow auld.

Tho' Sorrow's cloud may o'er us loom
    Or Death itsel' betide,
Yet we can look ayont the tomb,
    And "tak' the sunny side."

SARAH JANE STEWART.

THE BRAES ABUNE STOBHA'.

THE summer sun shines bonnilie on mountain, loch, and lea,
    An' life, an' love, an' beauty thrive whaure'er the e'e may fa';
Ilk livin' thing is happy like, an' heart-content but me,
    An' I am wae wi' thinkin' o' the braes abune Stobha'.

We've bonnie braes aroond us here, I view them a' day
    lang,
  An' aft an' sair I'm blamed because I sigh for else
    ava';
But, oh, our feet they wander gaets our hearts will
    hardly gang,
  An' mine I fear has never quat the braes abune
    Stobha'.

'Twas yonder I was born an' bred, an' ilka whinney
    knowe
  Is hallowed by some tale o' love that happen'd lang
    awa';
Yon roadside cot ayont the kirk held happy hearts, I
    trow,
  An', oh, they'll aye be dear to me, the braes abune
    Stobha'.

Ochone! but it's a thrawart fate that workin' bodies
    dree,
  Sin' maistly a' to win their bread maun wander far
    awa';
The family nests get herried sune by dour Necessitie,
  'Twas him, the loon, that twyned me frae the braes
    abune Stobha'.

Yet owre yon hills abune Dunblane, an' by the banks o'
    Tay,
  An', oh, gin I could waft me there but for an oor or
    twa,
I'd come again wi' pith anew to bide the hoped-for day,
  When I'll return, nae mair to lea' the braes abune
    Stobha'.

They're bonnie in the mornin', they're bonnier at noon,
  And, oh, they're ever glorious just ere the gloamin'
    fa';
The flow'rs that ha'e the sweetest scent, the birds the
    sweetest tune,
  Are those that bloom an' sing amang the braes abune
    Stobha'.

ROBERT FORD.

OOR AULD WIFE.

In a' the Lowlands wide, an' the Hielands e'en beside,
   Oh, ye ha'ena ance heard o', nor seen,
Sic a rare an' dear auld wife as is oor gude auld wife
   An' I ferlie gin her marrow's ever been.
She's dear unto the auld, the young fouk, an' the yauld,
   An' she's mair unto us a' than is oor life,
We could barter wi' oor health, we could sunder wi' oor wealth,
   But neither wi' oor dear auld wife.
      She's a dear auld wife, she's a fier auld wife,
      She's a fine auld wife, she's a kin' auld wife;
      A lichtsome, lithesome, leesome, blythesome,
      Free-gaun, hearty body, oor auld wife.

At dancin's on the green, in the bonnie simmer's e'en,
   She is there aye, wi' the speerit o' us a',
Gaily linkin' through the reels, an' shakin' o' her heels,
   Like a lassie on the laich o' twenty-twa;
If ye fain wad hae a joke, just try her wi' a poke,
   An' she'll cut yer gab as gleg as ony knife;
When there's shots o' wit agaun, there's no ane in a' the lan'
   Can haud his ain wi' oor auld wife.
      She's a slee auld wife, she's a spree auld wife,
      She's a smart auld wife, she's a tart auld wife,
      A lichtsome, lithesome, leesome, blythesome,
      Free-gaun, hearty body, oor auld wife.

Whaur sickness dulls a ha' she daurna be awa',
   She's sae lucky! sae skilly! an' sae kind!
There's no ane can row a sair wi' ae-half her canny care;
   No, nor speak sic words o' comfort to the mind;
Doctor Dozem, he declares, she's trick'd him o' his fares,
   An' oor minister is leavin' us for Fife,
For he says, "I canna see ony need ye hae for me,
   While ye hae sic a rare auld wife."

> She's a rare auld wife, she's a fair auld wife,
> She's a grave auld wife, she's a brave auld wife,
> A lichtsome, lithesome, leesome, blythesome,
> Free-gaun, hearty body, oor auld wife.

At comin' hame o' bairns, an' at marriages an' kirns,
  She is head-billie-dawkus aye, be sure :
For the bairnies wadna live, an' the waddin's wadna thrive,
  An she werena there the drappikie to pour—
Na! she winna pree hersel', binna just the hansel smell,
  Nor will gi'e o't whaur it micht breed ony strife,
An' she kens what a' can stan', to a dribble ilka man—
  Sic a skilly body's oor auld wife.
> She's a leal auld wife, she's a hale auld wife,
> She's a grand auld wife, she's a bland auld wife,
> A lichtsome, lithesome, leesome, blythesome,
> Free-gaun, hearty body, oor auld wife.

A treasure to the auld, a terror to the bauld,
  An' the brag an' joy o' a' that wad do weel,
For leal o' heart is she, an' fu' o' furthy glee,
  As the miller's ain big girnal's fu' o' meal ;
Ye will read o' heroines that flourished langsyne,
  But would you see their better in the life ?
Come owre some orra day to oor clachan on the Tay,
  An' get a glisk o' oor auld wife.
> She's a dear auld wife, she's a queer auld wife,
> She's a fine auld wife, she's a kin' auld wife,
> A lichtsome, lithesome, leesome, blythesome,
> Free-gaun, hearty body, oor auld wife.

ROBERT FORD.

BIGGIN' A NEST.

WE sat on the braeside, Jamie an' I,
  An' the sun was wearin' doun,
Twa pairtricks woo'd in the vale below
  In a sweet love-favour'd croon.

An' they whiddled about, they niddled about,
　　They chirm'd, they kiss'd, an' caress'd,
"Oh! Jamie," quo' I, "it's pairin' time,
　　I'se warrant they're biggin' a nest."

The sun was doun, an' the valley was lown
　　Ere ane o's neist opened a mou',
An' Jamie began, wi' a "hic" an' a stan',
　　Like ony whase heart's ower fu'.
An' hirsellin' near wi' a bashfu' care,
　　He fondled me ticht to his breast,
"Ay! Jeanie," quo' he, "it's pairin' time;
　　What think ye o' biggin' a nest?"

I didna say no, an' couldna say ay,
　　For my heart crap' up in my mou',
But the feckfu' grip, an' the heart-hove sigh,
　　Gae token o' sanction enou';
An' I'll tell ye a plot, tho' dinna speak o't,
　　For Jamie says quietness is best,—
Ye'll a' get a dance gin Whitsuntide;
　　We're busily biggin' a nest.

　　　　　　　　　ROBERT FORD.

A VALENTINE.

IN days gone by, when knights won maids
　　By dint of courage in the field,
By dashing skill in lawless raids,
　　When vanquished chieftains had to yield—

'Twas strong right hand that gained the heart
　　And doughty bearing charmed the eye;
But love now plays a gentler part,
　　And strives in other fields to vie.

I seek not men to overthrow,
    Nor rudely win thy praise in fight;
If e'er I'd like to strike a blow,
    'Twould be for thee and for the right.

But I would like thy love to gain
    By noble acts and honest worth—
By easing stricken hearts of pain,
    By giving hope a joyful birth;

I'd like to show that courage lends
    Itself to humble trials of soul;
That quiet patience oft transcends
    Great deeds proclaimed from pole to pole.

'Tis thus I fain would win thy smile,
    For this esteem thy word of praise,
When, happy, I with thee beguile
    An hour or two 'neath Luna's rays.

And, lassie dear, my fond desire
    Is that thy heart be ever mine—
'Twill make mine tuneful as a lyre—
    Accept me as THY VALENTINE!

                        JAMES CROMB.

THE SUMMONS OF LOVE.

"I WANT you!"—A summons I cannot resist,
    A summons I would not resist if I could;
So sweet its surprise, so cheering its tone!—
    A call that inspires me with happiest mood.

"I want you!"—I have read the same words before—
    The cry of a heart overburdened with pain
Finding vent in its grief to its chosen in love,
    And calling him back to itself once again.

"I want you!"—Not a trace of sadness or doubt!
　For I've looked close to see whether such were concealed;
"I want you!—e'en though I've nothing to say,"
　Is a message by which only love is revealed.

"I want you!"—A call that shall never fall dead
　On my ears, ever heark'ning the voice of thy heart.
"I want you!"—Brief phrase, yet it gladdens my soul,
　For it tells of thy life that I form a part.

"I want you!"—How pleasant the summons of love!
　I hasten to meet thee where named in thy line;
With heart-bounding rapture I'm waiting to greet thee—
　To kiss thee, to bless thee, to tell thee I'm thine!
JAMES CROMB.

TURLUM.*

Gin ye ha'e thochts o' warldly care,
　　An' fain wad hint ye birl them,
Juist tak' a waucht o' caller air,
　　An' stap awa' to Turlum!
　　　　To Turlum tap, hurrah, hurrah!
　　　　Through briery bush an' birken shaw
　　　　We'll warsel bauldly till we craw
　　　　　Upo' the tap o' Turlum.

It's a' oor ain, the lan' we see,
　　Oor lips at lairds we curl them,
Feint ane has mair o' richt than we,
　　Wha speil the heichts o' Turlum!
　　　　To Turlum tap, hurrah, hurrah!
　　　　The lairds had better bide awa',
　　　　Or aiblins they may get a fa'
　　　　　As heich's the tap o' Turlum!

---

* A wooded hill in the neighbourhood of Crieff.

There's Sandy wi' the pawky mou',
  My faith, an' he could dirl them!
An' Jock, an' Hal, though douce the noo,
  Micht len' a han' on Turlum!
      To Turlum tap, hurrah, hurrah!
      Gin we the lairds should meet ava,
      Let's houp they'll no begin to craw
        Upo' the heichts o' Turlum!

Hurrah, my lads, the tap at last!
  Oor throats wi' will we'll dirl them,
The triumph's oors, the labour's past,
  We've struck the heichts o' Turlum.
      Hurrah, hurrah, for Turlum tap!
      For on the tap there is a cap,
      An' in that cap there is a drap—
        Here's to ye, bauld auld Turlum!

An' here's to Scotland's hills and plains,
  While bonnets heich we birl them;
The Scottish bluid loups in oor veins
  Upo' the heichts o' Turlum!
      For Turlum, lads, hip, hip, hurrah!
      An' sweet Strathearn, the pride o' a'!
      We're Scotia's sons, an' weel may blaw
        Upo' the heichts o' Turlum!

Again we'll make the welkin ring,
  As Scotia's sangs we skirl them,
An' may we never dowfier sing
  Than noo we sing on Turlum!
      Hurrah, for Turlum tap, hurrah!
      Aince mair, hurrah! an' then awa'
      We'll ne'er forget this day ower a'
        Upo' the heichts o' Turlum!

HENRY DRYERRE.

TWA AULD FOUK.

THERE'S twa auld folk I lo'e richt weel,
   An' twa auld fouk lo'e me,
Twa hairts I ken are kind an' leal,
   Whate'er the lave may be;
Twa heids weel straiked wi' carefu' grey,
   That think for me an' mine,
Twa pair o' een that mony a day
   Grat sair for me langsyne.
      O douce auld fouk, O dear auld fouk,
         How could I've dune withoot ye?
      I kenna if to laugh or greet
         As noo I sing aboot ye.

It's faither, mither—ye're the twa
   That to my heart are dear,
An' mony a nicht, tho' far awa',
   In thocht I see ye near.
There's no a breath o' caller air
   That blaws frae hameward airt;
But brings fond memories to my min',
   King feelings to my heart!

Doon, doon the years, sae swiftly flown,
   I see ye baith again,
Ere heads an' hearts had weary grown
   Wi' carefu' thocht an' pain.
I hear ye singin' at my bed,
   An' greet I kenna hoo,
I feel your han's upo' my head,
   Your kisses on my mou'.

I see ye strugglin' thro' the years
   To keep us snod an' braw,
I see the saut, saut burnin' tears
   Frae weary een doonfa'.

It's late an' ear' ye're up an' doon,
  For bairns that gi'e nae heed;
While a' the warl' is sleepin' soon,
  Ye're toilin' for oor bread.

But little kent ye when ye thocht
  Us a' in slumbers deep,
The little min's that wrocht an' wrocht,
  An', thinkin', couldna sleep.
It's faither this, an' mither that,
  For us work nicht an' day—
Oh, when we're men an' women, what
  For them will we no dae?

An' noo, an' noo ye're auld an' grey,
  And in the gloamin' licht,
An' tho' it's little to gi'e we ha'e,
  Ye're welcome to it the nicht.
An' may ye live until ye dee!
  An' whan ye dee, gae whaur
There's nocht to frichten you or me,
  Or than this warl' waur!

     O douce auld fouk, O dear auld fouk,
       How could I've dune withoot ye?
     I kenna if to lauch or greet
       As noo I sing aboot ye.
                    HENRY DRYERRE.

IT'S A' OWRE.

IT'S a' owre! it's a' owre!
  She gaed last nicht at ten;
Come in, gude neebours, come awa',
  An' lat me tak' ye ben.
Ye see, she's sleepin' sounder noo
  Than last ye cam' to spier,
She's quiet enouch, the bonnie doo,
  She'll wauk nae mair, the dear!

Oh, ay! she spak' na muckle o't,
   An' tho' she suffered sair,
We never heard her mak' complaint,
   Except, maybe, in prayer.
For whan she thochtna we were by,
   She'd aften sab an' greet,
An' eh! 'twas pitifu' to hear
   Her tearfu' voice sae sweet.

Na, na; he never cam' ava,
   Tho' aft he would, she said,
An' ilka stap upo' the stairs
   Would mak' her lift her head.
An' then she'd clasp her wee bit haun's,
   An' glower wi' startin' een,
Until the door was opened wide,
   An' unco faces seen.

Then doon upon her pillow white
   She'd fa' wi' weary sigh,
The tear-draps tricklin' frae her een,
   That scarce were ever dry.
Owre to the wa' she'd turn her face
   An' greet till sleep wad come,
An' tho' I tried to comfort her,
   I micht as weel been dumb.

Ay, but she was a bonnie lass,
   An' kind an' leal forbye,
An' tho' she may hae dune some wrang,
   'Twas no her blame, say I.
O laddie, whaursoe'er ye be,
   I dinna ken or care,
But muckle is the doot in me
   Gin ye hae acted fair.

Eh? tak' a payment, did ye say?
   Na, na; I'm weel content
To keep this bonnie locket, slipt
   Aneath her head unkent.

Twa locks o' glintin' gowden hair,
    In lovers' knottie wrocht—
Eh! but there's mony a sair, sair heart,
    Aince kiss'd withoot a thocht!

HENRY DRYERRE.

GLEN OGIL.

OH, bonnilie on Ogil the simmer sunlicht fa's,
  An' cantie croon the burnies by hill an' wooded glen,
An' I wad barter a' I win, an' lea' these city wa's,
  To spend in dear Glen Ogil six simmer days again.

The city's dust is on me, an' I am far awa';
  Nor mavis' mellow sang is heard, nor happy burnie's croon;
But aft, when labour's ended quite, an' gloamin' shadows a',
  The crested lapwing Memory in the lane glen settles doon.

The moorfowl's whirring cry I hear the grey hill slopes alang,
  The whaup's disconsolate wailin', the brawl o' muirland streams,
And weird, as in the days langsyne, the deep glen glacks amang,
  The hill winds are hallooin' doon the gorges o' my dreams!

The Perthshire hills are bonnie, Schiehallion's steep and hie,
  An' grandly rows the buirdly Tay by hut an' lordly ha';
But, gazin' on the wondrous scenes, a tear but dims the e'e,
  An' thochts o' sweet Glen Ogil will rise an' whirr awa'.

The hills abune Glen Ogil! I see them a' the day
   As veive as when I speel'd them in summer days langsyne—
The heather purples in my heart, the hill mists gather grey,
   An' the licht that glints on tarn and stream my saul will never tyne.

I lived and loved in Ogil, and, ah! what wad I no
   To live again, and lo'e again, in the days that are awa'?
But, by St. Tarland's misty 'croon, an' the subject glens below,
   I vow to see sweet Ogil yet, when simmer breezes blaw.

DAVID M. SMITH.

THE DEIL'S STANE.

EH, bairns! siccan cantrip the muckle deil played
   In the gruesome days langsyne;
Whan's huifs were heard on the laich hoose taps,
   An' his voice i' the roarin' linn.

This grey stane, beddit i' the glack o' the glen,
   Ance lay on the heich hill tap;
An' roond it at nichts i' the licht o' the mune,
   The deil he skirled an' lap.

An' ance on a time, when the win's blew lood,
   He lifted it whaur it lay;
An' lauched as he held it in his het luif,
   Syne whumilt it doon the brae.

O, muckle he lauch'd, an' lood he skirled,
   An' doon the hill spanked he;
But when he stoopit to lift the stane,
   'Twas firm as a rock i' the sea.

"Ho, ho!" quo' the deil, "sae I canna lift up
   A stane flung by my richt han'!
But here let it rest; what the deil canna do
   Is no in the pooer o' man."

An' he danced roond an' roond, an' lanched an' skirled,
   Whaur the grey stane's lyin' the noo;
Havers o' Grannie!—weel, the deil's sair misca'd,
   But this, bonnie bairns, is true,

That the big, big stane o' his ugsome pooer
   He has flung on the sauls o' men;
An' neither oor strength, nor the deil himsel',
   Can lift it up again.

DAVID M. SMITH.

THE MAIDEN WHA SHORE IN THE BANDWIN WI' ME.*

O BONNIE blooms the heather on Formal hill,
   When waves the ripe corn aroun' Corrielea!
'Twas there I first saw bonnie Maggie Cargill,
   The maiden wha shore in the bandwin wi' me;
     A weel-faured young maiden,
     A winsome young maiden,
   The maiden wha shore in the bandwin wi' me.

---

* The days of "bandwins" passed with the extinction of the "hewk" as the universal implement in harvest work, and the introduction of the swing scythe, so speedily superseded by the reaping machine, and many persons even in country places will ere long not be able to tell what a "bandwin" was. In the days when the harvest fields were wholly cleared by the reaping hook—and that not so very long ago—one person, male or female, was delegated to bind, and set in stooks the sheaves shorn by a certain number of shearers, more or less according to the deftness of the operators and the quality of the crop, and each set so appointed formed a "bandwin." Universal as this custom was, and commonly as the word has been used to indicate the order of harvest work described, Mr. Robertson is the first, so far as I have seen, to celebrate it in song, For this fact, as well as for its inherent beauty, his song deserves to become popular.

An' O, but the lassie was gentle and lo'esome!
   I ne'er will forget the love-glance o' her e'e;
Her lang raven locks flowin' roun' her white bosom,
    A Ruth 'mang the reapers seemed Maggie to me;
       A dark-eyed young maiden,
       A lovely young maiden,
   The maiden wha shore in the bandwin wi' me.

Her mien i' the corn-field was gracefu' an' queenly,
   Though lowly her kindred aroun' Corrielea;
Native beauty an' grace shone aroun' her serenely:
    She was peerless wha shore in the bandwin wi' me—
       An artless young maiden,
       A matchless young maiden,
   The maiden wha shore in the bandwin wi' me.

In hairst-time we twa shore the same rig thegither;
   At high-twal we rested aneath the same tree;
At e'en fondly pairted, the ane frae the ither,
    Near her ain mither's cot richt abune Corrielea;
       A loving young maiden,
       A guileless young maiden,
   The maiden wha shore in the bandwin wi' me.

But ah, cruel Fate! when last autumn had gane,
   An' winter storms raged roun' the hills o' Glenshee,
The ill-starred young lassie gaed forth her lea-lane;
    Her ewie had strayed far ayont Corrielea.
       A tender young maiden,
       A kind-hearted maiden,
   The maiden wha shore in the bandwin wi' me.

We scoured hill an' dale till the gloamin', syne hurried
   A search in the glen as far up as Glenshee,
An' there in a snaw-wreath the lassie lay buried—
    Ah! lifeless, the maid wha my bride was to be!
       Waes me for the maiden!
       My loved an' lost maiden!
   The maiden wha shore in the bandwin wi' me.

Ceased the storm, an' through clud-rifts the munelicht
    fell streamin'
On her face—oh, I'll mind o't whaure'er I shall be !
An' I couldna hae tauld was I wauken or dreamin'
    When they bore my deid maid ower the snaw-covered
    lea.
        No a tear for my maiden,
        Nor a sab for my maiden ;
But my hert bruik, an' oh ! hoo I wished I micht dee !

In Ouchterga'en kirkyaird, all under the willow,
    She lies wha was sweeter than life unto me ;
Sae I will awa' ower the deep ragin' billow,
    For Maggie Cargill never mair I shall see !
        Alas ! the dear maiden !
        Alack ! the sweet maiden !
The maiden wha shore in the bandwin wi' me.

Frae scenes o' my youth nae mair joy can I borrow,
    Despairin' I wander aroun' Corrielea ;
On a far foreign strand I maun hide a heart-sorrow
    For the maiden wha shore in the bandwin wi' me ;
        Then adieu to the maiden !
        My fondly loved maiden !
And adieu to the loved scenes aroun' Corrielea !
                WILLIAM ROBERTSON.

A MAY SONG.

HILLY ho ! hilly ho ! hark the bugle horn,
Proclaiming the dawn of the glad May morn !
Come where the wild flowers the greenwood adorn—
    'Tis May, vernal May.

The young lambkin sports on the gowany lea,
The blythe birdie warbles love-notes on the tree,
The May sun is shining athwart the blue sea—
    'Tis May, gladsome May.

The greensward is gleaming with pearly dew,
The skylark is piping far up in the blue,
Come, my love, come, I am waiting for you—
    'Tis May, charming May.

May flowers are blooming on meadow and hill,
They bloom on the banks of the glittering rill;
They bloom round the homestead, the church, and the mill—
    'Tis May, blushing May.

Come, my love, come, to the woodlands gay,
While the sun's bright beams 'mong the dewdrops play,
For bright is the morn of the opening day
    Of May, beautiful May.

Let us hie o'er the heath to fair Murthly's dell,
Where the primroses grow and the fairies dwell,
And we'll pledge a love-cup o'er the Bog-bush Well—
    'Tis May, joyous May.

Hilly ho! hilly ho! 'tis the bugle horn,
Resounding afar o'er the wild Muir-o'-Thorn,
Where sparkles the dew of the bright May morn—
    Come away, love, away!

WILLIAM ROBERTSON.

SONNET.

To Chaucer.

CHAUCER! when in my breast, as autumn wanes,
  Sweet Hope begins to droop—fair flowers that grew
    With the glad prime, and bloomed the summer through—
Thou art my chiefest solace. It sustains
My faltering faith, which coming fogs and rains
  Might else to their dull element subdue,
  That the rude season's spite can ne'er undo
The spring perennial that in thee remains.

Nor need I stir beyond the cricket's chime
  Here in the ingle-nook—the cuckoo's cry
    Hushed on the hillside, meadows all forlorn—
  To breathe the freshness of an April morn.
Mated with thee, thy cheerful minstrelsy
Feeding the vernal heart through winter's clime.

DAVID M. MAIN.

SONNET.

To a favourite evening retreat, near Glasgow.

O LOVED wild hillside, thou hast been a power
  Not less than books, greater than preacher's art,
  To heal my wounded spirit, and my heart
Retune to gentle thoughts, that hour on hour
Must languish in the city, like a flower
  In wayside dust, while on the vulgar mart
  We squander for scant gold our better part
From morn till eve, in frost, and sun, and shower!
My soul breaks into singing as I haste,
  Day's labour ended, towards thy sylvan shrine
  Of rustling beech, hawthorn, and eglantine;
  And, wandering in thy shade, I dream of thee
As of green pastures 'mid the desert waste,
  Wells of sweet water in the bitter sea.

DAVID M. MAIN.

PISCATOR DOLOROSUS.

  YE see them a' there—
  Twa dizzen an' mair,
Fillin' up half o' the creel;
  They're bonnie an' fair,
  But they canna compare
Wi' the monster that broke frae my reel.

Deep, deep the stream in
I saw his sides gleamin',
He was four feet lang, an', nae boast,
Was twal pun' at least;
Look'd a saumon amaist,
This wonderfu' troot that I lost!

'Twas doon by the rushes
Whaur the stream hushes
Its sang for a maument awee;
Whaur in the still deep
It tak's a bit sleep,
Ere it sets its face to the sea:
Abune the greystane
That lies there its lane
As my flee was sailin' across't,
Far doon it was sookit,
An' sair he was hookit,
This terrible fish that I lost.

Wi' a wallop an' splash,
A rush an' a dash,
He snuived doon the river fu' braw;
O sair was my trouble,
My rod it bent double,
An' my breath it swarft clean awa'.
Hoo he lap an' flang
An' wi' a great spang
Ten feet in the air he was toss'd,
My heart gae a sten',
My hair stood on en',
A-playing that big fish that I lost!

His back fin—a sail;
The breadth o' his tail
Wad measure twall inches an' twa,
A great muckle felly—
An' O, what a belly,
'Twas just jike a hillside o' snaw!

    An' as for his length,
    An' as for his strength,
Thae baith I ken to my cost;
    My line's a' awa',
    My rod broke in twa,
Wi' that awfu' fish that I lost.

    In the stir an' the strife
    O' the river o' life,
This is what fouk tell us fu' aft,
    They mak' the lood maen
    Their fish that are gane
Are no' like the fish that they've gaff'd.
    When rinnin' a race,
    When gettin' a place,
Or landin' some canty bit post,
    Keep still an' say naething,
    But be sure o' ae thing,
It's aye their best fish that they've lost.

    But hover a blink,
    I'd hae ye to think,
When 'wailin' lost battles ye've focht,
    Hae ye nae a doot
    The loss o' yon troot
Was mair for your gude than ye thocht.
    Your mind it was on't,
    Your heart set upon't,
O' gudes it wad bring ye a host;
    But your courage up-pluck,
    An' thank mair than your luck
That yon braw "speckled beauty" ye've lost.

                    REV. PETER ANTON.

THE LAUCH IN THE SLEEVE.

THERE'S a smile that is bitter, a smile that is sweet;
There's the coarse loud guffaw o' the taproom and street;
There's the smile the-maiden gives to her lover,
The smirk that the hollow heart helps to discover.
At the jest o' the wise there's the smile that comes after;
And hark to that thunder, 'tis 'Teufelsdrockh's laughter!
But with Sara's I pass them, and give them their leave,
To sing the best o' them a', the lauch in the sleeve.
 The lauch in the sleeve, the lauch in the sleeve,
 It's skailin' wi' meanin', the lauch in the sleeve.

Is your heart ever sair wi' fouk's stories an' lees,
Wi' their tweedle-dee-dums and their tweedle-dee-dees?
Or broken in twa wi' their pride and assumption,
Their plenty o' cheek, and scant rummelgumption?
Is your heart ever sick o' their chit and their chat,
Wi' their reasons for this, and their reasons for that?
Fash ye never your thoomb, nor clench ye your nieve,
But just up wi' your elbuck and lauch in your sleeve!
 Aye lauch in your sleeve, aye lauch in your sleeve,
 Just up wi' your elbuck and lauch in your sleeve.

Are you ever sair tempted a letter to pen,
A just cause to mak' guid in the sight o' a' men?
Are you ever inclined at a word or a worry
To raise up your rung, or to get in a flurry?
Is your brain ever burnin' some fool to expose—
To shut up his coarse mouth, to disjoint a' his nose?
Sic designs put awa' wi', and find your reprieve
In that guid ancient comfort, the lauch in the sleeve.
 The lauch in the sleeve, the lauch in the sleeve,
 A glorious comfort's the lauch in the sleeve.

There's a story that comes frae auld Grecian days
O' twa* wise men well kent for their saws an' their says—
For the fauts o' his fellows the ane's heart was aye het,
And his cheeks wi' his tears they were never but wet;

---

* Heraclitus and Democritus.

But as for the ither—what a pawky auld man !—
No' to greet, but to lauch, he aye found the best plan ;
The ane sune dwined awa', for he ceased na to grieve,
But the ither lived lang, for he laucht in his sleeve.
   He laucht in his sleeve, he laucht in his sleeve,
   It's the way to lang life, to lauch in your sleeve.

To flee in a passion at you hardly ken what,
To gang argie and bargie wi' this ane and that ;
To see nae way ava' your wrangs how to heal up,
But gie this man a clour and that man a keelup—
Such thochts are a' vain. Brithers, ponder it well,
The far better plany—the bit lauch to yoursel',
Tak' you what scheme you like your fu' heart to relieve—
But you're sure to do weel if you lauch in your sleeve.
   If you lauch in your sleeve, just lauch in your sleeve,
   Aye victor you'll be if you lauch in your sleeve.

REV. PETER ANTON.

THE VALLEY OF THE SHADOW.

In the Valley of the Shadow
Dark the road is, rough and narrow.
We into the darkness staring
See no path for those wayfaring ;
On its cruel rocks and flowerless
Sure the foot of man were powerless,
And we hearken, but we hear nought
Save the murmurs to our ear brought,
Where the turgid swollen river
Sullenly flows on for ever
Through the Valley of the Shadow.

In the Valley of the Shadow
Dark the road is, rough and narrow.
Who shall guide our gentle sister—
Take her by the hand, assist her—

Timid is she, shrinking, tender—
Who shall from its perils defend her ?
Fitter path for her the meadows
With their chastened lights and shadows,
Where the placid flowing river
Calmly sings of peace for ever.
Give her in her pure white vestures
Quiet waters and green pastures;
Not for her the gloomy pathway
Where no sun is, gleam, nor star ray,
O'er the rocks and by the river
With its dirge which halteth never,
In the Valley of the Shadow.

In the Valley of the Shadow
Dark the road is, rough and narrow.
Still she lingers to us clinging
While the summons they are bringing,
For the fell decree is spoken,
And we cry in accents broken—
"Why should He, the Eternal, slay thee,
Perfect as a woman may be ?
Leave to earth the pure-souled maiden,
Take us rather, the sin-laden
Through the Valley of the Shadow."

In the Valley of the Shadow
Dark the road is, rough and narrow.
Unlike her, our gentle sister,
We have lost the morning lustre;
Dew of youth has from us faded;
Battle-scarred we are and jaded,
And our armour bright is rusted,
And our souls with stains are crusted.
We endured but yet have fainted,
And our lives are not untainted
With the darkening lines of error :
Still into the vale of terror
Would we go, the world-hardened,

Praying that our sins be pardoned,
So might she the pure and stainless
Find a pathway smooth and painless
Through the Valley of the Shadow.

From the Valley of the Shadow
(Dark the road is, rough and narrow)
Comes an answer—" Every mortal
Wends at last unto this portal."
Innocent she may be wholly,
Timid, still she enters solely ;
Human love can not attend her,
Human arms can not defend her ;
She must tread alone the pathway
Where no sun is, gleam, nor star ray,
O'er the rocks and by the river
With the dirge that halteth never :
Shield her cannot, friend or brother,
Sister dear, or father, mother !
Yet The Presence, all abiding,
Even in that gloom is hiding—
In the Valley of the Shadow.

In the Valley of the Shadow
Dark the road is, rough and narrow.
O, Divine Almighty Brother !
By the goodness, we implore Thee,
Of the gentle heart that bore Thee—
By Thy pure and virgin mother—
Be not Deity—be human,
Be to her as tender woman,
Keep her in Thy kind embraces
Through the dark and lonesome places,
Soothe her fears until she hear not
The hoarse murmurs of the river,
Give her courage till she fear not
Darkness there that broods for ever,
In the Valley of the Shadow.

In the Valley of the Shadow
Guide her through the gorges narrow,
Till the light of heaven, gleaming,
To the shadow-land is streaming,
Till the songs they sing for ever
Drown the murmurs of the river,
Till its waves, the gloom forsaking,
On the pearly gates are breaking,
Where the pure have their abode
In the citadel of God.

JAMES Y. GEDDES.

A TALE O' KIRRIE.

THE breath o' summer, the caller air,
Are no to be boucht wi' gathered gear;

The winter snell and bitter cauld
May be dear to breasts that are bare an' bauld.

Twa tinker bodies—a man and wife—
Had led for years a stravagin' life;

But auld age cam', an' the pair grew douce,
To settle doon they hae boucht a hoose.

They blankets boucht, and they boucht a bed,
An' sat them doon wi' a roof owerhead;

An' 'oors on end by the chimley cheek
Frae twa auld clay pipes they blew the reek;

An' there in state like a king and queen
They windered hoo tinkers they could hae been.

But the wastlin' winds cam' sighin' in;
O' a pratlin' burn they heard the din.

An' the wind broucht in the scent o' woods;
They saw through the panes the snaw-white cluds.

A hingin' branch that was blawn aboot
Tapped on the glass to wile them oot.

The sparrows cam' to the window pane,
Mavis an blackbird mony an ane.

They keekit in at the crouchin' pair
An' speered "What are they daein' there?"

An' they whistled—"A fig for reprobates
Wha turn their backs on their time-tried mates."

The pair at nicht couldna sleep a wink;
O' the stars they missed the freendly blink.

The rustlin' leaves an' the patterin' shower
Hushed na them ower as they did before.

O, uneasy lie on cauf the heads
That ken the fragrance o' heather beds.

The four stane wa's seemed creepin' in,
They scarce could breathe as they lay within.

In the morn they ta'en ilk ithers han's,
Hung ower their shouthers their pots an' pans,

An' leavin' behin' their but an' ben
They ta'en to their life in the woods again.

JAMES Y. GEDDES.

LORD RUTHVEN;
Or, THE WAES O' DUPPLIN FIELD.*

"FAUSE Baliol's bark is o'er the wave,
  It has touched the Scottish strand;
Then, hey! for the norlan' axe an' glaive
  'Gainst Southron bow an' brand.

---

* Donald, Earl of Mar, was Regent at the time of the battle of Dupplin.

'Gae licht a blaze on the castle knowe,
  Let the red cross speed thro' the glen,
For this deed will wauken a kindred lowe
  In the hearts o' my trusty men.

"Already brave Maxton an' stout Lord Grahame
  Hae up an' ridden awa';
An' sall Ruthven lag like a hind at hame
  When the gatherin' pibrochs blaw?"

Thus spake Lord Ruthven o' Huntin'tower.
  As he strode the chamber roun';
Like the simmer sun frae its mornin' bower
  Sweet Ellen cam' glintin' doon.

"Come, Ellen, lace ye my corslet fast,
  An' awa' wi' the lave I'll gae;
But, Ellen, why do you seem dooncast?
  O, my leddy, you look wae!"

She flung her arms around his neck;
  Was ever heart sae true?
The tears cam' drappin' doon her cheek
  Like the mornin' blobes o' dew.

An' saft her yellow ringlets bright
  Slid frae the silken band,
An' wandered doon like threads o' light,
  Till they touched his mailed hand.

She said: "My lord, you are sick an' sair,
  Wi' that auld scaur in yer side;
Tak' heed! tak' heed, ere forth you fare
  Ower anither field to ride.

"For I dreamt yestreen that my ain true knicht
  On a luckless field lay slain,
Never to ride by the Regent's side
  Wi' his bonnie bands again.

"O, I thocht I strayed through a forest wide,
　　An' mony a sheugh I cross'd;
An' the leaves fell doon on ilka side,
　　As though seared by sudden frost.

"An' syne I cam' to a dowie stream,
　　O, the bank was rough an' steep;
But a terrible shadow within my dream
　　Seem'd to urge me to the deep.

"An' aye I faucht wi' the jawin' wave,
　　Faucht sair, but never gat through;
For it hemm'd me in like a living grave,
　　Sae I clung mair close to you.

"Syne my dream was changed, an' on Dupplin heicht
　　I stood at the midnight hour;
The wan moon glimmered athwart the nicht
　　Wi' a cauld an' death-like glower.

"Then there cam' a soond frae the waterside
　　Like a steed's impatient neigh
When the mailed ranks to battle ride
　　An' the slogan swells on high.

"An' a lurking foe made sudden rush
　　Our startled tents amang;
On! on they did push through brake an' bush,
　　Till bills* an' broadswords rang.

"But our stately bands seemed a' in a rout,
　　An' the foe did them pursue;
O, I wat it wasna a Scottish shout
　　That pierced the welkin through.

"An' wha did I see but my ain gude lord
　　On that heath sae mirk an' chill;
A broken brand ye clutched i' yer hand,
　　But the hand was cauld an' still!"

* The bill was a weapon used by the English infantry.

Up spak her lord wi' a kind, kind glance:
  "Sweet Ellen, I gang awa';
But fear nae, love, that sic foul mischance
  Sall our bonnie bands befa'.

"For our youthfu' monarch's royal richt
  We ha'e drawn the sword this day;
An' yon fair sun sall be quenched in nicht
  Ere we own this king o' strae. *

"But my leddy will laugh at sic needless fears,
  An' dance me a sprightly fling,
When, to welcome our victorious spears,
  St. Johnstone's bells will ring."

The beacon blazed on the castle knowe,
  The red cross flashed through the glen,
An' Lord Ruthven marched frae St. Johnstone's gates
  Wi' a thousand kilted men.

O, I wat they were a comely sight
  That day, as they marched awa';
But Ellen gazed on that pageant bright
  Wi' cheeks maist like the snaw.

O, she waited lang, an' she waited late,
  The day broke sweet an' fair;
But a horseman stood at St. Johnstone's gate
  Wi' the tidings o' black despair.

An' St. Johnstone's bell rang a mournfu' knell
  As a bier came sad an' slow;
Then, as fa's the flower i' the bladdin' shower,
  The gowden head sunk low.

In their mailed arms they raised her up
  Frae the cauld turf where she lay;
An' they pressed the cup to her pallid lip,
  But the true heart throbbed nae mae.

---

* "King of Straw" was a name given to both the Baliols in derision.

So they brought her lord, an', side by side,
   They were laid in a stately tomb,
The knicht that had fa'en in manhood's pride
   An' the lady in beauty's bloom.

WILLIAM PYOTT.

SUNLICHT AN' MUNELICHT.

SUNLICHT an' Munelicht they met on the hill,
Says Sunlicht to Munelicht, "You're cauldrife an' chill,
Wi' your wan drumlie visage gae sleep i' the sea,
Or I'll kill ye outricht wi' ae glance o' my e'e.

"I'm the King o' the Dawn, I'm the darling o' day,
Frae the croon o' the lift a' the world I survey;
Frae the morn's rosy lap, as I whisk out my beams,
I straw pearls on the mountains an' gowd on the streams.

"But you, you gang glowerin' an' glimmerin' on high,
Fouk think you're a ghaist as you sail through the sky,
An' for licht or for warmth you are no worth a flee—
Losh! you buik unco sma' i' the big warld's e'e."

Said Munelicht to Sunlicht, "You shine unco bricht,
But if you're King o' Day, I'm the Queen o' the Nicht;
E'en the stars haud their breath as I rise ower the hill,
And mount on the breist o' the midnicht sae still.

"I girdle wi' silver the grey granite Ben,
I chase the dim shadows frae muirland an' glen;
An' the traveller belated aft blesses my ray,
When you're roamin' in far lands, thou bright god o' day."

Nae mair could I hear o' the crack o' the twa;
But as wee modest Munelicht slade canny awa,
I thocht to mysel' that some use we micht be,
Though we buik unco sma' i' the big warld's e'e.

Tho' we canna a' shine wi' the splendour o' morn,
Yet some cauld nook o' earth we may help to adorn;
E'en a kind word or look to some heart sunk in wae
Yet may bloom in the licht o' eternity's day.

There was Ane that cam' down frae the mansions o' licht
Though His glory was dimmed 'mid our warld's weary nicht,
Yet for puir fallen man He was willing to dee,
And to buik unco sma' in the big warld's e'e.

WILLIAM PYOTT

THE TOLLMAN'S LAMENT.*

Nae langer can I haud my peace,
Sad day to me an' a' my race,
The toll—the toll will hae to cease
    In half an-'oor,
Syne carts an' carriages an' bea's
    May pass like stoor.

Nae mair I'll hear the cheery cry
"T-o-a-l!" frae the drivers drawin' nigh,
Nor see them rype their pouch, while I
    Haud oot my loof,
But a' ken-kind my noo gae by
    Wi' prancin' hoof.

Already in my mind I see
Some farmer pass wi' chucklin' glee;
But whan they'll send him in a wee
    The amount in taxes,
A Heelan' wether's face 'ill be
    No half sae black's his.

---

* Toll-bars were abolished in Perthshire, as also in most other counties in Scotland, at midnight on the 15th of May, 1879, and by and by the custom of levying toll for vehicular traffic on the principal highways of the country may have to be explained, but so long as Mr. Craig's graphic and clever "Lament" survives, knowledge of the Tollman and his little ways will be obtainable.

Look hoo the schule rates gaed aboon
Fouks thochts, an' garr'd them change their tune—
You'll see a hash ere a' be dune,
    Wi' Boords creatin',
They need a gey lang-shankit spoon
        That sup wi' Satan.

I mind o' speerin' at a showman,
Aboot a beast wi' an uncommon
Humph on 't's back, just like Ben Lomon',
    Ere ye ascend it,
What was the matter wi't, an' so man
        He soon explained it.

He said that ance *ae* hin'most strae
Broke what he cau't its vertybrae,
An' what mair warnin' wad ye hae
    O what's to happen on 's,
Whan ance we're fixed aneath this a'e,
        Board mair they're stappin' on 's.

I'm sure *I* needna care for ane;
But lang afore a twalmonth's gane
Ye'll a' be wishin' that ye'd taen
    My soond advice,
An' left the tollman's gates alane
        At ony price.

As lang's they may lat fouk be jolly,
Richt soon they'll come to see their folly,
For though I've keepit on the toll aye,
    T' was nae to make o't,
This mony a year I've kept it solely
        Just for the sake o't.

Whan first my tollin' days began,
Langsyne whan the "Defiance" ran,
Thae were the times—oh they were gran'!
    Wi' ten-score droves,
An' strings o' carts—to think on't man
        My bosom hoves.

Weel micht my trade be ca't a roarin' ane,
I sell't a dram, an' keepit corn, an'
Hay for horses. Frae the forenoon
    I didna slack,
A' through the nicht until the mornin'
    Began to brak'.

Whan market nichts were wearin' late,
My fouk wad never tak' the gate,
So I bo'ed gie them for a treat
    A hool o' cheese,
Or dry cod fish, an' ham to eat
    As saut's the seas.

Syne ye may guess I had a yokin'
Afore their drooth began to slocken,
Aye i' the push the necks were broken
    Smash aff the bottles,
Fast as I broke they had them glockin'
    Adoon their throttles.

Thae times were far ower guid to last,
Misfortune followed, blast for blast,
Forbes MacKenzie's Act was pass'd,
    An' took awa
My "leeshince." Railways followed fast
    An' ruined a'.

Thae "lines" hae skaed puir fouk nae little,
Just look hoo mony a' ane they mittle,
Heich prices too for corn an' victual
    They've broucht to pass—
Tattie disease an' paddock spittle
    Upon the grass.

Noo-days, nae flesh-kind can we keep,
But chockit kye, an' braxy sheep,
The fatness o' the land, gaes wheep
    Awa to Englan',
An' what comes back—the laird's hae't deep
    I' their pouches jinglin'.

At this toll business few were smarter,
I ne'er compounded wi' a carter,
Nor wi' a hawker made a barter
    An' wasna't richt ?
I never ance allowed a quarter
    By twal at nicht.

Oh hoo my heart beat fast an' high
Whan i' the distance I did spy,
A dizzen caravans come nigh
    An' wasna't strange,
Aye whan a laird's turn-out gaed by
    I ne'er had change.

At the toll-roup I had nae nerve,
(I kept a bidder in reserve)
An' so whan I began to swerve
    The lave were scaured,
But whan the hammer fell—observe
    My name was heard.

For years its been my special likin',
In the bow-window to sit bykin',
Or stannin' starin' like a pike in
    Hope to see
A vehicle—syne I'm ready, rykin'
    Oot for my fee.

Laith frae the business I'm to part
It gaed sae kindly wi' my heart,
Stop, stop ! I see a cocker's cart
    Comin' pell-mell,
I'll maybe nailt—it's past my art !
    It's chappin' twel' !

Whan public servants quat their station
They a' get superannuation,
But in this great an' wealthy nation
    How is't the sole men
That canna win at compensation
    Are the puir tollmen ?

I'm thinkin' on a plan to calm
My speerits, an' to pour the balm
O' consolation on my palm.
    I'll try an' get
To watch—ance I hae learn't a psalm—
    Some kirk-door plate.

This change my heart has sorely stricken,
It's taen awa the wee bit pickin'
I made sae honestly to thicken
    My daily kail;
I'm maistly like to dwawm an' sicken,
    Sae deep's my wail.

Yea, up in Athole—I hae word
The Prince o' Tollmen's grane is heard,
Wi' droopin' head an' een a' blear't,
    Aneath his trees
He walks, while tear draps spot the yird
    Like lost bawbees.

Lament wi' lamentations deep;
My brethren a' bewail an' weep,
For if ye bang up through your sleep
    Whan carts gae by,
Toom-handit noo ye'll hae to creep
    Inower—Ou' aye!

                      JOHN CRAIG.

JEANIE BROWN.

O MONY a mornin' that glints fu' braw
    But heralds a dowie day,
An' flooers that sweet i' the springtime blaw
    Aft droop i' th' month o' May.
An' sae it happened in days lang gane
    That a sair grief bowed us doon,
As the shadow grew on the cauld hearthstane
    O' oor ain dear Jeanie Brown.

Our ain dear Jeanie, our sweetest wean,
   O her life ran on wi' glee,
Till the day that her hand was socht by ane
   Wha had nae true heart to gie.
He cam' wi' his pride, an' his gifts sae braw,
   An' he pressed sae hard an' lang
That our lassie e'en threw her life awa'—
   O hoo did we lat her gang?

He tane her awa wi' her leal young heart,
   Sae happy, an' pure, an' free,
To a hame where the joy o' the better part
   We kenn'd there wad never be.
A hame unhallowed by word o' prayer,
   Or thocht o' the land aboon,
Where grief aye grew into dark despair,
   Till her life's short day was dune.

O we're dowie aft i' the gloamin' noo
   As we sit where the shadows fa',
An' our een grow dim wi' a holy dew,
   For her that's been lang awa'.
But we're mindin' aye, the gudewife an' me,
   As the weary years gang roun',
O' the cludless land where we hope to see
   Our ain lost Jeanie Brown.

JAMES CRAIG.

THE SUN'S ON THE HEATHER.

Ho comrades! the skirmisher rain-clouds
   Are over the seas and away,
The lakes and the mountains are smiling,
   The sun's on the heather to-day.

The sun's on the heather, I trow, lads;
   There's light on the brown mossy brae;
There's joy in the bickering hill streams
   That fall in a glory of spray.

And here in the depths of the city
   My fancy is ever astray,
My heart's with the kings of the Highlands;
   I see them, I hear what they say.

Ben Lomond looks down his long valley,
   Afar to the Bass and the May,
And sees all the myriad flashes
   Of Forth on her wildering way.

There, too, is the lofty Ben Lawers—
   Breadalbane is under his sway—
His loch is a blaze of pure silver,
   The sun's on his heather to-day.

Schiehallion speaks only in Gaelic,
   I hardly know what he would say,
But Rannoch is heather all over,
   And—the sun's on the heather to-day.

See! there are the grand Cairngorms,
   Afar in the shimmering ray,
Their blue bonnets merrily bobbing—
   Hooch! reels to the music of Spey!

Let's off from the soot of the city!
   We're off for a month and a day
To the hills, and the glorious heather—
   Hooray! (caps in air, lads) hooray!

                    JAMES CRAIG.

MY FATHER AN' MY MITHER.

A JOY surpassin' feeble praise
   Brings tears aft to my een,
When pictures o' my laddie days
   Appear on memory's screen.

Wi' fitfu' flash they come an' go,
  Each following up the ither;
An' aye I see in sunny glow
  My father an' my mither.

> My father an' my mither, lads,
>   They've trauchled lang thegither;
> May blessin's fa' upon the twa—
>   My father an' my mither.

They struggled hard to gi'e us lear,
  That we micht a' obtain
A higher place, an' burdens bear
  Less heavy than their ain.
I bless them noo for what they've dune,
  An' while life's storm they weather
My heartfelt prayer shall rise abune
  For father an' for mither.

I mind we made the kettle sing,
  To cheer them, tired and lame;
An' cheerie did oor voices ring
  To gi'e them welcome hame.
At ilka cheek we set their chairs,
  While circled round we'd gather,
An' tell oor little griefs an' cares
  To father an' to mither.

When ower the earth nicht's mantle fell,
  An' joined us a' at e'en—
The picture mak's my bosom swell—
  I'll ne'er forget the scene—
Oor laddie cares awa' we hurled
  When rompin' a' thegither,
An' king an' queen o' oor sma' world
  Was father aye and mither.

Ye stirrin' pictures o' the past,
  I'm wae when ye depart;
I love to be thus backward cast
  To laddiehood in heart.

    Come aft an' guide my thochts awa'
      Frae earth's cauld heartless swither,
    To childhood's scenes sae artless a'—
      To father an' to mither.

        My father an' my mither, lads,
          They trauchled lang thegither;
        May blessings fa' upon the twa—
          My father an' my mither.
JOHN PAUL.

'ΕΣ 'ΑΕΙ.

O STARS, that will rise and shine
For other eyes than mine,
When these are rapt with the radiance of light divine;
O stars, will ye tell of me true;
As I have spoken of you,
Will ye shine far brighter than stars unsung could do?

O night, who hast trusted me
Such secrets deep and free,
As told ye had spoken with others, ere I with thee;
Wilt pass from mind as sight,
Because it is written: No night?
Will thy face lean forth from some gladsomer gleam of
    light?

O hills, that will catch the glow
When I'm in the Long-ago,
Will ye break yourselves open for other hearts to know?
Will one in the After say,
When the sunset's too fair for the day:
He is singing this scene on the hills that are far away?
REV. ROBERT W. BARBOUR.

A HIGHLAND FUNERAL.

"LORD, THOU HAST BEEN OUR DWELLING PLACE IN ALL GENERATIONS."

ONCE more we meet in the old retreat,
   The home roof over us once again ;
But the old walls wake to the bearers' feet,
   And the old rooms sob with the mourners' train—
  'Tis the old, old home again,
   But the old dwellers will not remain.

So we bear her out to the mountain side,
   For the hills are an older sort of home,
And better, they say, will the mountains bide
   And the heath thatch over the dark peat loom.
  Oh ! this is an older home,
   Where the feet of her childhood used to roam.

The hills rise round us as we rise,
   As they rose to Him who gave them birth,
Creation's dawn-look in their eyes,
   And their witness-feet fixt fast in earth,
  Attesting as at birth,
   Till our thoughts are spurred to the heavens' far-spanning girth ;

His heaven Whose home is everywhere,
   And all within His ken is home
Who sleeps with the dust we scatter here,
   Who sleeps not, over that crystal dome,
  Where she is awake and at home,
   Whither her spirit in living slowly clomb.

So we aye shall meet in an old retreat,
   A home-roof over us evermore,

One house to the lords whose rest is sweet,
  And the servants busy about the door,
One dwelling-place evermore,
In Whose going and coming we rest and rejoice and adore.

REV. ROBERT W. BARBOUR.

TWILIGHTS.

JUST when the night is casting
  Her curtain over me,
A sense of the everlasting
  A moment comes. I see
Strange lights in the westering sunward,
  And hasten it with a hymn;
When I turn my eyes again downward,
  My book is dim.

Just when the soul is weary
  With watching of herself,
And even the desk is dreary,
  And dreary is the shelf,
A calm clear call comes to me
  From the Blessed and the Beyond—
Bright fire-burst, oh how gloomy,
  Free fancy, oh how bond.

Just when the darkness presses
  I do not care to own,
And I cling to these strange caresses
  To make me not all alone,
When the silver streaks grow slender
  And the pencils shadow long,
I make the moment tender
  With a song.

REV. ROBERT W. BARBOUR.

THE WEAVER'S BAIRN.

A BONNIE bairn was Annie More,
    The flower o' a' the toun :
A guileless bairn, owre young to ken
    Her brow wore beauty's crown.

At gloamin', at the waterside,
    Amang the bairns was she;
And passers-by had wondered aft
    Wha that sweet bairn might be.

Her red lips parted wi' a smile
    That was like mornin' light,
And showed how that young heart looked out
    And saw the world a' bright.

A weaver's bairn was that sweet wean;
    Her faither at the loom
Worked late and early, thinkin' ne'er
    That labour's life was gloom.

For still between him and his toil,
    A lovely vision gleamed;
And when he dreamed of future days,
    'Twas for that bairn he dreamed.

She was the a'e flower o' his hame,
    A winsome flower o' spring;
'Twas nae mean hame, for round the hearth
    Were angels hovering.

For her sake, night and morn, he thought
    The angels aye cam' near,
Where that sweet bairn had lisped a prayer
    What could there be to fear?

Her mither, wi' her pale rose cheek,
    Was glad o' Annie's bloom;
She couldna think that ought sae fair
    Was near an earthly tomb.

She said, "Though painfu' days are mine
    And aft I'm droopin' sair,
This bonnie bairn uplifts my heart
    As health were mine ance mair.

"The queen has her bright crown o' gold,
    The duke his bonnie lands,
His lady has her jewelled rings
    For sma' and dainty hands.

"They canna think like John and me,
    Wha have our bread to earn,
We have nae wealth in a' the warld,
    But just oor bonnie bairn.

"The golden curls upon her head
    To us are gowd enou';
And ilka morn it's joy to meet
    Her laughin' e'en sae blue.

"Oh, bairnie! God in heaven is kind;
    I thank Him ever mair,
Wha lets me keep thee in my arms,
    Through grief, and pain, and care."

The bairnie, wi' her wonderin' e'en,
    Looked in her mither's face.
The mystery of death had yet
    In her young soul no place.

But fever to the toun was brought,
    And to the kirkyard sune,
Wee graves wi' new turned turf were seen
    Aneath the waxin' mune.

And Annie, in her loveliness,
    Lay meekly down to dee,
Just saying when her wee heart sank,
    "Oh, mither! bide wi' me."

"I'm here, my bairn," she said, but sune
   Ye canna ca' for me.
Yer rosy cheek is white as snaw;
   I'm feared ye're gaun to dee."

The bairnie opened her blue een,
   And saw her mother's tears.
A light seemed in her soul to wake,
   As from no childish years.

"Oh, mither! am I gaun to dee?
   Oh, faither dinna greet,
For Christ will take me np to heaven,
   Where a' the flowers are sweet,

"And when ye're comin' hame frae earth,
   I'll meet ye at the gate;
For there, ye ken, 'twill no be dark,
   However lang I wait."

They couldna speak, their hearts were fu',
   The wearied bairnie slept;
And through the darkness o' the night
   Their anxious watch they kept.

Small pain it seemed. The gushing tide
   Of earth's joy paused awhile,
And left a little space, before
   The soul took on heaven's smile.

With easy touch, Death took his prize
   Of beauty, for decay.
She drooped, and drooped, and in the morn
   She sighed her soul away.

ALICE PRINGLE.

SCOTLAND, LAND OF LIBERTY.

ONCE again from sordid slumbers would I wake my native lyre,
Tune its voice to bravest numbers, rouse to patriotic fire;
At the bugle-call of duty who would fail to sing of thee,
Home of valour, love, and beauty—Scotland, land of liberty?

> Swell with heart and voice the chorus, ringing over land and sea,
> Honour to the land that bore us—Scotland, land of liberty!

Many a field all grim and gory have thy kilted heroes trod,
Haloed with a flood of glory, fighting for their home and God.
Cowards fled and tyrants trembled when the watchword of the free
Sounded o'er their might assembled—"Scotland, land of liberty!"

Down the dark and misty ages my unbridled fancies go,
And I see in war's red pages Caledonia's records glow.
Rome's proud eagle, Norway's raven, crippled, flew back o'er the sea,
When they proved that Fate had graven—"Scotland, land of liberty."

Ever shall thy sons defend thee while there gleams a battle blade,
For the hearts are true and tender beating 'neath the tartan plaid.
As our fathers crushed oppression and enslaving tyranny,
We will guard the dear possession—Scotland, land of liberty.

Glory wraps thy name in grandeur, as the sunlight does the morn,
Bathing every vale in splendour, every rock and mountain tarn;
Of thy fame the woods are ringing, zephyrs catch the witching glee,
And the very birds are singing—"Scotland, land of liberty."

While the heather and the thistle on thy vales and mountains wave,
And the whaup and plover whistle requiems for thy storied brave;
While the martial fire that made thee glows in hearts born to be free,
Foreign foe shall ne'er invade thee, Scotland, land of liberty.

  Swell with heart and voice the chorus, ringing over land and sea,
  Honour to the land that bore us—Scotland, land of liberty!

THOMAS EDWARDS.

WHAUR SHAGGIE SINGS.

Aboon the dell whaur Shaggie sings
 Its wimplin' winnin' melody;
Whaur wagtails skip on wanton wings
 And keep perpetual holiday!
 Whaur water-bobbies jauntin'ly
Bow to their shadows in the stream,
 There would my fancy ever be
To share the poet's golden dream.

The warbler through the bracken glides,
   An' wriggles chatterin' on the spray;
While ilka spreadin' hazel hides
   A lintie at his e'enin' lay.
   Fair as when Nature's natal day
Swept o'er the earth on dewy wings,
   Are daisied nooks and arbours gay
Whaur lovers meet and Shaggie sings.

There first the throstle's maiden hymn
   Wells freely frae his mirly breast;
The shilfa seeks the forkit stem
   To big his cosy mossy nest;
   The restless wren wi' gowden crest
Plays gymnast on the birken tree,
   Till bluebells toll them a' to rest
'Neath Shaggie's leafy canopy.

O, earth has mony a fair domain
   To charm the wanderer's lingerin' e'e,
But nane can fire this bosom fain
   Like what this sunny spot can dae;
   Like ivy roond the aiken tree
My tendril fancy ever clings
   To what will ever be to me
Earth's Paradise, whaur Shaggie sings.
                THOMAS EDWARDS.

AROUND BENCHONZIE'S PURPLE CREST.

AROUND Benchonzie's purple crest
   The sun's last ray is clingin',
The burnie sabs itsel' to rest
   Aneath the hazels hingin';
The swallows left the westlin' licht
   When Nature's e'e grew weary.—
O why are ye sae late the nicht
   My only joy an' dearie?

Deep in the dell the woodland dove
    Its dreamy note is hummin';
The passin' zephyrs sing o' love,
    An' whisper o' your comin'.
But till your fairy form I see
    I canna be but eerie,
For thou art a' the world to me,
    My only joy an' dearie.

I mark the starnies up on hie
    That angel hands are guidin',
Wi' but a dull an' heedless e'e,
    For love kens nae dividin'.
The music o' your voice alane
    This nicht can mak' me cheerie,
Then haste an' lift this gnawin' pain,
    My only joy an' dearie.

                THOMAS EDWARDS.

THE CROAKER.

At dusk when the lovers seek a wattle-hid alcove,
In the shade an' soothin' scent o' the glee-givin' grove,
An auld crusty hoolit keeps the goers-bye in view,
An' for aye he seems to croon,
        "Come an' woo! come an' woo!"

Ae gloamin' a by-passin' lovin' couple took his rede,
An' a happy, happy while had the dear anes indeed;
But the weird singer's tones were to them ever new,
For when leavin' he enjoined them,
        "Oh, be true! oh, be true!"

Ance mair cam' the wooers, like a saint to the shrine
Whaur his spirit is refreshed wi' a rapture divine,
An' they interchanged their troth 'mang the brackens'
    drippin' dew,
But the Croaker screiched aloud—
        "Ye will rue! ye will rue!"

A' heedfu' o' what the hidden prophet had declared,
To the place o' dootfu' omen they anither nicht repaired,
An' they questioned, an' they quarrelled. Said the lad,
    "It's 'ye will rue.'"
But the lass maintained wi' micht 'twas
        "Oh, be true! oh, be true!"

Sae they battled, an' they sundered, an' the feathered tattler fled;
The laddie banned the gentle sex, an' vowed he'd never wed;
The lassie raved ower thwartit love, an' aft she'd fain beshrew
The fatefu' 'oor when erst they
        Met to woo, met to woo.

Let the double-throated Croaker deal a counsel to us a',
Lest imaginary evils filch oor present peace awa';
An' let happy-hearted lovers never reck the blabbin' crew,
Wha would rive their souls asunder
        When they're true, when they're true.
            REV. JAMES PAUL.

MY GRANNIE'S BIBLE.

I'VE glowered aroond museums fu' o' ancient art an' lore,
An' rummaged wizard relics o' the sage an' skilled o' yore,
But what has richer charms for me, an' far excels them a',
Is grannie's Gaelic Bible in the crevice o' the wa'.

They tell's, atweel, my grandsire's earthly day was early dune;
The auld book was a lamp to licht his road to realms abune;

Wi' weetit een I've heard them crack his gracious rede
    an' wise;
The gloamin' prayers ahint the hoose, the hallowed
    times he'd prize.

It wants a brod, an' if ye touch't, it near-hand sindry
    comes;
Its leaves are strung thegither slack wi' strengthless
    threeds an' thrums;
It's a' sae stained wi' stour ye scarce can scan a verse
    ava;
It ochtna to be hau'led e'er, but hod aye in the wa'.

It's easy seen it bears the blurs o' saut repentant tears;
They're brawly kent frae damp an' dust, an' a' the scaith
    o' years;
The sacred draps that drenched the page thae roundit
    flecks maun be—
There's ane juist richt abune the text—Ha'e mercy,
    Lord, on me.

A tawny tattered leaf atween the Auld Will an' the
    New
Contains the family register, wi' care an' rev'rence due;
The crispit rim an' welkit write precludes the anxious
    e'e
Frae facts o' life an' death, an' what my grannie's age
    may be.

Though far frae hame I sune may be, ower beildless tilth
    an' tide,
Whare savage hirsels ramp an' roar, an' dun barbarians
    bide,
I'll aye revere an' bear in mind, whare'er my lines may
    fa',
My grannie's Gaelic Bible in the crevice o' the wa'.

                        REV. JAMES PAUL.

LIFE IS SHORT, BUT LOVE IS LONG.

OH! life is short, but love is long,
    And youthful hearts beat warm and light;
The days of youth pass like a song—
    Like twilight merging into night.

But love is long, and cannot die,
    It lives when other passions fade,
And is the dearest human tie
    That heavenly God with man has made.

Yes, love is long; it gathers strength
    As life is hastening to its close,
And time imparts to love at length
    A sweeter perfume than the rose.

Though life is short, yet love is long,
    And emanates from God alone;
It rules the right, yet pities wrong,
    And makes two hearts melt into one.
        REV. R. M. FERGUSSON, M.A.

ALLAN WATER.

WHERE can you find a sweeter spot
    Than by clear Allan Water,
The classic ground where poets sought
    The Miller's lovely daughter?

'Tis dear to me this winding stream,
    Where maids and lovers banter;
For here there came a charming dream
    To roving "Rob the Ranter."

But sweeter far the song it sings
   Of peace and joy and beauty,
For to my heart it solace brings
   To aid me in my duty.

The Ochil hills invite my feet
   To tread the soft moss under,
But still for thee my heart shall beat
   Although thy waters thunder.

In summer days I sit by thee
   And listen to thy singing;
And as I sit there comes to me
   The sound of church bells ringing.

'Tis marriage bells that sound so clear,
   And set the air a-throbbing;
But dear to me, and still more dear
   Is thy soft waters sobbing.

O, who can find a lovelier stream,
   Than that of Allan Water?
And who can sing a sweeter theme
   Than the Miller's lovely daughter?

            REV. R. M. FERGUSSON, M.A.

THE VIKING'S BRIDE.

AN ORCADIAN BALLAD.

IN the cold grey dawn of an autumn day,
   As the sun peeped over the sea,
A Norseman's bark sailed out of the bay,
With the sails full set and all so gay,
   Away to the west went he.

'Twas a Viking bold from the Norway shore,
    And a tall sea king was he ;
But he sailed away to return no more,
Nor to hear again it's deep-toned roar ;
    For he sank 'neath the foam of the sea.

The Orcadian isles was the land he sought,
    And a royal bride to wed,
Who was waiting now till the north wind brought
To her watching—that looked for nought—
    The sight of the Dragon Head.

And this brave sea king, with his crew so gay,
    Were as happy as men could be ;
For they left their shores at the break of day,
And they cheered their friends as they passed the bay,
    And steered for the open sea.

As their hearts were light and their bark was tight,
    And their limbs so stout and strong,
They would fear no foe, nor the dark wild night,
As they steered their bark by the pale moonlight
    But sang this Orcadian song :—

    "The sea is wild and free, my boys,
        The sea is wild and free,
    And o'er the back of the ocean wide,
    We steer onr barks by wind and tide,
        And sing aloud in our glee, my boys,
        And sing aloud iu our glee.

    "We play with the foam of the deep, my boys,
        We play with the foam of the deep,
    That gleams in the light of the moon so bright,
        And sinks with the stars to sleep, my boys,
        And sinks with the stars to sleep.

    "We fish at the turn of the tide, my boys,
        We fish at the turn of the tide,
    And whisper low, while the breezes blow,
        Of the girl that's to be our bride, my boys,
        Of the girl that's to be our bride.

"Oh, we are happy and gay, my boys,
   Oh, we are happy and gay,
We love to sail with breeze or gale,
   And then return to the bay, my boys,
   And then return to the bay."

When the music ceased there arose a gale
   That became a hurricane blast,
And the cheek of the Norse sea king turned pale
As he heard the sound of the ocean's wail,
   And saw the bending mast.

With a shriek and moan all the shrouds were rent,
   And the mast went by the side,
While the brave Norsemen 'neath the billows went
With their bark, and all that the king had sent
   To deck his bonnie bride.

      *   *   *

In Jarl's home, on a lofty tower,
   Sits a maid by Orcadia's sea,
And she weeps and sighs from hour to hour,
For the Viking bold to claim her dower,
   But he sleeps in the moaning sea.

          REV. R. M. FERGUSSON, M.A.

MY BONNIE BIT LASSIE.

THE miser may gloat ower his gear,
   The toper may smirk ower his tassie,
But their pleasures can never compare
   Wi' the raptures I feel wi' my lassie.
Like the violets blue are her een,
   In her breath the balm breezes are blawin',
And suffused are the cheeks o' my queen
   Wi' the roseate flush o' the dawin'.

   I carena for riches or micht,
      I carena for wine in a tassie,
   When I quaff the rich drauchts o' delicht
      Frae the lips o' my bonnie bit lassie.

Like the sunblinks that brichten the brae
   Her smile gladdens a' that's aboot her,
Noo I've tint her, fair Nature looks wae,
   For simmer's nae simmer withoot her.
Yet aft at that oor we did pairt,
   When a' the deep wast is a-lowin',
Her memory fa's on my heart
   Like pearly dew-draps on the gowan.

     Then awa' wi' yer riches and micht,
       Awa' wi' yer wine in a tassie,
     Oh! gie me ae draucht o' delicht
       Frae the lips o' my bonnie bit lassie.

                      JOHN ANDERSON.

THE ROMANCE OF THE ROSE.

A ROSE hung high on the castle wall
   On a summer morning fair,
'Twas fed by the dews that sweetly fall,
   And fanned by the sunny air.
Its odorous breast was all bedight
   With the diamond's sparkling sheen,
Its silken petals were soft and white,
   Its leaves a tender green.

     Then, O, I said, as I looked at the rose,
       Thou art fair as fair can be,
     But who will gather thee, lovely flower,
       O, who will gather thee?

A lady looked o'er the castle wall,
   So gentle, so sweet, so shy,
Like the stately pine, she was slender and tall,
   The lovelight lay in her eye.
And the fame of her beauty spread like a breeze
   That is laden with perfumes sweet,
And lovers of low and of high degrees
   Came flocking around her feet.

Then I sighed and said, as I looked at the maid,
 Thou art fair as fair can be,
But who will gather thee, lovely flower,
 O, who will gather thee?

The sunlight gleamed on the castle wall,
 And a silken ladder swung,
But a bowshot from the Baron's hall,
 Where the dainty roselet hung.
And I swam the moat, I clomb the height,
 Plucked the rose with my fingertips,
Low murmuring words of soft delight
 Fell from my lady's lips.

And I said, as she placed it in her breast,
 O rose thou wert fair to see,
But I have gathered thee, lovely flower,
 O, I have gathered thee.

Then gaily and lightly my lady smiled,
 And my heart leapt high for love,
For my foolish fears were now beguiled,
 And I swore by the heavens above
"What man may do, what man may dare,
 Shall be done and dared by me.
And all for the love, sweet lady fair,
 My heart hath given to thee.

And when in triumph I come from the wars,
 If fortune favour me,
O, I shall gather thee, lovely flower,
 O, I shall gather thee."

JOHN ANDERSON.

"A MIDSUMMER NICHT'S DREAM."

Ae e'enin' I laid mysel' doon to sleep
   'Mang the moss that cushioned a burnie's brim,
An' some eldrich pooer 'gan my senses steep,
   An' the munelicht was thrangit wi' shapes fu' grim.

Frae 'neath leaves o' dockens an' ilka grass blade
   Cam' unearthly bodies wi' coats o' green,
An' wee red Kilmarnocks on touzled head,
   And the wizendest faces that e'er war' seen.

Ilk warlock was hotchin' an' lauchin' wi' glee,
   An' they paidl't aboot an' they wadna be still;
Till a fiddler loon, wi' his bonnet agee,
   Was cannily stanced in his seat on a hill—

A cosy bit nook in the fair dingle side,
   Whar the mune glinted bricht on the dewdraps wat;
But the rest o' the company still couldna bide,
   But waitin' the fays, by the burnie sat.

Some leaves o' last autumn cam' sailin' doon,
   Ilk riggit wi' moonbeams an' helm o' fate;
An' steered wi' a stalk o' hemlock broon—
   The barges o' fairies travellin' in state.

It was awesome to see ilk enchantit carle
   Handin' out a fair leddy wi' auld farrant grace;
But the bonniest sicht I hae seen i' this warl'
   Was the blithesome blink o' ilk fairy face.

Their goons war' o' thistledoon, fa'in' like air,
   An' their gems o' the dewdraps' glimmerin' sheen;
An' never a Queen, be she bonnie or fair,
   Was drest like thae fairies this midsummer e'en.

They stude i' their places a' ready to reel,
   An' the music struck up, an' the dance began;
An' they turned an' linkit and trippit fu' weel,
   Ilk fairy white wi' a warlock man.

I turned me aboot to see mair o' the fun,
    But a wailin' *sough* ower the gatherin' fell;
I was fear'd they'd hae meltit like snaw 'neth the sun
    Had they kent mortal een lookit doon on the dell.

Sae I keppit my breath, an' I lay fu' still,
    Juist keekin' wi' ane o' my een at the ploy,
Till the fiddler wight frae his seat on the hill
    Played up, an' the company fell to wi' joy.

At last a great supper was laid oot at twal
    On a patch o' muneshine aneath a tree,
A' deckit wi' wild flooers an' goblets tall,
    An' sparklin' wi' red wine frae Normandy.

An' warlocks an' fairies, wi' daffin' an' mirth,
    Sat doon to the feast an' the red wine quaſft;
I fairly forgot what my silence was worth,
    An' clean lost my gumption an' roared an' laucht.

Like the shadowy munelicht they meltit awa',
    An' left nae a ribbon to tell o' their joy;
But I'll no be persuadit by ony ava
    That I didna tak' part in a fairy ploy.
JESSIE M. KING.

AUTUMN THOUGHTS.

THE year is slowly dying down
    In mist and storm into the past,
    That seemed at times too fair to last,
So bright it was with beauty's crown.

The glorious sky that round us shone,
    The summer fires that gladdened us,
    Throughout the long days luminous
Of golden prime, have passed and gone.

The summer trees are leafless now,
   And fling their gaunt arms drearily
   About the fields, and wearily
In autumn breezes creak and bow.

And, oh, my heart is sad and lone,
   I mourn the golden summer dead;
   I almost think the brown leaves shed
In sadness that can match my own.

On every house, on every tree,
   Glad birds of passage sit and sing,
   Ready to speed on eager wing,
To summer skies beyond the sea.

Oh, could I leave this misty air,
   Where fogs from sluggish marshes creep,
   To veil the genial sun, and steep
My soul in southern sunshine fair.

But as I raise my aimless cry,
   Some other voices rise to charm,
   Some other sights win me from harm,
From wishes which are but a sigh.

I see our northern autumn stand
   With blithesome shouts in all its fields,
   I see the tints September yields
In largesse to the painter's hand.

Of nut and berry dropping brown,
   And scarlet clusters of the ash;
   I hear the jocund winds that lash
The bending tree-tops' fiery crown.

I see the splendid fires that gild
   The evening gateway of the sun,
   Telling of crimson honours won,
And life with gen'rous action filled.

And though, in darkness gleaming white,
  I see the snowflakes cloud the air,
  And frost and ice in masses fair,
Which mark our iron winter night.

I look on these with opened eyes,
  Knowing their bleakness holds the spring,
  Rising from wintry frosts to bring
Another summer's mysteries.

JESSIE M. KING.

FALLEN LEAVES.

I STAND where evening breezes blow,
I hear the tinkling streamlet's flow,
  Meandering in the wood;
There's music in the woodland's din,
The winds give voice to Nature's hymn
  In sad and solemn mood.

Oft have I stood beneath these trees,
When grasses kissed the evening breeze,
  In glorious summer eves;
But now I stand when flowers are dead,
When wintry winds weep o'er their bed,
  Amid the fallen leaves.

Pleasant it was at evening's close
To court the shelter of these boughs,
  And dream bewitching dreams.
High hopes I had, fair as the flowers
That ever bloomed in fancy's bowers,
  Or were a poet's themes.

Sweet voices spake in this dim wood;
I heard songs in the solitude,
  Like strains from Fairyland.
All care and sorrow fled with fright,
The smiling flowers glowed with delight;
  But now 'mongst leaves I stand.

Ah me! how strange a tale life weaves;
Each heart has had its fallen leaves
   In winters long ago.
Some weep o'er withered flowers to-night;
Some lay their dead leaves out of sight;
   But still life's stream doth flow.

Just as I learned the matchless song
The woods grew dumb—a speechless throng
   In winter's cold embrace;
So loving hearts and dead ones gone,
Whose souls we just had searched, are flown,
   And hide from us their face.

Yet as I mourn the leaflet's death,
Methinks I feel the summer's breath,
   And see the flowers once more.
What though the woodlands cannot sing,
I know with joy they soon shall ring
   As I have heard before.

What though 'mid fallen leaves we stand,
In faith stretch forth thy doubting hand—
   He who believes receives.
Thy withered flower will fairer grow,
In fields of light thou'lt see it blow,
   When gathered are our leaves.

          PETER GALLOWAY FRASER.

OCH, HEY, HUM.

WHEN hearts are bleedin' sair wi' grief and care has knit the broo,
And time has made the auld head bare whaur bonny ringlets grew;
A weary sigh steals frae the soul that's almost overcome,
Yet buried grief aft finds relief in "Och, hey, hum."

The faithfu' shepherd leads his flock oot owre the green hillside,
And tak's them to the choicest knowes whaur a' may safe abide;
But when the sun sinks frae his view, and cares his heart benumb,
Kind Heaven hears his waesome cry of "Och, hey, hum."

The labourin' man, wi' busy hand, wha toils frae morn till nicht,
And prays betimes that a' his bairns may grow up to do richt,
When borne doon aneath a load owre heavy far for some,
Gets cheerfu' comfort when he utters "Och, hey, hum."

The mither by the cradle side sits watching there alane,
To keep the messenger o' death awa' frae her doorstane;
She hides the tears that nature sends when death at last has come,
Yet noo and than you'll hear her sobbin' "Och, hey, hum."

Yet let us a' be thankfu' that we're no sent here to bide,
The day will come when a' will meet owre on the ither side;
Nae trachle sair, nor sorrow there; nae lip will there be dumb;
Nae tears will flow, nae lips will utter "Och, hey, hum."

Rev. D. G. Mitchell.

"WEEL THRO' THE VALLEY."*

Aweary is my auld grey head, a mist steals ower my e'e,
Earth's lower lichts are growin' dim, the journey's end I see;
Up mony a hill I've warstled sair, and mony a rugged steep;
But I'm weel thro' the valley noo, and would fain fa' asleep.

I've trauchled lang an' fochten hard 'mid sin, and storm, and strife,
And aft, tho' kennin' richt, dune wrang—I mourn a sinfu' life;
In heart I've broken a' God's laws, the least I couldna keep;
But I'm weel thro' the valley noo, and would fain fa' asleep.

Oh! langsome, dreary road o' life, oh! sorrow-laden years,
Ye've cost me mony a weary climb and mony bitter tears;
But see, the sun is sinkin' fast adoon the Western deep,
For I'm weel thro' the valley noo, and would fain fa' asleep.

Some leaves fa' green, some withered fa', when winds are calm and still,
And withered too, I soon maun fa', yet wait Jehovah's will;

---

*These were the last words of an old woman as she lay on her deathbed. She lived in the top flat of a dingy old house in the Pleasance in Edinburgh; and as a few poor friends gathered round her humble bed to watch her breathing out her last, after commending them to the Saviour, and expressing her hope in a happy immortality, she "fell asleep." Over and over again these words fell from her dying lips—"I'm weel thro' the valley noo, and would fain fa' asleep."

The thocht o' quittin' earth for heaven, it gars my auld heart leap,
For I'm weel thro' the valley noo, and would fain fa' asleep.

Oh, dinna greet, freen's, dinna greet, though I maun gang awa',
We'll a' forgaither up aboon inside oor Father's ha';
Nae sair, sad scenes, nae heartbrak's there, nane there will sit and weep;
I'm far thro' the valley noo, and will lay me doon and sleep.

Rev. D. G. Mitchell.

THAT HORN SPOON THE TINKLER MADE.

Ae mirky nicht, when winds blew cauld,
   And sour an' surly clouds drove past,
A tinkler, sair in rags, and auld,
   Crawled to the shed to scoug the blast.
And as the dawn dang oot the dark,
I met him, settin' aff to wark,
And, pairtin', vowed he'd mak' a spoon
Wad ne'er be matched by mortal loon.

Chorus—There's no a spoon in a' the toon
      Sae mony hungry mou's has fed;
   And nane I'd like to praise aboon
      That horn spoon the tinkler made.

Twa winters passed, when ae dreich nicht—
   I just had supper't Bett the pony—
And, stappin' roon withoot lamp licht,
   I ran against my tinkler crony.
"Weel met, my man, here, there's yer spoon,
'Twas feenished i' the wuds o' Scone;
And whan through this wide warl' yer led
Aye mind the spoon the tinkler made."

    Chorus—There's no a spoon, etc.

He telt me hoo, in yon wild den,
  Whaur hoolits screiched and winds howled dreary,
An' birds an' cushies cam' to speu'
  The nicht amang the firs sae eerie,
There in his tent, roun' blazin' fire—
His wife and bairns asleep wi' tire—
He shap'd it, till his heart was glad,
That horn spoon the tinkler made."

      Chorus—There's no a spoon, etc.

Gin I had time, an' space, an' wit,
  This spoon—what screids I'd tell aboot it—
Hoo ilka mou' it seems to fit,
  E'en grannie canna sup withoot it.
At cogs o' brose an' reekin' kail
Hoo aft we've met I needna tell;
Gin ere 'twas lost saut tears I'd shed,
For the horn spoon the tinkler made.

      Chorus—There's no a spoon, etc.

A lad may coort, an' nichtly woo
  The lass he likes the best o' ony;
A lass may boast her lover's mou'
  Tastes better than the sweetest honey;
But I'll ne'er brag o' bonnie lass,
Although her charms nane may surpass,
I'll blaw my horn an' praise instead
The braw, braw spoon the tinkler made.

Chorus—There's no a spoon in a' the toon
    Sae mony hungry mou's has fed,
  An' nane I'd like to praise aboon
    That horn spoon the tinkler made.

            REV. D. G. MITCHELL.

THE GRACES' SPELL

Twas summer time, and eventide,
The Graces met by a fountain-side.
In its glassy pool each viewed her form,
Lovely, untouched by passion's storm.
Near Olympus' mount this fountain stood
Close by a rich and shady wood;
And as Apollo went to rest
A glorious blush suffused the west.
The Graces sported by the pool,
And praised its waters fresh and cool,
But when its wondrous powers they found,
With songs they made the groves resound.
'Twas thus the artless trio sang,
And first Thalia thus began—
"How can we this to mortals give,
That they in purity may live?
A subtle essence let us make
Which of its nature shall partake.
To mother Venus let us go,
For she'll advise us well, I trow."
Aglaia and Euphrosyne
With one accord did answer "Yea."
Olympus' top they soon did reach,
Their goddess mother to beseech;
And when their purpose they had told,
Venus her plan did then unfold.
"Your little brother, Cupid, dear,
He grows not old from year to year,
But still a chubby boy remains,
Though he a manly mind retains.
A vicious imp has ta'en his name,
Of Erebus and Nox he came.
Both old and young he doth deceive,
That he's my son he'd make believe.
Let's arm our Cupid for the fight;
I'll clothe him in Love's armour bright,
And give to him a little bow,
Which mortals cannot see, I know.

Quiver and arrows he'll require,
Points tempered by celestial fire;
These arrows first you all must take
And carefully your essence make,
Next dip the arrow heads in it;
For service then they will be fit.
Our Cupid dear will ne'er be still,
And he may hide where'er he will.
At one time in young maiden's eye,
Or from the curling locks he'll spy;
Then shoot his dart, which cannot miss,
And falls as lightly as a kiss.
No one against him shall be proof,
'Neath homely thatch or palace roof.
It matters not, he knows his way
At dead of night or break of day.
The soldier bold he will not fear,
Nor learned man, nor poet seer.
The pain he gives they'll say is sweet,
And makes their happiness complete.
Poor mortals! well I'm glad 'tis so;
The feigning imp may they ne'er know;
But saved, perchance, by our dear boy,
Pass daily on from joy to joy,
Till when they leave this world, I trow,
'Twill cause them not a pang to go."

. . . . .

Quickly the Graces hied away,
And from that time until this day
The chubby boy doth vict'ries gain;
To know him well may you attain,
And from his paths may you ne'er stray,
Lest Cupid false make you his prey.
Oh! what a life would then be thine
If round your heart his tendrils twine;
Dispel the thought! It must not be.
Let one bright star be guide to thee;
Tho' far away at first it seem,
And through the clouds it oft may beam;

Sometimes perchance quite lost to sight,
And all your hope's grow dark as night;
Yet love's strong laws will draw it near
If you yourself but be sincere;
Then, all your early struggles past,
You'll reach your haven safe at last.

. . . . .

The age of Grecian Myth has gone,
A love Divine on earth hath shone;
And only those who know Him well,
The purest joys of love can tell.

W. T. TOVANI.

IN THE GLOAMING.

THE sun has sunk, and soft and grey
The shadows fall of closing day
   Across the snow-clad lawn;
And far o'erhead 'mid deepest blue,
Emblems of love steadfast and true,
   The stars begin to dawn.

Now flickering lights of fireshine fall
Across the room, while from each wall
   Old pictured faces smile,
That once have lived and loved like we
And found the world as fair to be
   In their brief "little while."

The shadows fall, and to and fro
The flickering firelights come and go
   While I sit here alone;
Yet quiet footsteps cross the floor,
And voices that I heard of yore
   Once more, in softest tone,

Whisper to me they love me yet;
Not they who pass the veil forget
   The loved they leave behind.
And we who part with them in pain
Can know that when we meet again
   Shall still them faithful find.

Oh! dearest hour of all the day,
When work is done, and put away
   All thoughts of care awhile,
When resting in my cosy chair,
While rubby firelights gleam and glare,
   And all my thoughts beguile.

Outside the storms of life may beat,
Inside there is a lull most sweet
   For wearied heart and brain.
Then oftentimes I read anew
Old words of love as dear and true
   As if they lived again.

Old letters writ by those long dead,
Remembered speech by them once said,
   Before we had to part;
What though the light's too dim and low
The faded writing plain to show—
   I know them all by heart.

And sometimes musing thus I see
The time that soon must dawn for me,
   When my life's day is done.
Ah! then the gates will open wide
That are beyond Death's awful tide
   Where shines for aye the sun.

When all earth's cares and pains are past,
The rest eternal won at last,
   For which I weary here,
Then I shall meet to part no more
With those that once on earth's dark shore
   Were unto me most dear.

If then I may remember aught
Of all that on the earth was wrought
   It shall be this dear hour;
When flickering firelights come and go
And win me with their quiet glow
   From sorrow's cruel pow'r.

M. BUCHANAN WHITE.

SONNET.—SCOTTISH HEATHER.

FAR from the haunts of men it grows this flower;
   Lonely it reigns, queen of the mountain peak,
The Bride of storms: through sunshine and in shower
   Faithful to all small lives that safety seek
From its outspreading arms. Yea! I would sing
   Thy praises, flower, too little sung as yet—
For far across wild moors where songsters wing
   These soulless poets do not thee forget.
Thy sturdy beauty wins the wooing wind,
   To thee the roving bee most constant proves
Nor underrates thy worth. So do I find
   In thee a fitting type of all true loves—
For year by year upon the hillside bare
Ever the same, we search and find thee fair.

M. BUCHANAN WHITE.

TO WORDSWORTH.

THOU dost not take us, Wordsworth, where the stream
   Of unpent fancy rushes bold and free,
Nor where the falling rapids whitely gleam
   Thro' rocky chasms and overbending tree.
Thine is the under-current, calm and slow,
   Untouched by surface storms or wintry cold.

Quietly unruffled all thy verses flow
  By meadow grasses and the shepherd's fold.
The every-dayness of our common life
  Is wrought with mystic meaning in thy hand,
And somewhat calmer grows our earthly strife
  When at thy side we, leaning, meekly stand
With the blue sky above us, and the breeze
  Roaming at will among the whisp'ring trees.
M. BUCHANAN WHITE.

HANSEL-MUNONDAY.

COME haste ye, haste ye, noo, guidman,
  And redd yersel' and mak' ye braw,
We'll hae the strangers on oor haun'
  Afore the mornin's weel awa';
The frost is nippin' shairp and keen,
  The hill-taps a' are flichten'd grey;
It's juist as brisk a morn's I've seen
  For mony a Hansel-Munonday.

Gae pit ye on yer coat o' grey,
  And I'll pit on my feckfu' goon;
We kenna wha may come the day
  Wi' a' oor bairns frae the toon;
For we'll hae Maggie and her man,
  And John will be frae ower the way;
We maun be snod and braw, guidman,
  To haud oor Hansel-Munonday.

Oor Davie will be here frae Fife,
  An' he'll be prood to see's sae fine;
'Twill be anither tack o' life
  To haud his haund again in mine.
And oh, my bairn, my Sandie dear,
  Guid send him safe across the Tay,
I wat, guidman, if he's no here
  'Twill be nae Hansel-Munonday.

O gi'e oor Maker praise, guidman,
    For a' the mercies we hae met ;
We've ha'en oor sorrows noo and than,
    But here we're baith thegither yet ;
Tho' we hae won life's tapmost heicht,
    An' noo we're toddlin' doon the brae,
We're aince mair gladden'd wi' the sicht
    O' anither Hansel-Munonday.

What mak's the saut tear fill my e'e ?
    It's fecklesslike o' me, I ken,
But oh, guidman, I lang to see
    Oor lassies and oor muckle men ;
The time is swiftly wearin' near
    Whan we'll be baith laid in the clay,
And never mair they'll gaither here
    To spend their Hansel-Munonday.

But, come, get on yer thrifty grey,
    Ye maun be buskit clean and snod :
The mornin's wearin' on to day,
    There's folk already on the road ;
We'll hae the bairns in an 'oor,
    And we maun baith be trig and gay
To mak' for them wi' a' oor power
    A canty Hansel-Munonday.

ALEXANDER M. SCOTT.

KINNAIRD.

FAIR fa' bright Phœbe's gowden rays
    Around thy rising breast, Kinnaird,
May seasons' beauty fill thy braes
    And peaceful joy be widely shared.
There summer's gladness filled my heart
    There stern winter pleased my e'e,
For Nature strove her kindest part
    To spread her winsome charm o'er thee !

I speeled thy braes in happy hour
   In childhood's merry harmless play,
And ranged thy woods from bower to bower
   When life seemed but a summer's day;
Each rugged path that skirts a brae,
   Each muckle stane wi' mossy beard,
That meet my gaze where'er I gae
   Awaken thochts o' loved Kinnaird.

How oft upon thy ruddy tower,
   A royal wand'rer's ready hold,
In dreams' mysterious, happy power
   Iv'e sat and viewed the scenes of old—
The village basked in sunny ray,
   The level Carse in farming pride,
And silvery waters of the Tay,
   That like my dreams in swiftness glide.

How fondly in our bosoms rise
   The thoughts of early happy hours,
Like sudden glints in cloudy skies
   Or earth renewed by summer showers;
What happiness to mortal mind
   The memory of childhood's age,
One guileless hour of bliss to find,
   One bright word on Life's blotted page.

Fair fa' bright Phœbe's gowden rays
   Around thy rising breast, Kinnaird,
May seasons' beauty fill thy braes
   And Nature's joy be widely shared;
On ilka bank, by ilka bower
   May Nature's arts still brightly reign,
And hasten, hasten, happy hour
   I tread thy weel-kent paths again!

                ALEXANDER M. SCOTT.

THE BRAES ROUN' ABOOT AUCHTERAIRDER.

At times when I think on my boyhood's bricht oors
Its joys and its sorrows, its sunshine and shooers;
I'm a laddie again, and I'm puin' the flooers
   On the braes roun' aboot Auchterairder.

I'm list'nin' again to the hum o' the bee,
As it scans ilka flooer on the wet dewy lea;
Or list'nin' the laverock that sings blythe and free
   'Bune the braes roun' aboot Auchterairder.

I'm paidlin' ance mair in the cool o' the burn,
And chasin' the big troots at maist ilka turn;
Or landin' them oot wi' my new horse-hair gurn,
   On the braes roun' aboot Auchterairder.

I'm lyin' again on the green whinny knowes,
And watchin' the sheep as they lazily browse;
Or I'm puin' the heather whaur wildly it grows,
   On the braes roun' aboot Auchterairder.

In fancy I'm hearin' the heart-stirrin' note,
O' the siller-voiced cuckoo frae yon woody grot,
As loodly it pipes frae its clear trebly throat
   O'er the braes roun' aboot Auchterairder.

I'm stannin' again whaur the grass grows knee-deep,
Whaur the saft gloamin' shadows their lanely watch keep,
And I bend o'er a mither that sleeps her last sleep
   In the kirkyaird o' auld Auchterairder.

Oh! scenes o' my childhood, you're dear, dear to me,
My heart's like to break, and the tear blin's my e'e,
When I think that I'll maybe again never see
   The braes roun' aboot Auchterairder.

But when my lamp's oot—when my sun's shone its best,
And draps ower the hills in the far distant West;
I'd like just to think I could lie down and rest
   On the braes roun' aboot Auchterairder.
WILLIAM NEISH.

THE BURNIE'S SANG.

OH hoo bonnie rows the burnie
   At the breakin' o' the morn,
When the fragrant breath o' simmer
   Moves the blossoms on the thorn,
When the birdies still are sleepin',
   And the zephyr scents the hay;
Oh hoo sweetly sings the burnie
   At the breakin' o' the day.

Oh hoo bonnie rows the burnie
   When the simmer sun is high,
And naething but a fleecy cloud
   Floats through the azure sky,
When the birds are whistlin' blythely,
   And the lambkins frisk and play,
Oh hoo sweetly sings the burnie
   On a sunny simmer day.

Oh hoo bonnie rows the burnie
   When the nicht-clouds settle doon,
And the glamour o' the gloamin'
   Flings its mystic shadows roon',
When the birdies a' are nested,
   And the sun draps ower the moor,
Oh the burnie sings the sweetest
   At the gloamin's witchin' oor.

Oh the music o' the burnie,
   Heard far back in childhood's days,
Mak's me aftentime's grow weary
   O' the city's buzz and blaze,

Yet at times ower rigid manhood
  Childhood sheds its sunny beams,
For I hear the burnie singin'
  In the midst o' happy dreams.

WILLIAM NEISH.

PERTHSHIRE SONGS AND POEMS.

BY OUTSIDE AUTHORS.

THE BIRKS OF ABERFELDY.*

Bonnie lassie, will ye go,
Will ye go, will ye go;
Bonnie lassie, will ye go
    To the birks of Aberfeldy?

---

* Burns explains that this song, which was first printed in Johnson's *Museum*, was composed consequent on a visit which he paid to the beautiful falls of Moness in 1787, when he and his friend, William Nicol, of the High School, Edinburgh, were on their tour in the Highlands. Like many another of the National poets' celebrated lyrics, the "Birks of Aberfeldy" sprang Phœnix-like from the ashes of a less worthy sire. In the present instance, he takes his cue from the simple old song entitled, "The Birks of Abergeldy," which celebrates a beautiful district on Deeside, in close proximity to the Royal residence of Balmoral. This older song, which is of unknown date and authorship, is worth quoting, though but to show how much, or how little Burns owed to it.

    Bonnie lassie, will ye go,
    Will ye go, will ye go;
    Bonnie lassie, will ye go
        To the birks of Abergeldy?

    O ye shall get a goun o' silk,
    A goun o' silk, a goun o' silk;
    O ye shall get a goun o' silk,
        And a coat of calimanco.

    Na, kind sir, I darena gang,
    I darena gang, I darena gang;
    Na, kind sir, I darena gang,
        For my Minnie she'll be angry.

    Sair, sair wad she flyte,
    Wad she flyte, wad she flyte;
    Sair, sair wad she fiyte,
        And sair wad she ban me.

Now simmer blinks on flow'ry braes,
And o'er the crystal streamlet plays;
Come let us spend the lightsome days
   In the birks of Aberfeldy.

The little birdies blythely sing,
While o'er their heads the hazels hing;
Or lightly flit on wanton wing
   In the birks of Aberfeldy.

The braes ascend like lofty wa's,
The foaming stream deep-roaring fa's,
O'erhung wi' fragrant spreading shaws
   The birks of Aberfeldy.

The hoary cliffs are crowned wi' flowers,
While o'er the linns the burnie pours,
And, rising, weets wi' misty showers
   The birks of Aberfeldy.

Let Fortune's gifts at random flee,
They ne'er shall draw a wish frae me;
Supremely blest wi' love and thee,
   In the birks of Aberfeldy.

ROBERT BURNS.

BLYTHE, BLYTHE, AND MERRY WAS SHE.*

BLYTHE, blythe, and merry was she,
   Blythe was she but and ben,
Blythe by the banks of Earn
   And blythe in Glenturrit glen.

The sprightly melody to which the songs are sung was published in Playford's *Dancing Master* as early as 1657, and is there styled "A Scotch Ayre."

Aberfeldy and the falls of Moness are dearer to the heart of every Scottish tourist from their association with Burns' exquisite song, and nothing strikes the visitor to the locality more than the truthfulness of the song-picture—for this it fully is, in addition to being a spirited and beautiful love-lyric.

* The heroine of this beautiful song was Miss Euphemia Murray of Lintrose, distinguished in her teens by the appellation of "The

By Ochtertyre grows the aik,
  On Yarrow banks the birken shaw:
But Phemie was a bonnier lass
  Than braes o' Yarrow ever saw.

Her looks were like a flower in May,
  Her smile was like a summer morn;
She trippèd by the banks of Earn,
  As light's a bird upon a thorn.

Her bonnie face it was as meek
  As ony lamb upon a lea;
The evening sun was ne'er sae sweet
  As was the blink o' Phemie's e'e.

The Highland hills I've wandered wide,
  And owre the Lowlands I ha'e been;
But Phemie was the blythest lass
  That ever trod the dewy green.
                                ROBERT BURNS.

STRATHALLAN'S LAMENT.*

THICKEST night, o'erhang my dwelling!
  Howling tempests, o'er me rave!
Turbid torrents, wintry swelling,
  Still surround my lonely cave!

Flower of Strathmore." The poet met her while on a visit to the house of her cousin, Sir William Murray of Ochtertyre, in 1787, and seems to have been charmed by her beauty and affability. She was married in 1794, to Mr. Smythe of Methven, afterwards a judge of the Court of Session under the title of Lord Methven, the main branch of whose family-tree finds its present-day representative in the popular occupant of Methven Castle.

* This pathetic lament was written by Burns for Johnson's *Museum*, and is supposed to express the feelings of James Drummond, fifth Viscount of Strathallan, who escaped to France after the battle of Culloden, where his father was slain, and died after twenty years' exile. Both Cunningham and Chambers apply the verses to William, fourth Viscount, but William never was attainted; for, although out in the "Fifteen," no proceedings were taken against him, and he was under the turf at Culloden before his name was included in the Act of Attainder, 1746.

Chrystal streamlets, gently flowing,
    Busy haunts of base mankind,
Western breezes, softly blowing,
    Suit not my distracted mind.

In the cause of right engagèd
    Wrongs injurious to redress,
Honour's war we strongly wagèd,
    But the heavens denied success.

Farewell, fleeting, fickle treasure,
    'Tween Misfortune and Folly shared!
Farewell Peace, and farewell Pleasure!
    Farewell flattering man's regard!

Ruin's wheel has driven o'er us,
    Not a hope that dare attend,
The wide world is all before us—
    But a world without a friend!

                      ROBERT BURNS.

BY ALLAN STREAM.[*]

By Allan stream I chanced to rove,
    While Phœbus sank beyond Benledi;
The winds were whispering through the grove,
    The yellow corn was waving ready;
I listen'd to a lover's sang,
    And thought on youthfu' pleasures many;
And aye the wild wood echoes rang—
    Oh, dearly do I love thee, Annie!

---

[*] In a letter to George Thomson, dated, August, 1793, Burns writes:—
"I walked out yesterday evening, with a volume of the *Museum* in my hand; when, turning up 'Allan Water,' 'What numbers shall the muse repeat,' etc., as the words appeared to me rather unworthy of so fine an air, and recollecting that it is on my list, I sat and raved under the shade of an old thorn, till I wrote one to suit the measure. I may be wrong; but I think it is not in my worst style. You must know that in Ramsay's *Tea Table*, where the modern song first appeared, the ancient name of the tune, Allan says, is 'Allan Water' or 'My

Oh, happy be the woodbine bower,
   Nae nightly bogle make it eerie;
Nor ever sorrow stain the hour,
   The place and time I met my dearie!
Her head upon my throbbing breast,
   She, sinking, said "I'm thine for ever!"
While mony a kiss the seal imprest,
   The sacred vow,—we ne'er should sever.

The haunt o' Spring's the primrose brae,
   The Summer joys the flocks to follow;
How cheery, through her shortening day,
   Is Autumn in her weeds o' yellow!
But can they melt the glowing heart,
   Or chain the soul in speechless pleasure,
Or through each nerve the rapture dart,
   Like meeting thee, my bosom's treasure?

                              ROBERT BURNS.

MARY OF TOMBEA.*

THE heath this night must be my bed,
The bracken curtain for my head,
My lullaby the warder's tread,
   Far, far, from love and thee, Mary;
To-morrow eve, more stilly laid,
My couch may be my bloody plaid,
My vesper song, thy wail, sweet maid!
   It will not waken me, Mary!

---

love Annie's very bonny.' This last has certainly been a line of the original song; so I took up the idea, and, as you will see, have introduced the line in its place, which, I presume, it formerly occupied; though I likewise give you a choosing line, if it should not hit the cut of your fancy. Bravo! say I; it is a good song, . . . Autumn is my propitious season, I make more songs in it than all the year else. —God bless you. R. B."

  * This is the song of Norman in "The Lady of the Lake," canto third. Mary of Tombea had just been married with great ceremony to Norman, heir of Armandave, and as the bridal party were leaving the chapel of St. Bride, Angus of Duncraggan dashed through the

I dare not, dare not, fancy now
The grief that clouds thy lovely brow;
I dare not think upon thy vow,
   And all it promised me, Mary!
No fond regret must Norman know;
When bursts Clan-Alpine on the foe.
His heart must be like bended bow,
   His foot like arrow free, Mary!

A time will come with feeling fraught,
For, if I fall in battle fought,
Thy hapless lover's dying thought
   Shall be a thought on thee, Mary!
And if restored from conquered foes,
How blithely will the evening close,
How sweet the linnet sing repose,
   To my young bride and me, Mary!

Sir Walter Scott.

---

flooded Teith, "panting and travel-soiled," carrying the "Fiery Cross"—"the fatal sign of fire and sword." Holding this forth, he spoke the appointed words:—

   "The master-place is Lanrick mead,
   Speed forth the signal! Norman, speed!"

This summons dread, brooks no delay, Norman must tear himself from his blighted bride, and the song is the expression of his feelings at parting, mingled with love's impatience and the manly thirst for martial fame.

"There is so much genuine feeling, so much tenderness in the reiterations of Mary's winning name," says the late Mr. P. R. Drummond, "that the reader is naturally led to enquire if it had no real inspiring first cause. In one of his early rambles into Perthshire, Scott met at Pitkellony, William and Mary Ann Erskine, children of the Rev. William Erskine, Episcopal minister of Muthill. William went to the bar, and eventually became Lord Kinnedder. Mary, after her father's death, lived with her brother at Edinburgh, and the talented young advocate became deeply attached to her; but he temporized, and Mr. Colquhoun, also an advocate, and Sheriff of Perthshire, carried off the much-envied Mary. This lady subsequently became well known as the confidential correspondent of Carolina Oliphant, from whom she received the first draft of 'The Land o' the Leal,' as a hymn of consolation on the death of one of her children. It does not therefore appear any very hazardous journey to walk down Glenartney, and identify Mary of Tombea with Mary of Pitkellony. An early, but long-deceased, friend of mine lived on intimate terms with the Erskine family so long as they remained at Muthill. He spoke with

HAIL TO THE CHIEF.*

FROM "THE LADY OF THE LAKE," CANTO II.

Hail to the Chief who in triumph advances!
  Honour'd and bless'd be the ever-green Pine!
Long may the tree in his banner that glances,
  Flourish, the shelter and grace of our line!
      Heaven send it happy dew,
      Earth lend it sap anew,
Gaily to bourgeon, and broadly to grow,
      While every Highland glen
      Sends our shout back again,
"Roderigh Vich Alpine dhu, ho! ieroe!"

Ours is no sapling, chance-sown by the fountain,
  Blooming at Beltane, in winter to fade;
When the whirlwind has stripp'd every leaf on the mountain,
  The more shall Clan-Alpine exult in her shade.
      Moor'd in the rifted rock,
      Proof to the tempest's shock,
Firmer he roots him the ruder it blow;
      Menteith and Breadalbane, then,
      Echo his praise again,
"Roderigh Vich Alpine dhu, ho! ieroe!"

Proudly our pibroch has thrill'd in Glen Fruin,
  And Banochar's groans to our slogan replied:
Glen Luss and Ross-dhu, they are smoking in ruin,
  And the best of Loch-Lomond lie dead on her side.
      Widow and Saxon maid,
      Long shall lament our raid,

---

enthusiasm of Scott's visits to them, and asserted that his marriage to Miss Carpentier was facilitated by his losing Mary Ann Erskine." Lockhart admits the attachment to Mary Erskine, but it is to the daughter of some mysterious northern baronet that he attributes Scott's early disappointment.

  * Readers of Scott will remember this as the spirited boat-song sung by the retainers of Roderick Dhu, while rowing down Loch Katrine.

  Think of Clan-Alpine with fear and with woe;
   Lennox and Leven-glen
   Shake when they hear again,
"Roderigh Vich Alpine dhu, ho! ieroe!"

Row, vassals, row, for the pride of the Highlands!
Stretch to your oars, for the ever-green Pine!
O! that the rose-bud that graces yon islands
Were wreathed in a garland around him to twine!
   O that some seedling gem,
   Worthy such noble stem,
Honour'd and bless'd in their shadow might grow!
   Loud should Clan-Alpine then
   Ring from the deepmost glen,
"Roderigh Vich Alpine dhu, ho! ieroe!"

SIR WALTER SCOTT.

THE BROOCH OF LORN.*

FROM "THE LORD OF THE ISLES," CANTO II.

WHENCE the brooch of burning gold,
That clasps the Chieftain's mantle-fold,
Wrought and chased with rare device,
Studded fair with gems of price,
On the varied tartans beaming,
As, through night's pale rainbow gleaming,
Fainter now, now seen afar,
Fitful shines the northern star?

---

* Between Crianlarich and Tyndrum, at a place called Dalree, or the King's Field, King Robert Bruce was encountered and repulsed, after a very severe engagement, by Alexander Macdougall, Lord of Lorn, at the head of a thousand men. "Bruce's personal strength and courage," says Sir Walter Scott, "were never displayed to greater advantage than in this conflict. There is a tradition in the family of the Macdougalls, that their chieftain engaged in personal battle with Bruce himself, while the latter was employed in protecting the retreat of his men; that Macdougall was struck down by the king, whose strength of body was equal to his vigour of mind, and would have been slain on the spot, had not two of Lorn's vassals, a father and son, whom tradition terms MacKeoch, rescued him, by seizing the mantle of the

'Gem! ne'er wrought on Highland mountain,
Did the fairy of the fountain,
Or the mermaid of the wave,
Frame thee in some coral cave ?
Did in Iceland's darksome mine
Dwarf's swart hands thy metal twine ?
Or, mortal-moulded, comest thou here,
From England's love, or France's fear ?

No! thy splendours nothing tell
Foreign art or faery spell.
Moulded thou for monarch's use,
By the overweening Bruce,
When the royal robe he tied
O'er a heart of wrath and pride ;
Thence in triumph wert thou torn,
By the victor hand of Lorn !

When the gem was won and lost,
Widely was the war-cry toss'd !
Rung aloud Bendourish fell,
Answer'd Douchart's sounding dell,
Fled the deer from wild Tyndrum,
When the homicide, o'ercome,
Hardly 'scaped with scathe and scorn,
Left the pledge with conquering Lorn !

---

monarch, and dragging him from above his adversary. Bruce rid himself of these foes by two blows of his redoubted battle-axe, but was so closely pressed by the followers of Lorn, that he was forced to abandon the mantle, and brooch which fastened it, clasped in the dying grasp of the MacKeochs. A studded brooch, said to have been that which King Robert lost upon this occasion, was long preserved in the family of Macdougall, and was lost in a fire which consumed their temporary residence."

Another account says that the worst that befel the brooch was that it was carried off during the Civil War of the seventeenth century, but was afterwards restored to the family. And the latter must be true if at Taymouth, on the occasion of the Queen's visit in 1842, as stated in Her Majesty's *Leaves from the Journal of Our Life in the Highlands*, the real Brooch of Lorn was shown to the Royal party by Captain MacDougall of Dunolly.

Vain was then the Douglas brand,
Vain the Campbell's vaunted hand,
Vain Kirkpatrick's bloody dirk,
Making sure of murder's work;
Barendown fled fast away,
Fled the fiery De la Haye,
When this brooch, triumphant borne,
Beam'd upon the breast of Lorn.

Farthest fled its former Lord,
Left his men to brand and cord,
Bloody brand of Highland steel,
English gibbet, axe, and wheel.
Let him fly from coast to coast,
Dogg'd by Comyn's vengeful ghost,
While his spoils, in triumph worn
Long shall grace victorious Lorn!

Sir Walter Scott.

THE MACGREGOR'S GATHERING.*

The moon's on the lake, and the mist's on the brae,
And the clan has a name that is nameless by day;
   Then gather, gather, gather, Grigalach!

Our signal for fight, which from monarchs we drew,
Must be heard but by night in our vengeful haloo,
   Then haloo, haloo, haloo, Grigalach!

Glen Orchy's proud mountains, Coalchuirn and her towers,
Glenstrae and Glenlyon no longer are ours;
   We're landless, landless, landless, Grigalach!

But, doom'd and devoted by vassal and lord,
Macgregor hath still both his heart and his sword!
   Then courage, courage, courage, Grigalach!

---

* These popular verses, in which the severe treatment of the Clan Macgregor, their outlawry, and the very proscription of their name, are feelingly alluded to, were written for *Albyn's Anthology*, in 1816.

If they rob us of name, and pursue us with beagles,
Give their roofs to the flame, and their flesh to the eagles!
    Then vengeance, vengeance, vengeance, Grigalach!

While there's leaves in the forest, or foam on the river,
Macgregor, despite them, shall flourish for ever!
    Come then, Grigalach! come then, Grigalach!

Through the depths of Loch Katrine the steed shall career,
O'er the peak of Ben Lomond the galley shall steer;
And the rocks of Craig Royston like icicles melt,
Ere our wrongs be forgot, or our vengeance unfelt!
    Then gather, gather, gather, Grigalach!

SIR WALTER SCOTT.

CAM' YE BY ATHOL?*

CAM' ye by Athol, lad wi' the philabeg,
  Doun by the Tummel, or banks o' the Garry?
Saw ye our lads, wi' their bonnets an' white cockades,
  Leaving their mountains to follow Prince Charlie?
    Follow thee, follow thee, wha wadna follow thee?
      Lang hast thou lo'ed an' trusted us fairly!
    Charlie, Charlie, wha wadna follow thee?
      King o' the Highland hearts, bonnie Prince Charlie.

I ha'e but a'e son, my gallant young Donald,
  But if I had ten they wad follow Glengarry;
Health to Macdonald an' gallant Clanronald,
  For these are the men that will die for their Charlie.
    Follow thee, follow thee, etc.

---

* This is not only a Perthshire song in the matter of its subject, but the rousing melody to which it is sung was composed and arranged for the pianoforte by Nathaniel Gow, son of the more celebrated Neil, whose humble abode at Inver is still a feature of curious interest to the intelligent visitor of Dunkeld and surrounding district.

I'll to Lochiel an' Appin' an' kneel to them,
   Doun by Lord Murray an' Roy of Kildarlie;
Brave Mackintosh, he shall fly to the field wi' them;
   These are the lads I can trust wi' my Charlie.
      Follow thee, follow thee, etc.

Doun through the Lowlands, doun wi' the whigamore,
   Loyal true Highlanders, doun wi' them rarely;
Ronald an' Donald drive on wi' the braid claymore,
   Over the necks o' the foes o' Prince Charlie.
      Follow thee, follow thee, etc.

JAMES HOGG.

THE BOWER OF TAY.

WEAR away, ye hues of Spring;
   Ye blooms of Summer, fade away;
Round the welcome season bring
   That leads my steps to Highland Tay.
Dear to me the day—the hour,
   When last her winding wave I saw,
But dearer still the bonnie bower
   That lies aneath yon greenwood shaw.

Aye we sat, and aye we sighed,
   For there was one my arms within;
Aye the restless stream we eyed,
   And heard its soft and soothing din:
The sun had sought Glenlyon's glade,
   Forth peered the evening's modest gem,
And every little cloud that strayed
   Looked gaudy in its gowden hem.

The playful breeze across the plain,
   Brought far the woodlark's wooer tale;
And gambolled o'er the mellow grain
   In mimic waves adown the dale.

I saw the drops of dew so clear
   Upon the green leaf trembling lie,
And, sweeter far, the crystal tear
   That trembled in a lovely eye.

When lovers meet, 'tis to the mind
   The Spring-flush of the blooming year;
But oh! their parting leaves behind
   A glow to memory ever dear.
Ettrick's fairy banks are green,
   And Yarrow braes are mooned with gray,
But gloamin' fall was never seen
   Like that I viewed in bower of Tay.

JAMES HOGG.

ATHOL CUMMERS.*

DUNCAN, lad, blaw the cummers,
Play me round the Athol cummers,
A' the din o' a' the drummers
Canna rouse like Athol cummers.
When I'm dowie, weet, or weary,
Soon my heart grows light an' cheerie;
When I hear the sprightly nummers
O' my dear, my Athol cummers.

When the fickle lasses vex me,
When the cares o' life perplex me,
When I'm fley'd wi' frightfu' rumours,
Then I lilt the Athol cummers.

---

* One evening in the winter of 1800, I was sawing away on the fiddle with great energy and elevation; and having executed the Strathspey called "Athol Cummers" much to my own satisfaction, my mother said to me, "Jemmie, are there ony words to that tune?" "No, that ever I heard, mother." "Oh, man, it's a shame to hear sic a guid tune an' nae words till't. Gae awa ben the house, like a guid lad, an' mak me a verse till't," and awa I gaed, an' here they are.—AUTHOR'S NOTE.

'Tis my cure for a' disasters,
Kebbit ewes and crabbit masters;
Drifty nights and dripping summers—
A' my joy is Athol cummers.

Ettrick banks and braes are bonny,
Yarrow hills are green as ony;
But in my heart nae beauty nummers,
Wi' my dear, my Athol cummers.
Lomond's beauty nought surpasses,
Save Breadalbane's bonnie lasses;
But deep within my spirit slummers
Something sweet of Athol cummers.

JAMES HOGG.

THE BANKS OF ALLAN WATER.*

On the banks of Allan water,
  When the sweet springtime did fall,
Was the miller's lovely daughter,
  Fairest of them all.
For his bride a soldier sought her,
  And a winning tongue had he,
On the banks of Allan water
  None was gay as she.

---

* This beautiful and popular song first appeared in the opera of "Rich and Poor." The plaintive air to which it has always been sung is said to have been composed by Lady Charlotte Campbell of the House of Argyll, the clever musician and novelist, afterwards known as Lady Charlotte Bury. Its *locale* has been claimed for Northumberland, and for Teviotdale, but Perthshire alone—in Strathallan—possesses the various features receiving prominent mention in the verses. Properly speaking, there is no river Allan in Northumberland. The Teviotdale Allan is small, and could have few millers or soldiers on its banks; whereas the Perthshire Allan has had many mills, and a garrison in its immediate vicinity. Further, the author's visits to this district, though affording no direct proof, are not without significance in the connection.

On the banks of Allan water,
    When brown autumn spread its store,
There I saw the miller's daughter,
    But she smiled no more.
For the summer grief had brought her,
    And the soldier false was he,
On the banks of Allan water,
    None was sad as she.

On the banks of Allan water,
    When the winter snow fell fast,
Still was seen the miller's daughter,
    Chilling blew the blast!
But the miller's lovely daughter
    Both from cold and care was free,
On the banks of Allan water
    There a corse lay she.
                  MATTHEW GREGORY LEWIS.

POOR ANNE.

Written at Callander in presence of Sir Walter Scott.

THE heart of Anne young Henry won,
    But love much sorrow wrought her,
For Henry was a monarch's son,
    Poor Anne—a shepherd's daughter.
He said, "A queen must be my bride,"
    Of Anne his last leave taking,
She kissed his hand, but nought replied,
    Poor girl! her heart was breaking.

He who her simple heart had won,
    And love and sorrow taught her,
Would he had been a shepherd's son,
    Or she some lordling's daughter!
His parting step she fondly eyed,
    But not one word was spoken;
Then down she laid her head, and died,
    Poor girl! her heart was broken.
                  MATTHEW GREGORY LEWIS.

THE FLOWER O' DUNBLANE.*

The sun has gane down o'er the lofty Benlomond,
    And left the red clouds to preside o'er the scene ;
While lanely I stray, in the calm summer gloamin',
    To muse on sweet Jessie, the flower o' Dunblane.
How sweet is the brier, wi' its saft faulding blossom !
    And sweet is the birk, wi' its mantle o' green ;
Yet sweeter and fairer, and dear to this bosom,
    Is lovely young Jessie, the flower o' Dunblane.

She's modest as ony, and blythe as she's bonnie,
    And guileless simplicity marks her its ain ;
And far be the villain, divested o' feeling,
    Wha'd blight in its bloom the sweet flower o' Dunblane.
Sing on, thou sweet mavis, thy hymn to the e'ening,
    Thou'rt dear to the echoes o' Calderwood glen ;
Sae dear to this bosom, sae artless and winning,
    Is charming young Jessie, the flower o' Dunblane.

---

* Few songs in the native dialect have taken a higher place and kept their popularity for a longer period than this beautiful love lyric. It has been sung in succession by Paton, Stephens, Tree, Wilson, Templeton, Sinclair, Milne, Taylor, Kennedy, and other vocalists of more than local fame. And many a bonnie lass whose name chanced to be the same with that in the song has been in her time the suppositious heroine of it, and got the blame of having "cuist the glamour" over the poet. There is no reason for believing, however, that the author had any particular fair one in his eye at the time. The truth is, Tannahill wrote the words to supplant the old coarse song " Bob o' Dunblane "—hence the title—and Jessie was quite an imaginary personage.

"The third stanza of the song was not written," says Mr. R. A. Smith, to whom the world is indebted for the music, "till several months after the others were finished, and, in my opinion, it would have been more to the author's credit had such an addition never been made. The language falls considerably below that of the first two verses."

A good deal has been made by some writers of the somewhat frivolous circumstance that Benlomond cannot be seen from Dunblane ; but I think it is true, as Mr. P. R. Drummond remarks, that one would not require to stray far therefrom in the calm summer gloamin' when he would see Benlomond between him and the setting sun.

How lost were my days till I met wi' my Jessie!
    The sports o' the city seemed foolish and vain;
I ne'er saw a nymph I could ca' my dear lassie,
    Till charmed wi' sweet Jessie, the flower o' Dunblane.
Though mine were the station o' loftiest grandeur,
    Amidst its profusion I'd languish in pain;
And reckon as naething the height o' its splendour,
    If wanting sweet Jessie, the flower o' Dunblane.
ROBERT TANNAHILL.

THE BRAES O' BALQUHITHER.

LET us go, lassie, go
    To the braes o' Balquhither,
Where the blaeberries grow
    'Mang the bonnie Highland heather;
Where the deer and the rae,
    Lightly bounding thegither,
Sport the lang simmer day
    On the braes o' Balquhither.

I will twine thee a bower,
    By the clear siller fountain,
And will cover it o'er
    Wi' the flowers o' the mountain.
I will range through the wilds,
    And the deep glens sae dreary,
And return wi' their spoils,
    To the bower o' my dearie.

When the rude wintry win'
    Idly raves round our dwelling,
And the roar of the linn
    On the night breeze is swelling;
So merrily we'll sing,
    As the storm rattles o'er us,
'Till the dear shieling ring
    Wi' the light lilting chorus.

Now the simmer is in prime,
  Wi' the flowers richly blooming,
And the wild mountain thyme
  A' the moorlands perfuming ;
To our dear native scenes
  Let us journey thegither,
Where glad Innocence reigns
  'Mang the braes o' Balquhither.

ROBERT TANNAHILL.

NEIL GOW'S FAREWELL TO WHISKY.*

You've surely heard of famous Neil,
The man wha played the fiddle weel,
He was a heartsome, merry chiel',
  An' weel he lo'ed the whisky, O.

---

* "Everybody knows Neil Gow. When he was poorly the physicians forbade him to drink his favourite liquor. The words following were composed, at his particular desire, to a lamentation he had just made."—AUTHOR'S PREFATORY NOTE.

"Mrs. Lyon," says Dr. Charles Rogers, "became acquainted with Gow when she was a young lady, attending the concerts in Dundee, at which the services of the great violinist were regularly required."

Commenting on the song, the author's note, and Dr. Rogers' remarks, together, the late Mr. P. R. Drummond, while admitting that Neil "liked a wee drap Highland whisky, and took occasional sprees," declares that to represent him as a retributive abstainer at the instance of a conclave of doctors, while he was in good health and living a comparatively sober life, was not only cruel in itself, but has mainly led to the popular falsehood that Neil Gow was a drunken man. It were a matter of regret," he adds bitterly, " if the memory of a man who, for half a century, was the delight and admiration of the nobles and educated people of Scotland, from the Tweed to the Spey, should, by the indiscretion of an individual who knew so little of him that she could not even spell his name, go down to future generations tainted by the unmeri'ed blemish that he was a devout worshipper ot Bacchus."

As to the libel, well, perhaps the "famous Neil" himself would not have protested so stoutly as his champion has done. And if Neil Gow chose to spell his Christian name *Niel* rather than *Neil*, as every previous bearer of it was content to do, there is little reason for blaming, or charging with ignorance, any one who may fail or refuse to fall in with his whim.

For e'er since he wore the tartan hose
He dearly liket Athole brose !
And grievèd was, you may suppose,
   To bid " Farewell to whisky," O !

" Alas ! " says Neil, " I'm frail and auld,
And whiles my hame is unco cauld ;
I think it mak's me blythe and bauld,
   A wee drap Highland whisky, O !

"But a' the doctors do agree
That whisky's no the drink for me ;
I'm fley'd they'll gar me tyne my glee,
   By parting me and whisky, O !

"But I should mind on auld lang syne,
How Paradise our friends did tyne,
Because something ran in their mind—
   Forbid—like Highland whisky, O !

" Whilst I can get guid wine and ale,
And find my heart and fingers hale,
I'll be content, though legs should fail,
   And though forbidden whisky, O !

" I'll tak' my fiddle in my hand,
And screw its strings whilst they can stand,
And mak' a lamentation grand
   For guid auld Highland whisky, O !

" Oh ! all ye powers of music, come,
For, deed, I think I'm mighty glum,
My fiddle-strings will hardly bum,
   To say ' farewell to whisky, O ! ' "

MRS. AGNES LYON.

ROB ROY'S GRAVE.*

A FAMOUS man is Robin Hood,
The English ballad-singer's joy!
But Scotland has a thief as good,
An outlaw of as daring mood;
She has her brave Rob Roy!
Then clean the weeds from off his grave
And let us chant a passing stave
In honour of that hero brave.

Heaven gave Rob Roy a dauntless heart,
And wondrous length and strength of arm;
Nor craved he more to quell his foes,
  Or keep his freends from harm.

Yet was Rob Roy as *wise* as brave;
Forgive me if the phrase be strong;—
A poet worthy of Rob Roy
  Must scorn a timid song.

Say, then, that he was wise as brave:
As wise in thought as bold in deed;
For in the principles of things
  He sought his moral creed.

Said generous Rob, "What need of books?
Burn all the statutes and their shelves;
They stir us up against our kind;
  And worse, against ourselves.

"We have a passion, make a law,
Too false to guide us or control!
And for the law itself we fight
  In bitterness of soul.

---

* The history of Rob Roy, over which Scott has thrown the glamour of his genius, is sufficiently known. His grave is in Balquhidder churchyard, where for many years his tombstone was only distinguished by a rude attempt at the figure of a broadsword. Recently, at the instance of the chief of the clan Macgregor the place has been marked by a handsome and substantial monument.

"And, puzzled, blinded thus, we lose
Distinctions that are plain and few;
These find I graven on my heart;
   That tells me what to do.

"The creatures see of flood and field,
And those that travel on the wind!
With them no strife can last; they live
   In peace, and peace of mind.

"For why?—because the good old rule
Sufficeth them, the simple plan,
That they should take who have the power,
   And they should keep who can.

"A lesson which is quickly learn'd,
A signal this which all can see!
Thus nothing here provokes the strong
   To wanton cruelty.

"All freakishness of mind is check'd;
He tamed, who foolishly aspires:
While to the measure of his might
   Each fashions his desires.

"All kinds, and creatures, stand and fall
By strength of prowess or of wit:
'Tis God's appointment who must sway,
   And who is to submit.

"Since, then, the rule of right is plain,
And longest life is but a day;
To have my ends, maintain my rights,
   I'll take the shortest way."

And thus among these rocks he lived,
Through summer's heat and winter's snow:
The eagle, he was lord above,
   And Rob was lord below.

So was it—*would*, at least, have been
But through untowardness of fate;
For polity was then too strong;
   He came an age too late.

Or shall we say an age too soon?
For, were the bold man living *now*,
How might he flourish in his pride,
   With buds on every bow!

Then rents and factors, rights of chase,
Sheriffs, and lairds and their domains,
Would all have seem'd but paltry things,
   Not worth a moment's pains.

Rob Roy had never linger'd here,
To these few meagre vales confined;
But thought how wide the world, the times
   How fairly to his mind.

And to his sword he would have said,
"Do thou my sovereign will enact
From land to land through half the earth!
   Judge thou of law and fact!

"'Tis fit that we should do our part;
Becoming, that mankind should learn
That we are not to be surpass'd
   In fatherly concern.

"Of old things all are over old,
Of good things none are good enough:—
We'll show that we can help to frame
   A world of other stuff.

"I, too, will have my kings that take
From me the sign of life and death:
Kingdoms shall shift about like clouds,
   Obedient to my breath."

And, if the word had been fulfilled,
As *might* have been, then, thought of joy!
France would have had her present boast,
   And we our brave Rob Roy!

Oh! say not so; compare them not;
I would not wrong thee, champion brave!
Would wrong thee nowhere; least of all
   Here standing by thy grave.

For thou, although with some wild thoughts,
Wild chieftain of a savage clan!
Hadst this to boast of; thou didst love
   The *liberty* of man.

And, had it been thy lot to live
With us who now behold the light,
Thou wouldst have nobly stirr'd thyself,
   And battled for the right.

For thou wert still the poor man's stay,
The poor man's heart, the poor man's hand!
And all the oppress'd who wanted strength,
   Had thine at their command.

Bear witness many a pensive sigh,
Of thoughtful herdsman when he strays
Alone upon Loch Veol's heights,
   And by Loch Lomond's braes!

And, far and near, through vale and hill,
Are faces that attest the same;
And kindle, like a fire new stirr'd,
   At sound of Rob Roy's name.

WILLIAM WORDSWORTH.

OSSIAN'S GRAVE.*

In this still place, remote from men,
Sleeps Ossian, in the "Narrow Glen;"
In this still place, where murmurs on
But one meek streamlet, only one:
He sang of battles, and the breath
Of stormy war, and violent death;
And should, methinks, when all was past,
Have rightfully been laid at last
Where rocks were rudely heap'd, and rent
As by a spirit turbulent;
Where sights were rough, and sounds were wild,
And everything unreconciled;
In some complaining, dim retreat,
For fear and melancholy meet;
But this is calm; there cannot be
A more entire tranquility.

Does then the bard sleep here indeed?
Or is it but a groundless creed?
What matters it?—I blame them not
Whose fancy in this lonely spot
Was moved; and in this way express'd
Their notion of its perfect rest.
A convent, even a hermit's cell
Would break the silence of this dell:
It is not quiet, is not ease;
But something deeper far than these:
The separation that is here
Is of the grave; and of austere
And happy feelings of the dead:
And, therefore, was it rightly said
That Ossian, last of all his race!
Lies buried in this lonely place.

WILLIAM WORDSWORTH.

---

* At the head of the "Sma' Glen," and on a grassy plot of ground at the side of the public road, stands a conspicuous relic of the past, an immense block of stone, cubical in form, eight feet high, and

ARCHY O' KILSPINDIE.*

WAE worth the heart that can be glad,
  Wae worth the tear that winna fa',
For justice is fleemyt frae the land,
  An' the faith o' auld times is clean awa'.

Our nobles they hae sworn an aith,
  An' they gart our young king swear the same,
That as lang as the crown was on his head,
  He wad speak to nane o' the Douglas name.

---

twenty-one feet in girth. It is called *Clach-na-Ossian*, and, according to unvarying tradition, was raised to mark the grave of the renowned Celtic bard.

* Archibald Douglas, the youngest son of the fifth Earl of Angus, when a child, was a great favourite of James V., who called him his "Grey-steel," and, when he grew up, made him High Treasurer of Scotland. On the attainder and forfeiture of the Douglases in 1528, Archibald of Kilspindie was banished into England. Wearied of his exile he ventured back to Scotland, and threw himself in the king's way as he returned to the Castle of Stirling from hunting in the neighbourhood. Seeing him in the distance, James said to one of his courtiers, "Yonder is my Grey-steel, Archibald of Kilspindie, if he be alive," to which the courtier replied that it could not be he, as a Douglas could not come into His Majesty's presence. On James's approach, Archibald fell on his knees, cast himself on the royal clemency, and promised that, if pardoned, he would never meddle with public affairs, but would lead a quiet and private life. James's heart yearned over him lovingly and tenderly; but remembering his vow against the Douglases, he deigned no reply, but trotted up the hill to the castle. The suppliant kept pace with him in the vain hope of his relenting; and exhausted with fatigue, sat down on a stone within the gate of the castle, and begged a drink of water, which none would give him, for fear of the royal displeasure. Hearing of this, James upbraided his servants for their inhumanity, saying that, but for his oath's sake, he himself would have taken Kilspindie into favour. He then ordered him to Leith, to wait his pleasure, whence he was sent to France, where he died soon after. It is pleasing to have to add that his forfeiture was rescinded, in 1543, and that his son and heir, also Archibald, was restored to his estates, and was twice Lord Provost of Edinburgh.—*Dr. Marshall's "Historic Scenes in Perthshire."*

Finlay, the author of the ballad, was a native of Glasgow. He was born in 1782, and died at Moffat in 1810.

An' wasna this a wearifu' aith ;
   For the crown frae his head had been tint an' gane
Gin the Douglas' hand hadna held it on,
   When anither to help him there was nane.

An' the king frae that day grew dowie an' wae,
   For he liked in his heart the Douglas weel;
For his foster-brither was Jamie o' Parkhead,
   An' Archy o' Kilspindie was his Grey-steel.

But Jamie was banisht an' Archy baith,
   An' they lived lang, lang ayont the sea,
Till a' had forgotten them but the king!
   An' he whiles said, wi' a watery e'e—
"Gin they think on me as I think on them,
   I wat their life is but drearie."

It chanced he rode wi' hound an' horn
   To hunt the dun an' the red-deer down,
An' wi' him there was mony a gallant earl
   An' laird, an' knight, an' bold baron.

But nane was wi' him wad ever compare
   Wi' the Douglas so proud in tower and town,
That were courtliest all in tower and hall,
   And the highest ever in renown.

It was dawn when the hunters sounded the horn,
   By Stirling's walls, so fair to see;
But the sun was far gaen down i' the west
   When they brittled the deer on Torwood-lee.

An' wi' jovial din they rode hame to the town
   Where Snawdon * tower stands dark an' hie;
Frae least to best they were plyin' the jest,
   An' the laugh was gaun round right merrily.

* An ancient name of Stirling.

When Murray cried loud,—" Wha's yon I see ?
   Like a Douglas he looks, baith dark and grim ;
And for a' his sad and weary pace,
   Like them he's richt stark o' arm and limb."

The king's heart lap, and he shouted wi' glee—
   " Yon stalwart makedom * I ken richt weel ;
And I'se wad in pawn the hawk on my han'
   It's Archy Kilspindie, my ain Grey-steel ;
We maun gi'e him grace o' a' his race,
   For Kilspindie was trusty aye, an' leal."

But Lindsay spak' in waefu' mood—
   " Alas ! my liege, that mauna be."
And stout Kilmaurs cries—" He that daurs,
   Is a traitor to his ain countrie."

And Glencairn, that aye was doure and stern,
   Says—" Where's the aith ye sware to me ?
Gin ye speak to a man o' the Douglas clan,
   A gray groat for thy crown and thee."

When Kilspindie took haud o' the king's bridle reins,
   He louted low down on his knee ;
The king a word he durstna speak,
   But he looked on him richt wistfullie.

He thought on days that lang were gane,
   Till his heart was yearnin' and like to brast ;
As he turned him round, his barons frowned ;
   But Lindsay was dichtin' his een fu' fast.

When he saw their looks, his proud heart rose,
   An' he tried to speak richt hauchtillie—
" Gae tak' my bridle frae that auld man's grip ;
   What sorrow gars him haud it sae sickerlie ? "

---

* Stout body.

And he spurred his horse wi' gallant speed,
    But Archy followed him manfullie,
And, though cased in steel frae shoulder to heel,
    He was first o' a' his companie.

As they passed, he sat down on a stane in the yett,
    For a' his grey hair there was nae ither biel;
The king staid the hindmost o' the train
    And he aft looked back to his auld Grey-steel.

Archy wi' grief was quite fordone,
    An' his arm fell weak that was ance like airn,
An' he sought for some cauld water to drink,
    But they durstna for that doure Glencairn.

When this was tauld to our gracious king,
    A red-wud furious man woxe he,
He has ta'en the mazer cup in his hand,
    And in flinders he has gart it flee—
"Had I kent my Grey-steel wanted a drink,
    He should hae had o' the red wine free."

And fu' sad at the table he sat him down,
    And he spak' but a'e word at the dine—
"O I wish my warst fae were but a king,
    Wi' as cruel counsellours as mine."

JOHN FINLAY.

THE BATTLE OF LUNCARTY.*

THE beacon lights are blazing bright, the slogan's on
    the blast;
The clansmen muster rapidly, the fiery cross flies fast;
Chiefs hurry from their towers of strength, and vassals
    from their shiels;
For Albyn's strand's polluted by an hundred hostile
    keels.

---

* In the year 980, when the Danes had invaded Scotland, and prevailed in the battle of Luncarty, near Perth, the Scots were worsted, and gave way. In their flight through a narrow pass they were stopped by a countryman and his two sons, who encouraged them to

Oh! vermil cheeks shall pallid grow, and sunny eyes
    shall weep;
But not from fear or sorrow, but from indignation deep;
To see these Scandinavian wolves, a wild, unhallow'd
    band,
Like demons of destruction come to wreck our father-
    land.

The robber hordes are all debarked—their raven-banners
    wave—
Their swords are out, and fair Strathmore is one pro-
    miscuous grave;
The Esk, the Brothick, Lunan, Tay, run ruddy to the
    sea;
While altar, temple, tower, and town, are levelled with
    the lea!

---

rally and renew the fight, and upbraided those who would fly like cowards when all was at stake. The more timorous stood still, and many of the stout men, who fled more by the desertion of their companions than from want of courage, joined with the old man and his two sons to stop the rest, till there was a good number together. The countrymen, who are said to have been armed with only their plough coulters, backed by the rallied forces, made a furious attack on the approaching Danes, crying aloud, "Help is at hand!" whereupon the Danes, thinking a fresh army was falling on them, were partially paralysed, and the Scots thereby totally defeated them, and freed their country from servitude. The battle over, the old man, afterwards known by the name of Hay, was brought to the King, who, assembling a Parliament at Scone, gave Hay and his sons, as a just reward for their valour, so much land on the river Tay, in the district of Gowrie, as a falcon from a man's hand flew over till it settled; which, being six miles in length, was afterwards called Errol. And the King being willing to promote the said Hay and his sons from the rank of plebeians to the order of nobility, he assigned them a coat of arms, which was —Argent, three escutcheons, gules—to intimate that the father and two sons had been the three fortunate shields of Scotland. Such is the story as told in "The Scottish Peerage" (art. Hay), the authenticity of which has, however, been questioned by subsequent writers. We have before us three ballads composed on the battle of Luncarty—one by David Miller, the author of "The Tay—a Poem;" another by James Ferguson of Stanley; and the third the one we have chosen, and which is certainly the best, from the pen of David Vedder, the well-known sailor-poet of Orkney.

The hut, the cottage, and the grange, are blazing up to heaven;
Decrepit eld, and babes alike, are to this carnage given;
And beauteous maids and matrons fair leap from the dizzy steep,
And perish—pure as snow from heaven—upon the ocean deep.

The spoilers move exultingly, o'er Gowrie's fertile fields,
Their deadly spears a forest seem'd, a solid wall their shields;
Like locusts in their mortal flight upon the orient wind,
A paradise before them lay, a blighted waste behind.

Bathed in the setting light of heaven, imperial Bertha shone,
Like some empurpled orient queen upon her emerald throne.
The waving woods, her gorgeous train, seem'd paying homage meet;
And Tay, emitting silver sounds, lay crouching at her feet.

"Now by the sacred mead that flows in Odin's palace high—
And by the blessed light that beams from Thor's immortal eye,
If there's a recreant in my host," the giant Sweno cries,
"His craven corse shall flesh my hounds—his odious memory dies.

"See, mountain, meadow, strath, and stream—behold the glorious prize,
The bright Valhalla of my dreams, when sleep had scal'd mine eyes,
There lies the land of my desire—the home of all my love;
And *there* the Danish diadem shall shine all crowns above."

Ten thousand voices burst at once in one loud chorus swell;
Whilst echo from her mountain caves prolonged the savage yell;
Ten thousand brands on brazen shields in dire collision clash'd—
Ten thousand darts were hurl'd in air, or in the sod were dash'd.

But, hark! a shout has answered theirs, like mountain torrents loud—
A marshalled host comes moving on dense as a thunder cloud—
And like that cloud, surcharged with death, and rolling rapidly;
That thunder cloud is Scotland's king, and Scotland's chivalry.

In fiery haste the Scots advance, and with the invaders close—
Like tigers of their cubs bereaved, they spring upon their foes,
And thousands fall no more to rise, gash'd o'er with many a wound;
And shrieks, and shouts, and groans are blent, and life-blood stains the ground.

The Scottish monarch marked his track along the gory plain,
His beacons in that sea of blood were pyramids of slain.
He spurr'd his foaming charger on along the embattled line,
And with his ponderous battle-axe clove Sweno to the chine.

Now clan with clan, and son with sire, and chief with chieftain vied,
To pierce the Danish phalanx through, and turn the battle's tide,

For vassal, knight, and thane, alike, their blood ran hot
    and high ;
Death glared from every falchion's edge, and vengeance
    from each eye.

What boots it now how well they fought, for ah! they
    fought in vain ;
Their squadrons reel, their ranks are broke, they fly
    before the Dane ;
The banner of the silver cross lies trampled in the clay,
And for the glorious battle-cry 'tis " Save himself who
    may."

See how they flee o'er moor and dale, like fugitives
    forlorn ;
Where is thine honour, Scotland, now ? 'tis like thy
    banners—torn ;
Yes, there is honour—there is hope—for by this blessed
    light,
Three gallant men have left their teams, and check'd
    the shameful flight.

And now they rally, form, and charge, and gory gaps
    they hew'd ;
With tenfold fury in their souls the battle was renew'd.
'Twas hand to hand, and brand to brand, and dirk and
    dagger met,
And flane and flane alternately in red heart-blood were
    wet.

On, on, ye glorious peasants three, the bloody die is cast;
The Danes are routed—See, they fly like snowflakes on
    the blast.
On, on, ye peasant heroes, on, and win your deathless
    mead—
The gory die at length is cast, and Scotland's soil is
    freed.

There's mirth and kingly revelry in Scone's imperial
    hall ;
And squire and knight and lord and thane grace that
    high festival,

And royalty, in robes of state, and beauty's bright display;
But every eye in homage turned upon the patriots Hay.

There's mimic warfare on the lawn, beneath the royal eye,
There's lances shiver'd—knights unhorsed—the flower of chivalry;
And high-born dames, lit up with smiles, bright as the milky way—
But O! their smiles beamed brightest on the stalwart peasants Hay.

Then royal Kenneth left his throne, and laid his crown aside—
"Are you the glorious peasants three that turned the battle's tide?
Your patent of nobility Heaven gave you at your birth,
Alas! a king can only add the splendours of the earth.

"Such as we have we give. Be lords of Errol's fertile fields,
And be your scutcheon blazon'd with three blood-stain'd Scottish shields;
And may your fame, your glory, last for ever and for aye,
For Scotland, to the end of time, shall bless the name of Hay."

DAVID VEDDER.

BIOGRAPHICAL NOTICES OF PERTHSHIRE POETS.

BIOGRAPHICAL NOTICES.

HENRY ADAMSON,

Author of "The Muses' Threnodie, or Mirthful Mournings on the Death of Mr. Gall," is the earliest, and only known poet of the old classic order, which the City of Perth can lay claim to. According to James Cant, who edited an edition of his poems, with notes and observations, which was published at Perth in 1774, Adamson was educated for the pulpit, and was a gentleman of considerable talent, a good classical scholar, and the author of some Latin poems above mediocrity. He was the son of James Adamson, who was Dean of Guild in Perth in the year of the Gowrie Conspiracy, and Provost in 1610 and 1611. As a poet he was known and esteemed by Drummond of Hawthornden, the Poet-Laureate of the time, at whose solicitation, he, in 1638, issued the first edition of his poems. Prefixed to this is the following address to the "Courteous Reader." "It is not amiss," says the poet, "thou be a little informed concerning the persons of the defunct Mr. Gall, and the mourner, Mr. Ruthven. The poet wrote this for his own exercise, and the recreation of his friends, and this piece, though accomplished to the great contentment of many that read and heard it, yet could not the author be induced to let it thole the press, till the importunity of many learned men urged him unto it; and the last brashe (effort) was made by a letter of the prime poet of our kingdom, whereof this is the just copy

"'To my worthy friend Mr. Henry Adamson.

"'Sir,—These papers of your Mournings on Mr. Gall, appear unto me as *Alcibiadis Sileni,* which ridiculously look with the faces of Sphinges, Chimeras, Centaurs, on their outsides; but inwardlie containe rare artifice, and rich jewels of all sorts, for the delight and weal of man. They may deservedlie bear the words *non intus ut extra*. Your two champions, noble zanys (buffoons) discover to us many of the antiquities of this country, more of our ancient town of Perth, setting down her situation, founders, her huge colosse or bridge, walls, aqueducts, fortifications, temples, monastries, and many other singularities. Happie hath Perth been in such a citizen, not so other towns of this kingdome, by want of so diligent a searcher and preserver of their fame from oblivion. Some Muses, neither to themselves nor to others, do good, nor delighting, nor instructing. Yours perform both, and longer to conceal them, will be, to wrong your Perth of her due honours, who deserveth no less of you than that she should be thus blazoned and registrate to posterity, and to defraud yourself of a monument, which, after you have left this transitory world, shall keep your name and memory to after-times. This shall be preserved by the towne of Perth, for her own sake first, and after for yours; for to her it hath been no little glory, that she hath brought forth such a citizen, so eminent in love to her, so dear to the Muses.

"'W. D.

"'Edinburgh, 12th July, 1637.'"

Adamson appears not to have been ambitious of fame, and, presumably, but for the patronising solicitude of "the prime poet," neither "Gall's Gabions," nor "The Muses' Threnodie," would ever have seen the light of print. As to the first poem, of which no idea can be formed from the title, it consists of a ludicrous and Hudibrastic inventory of the furniture and collection of curiosities contained in Mr. George Ruthven's closet, all of which the venerable owner was wont to succinctly describe as his "Gabions."

The "Threnodie" is an elegiac poem on the death of Mr. John Gall, a young gentleman, handsome, facetious, and learned. The poet keeps himself behind the curtain, and introduces Ruthven and Gall upon the stage, who give an account of the antiquities of Perth, and its environs. Ruthven was descended from the noble family of the same name, and was a physician and surgeon in Perth. Gall was a merchant, well educated, of sweet disposition, and pregnant wit, and much esteemed. His premature death, of consumption, afforded occasion for the poem.

Adamson died, unmarried, in 1629, the year after the publication of his book, and was much lamented, the following tribute to his memory showing the high esteem in which he was held by the "makkirs" of his time :—

> Dear soul, thou hast obtained more lasting fame,
>   In Folly's colours wisdom setting forth ;
> Than if ten fabricks like *Mausolus*' frame,
>   Were for thee rear'd in witness of thy worth.
> Thy *Perth* may boast of such a grateful son,
>   Who thus hath honour'd his dear aged mother ;
> Thy Muse such glory and such fame hath won
>   To her, as no oblivion can it smother.
> Art, wit, and learning, learning, wit, and art,
>   Do jointly jostle here, each of them striving,
> Which carry shall the prize, and bear chief part
>   In these thy lays, thy native town describing.
> Thy *George's Gabions* shew to underlings
>   That all things triffles be that Heaven not reaches;
> By what thy *Gall* and he, in rapture sings
>   Much wisdom divine and humane thou teaches.
> Thy death the Muses' darlings all shall mourn,
>   And shall a tomb erect unto thy name ;
> Of tears turned *cristal*, and upon thine urn,
>   These words shall write as blazon of thy fame.
>   Here lies his dust by whose most learned quill,
>   He and his *Perth* do live, and shall live still.
>   Jo. MOORE.

PETER AGNEW.

A house-painter to trade, and a poet by chance, Peter Agnew was a native of Perth, and lived in the South

Street in 1793. Very early in life he gave evidence of being possessed of rare musical talent, and learned to play on the violin, an instrument over which he soon obtained an almost complete mastery, and with which he lived to charm the ills of many a luckless day. On the completion of his 'prentice time Agnew went to Glasgow, and from thence, in a few years, to London, from whence he again, after a few more years, returned to the commercial capital of his native Caledonia, where he wore out the bulk of his after-lease. His life appears to have been a somewhat chequered one, the grim visage of poverty frequently staring him in the face, and, if not actually sconcing herself at his fireside, being represented there on an occasion by her foster-friend, the beagle. An excellent violinist, a fair landscape painter, a capital singer of songs, a pleasing writer of verses, and an entertaining story-teller, perhaps Peter Agnew had too many accomplishments to be eminently successful in any.

REV. JOHN ANDERSON, D.D.

A profound preacher, a genial and subtle essayist, a graceful poet, and a keen angler, the Rev. Dr. John Anderson, of Kinnoull, is the only child of the Rev. Dr. John Anderson, minister first at Dunbarney, near Bridge of Earn, and afterwards at Newburgh-on-Tay, and was born at the latter place in 1822. "My father," he says, "always, in his mind, designed me for the Church; but for some time it seemed doubtful if such a special nugget was destined to enrich the treasury of the dear Auld Kirk. . . . The sons of the manse have earned the name of proverbial 'Pickles,' and the writer of these lines, I greatly fear, was closely allied to that family. My 'schooling' began under the kindly care of old Tom Scott, who died not long ago, the minister of Shapinshay in the far off misty Shetlands. It was no fault of his that his boy failed to become a star. . . . However, in one way I made my 'mark;' for if I had not a pair of handsome black eyes once a quarter some other fellow was certain to wear the sable livery. These things I can afford to write, keeping nothing back, being now a greyhaired man, much sobered and subdued by the stern realities of life, and gazing with a placid sadness down the sombre far-stretching vista of more than half a century." "A ragged cowte has aft been kent to mak' a guid gelding," says the old Scotch proverb, and by and by "the minister's wild laddie," as he was called, became "cannie," and sought to excel at school, and succeeded. At the age of fourteen he was sent to St. Andrews University, and there for six years worked hard, with honours. Proceeding to Edinburgh, he there completed his theological course, and justified the hope which was entertained of him whilst a student at St. Andrews. He was the only alumnus of the period whose contributions were accepted by the leading serials. To *Fraser's Magazine* he contributed a series of papers on "Christopher North in his Fishing Jacket," which subsequently secured him Professor Wilson's personal regard. His literary powers also attracted the notice of Principal Lee, who evinced exceptional interest on his behalf. The Principal offered him important preferment abroad, but, in deference to his parents' entreaty, he remained at home. In 1844 he was elected minister of St. John's Church, Dundee. In the year following he was translated to St. John's Parish, Perth. Here he laboured with much acceptance for about seven years, when he was appointed to the church living of Kinnoull, where he still remains and ministers to a much-devoted and proudly-appreciative congregation. "A graceful and effective preacher," says the *Christian Leader*, "Dr. Anderson, had he encouraged proposals made to him, might have occupied important charges either at Glasgow or Edinburgh. But a town life had no attractions for him, and he has expressed his determination not to abandon his present sphere. At Kinnoull he lives among an attached people and kindly appreciative neighbours, while he daily enjoys a spectacle of landscape beauty singularly adapted to his tastes. A vigorous prose writer, he might as a poet have obtained fame had his ambition been equal to his genius." As it is, he is well known as a Christian lyrist. His beautiful compositions adorn the pages of "Lyra Britannica," the "Harp of the Christian Home," and other collections. His published works include "Visions of a Night," "The Pleasures of Home," "A Legend of Glencoe," "Bible Incidents," "Holy Ground," "Autumn Gleanings; or Ears of Barley," and "Sprigs of Heather; or the Rambles of May-fly with his Old Friends," all giving evidence of a mind enriched with the stores of varied scholarship; an eye keenly alive to the beauties of nature; and a heart as tender and sympathetic as it is frequently joyous and strong.

JOHN ANDERSON.

A frequent contributor of prose and verse to the periodical press, John Anderson, the second, presently employed as an assistant teacher in Yardheads Public School, Leith, is a native of Auchterarder, and was born on 30th March, 1860. When little more than a mere child he exhibited an unusually fine faculty for the acquirement of knowledge, and became a pupil teacher in his *Alma Mater* before he was fifteen years old. He attended the E. C. Training College in Glasgow, in 1879-80, and has since held important appointments as a teacher both in Scotland and in England. An esteemed member of the literary staff of *Illustrations*, conducted by Mr. Francis G. Heath, since 1886, he recently contributed to that Magazine an important series of articles on the educational establishments, public and private, of the United Kingdom, and another on Scottish artists and their studies, which merit the permanency of collective book form. Adding to a fine literary taste, a good ear, and a cultured imagination, Mr. Anderson's lyrics, if not powerful, are graceful and pleasing.

REV. PETER ANTON,

Parish minister of Kilsyth, and author of "Masters in History," and "England's Essayists"—two of the most popular books of their class—was born about forty years ago on the braes of the celebrated Carse of Gowrie, where his family circle has still its centre, and whence his heart yet sends his memory on many a pleasant excursion. He received his scholastic education in Perth and Dundee, and at an early age entered the University of St. Andrews. Adding to a powerfully athletic body an equally powerful mind, and a finely retentive memory, Mr. Anton distinguished himself at college by carrying off first honours both in the literary classes and in the gymnasium; and even at this early time his contributions to the literary journals of the day were not unfrequent. Immediately after being licensed by the Presbytery of St. Andrews, he was appointed assistant in St. Paul's Parish—the South Kirk—Dundee. After a few weeks here, he was presented by the late Earl of Rosslyn to the Parish of Dysart, from whence, six years subsequently, he received an unanimous appointment to Kilsyth, where he presently ministers to a large and highly appreciative congregation. Mr. Anton's fame as a biographical essayist—a line of work in which he specially excells—is co-extensive with the circulation of the *People's Friend*, perhaps the most popular and widely read miscellany of its class, to the pages of which he has been a regular and welcome contributor for many years. He has also written for *The Scots Magazine*, *The Scottish Church*, *Life and Work*, *Fraser's Magazine*, etc. Poetry has been but the mere by-play of his life—the study with which he has been accustomed to fill in an otherwise idle half-hour; but so fresh and inspiriting are some of his numbers that his many friends and admirers will be disposed to hope with the present writer that those "orra" half-hours will occur to him more frequently in the future than they have been permitted to do in the past.

CHARLES BALFOUR,

For many years station-master at Glencarse, was born at Panmure, near Carnoustie, in 1819. He was early sent to work, and has, on the stage of life and labour, played in his time many and varied parts. Beginning with cow-herd, he has been successively apprentice brewer, factory worker, soldier, railway parcel-deliverer, goods guard, passenger guard, and station-master. When employed as a guard, in 1852, the train to which he was attached was thrown over the bridge which crosses Invergowrie Quarry, and, going down with it, he sustained such fearful injury that for months he lay in Dundee Infirmary, his life trembling in the balance. Rallying at length, he was appointed station-master at Glencarse, where he remained until his retirement, recently, respected and esteemed by all with whom he came into intimate contact. His one popular song, "The Iron Horse," was first sung in public at a festival of railway servants, held in Perth in 1848.

MRS. M. F. BARBOUR.

A grand-niece of Lady Nairne, the authoress of "The Land o' the Leal," Margaret Fraser Sandeman, born 24th March, 1823, possessed not a little of the poetic fire that percolated through the veins of her saintly mother, Mrs. Sandeman of Springland, and descended to her own son, the late Rev. Robert W. Barbour of Bonskeid; and the examples of her muse which we have been able to secure for this work through the kindly offices of her daughter, Mrs. Simpson, of Edinburgh, reflecting as they do the gentle and devout spirit of their author, will be much esteemed.

Part of our subject's childhood, it is worth noticing, was spent with her illustrious grand-aunt on the Continent, and many of the leading events and incidents contained in the Memoir of the Baroness, which was published some years ago, were gathered from a narrative supplied by her facile pen.

On the 24th April, 1845, she was married, in her mother's house at Springland, to George Freeland Barbour, Esq. Her brother, the Rev. David Sandeman, who was groomsman, then said to her, "Do not go to your home as a Mistress, go as a Door-keeper, to let in whomsoever Christ sends." And this advice she obeyed to the letter. To the end of her days the doors of Bonskeid House were ever open to the servants of the Master, and, like her mother, she was never so happy as when she had a house full of evangelists, to minister to whom was one of the supreme pleasures of her life. She was an eloquent and effective speaker as well as ready with her pen, and although she did not appear on public platforms, those who have heard her on semi-private occasions will never forget her powerful and impassioned addresses. A devoted member of the Free Church for many years, China and its people occupied the chief place in Mrs. Barbour's thoughts. Her interest in that great empire dated from the time when the Rev. William C. Burns, who manifested a powerful influence on her life, and her brother, the Rev. David Sandeman, a man of noble character, devoted themselves to missionary work in China. To all the missionaries in China and to students from that land attending the University of Edinburgh she showed unbounded kindness, and gave freely of her means for the work of the mission, as she gave, indeed, for every good object. The present age with its artificialities and proprieties is not likely to produce many women of such a high order as Mrs. Barbour of Bonskeid, and it will be difficult to fill her place. The death of her husband, six years ago, and of her gifted son, Rev. Robert W. Barbour, early in the summer of 1891, darkened the close of her life, but her friends never knew any change in the geniality of her disposition and in her largeness and kindness of heart. She died in the beginning of February last year.

As a book writer, Mrs. Barbour acquired considerable fame. "The Way Home," which records the lives of her two eldest sons, who met their death in a railway accident at an early age, has had a wide circulation, and the loving and delightsome Memoir of her Mother, "The Soul-Gatherer," and other works, attest her literary skill. But her great work—her great poem—was her life.

REV. ROBERT W. BARBOUR.

A second M'Cheyne, Robert William Barbour, recently deceased, was the eldest son of the late George Freeland Barbour, Esq. of Bonskeid, and the subject of the preceding notice, and was born at Edinburgh, on the 29th November, 1854. In early boyhood he gave himself to the Christian life, and at Edinburgh University came at once to the front and achieved a very brilliant career. After visiting the mission fields of several churches in Africa, Mr. Barbour entered the ministry of the Free Church, and was settled at Cults, near Aberdeen, in 1881. After labouring at Cults with much success and acceptance for five years, he was obliged to resign his charge on account of the state of his health. During the absence of Professor Lindsay in India, he occupied the Chair of Church History in the Free Church College in Glasgow, where his services were greatly appreciated by the students. At the request of the College Committee of the United Presbyterian Church, Mr. Barbour had agreed to discharge for a session, along with Professor Calderwood, the duties of the Chair of Church History, rendered vacant by the death of Professor Duff, but, to his regret, he was prevented by medical orders from fulfilling the engagement. During the winter of 1891-2 he was confined to the house, and in the month of February he went to Mentone, tended by his devoted wife and some friends; latterly he removed to Aix-les-Bains, where he lingered till the end of May, when he sank out of great weakness into everlasting rest. On the 3rd June his remains were interred beside those of his father and his son in the private burying-ground at Bonskeid.

Mr. Barbour early discovered a true poetic faculty, and more than a dozen years ago published a volume of his poems under the title of "Jeroveam's Wife and other Poems," which was very favourably received. Writing of this and the intellectual side of his friend and fellow-student's character generally, Professor George Adam Smith of Aberdeen recently said, "I do not think that the poetry of his book ever came near the poetry of his life. He saw the ideal in everything, especially in common Christian work and in our Scottish life, in both of which it is so difficult for ordinary hearts to rise above the commonplace. He saw the blush of the heart's blood through the meanest face, and had a way all his own of glorifying the humblest means of grace. He was a thorough Scot, with a love for his land, her history, and her songs, that was very beautiful. He knew Scottish life to the bone, Scottish history to the fountainhead; and it was delightful in conversation about parish politics and every-day matters, to be surprised by his emphasis of the historical meaning and national virtue of some ordinary event or institution. If he has failed to build any monument worthy of his intellectual strength, it is largely because he consecrated his powers to pastoral work."

REV. JOHN BARCLAY,

Sometimes called "John the Berean," by reason of his being the founder of the old and now totally defunct religious sect bearing that name, was born at Strageath, in the parish of Muthill, in 1734. His father, Ludovic Barclay, from the first designed his son for the Church, and, after running the course of the parish school and studying at St. Andrews University, he was licensed to preach the Gospel by the Presbytery of Auchterarder on the 27th September, 1759. Acting for three or four years as assistant minister of Errol, and afterwards for nine years occupying the same position at Fettercairn, he was hunted for heresy, and seceded from the Church of Scotland in 1773. Subsequently he preached the Gospel, according to his own interpretation of it, in Edinburgh and London, in both of which centres he established a church, and disputed in public with whoever might be inclined to call his doctrines in question. In the Scottish capital he formed a large congregation. He died there of apoplexy on the 29th July, 1798. His remains were interred in the Calton old burying-ground, where a monument bearing a suitable inscription has been erected to his memory. In addition to several volumes of a polemical character, Barclay wrote and published a metrical version of the Psalms, and was, according to Burns and others, the author of the version of the "Battle of Shirramuir," placed above his name in this work.

During his career as a "gospeller," he occasionally visited his native locality, and he formed a church in Crieff, which flourished up till about forty years ago, when the survivors divided the collection plate, plate-stand, forms, etc., by lot. When resident here he generally lodged with a family who lived on the east side of King Street; and tradition tells that after an animated discourse on the people of Berea, in a malt barn, which occupied the site of the present Free Church, some one wrote with chalk on the door of the house in which he lodged, "Noble Bereans," which so pleased him that he adopted "Bereans" as the title of his sect.

JAMES BEATTIE

Was a native of Leetown, near Errol, in the Carse of Gowrie, and was born in the year 1796. The son of a stone mason, he learned his father's handicraft, and—a brief interval excepted, in which he vainly endeavoured to establish himself as an architect and contractor—he continued an operative stone-worker until the end of his days. We have not been able to learn very much of what one may appropriately term Beattie's every-day walk; but the sorry fact is on record that while yet in the prime of life he contracted irregular habits, and hastened his end by insistent intemperance. He died at Leetown in the winter of 1838, and lies buried in St. Madoe's Churchyard.

A volume of his poems, extending to 64 pages, was published during the poet's lifetime by John Taylor, Perth, but the book bears no date. Many of his poems are of surprising excellence, especially as the lucubrations of a working man. His style, formed on some of the best models, is substantially English; and he displays, in vigorous diction, great wealth of poetic thought and refined sentiment.

REV. GEORGE BLAIR.

A distinguished student of St. Andrews University, George Blair was ordained to the pastorate of Monzie parish in September 1843. In October of the following year, he resigned his pastoral charge, and was at the same time suspended from the office of the holy ministry. After engaging for a short time in journalistic work in Glasgow he went abroad. In 1877, when the late Principal Tulloch visited America, he met Mr. Blair, who then occupied the responsible position of an Inspector of Schools in Canada. Acting on the Principal's advice, he at that time applied to the Presbytery of Auchterarder to remove the sentence of suspension passed on him thirty-three years before; and the application being accompanied by testimonials from some of the best known men in Canada, this was accordingly done. A mixed volume of poetry and prose, of supreme local interest, from Mr. Blair's pen, entitled "The Holocaust; or the Witch of Monzie: a poem illustrative of the cruelties of superstition; Lays of Palestine, and other poems, to which is prefixed Enchantment Disenchanted; or a treatise on Superstition," appeared in 1845, and is now very scarce. The example of his verse herein contained is taken from that work.

REV. WILLIAM BLAIR, D.D.,

The venerable and esteemed U.P. Minister of Dunblane, whose contributions to literature are neither few nor unimportant, was born at Clunie, in the parish of Kinglassie, in 1830. After a distinguished University career, which terminated in 1854, he simultaneously received a call to Whitby, in England, and another to

Dunblane; and, choosing the latter, was ordained as minister there in April, 1856, where he has since laboured assiduously, and without interruption, to a large and attached congregation. As a student and a minister Dr. Blair's mind has continued in unceasing activity. While yet at college he published "The Chronicles of Aberbrothock," a traditionary work of considerable extent. In 1857 "Rambling Recollections" appeared, and three years subsequently "The Prince of Preachers," a sermon and a biographical sketch of the late Dr. Fletcher of London, which was followed a year later by an interesting account of a tour he made through France, Switzerland, and Italy. In 1873 he edited M'Kelvie's "Annals and Statistics of the U. P. Church," and ten years later published "Selections from Archbishop Leighton, with Notes and Biography," a work which has been greatly esteemed. In addition to the books named, Dr. Blair has written largely for the newspapers, magazines, and reviews of the day, as well as articles for biographical dictionaries. The University of St. Andrews conferred upon him the honorary degree of D.D. in 1879, and he has since been made an F.S.A. Scot. It will surprise many who know the reverend gentleman well to find him ranked among the poets of the shire to which by lengthened residence within its borders he very essentially belongs; but the pieces which appear here, selected from a number in our possession, will show that his title to do so is, beyond question, valid.

DUGALD BUCHANAN.

A Gaelic poet of distinction, and justly celebrated as a writer of hymns, Dugald Buchanan was born at Strathyre, on the "Braes o' Balquhidder," in 1716. His father, who was a farmer and miller, gave him a more than ordinary country education, and was led to do so from having discovered that the lad was unusually "gleg in the uptak'." For a number of years young Buchanan led a somewhat irregular life, but at length reformed. In the stormy times of the '45 he did not himself actually take up arms in the Pretender's cause, but many of his friends did, and were massacred at Carlisle. In 1755 the Society for Propagating Christian Knowledge appointed him schoolmaster and catechist at Kinloch Rannoch. Here he laboured with diligence, writing hymns and lyrics in his spare hours; and here, in 1768, he died. A fountain was recently erected to his memory in Strathyre. He was an earnest preacher and evangelist; assisted in the preparation of the first edition of the New Testament in Gaelic, and did much by his faithful and civilising influence to pacify the wild district in which he lived. His "Spiritual Songs" appeared in 1766. In general estimation Buchanan is inferior as a poet to Duncan Ban M'Intyre, but is admittedly the greatest sacred poet the Scottish Highlands have produced. His "Day of Judgment," displaying great power of imagination, is amongst the most popular poems in the language. It reflects accurately the religious opinions of his riper years, and, indeed, of his time and country; preaching, as it does, Calvinism pure and simple, without one softening touch of humanity. "The Skull" is the poem, however, that will have most attraction for readers of to-day.

FRANCIS BUCHANAN,

Author of "The Crusader and other Poems and Lyrics," and "Sparks from Sheffield Smoke," is a native of Perth, and was born in 1825. In the course of his teens he was apprenticed to the drapery trade, at which occupation—pursued throughout the united kingdom—he continued until within recent years. Mr. Buchanan early discovered a versatile and melodious poetical faculty, and had the honour, when only twenty-two, to be elected Bard of the Worshipful Brotherhood of the Royal Arch Free Masons of Perth. For many years he has been settled in Sheffield; but though he has found a home in the sister country, his heart still turns fondly to dear old Scotland; his "Lines written on Kinnoull Cliff," his songs, "The Exile's Lament,"

"School Days," and "My Fatherland," and others, showing how deeply the scenes and recollections of his early days are engraven on his memory.

ALEXANDER CAMPBELL,

A poet, musical composer, and miscellaneous writer, was born at Tombea, on the banks of Loch Lubnaig, in February, 1764. An early taste for music induced him to cultivate a systematic acquaintance with the art, which he acquired under the celebrated Tenducci and others. He became a teacher of the harpsicord, and of vocal music, studied physics, and gave lessons in the art of drawing. While employed as organist in a church in Edinburgh he had the good fortune to form the acquaintance of Robert Burns. At a later period he became intimately acquainted with Sir Walter Scott, James Hogg, Professor Wilson, and other eminent men of letters. A man of real ability, he was perhaps too erratic in his tastes to arrive at very marked distinction. "Had he been a little less florescent," says a recent writer, "and had he economised the abilities bestowed on him, his capacity would have set him high amongst men; but he aimed at being a second Admirable Crichton, and as a matter of necessity broke down in the attempt. He speculated in wives too, his second wife being the widowed chieftainess of a wealthy clansman, from whose awfully grand connection he dreamed of great halls covered with broadswords, and years of Celtic grandeur; but not only did the superstructure crumble down, but the foundation itself gave way, by the lady suddenly levanting, and taking up house on her own account, in one of the fastnesses of her first lord's domains, leaving Campbell to make his way in the world as best he could. After a life much chequered by misfortune, Mr. Campbell died of apoplexy on the 15th of May, 1824. His best known works are "An Introduction to the History of Poetry in Scotland," published in 1798, "The Grampians Desolate," a poem on the depopulation of the Highlands, issued in 1804, and "Albyn's Anthology; a select collection of the

Melodies and Vocal Poetry Peculiar to Scotland and the Isles, hitherto Unpublished." The latter appeared in 1816; and contains, in addition to contributions from Scott, Hogg, Wilson, Boswell, and others, several lyrical pieces by the editor himself, which compare favourably with the run of the work.

JOHN CAMPBELL ("Will Harrow"),

A shrewd and quaint observer of human life and character, who died only a few months ago in the Poor's house at Perth, was a native of the parish of Kinclaven, where his father held a small farm, and was born in 1808. His youth was spent as a son of the soil, in hedging and ditching, etc. At the age of twenty-five he went to Dundee, where he remained for seven years, after which "I went back to the spade again," he says in his own quaint style, "and dug my way from Dunblane to Lintrathen, in Forfarshire." A long "delve" and no mistake! Twice he laid the spade aside, and spent three years in Glasgow and six in South Africa. He was twice married, and at an age considerably beyond the allotted span of human life as fixed by the Psalmist—childless and alone—he spent the gloaming of his career in the village of Stanley, where he found more true kindliness than in all the world beside. John had many "ups" and "downs" in his time, and all along, we fear, the "downs" had the best of it. If fickle Fortune resisted his approaches, however, the divinities did not each and all hold him at bay. The muses deigned to smile upon him, and in their society, we know, he was often happier than ever was Kaiser, Pope, or King. During a long course of years, with irregular intervals between, "Will Harrow's" screeds of Scottish rhyme enriched the columns of the local press; and twenty years ago, there was a spring in his measure and a "snap" in his style which caused his contributions to be looked for with anticipations of delight.

WILLIAM CLYDE,

A lyric poet of considerable culture, was a native of Perth, and was born in 1791. His father—a much-respected and successful citizen of the Fair City—was a bookseller, in easy circumstances, who pushed his trade by making stated circuits through the surrounding districts, and attending the fairs in the principal country towns of Perth, Fife, and Kinross-shires, and disposing of his stationery and literary stock by public auction in the open air. Old Mr. Clyde's shop—his own property—was on the north side of the High Street, almost directly opposite the Meal Vennel; and the literary wares in which he dealt were chiefly old fashioned religious works, popular histories, school books, and chap-books. To this business William, on the death of his father, succeeded in 1820. "The father had been much respected," says a recent writer, "for kindly manners and sterling integrity, and the son was looked upon as holding forth the fairest promise of worthily treading in the old man's footsteps. But Clyde's good prospects were soon clouded. It seemed that on becoming his own master, and the head of a household, his attention was gradually diverted from his business to objects of ambition beyond his reach in Perth. Whether poetry and dreams of fame had any share in his imprudence we cannot tell; but it was obvious that his aims, whencesoever arising, and whatever they pointed at, overshot the limited plodding sphere in which he was placed. Neglect of his affairs entailed the usual consequences. Difficulties grew about him, out of which he might have extricated himself with steady exertion; but lacking energy he gave way to them, and in 1825 left Perth, resolving to try his luck in the Metropolis."

After many years, spent south of the Tweed, William Clyde returned, and wove in the "thrum-keel" of his life in his native city. His circumstances after the date of collapse never very appreciably improved, and his later years were passed in a state of semi-genteel poverty. He died in 1873.

JAMES CRAIG,

A native of the village of Burrelton, in the parish of Cargill, was born in 1848. His education commenced at Woodside School under Mr. James Kiellor—a teacher widely known in his day—and afterwards he attended the parish school, at Newbigging, then as now conducted by Mr. Alexander Fergusson, one or two of whose poetical pieces find housing here along with those of quite a number of his old pupils. Mr. Craig learned the Banking profession in the office of Messrs. Clark and Boyd, National Bank, Coupar Angus, and in 1871 was transferred to the head office of the same Bank in Edinburgh, where he still remains. He devotes his leisure almost entirely to art, but at times he lays aside the pencil and brush for the poet's pen, the which he wields with almost equal grace and facility.

JOHN CRAIG,

A younger brother of the foregoing subject, was born in the village of Burrelton, in June, 1851, and has resided there during the greater part of his life; growing strawberries, attending to School Board matters, corresponding to the newspapers, etc., etc. He has given more attention to the tuneful sisters than his elder brother, and enjoys a well-merited reputation as a poet and essayist. The Burrelton and Woodside Young Men's Mutual Improvement Society—which has been heard of far beyond the limits of the parish—owes its origin and respectable old age almost entirely to his literary energy and skillful and persevering management. For the delectation of this coterie of the rural "lichts," and their friends, Mr. Craig has, in addition to scores of essays of an educative and debatable character, written about half-a-dozen original dramas, which have been acted in character by himself and the leading members, and proved each in their turn the proverbial "nine day's wonder" of the district. The latest performance of this kind—"The Cobbler o' Greenha', or a Warpit Wooin'"—with which he received some little assistance, caused such a *furore* about a year ago, that it has since been taken up and submitted to the public by an enterprising Edinburgh publisher, and is likely to become popular over the length and breadth of the land. To considerable skill in versification John Craig adds a pleasing humour and power of narrative which raise his numbers above the mediocrity of amateur verse.

DUNCAN MACGREGOR CRERAR.

Familiarly known in Scottish circles in America as "The Breadalbane Bard," and beloved of every song-loving Scot at home and abroad, Duncan MacGregor Crerar, author of the exquisite lyric "Caledonia's Blue Bells," is a native of Amulree, in Glenquaich, and was born on the 4th of December, 1837. His early life, like that of many another who has ultimately attained fame, was uneventful. His parents, of whom he cherishes the fondest regard, intended him for the ministry, and to this end supplied him with a good scholastic education. The early death of his father, however, defeated the cherished hope of his one day "waggin' his pow in a poopit," and, accordingly, in 1857, Mr. Crerar turned his eyes in the direction of a sphere of labour across the Atlantic, and set out for Canada. There he located in the County of Perth, where he met numerous parties who had been evicted from Glenquaich and other parts of Breadalbane, many of them relatives, and not a few of them old acquaintances. In Canada he embarked at once in mercantile pursuits, manifesting in his business that shrewdness and activity for which the Scot abroad has achieved a merited reputation, whilst the evening of each day found him busy adding to his store of knowledge on scientific and other subjects. By and by an opportunity occurred which brought him distinction in Her Majesty's service. He entered the Active Militia, and during the Fenian troubles of 1865, served with his company for several months on the frontier. As a reward for his efficiency in this capacity, he was gazetted by the Canadian Government, under the direction of his warm friend the Honourable Alexander MacKenzie, Honorary Lieutenant of his corps, which rank, with its privileges, he still retains. Between the posts at the front he used a diligent pen, and was the well-known correspondent of the *Stratford Beacon*, an influential paper published in the county town of Perth. When the Active Service Battalions were recalled, Mr. Crerar made his way to Toronto, and entered a college for a short season. From thence he proceeded to New York, where, with the exception of a summer spent in Scotland, he has since remained. He has been Secretary to the Burns Society of New York since its inauguration; and perhaps the finest of all his productions, his poem on Robert Burns—afterwards published in beautifully illustrated book-form by Marcus Ward & Co.,—was composed for and read at one of the annual dinners of that Society. With the exception of the above poem, none of Mr. Crerar's writings have appeared in volume form. He is, indeed, not at all ambitious of fame, many of his song and longer [productions have never been printed, even although most of those which he has contributed to the papers have been reproduced again and again by the home and foreign journals. A Scotchman of the truest fibre, he manifests the keenest interest in all matters appertaining to the good and glory of his native land. Among his literary friends in America he speaks of none with more pride than the venerable Thomas C. Latto, author of "When we were at the Schule," old Evan M'Call, author of "The Mountain Minstrel," etc., Alexander M'Lachlan, the well-known Scoto-Canadian poet, James Kennedy, author of "Auld Scotia in the Field," and other lyrics, and Donald Ramsay, another Scottish-American poet, recently deceased. Among literary personages in the home-country whose hands he has touched on the other side, and who are proud to call him friend, may be named William Black, the novelist, Dr. George MacDonald, Professor Blackie, the

Earl of Rosebery, and others almost equally distinguished. William Black, indeed, makes honourable mention of Mr. Crerar as "the Bard of Amulree" in his recently published novel, "Stand Fast, Craig Royston."

JAMES CROMB,

Chief sub-editor of the *Dundee Evening Telegraph*, and a writer of military novels scarcely less fascinating than those of the author of the "Romance of War," is a native of Cargill, and was born in 1849. When seven years of age he went to reside in Coupar Angus, where he learned the shoemaking craft and subsequently formed a contributing connection with various newspapers. By and by, he abandoned the awl and took to serial story writing, his first tale, "Marion Ogilvie," appearing in the *Dundee Weekly News*. About twenty years ago, on the invitation of Mr. John Leng, he joined the staff of the *Dundee Advertiser*, and became one of the permanent serial writers for the *People's Journal*, as well as a regular contributor of essays, critical and biographical, to the *People's Friend*. The more popular of his serials to the *Journal* include "Gentle Alice: a story of Cluny in the Forty-five," "Highland Jessie's Dream: a story of the Indian Mutiny," and "Lilian Ray: a story of Glasgow and the Crimea." In book-form he has published "Working and Living," a volume of essays, "The Highlands and Highlanders of Scotland," "The Highland Brigade: Its Battles and its Heroes," now in its second edition, and "The Majuba Disaster." In 1877, on the commencement of the *Evening Telegraph*, Mr. Cromb was appointed to the important position on its editorial staff which he still occupies with credit and renown. Though of a warmly poetic temperament, and a good judge of verse, he has given little direct attention to the muses; the few pieces he has written being intended chiefly to embellish his fiction, and to be introduced into the text of his stories.

GAVIN DOUGLAS,

Bishop of Dunkeld, whom the Scottish antiquary John Pinkerton pronounced the fifth of the seven classic poets of Scotland whose works would "be reprinted to the end of the English language"—the others being Barbour, James I., Blind Harry, Dunbar, Sir David Lyndsay, and Drummond of Hawthornden—was the third son of Archibald, fifth Earl of Angus, popularly known as "Archibald Bell the Cat," and was born at Brechin in 1474. He was educated for the Church at St. Andrews, and became successively Rector of Hawick in 1496, Provost of St. Giles, Edinburgh, in 1509, and Bishop of Dunkeld in 1515. Living in the stormy and anarchic period, when the kingdom was embroiled with the disputes of the Queen Mother and the Duke of Albany, and others, his entry to the See was opposed by the Duke of Albany, and the Athole family, and on a charge of contravening the laws of the realm in obtaining bulls from Rome, he was imprisoned for a year in the Castle of Edinburgh. In 1517 he accompanied the Duke of Albany to France, but soon returned to Scotland, and repaired to his diocese, where he applied himself diligently to the duties of his episcopal office. In 1521 he was compelled by the disputes between the Earls of Arran and Angus to take refuge in England, where he was kindly received by Henry VIII., and formed the acquaintance of Erasmus. He died in London, of the plague, in September, 1522, and was interred in the chapel-royal of the Savoy.

The character of Bishop Douglas is thus drawn by the classical pen of Buchanan:—"To splendour of birth, and a handsome and dignified person, he united a mind richly stored with the learning of the age, such as it then existed. His temperance and moderation were very remarkable; and living in turbulent times, and surrounded by factions at bitter enmity with each other, such was the general opinion of his honesty and uprightness of mind that he possessed a high influence with all parties. He left behind him various monuments of his genius and learning of no common merit, written in his native tongue."

Besides translations of Ovid's *De Remedio Amoris*, and Virgil's *Æneid*, Douglas is the author of two allegorical poems entitled respectively "The Palace of Honour" and "King Hart," the latter containing what Dr. Irving styles "a most ingenious adumbration of the progress of human life."

DAVID DRUMMOND,

A native of Crieff, was born in the end of the last century. In 1812 he proceeded to India, and attained considerable wealth as the conductor of an academy and boarding establishment at Calcutta. From early youth he had cultivated a taste for literary composition, both in poetry and prose, and ultimately, in India, became an extensive contributor to public journals and periodical publications. He died at Calcutta in 1845, about the age of seventy, lamented by a wide circle of friends and admirers.

HENRY DRYERRE,

Bookseller, Blairgowrie, is a Scotchman by birth and breeding, though of German extraction, and was born in the Lawnmarket of Edinburgh, in 1848. In 1858 his father joined the 72nd Highlanders, and the family removed to Aberdeen, where they remained for a short time, moving from thence to India. In India Henry commenced his apprenticeship as a compositor in the regimental printing office. Before he had had time to master the intricacies of his adopted handicraft, the father was invalided home, and the family, moving with him, and settling down in Perth, Henry "finished his time" in Perth, with Mr. Robert Whittet, printer and poet, now of Richmond, Va., North America, than whom, he says, he never met a more sympathetic, tender-hearted, and considerate master, or one with purer and loftier aspirations, and with more ability to fulfil them. In

1870 Mr. Dryerre proceeded to London, where, after working for a time "at the case," he acted as head reader on a daily newspaper. Nightwork, however, acted injuriously on his health, and necessitated his returning home. He resumed his trade in the Fair City, occupying his spare hours in writing tales and sketches for the press, teaching music, and perfecting his knowledge of the French, Latin, and Greek languages. In 1878 he removed to Blairgowrie, where he still continues engaged in business on his own account as music-seller and stationer, and teaching languages, music, etc., making good violins, and composing excellent music. Mr. Dryerre is a thoughtful, sweet-voiced poet. There is the evidence of mental culture on the face of everything he writes, and an ardent lover of nature in all her aspects, moods, and seasons, he ever finds his highest joy in the contemplation of her manifold charms; hearing the tongues in the trees, reading the books in the running brooks, listening to the sermons in the stones, and beholding and adoring the good in everything. He writes without apparent effort—in fact with extreme fluency—composing frequently three and four poems within as many hours. In the course of a letter to the present writer, he says, " In anything I write, it is as a rule the assertion of my own genuine feelings, opinions, or fancies, my own experiences, and, in many cases, my own sufferings (lightly disguised) that finds utterance in verse, and were I to lay down a rule for writing poetry, it would be—utter what is within, and fear not; it will reach a heart somewhere if it comes from your own. I have no sympathy with those who talk of poetry as an 'art;' the true poet, I opine, employs art as a means of expression, but the art itself is not poetry, and unless he has an impulse deeper than the mere desire to cut and carve images out of words, he is—not a poet, at any rate. For myself, I am as unable to account for anything I may have done myself thought worthy of notice as I am to command the ability to write such. With few exceptions, all I have written are individually the unpremeditated offspring of the time." A volume of his poems entitled "Love Idylls" was published in 1884.

JAMES DUFF,

Known as "the Methven poet," was a gardener to trade, and flourished in the early years of the present century. A volume of his poems published at Perth, in 1816, and containing a somewhat flabby and diffuse version of "Bessie Bell and Mary Gray," is now scarce. His song "Lassie wi' the yellow Coatie," contained in this work, is the only one of his productions which has attained any popularity.

THOMAS EDWARDS,

Author of "Strathearn Lyrics," and well-known by his pen-name of "Ned Thomas," is a native of Crieff, and was born at the old mill of Milnab in 1857. On leaving school in his fifteenth year he was sent to learn the house-painting business, which he has followed ever since and practised in all its branches. For a time he wrought as a journeyman in Edinburgh; but his love of the country soon brought him back to his native town, where he continues to reside, alternating the handling of the brush with the play of the pen, and making life noble and sweet by the excellent display of each. The volume of Mr. Edwards' poems and songs appeared in 1889. One of the first to recognise the merits of its contents was the Rev. Dr. Stalker of Glasgow, himself a gifted son of Crieff, who has enriched our theological literature by several works from a brilliant pen. In a letter dated Glasgow, January 11, 1890, the author of "Imago Christi" writes:—

"Chancing to be in Crieff the other day, I picked up in one of the book shops a copy of Thomas Edwards' *Strathearn Lyrics*. Mr. Edwards is not known to me, and I confess that I opened the book with little expectation of pleasure, knowing how halting and ineffectual the efforts of the provincial muse generally are, if she ventures to expand them to the dimensions of a volume. But I had not read far when I opened my eyes with astonishment at the power and mastery displayed by the author, and I have read his book through again and again with deep and growing delight. We have at last got a true poet in Strathearn, who, I venture to say, has not had his match in Perthshire since Robert Nicoll. Indeed, in some respects, especially in the sweetness of his melody and his easy command of language, Mr. Edwards seems to me superior to Nicoll, though Nicoll excels him in those shrewd and pithy observations on life and character of which Burns set so great an example." With these remarks we thoroughly agree, in all but the comparison with Robert Nicoll, which is not a happy one. Each excellent in his way, their notes are yet as distinct as those of the lark and the thrush.

FINLAY FARQUHARSON

Was a native of Killin, and was born sometime between 1810 and 1820. He learned the shoemaking trade, and was located for many years at Lundie, near Newtyle, where many of his best pieces were composed. Latterly he removed to Balquhidder where he died about seven or eight years ago. "Farquharson was entirely self-taught" writes a correspondent, who had heard him recite his own compositions at concerts with the greatest gusto, "but was very intelligent, and had a wide acquaintance with the works of the Scottish poets, especially Burns. His own effusions, though rugged in construction were written in a fresh, happy, and humorous style, and he had a vein of satire which he sometimes wielded unsparingly. I have heard him repeat a piece in which he administered a severe castigation to a character he called 'Tailor Whin.' The first verse ran—

> 'There's curious fouk in mony a place,
> In Fowlis, Lundie, an' Callace,
> But the queerest o' the curious race
> Is brawlin' Tailor Whin, O.

'The tailor never grew a man,
For that's beyond a tailor's span,
But monkeys learn to tak' a dram,
An' sae did Tailor Whin, O.'"

Besides his Doric pieces, Farquharson was complete master of Gaelic, and has left some standard translations of Scotch and English poetry. He was highly praised by Professor Blackie for a splendid translation of "Tam o' Shanter;" and he also translated "Kate Dalrymple," "Watty and Meg," and "Captain Fraser's Nose," etc."

ALEXANDER FERGUSSON,

Schoolmaster, Cargill, is a native of Pitlochry, where several members of his family still reside, and was born in 1828. He was educated partly in his native village, and latterly in Edinburgh. At the age of twenty-one he was appointed parochial teacher at Blacklunnans, in the neighbourhood of Mount Blair, and remained there for four years, after the expiry of which period he removed to Cargill. This latter appointment (though now under the "Board" instead of the Parochial regimè) he still retains, and is much esteemed throughout, and beyond the wide circle of his labours, alike for his merits as a teacher, and for the hearty readiness with which he enters into every scheme calculated to advance the worldly interests and moral well-being of the community. An effective lecturer on various subjects, he also enjoys more than local fame as a reliable antiquary, and rendered valuable service to the late Sir James Simpson when the latter visited Cargill in connection with the preparation of his work on "Archaic Sculpturings." The weighty and exacting nature of Mr. Fergusson's professional duties—for, besides being schoolmaster, he is parochial registrar, etc., etc.—leaves him very little time to dally with the tuneful Nine— and they seek his company rather than he seeks theirs. Taken at his own estimate he has no claim to a place among the song-writers of his native county; but, naturally of a genial disposition, and raticnally conciliatory even in extremities, when he finds a large majority holding an entirely opposite opinion, if he does not meekly give in, he will, when he sees his name here, assuredly not boldly protest.

JAMES FERGUSON.

People who are in the habit of turning to the poetical corner of their weekly newspaper have long been familiar with the signature of "Nisbet Noble," the *nom de plume* of James Ferguson. Mr. Ferguson is a native of Stanley, and was born in 1842. Up to his fourteenth year he resided in his native village, spending his sunny hours on the all-beautiful banks of the adjacent river Tay, drinking in the inspiration that, ever since may be said to have continued to flow from his heart in lays and lyrics fresh and sweet as the ripple of the mountain rill. He is presently employed in the Spinning Mills at Stanley, but in his time has been many things to many men. First a mill boy in his native village, secondly an apprentice to the grocery business in Dundee, next in Glasgow, employed successively as labourer, engine-keeper, time-keeper, and counting-house clerk. Then in Perth, employed in the Messrs. Pullar's dyeing establishment, clerk in the Inland Revenue office, back to the dyehouse again, and afterwards in the Co-operative Store. His early recollections are love for woods and waters in summer, and fireside reading during winter. He remembers well when first he came across the "Lady of the Lake" and Aytoun's "Death of Montrose." He seemed to have entered a new world. Mr. Ferguson's first publication in book form appeared in 1873, and is a somewhat ambitious performance, viz.—a secularized version of "The Song of Solomon," in a series of lyrics. Viewed from a literary stand-point the work is excellent; but whether he has been successful in the debatable part of the subject is still matter of opinion, and need not be entered on here. In 1880 he issued a little volume of "Lays of Perthshire," which deserves to be thoroughly well known. The pieces are fourteen in number, and include "The Battle of the Inch," "The Stone of Destiny," and "The Battle of Luncarty," etc., and form a contribution to Perthshire literature eminently worthy of preservation. What he has published in book form does not however form a tithe of what Mr. Ferguson has written—nor, perhaps, the best. His muse is essentially lyrical, and of songs and lyrics he has written, he says himself, far more than he knows anything about, as he rarely keeps a copy of anything he writes. The essential elements to successful song-writing he certainly possesses in no stinted measure—music, humour, pathos, and fire—and few among our living Scottish lyrists are more likely to send their numbers ringing down through the corridors of Time.

REV. R. M. FERGUSSON, M.A.

Well known as a writer of vigorous and descriptive prose, as well as a graceful and pleasing poet, the Rev. Robert Menzies Fergusson, M.A., minister of Logie parish, Bridge of Allan, is the eldest surviving son of the late Rev. Samuel Fergusson, author of "The Queen's Visit and other Poems," and was born in the manse of Fortingall in the year 1859. He received his early education at the Public School of Stanley, a village and district which are still dear to his heart, and which retain fragrant and cherished memories of his youthful days. In the autumn of 1877 he entered as a student the University of Edinburgh, where, after a successful course, he graduated M.A. in 1881. From Edinburgh he passed over to St. Andrews, and studied theology in St. Mary's College there. From St. Andrews he went to Oxford, where he carried on for a time the ministerial work of the late Rev. Henry Bazely, B.C.L., attending at the same time several of the classes in the University. Returning to Scotland, Mr. Fergusson was licensed as a preacher of the Gospel by the Presbytery of Perth in May, 1884. Subsequently he acted for nine months as assistant to the late Rev. Dr. Rankine, of Sorn, in Ayrshire, and was elected minister of Logie parish and ordained to his charge there on the 2nd of April, 1885.

He commenced to toy with the Muses at a very early age, and while a student at the University of Edinburgh occasionally wrote short pieces—principally translations from the Greek and Latin poets—for the learned and genial Professor Blackie. Himself a true son of song, Blackie delighted to foster the poetical spirit among the members of his classes, and many a student of Edinburgh who has since won his spurs in the field of poetic literature can look back with a feeling of pride and gratitude to the encouragement and advice awarded him by the popular ex-Professor of Greek. Our subject was also in his year one of the competitors for the prize which is annually awarded for the best poem in the class of English Literature; and, though unsuccessful, his poem was distinguished by receiving the high commendation of Professor Masson. For several years Mr. Fergusson has been a contributor to the *Edinburgh University Quarterly*, and other magazines. His published works are "Rambles in the Far North," now in its second edition; "My College Days," a volume descriptive of student life, and "Quiet Folk," a collection of essays on various subjects.

REV. SAMUEL FERGUSSON.

For more than eight years pastor of the parish church of Fortingall, the Rev. Samuel Fergusson, author of the "Queen's Visit and other Poems," was born at Dalchonzie, near Comrie, on the 2nd of January, 1828. Early destined by his parents to "wag his pow in a poopit," he was educated at St. Andrews University, and received a license as a probationer of the Church of Scotland from the Presbytery of Auchterarder in 1854. In 1857 he was presented to the parish of Fortingall, where he laboured with much energy and acceptance until the year 1865, when, his health breaking down, he retired in favour of an assistant and successor, and went on a voyage round the world in the hope of rebuilding his shattered constitution. In returning from abroad, it is worth mentioning, Mr. Fergusson came home in the ill-fated steamship *London*, which, the very next time she sailed from the port of London, foundered in the Bay of Biscay, and went down with two hundred and twenty souls aboard. "The Queen's Visit" was published in 1869, and on the evening of the day of its issue—the 27th of September—its author, mistaking his way, walked into the Tay at Perth, and was drowned. He left behind him a widow and five sons, the eldest of whom was drowned while bathing in Loch Voil, Balquhidder, in July, 1876.

The Rev. Samuel Fergusson, was well-known as a ripe Celtic scholar, and wrote Gaelic poetry, we have been told, which was much superior to his English verse. He was a member of the Committee on the Revision of the Gaelic Scriptures, and wrote an account of Dugald Buchanan and his poetry, which has never been published. Many of his Gaelic poems were published separately, but none of them in book form. Shortly before his death he had begun a history of Perthshire, having been advised thereto by his friend, the late Principal Tulloch, and others.

"The Queen's Visit," as the title half reveals, is a poem in celebration of Her Gracious Majesty Queen Victoria's first visit to Scotland, in the autumn of 1842. We have had the foremost lady of all the land so frequently amongst us since Balmoral became her favourite residence that a Royal visit has come to be regarded as a thing of little moment by us. It was very different in the days of yore. It had been the fashion for Royalty to give Scotland "the cold shoulder," and when Victoria and her good Consort declared their intention of coming northwards—

"Old Scotland, south, north, east, and west,
Was mov'd to hear the tale,"

and there was an outburst of loyalty the like of which has seldom been seen and heard in these realms. Poet vied with poet to describe the scene, and express the jubilation; and it is not claiming more for our author than is his due to say that the simple narrative of the event which he produced—bald as it frequently is—being a faithful description of the Royal visit from the moment that Her Majesty and Prince Albert disembarked at Granton pier, on the 1st of September, 1842, until they re-embarked at the same place at 5 o'clock in the afternoon of the 13th day of the same month—will be read and cherished long after all the others are entirely forgotten. The poem is in six cantos, and extends, notes and all, to 214 octavo pages.

ROBERT FORD,

Editor of this work, was born in Wolfhill village, parish of Cargill, on the 18th of July, 1846. At the age of eighteen he went to Dundee, where he was employed for a period of ten years, most of the time in the works of Messrs. Baxter Bros., & Co. In 1874, he removed to Glasgow, where he still remains employed as a clerk in one of the larger warehouses in the city. Is author of "Hame-spun Lays and Lyrics," "Humorous Scotch Readings in Prose and Verse," "Glints o' Glentoddy," and "Thistledown: a book of Scotch Humour." Has edited "Auld Scots Ballants," "Popular Readings: Scotch, English, Irish, and American," etc.

PETER GALLOWAY FRASER,

Who has seemingly "hung his harp on the willow," was for a number of years a frequent contributor of poetical pieces to the Dundee papers over the *nom de plume* of "Ariadne." Mr. Fraser was born in Errol on the 4th of January, 1862, and when four years old removed with his parents to Dundee, where he received his elementary education. In 1882 he entered Glasgow University, with a view to the Church, and studied there during several subsequent sessions, taking respectable places in all his classes, but distinguishing himself in the department of English literature. During this period he contributed to *Scottish Nights* a series of articles on "Studies in Scottish Literature," in which much desirable information interwoven with healthy pointed criticism was afforded concerning the early poets and song-writers of the North. By and by he was induced to join the Parliamentary staff of the *Dundee Courier.* But this office he relinquished after a couple of sessions, and, still bent on " wagging his pow in a poopit," proceeded to Edinburgh to qualify for the kirk. While studying divinity he edited the *Scottish Liberal* during the latter days of its brief and sickly career, and formed a corresponding connection with *Tit-Bits.* Very soon Mr. Newnes called him to fill the editorial chair of this popular miscellany; and here Mr. Fraser continues, as we hope and believe, "prospering, and to prosper."

ROBERT GAIRNS,

Author of "Rustic Rhymes," was born in the year 1804, and in the same house at New London, on the estate of St. Martins, in which he lived his long life-lease of eighty-six years, and in which he died in May 1890. In his youth he learned handloom weaving; but on the inauguration of the steamloom, the handloom weaver found his occupation gone, and from that time Mr. Gairns became a day labourer to the farmers in the neighbourhood. Ultimately he was content to tend his own little croft, abandoning the more active scenes of labour to those better able to bear the burden. He was forty years old before he wrote a line of verse, and aspired to be the Poet-Laureate of St. Martins—the which he was in very truth. No big meeting in the district could be regarded as complete unless he was there, and raised his voice in a rhyme pat to the occasion. Was there a ploughing match of more than usual interest, a cattle show, or a concert in St. Martins, its story was faithfully told in graphic Scotch rhyme. Then occasionally he sang of the loves and the lives of the people around him, painting a sage moral, as in

"Fifty Years Ago," and "Strong Drink," and teaching wisdom under a glamour of humour, as in "The Farmer's a'e Dochter," "A Penny the Ell," and "Willie's Hay-Stack."

JAMES Y. GEDDES.

A writer of pungent and eloquent prose as well as of thoughtful and animated verse, James Young Geddes, born in Dundee in 1850, has resided in Alyth for upwards of twelve years, and serves the community in the capacity of a junior Commissioner. Mr. Geddes early discovered a faculty for verse-writing, and while yet in his teens was a frequent and welcome contributor to the poet's corner of the local journals. In course of time, yielding to the pressure of many friends and admirers, he collected the scattered creatures of his imagination within the boards of a book, which was published in 1879 under the title of "The New Jerusalem, and other Verses." The work was well received, not only by our author's friends, but by the Scottish press and the public at large, and the happy result was that it soon ran out of print. This was just as it ought to have been, for the work is truly meritorious. At no page or point in the volume does the reader find himself in shallow water, but is borne along on a broad and ample current of ready thought and sparkling fancy. Of the varied contents, "The New Inferno" is a thoughtful and able poem; so is also "The New Advent," while the sonnets on Carlyle, Emerson, and Tennyson, display artistic taste and poetical susceptibility of a decidedly exceptional character. Mr. Geddes next issued "The Spectre Clock of Alyth, and other Selections;" and recently, "In the Valhalla and other Poems" appeared. Our selections are from his latest, which is in most respects his best work.

REV. GEORGE GILFILLAN.

It is scarcely possible to give anything approaching to an adequate idea of the life and work of a man like George Gilfillan within the brief scope of a mere *note*, and such a thing will not be attempted here. Indeed it is not necessary. One of the greatest men that Scotland has produced in the present century, he is far and away the brightest star in the literary firmament of Perthshire, and Perthshire men everywhere know all about him—or all that is worth the knowing. They know him as a man, a preacher, a critic, and a poet who was esteemed and honoured while he lived, widely lamented when he died, and whose memory, together with much that he wrote, will be cherished by his countrymen for many generations. The eleventh child of a family of twelve, Gilfillan was born in the village of Comrie on the 13th of January, 1813. His father, Samuel Gilfillan, was the saintly minister of the Secession Church there, and the author of several works of a religious character. George was educated in the village school, and in his thirteenth year entered the University of Glasgow. Subsequently he studied in Edinburgh, attending the moral philosophy class of the immortal Professor Wilson, to whose genius, in his later life, he delighted to pay frequent and noble tribute. Licensed to preach the Gospel in 1835, he was, in March of the following year, ordained to the charge of School Wynd Church, Dundee, where he continued to minister to a large and devoted congregation till his death, on the 13th of August, 1878. On the Sabbath previous, the 11th of August, he had preached in School Wynd, the subject of his sermon being, somewhat strangely, "Sudden Death." On the Monday he went to Brechin to officiate at the wedding of his niece, at Arnhall, near Edzell.

Early on the morning of Tuesday he complained to Mrs. Gilfillan of feeling ill, and a doctor was called. On his arrival Gilfillan at once said, "I am dying, doctor," and the physician replying that it was so, he said, "The will of the Lord be done." In a few minutes more he had entered the "silent land." He was laid to rest in Balgay Cemetery, Dundee, receiving the melancholy honour of a public funeral. In Dundee Gilfillan was honoured and esteemed not more by his own congregation than by the whole body of the people. He was the mental light and leader of the community, and no public platform was regarded as complete if it lacked his genial and inspiring presence. As a lecturer he was popular everywhere, and constantly in demand all over the united kingdom; and few, I presume, who have listened to the rolling undertones of his voice in an impressive passage will ever forget them—they were vocal majesty. His literary career must be summed up in a few words. He began to write early; his first contributions being, curiously, sent to a periodical called *The Farmer's Magazine.* Subsequently he wrote several critiques for the *Edinburgh University Magazine.* These were followed by his celebrated "Gallery of Literary Portraits," originally contributed to Thomas Aird's *Dumfries Herald.* Then came "Hades, or the Unseen," a sermon, "Bards of the Bible," (his most beautiful work), "Martyrs, Heroes, and Bards of the Scottish Covenant," "History of a Man," (since withdrawn from publication), "Life of Scott," "Remoter Stars," "Life of Dr. William Anderson," "Burns," "Night, a Poem," etc., etc.

Altogether, according to his own computation, Gilfillan produced from ninety to a hundred volumes, and, in addition, his contributions to the magazines and reviews, which were not republished, were very considerable. His poem "Night" has not been greatly esteemed—perhaps he was a better judge of poetry than a writer of it. Notwithstanding, "Night" is a great poem. As to his quick perception of the true poetic metal, as well as the proof of his large warm-heartedness, he was the first to discover the genius of Alexander Smith, the author of "A Life Drama," of Robert Buchanan, Sydney Dobell, George MacDonald, Gerald Massey, Alexander Anderson ("Surfaceman"), and many others, all of whom he rang into fame, and gloried in their success.

Take him all in all, Scotland may not look on Gilfillan's like in a hurry again; and it is no small thing for Perthshire to be able to say " he was my son."

WILLIAM GRAHAM, LL.D.

Well-known for his scholarly, poetical, and recreationary attainments, Dr. William Graham, recently deceased, was a native of Dunkeld, and was born in October, 1800. In the early years of the century the family removed to Perth, and the only memory which Dr. Graham cherished of his native city of Dunkeld was, that while there he sat on the knee of Neil Gow, the famous fiddler. After receiving an ordinary education, partly from his father, who was a well-known teacher in Perth, he studied at Edinburgh University. On the completion of his college curriculum he was appointed a teacher—first at Perth, where he acted for some time as an assistant to his father—and afterwards as teacher of English in the Academy of Cupar, in Fife. In 1831 he removed to Edinburgh, where he received the appointment of teacher of English literature, history, and elocution in the Naval and Military College. His capacity for work is shown by the fact that to these duties he subsequently added an academy of his own, which he opened in Queen Street, and, with some other teachers, founded the Scottish Institute for the Education of Young Ladies in Moray Place; and over and above all this, taught elocution to divinity students, and gave lessons in English and History in several boarding schools in Edinburgh. In this way he worked ten hours a day, and frequently more, yet found time for occasional literary work, now in the form of a lecture, now a breezy song of golfing or fishing—both of which pastimes he entered into with a fine relish—or it was a treatise on elocution, or an essay on Scottish life and manners. He edited the *Educational Journal* for some time, with much tact and ability, and frequently appeared before the public as a popular lecturer and reader. He was peculiarly fond of the study of Scottish manners and customs, and many a good story of old world ways he would tell, while his recollections of distinguished contemporaries were singularly interesting. At the instigation of many of his old pupils, he published in 1873, " Lectures, Sketches, and Poetical Pieces." A good deal of the matter in the volume is connected with schools and teaching, but embraces such subjects as " Neglect of National Music," " Scottish Life in the Past," " The Scotch Accent," etc. Dr. Graham taught for upwards of fifty years in Edinburgh, and died there in the autumn of 1891, at the ripe age of eighty-six. He was a keen golfer and angler, as we have said, and many of his songs turn on the pleasures derived from these pursuits. Parodying Henry Scott Riddell's well-known song of " Scotland Yet," he sings :—

" Gae bring my guid auld clubs ance mair ;
  Rin, laddie, bring them fast,
For I maun ha'e anither game
  Ere the autumn season's past.

And trow ye as I play, my lads,
  My song shall ever be
Auld Scotland's Royal game o' gouf—
  Our country's game for me."

His graphic and clever poem, " My First Saumon," will suffice to keep his memory green for many a day.

CHRISTIAN GRAY,

The blind poetess of Aberdalgie, published a slim volume of her miscellaneous pieces in verse in 1809, and another in 1821. In the course of her preface to the latter, she says, "My artless rhymes may not excite a very powerful interest in the hearts of others ; but, in my own, on account of the circumstances and recollections from which they originated, they have long been cherished with the complacency and fondness of affectionate regard." Her rhymes are in general truly artless enough, at the same time the verses in imitation of

"The Land o' the Leal," even in this way, are tender, graceful, and pleasing.

DAVID IMRIE,

Was born in Perth in 1809, and received his education at Kinnoull Parish School. He learned shoemaking, with his father, and after working for some time in Perth and Dunkeld, he crossed the Border and settled, in 1848, in Newcastle-on-Tyne. Subsequently he studied medical botany and chemistry. On the passing of the Pharmacy Act, in 1868, he was admitted a member of the Pharmaceutical Society, since which he has carried on business in that capacity in Consett, in Durham.

REV. GEORGE JACQUE,

For fifty-eight years the esteemed minister of Auchterarder U. P. Congregation, died on the 13th February last, at the ripe age of eighty-eight. He wrote and published extensively, both in prose and verse—if the word prose may be fittingly applied to anything that came from his pen—for, as a recent writer truly remarked, concerning such of his writings as are not in verse, "They only differ from poems because they lack distribution into fixed numbers of syllables." His tales are simply prose poems; and of these, "Wandering Menie," and "The Three Street Orphans," have enjoyed wide popularity, the latter having been translated into Danish and Icelandic. To the realm of poetry, strictly speaking, Mr. Jacque contributed "The Clouds," a descriptive poem in the heroic stanza, extending to ten cantos, and "Hope: Its Lights and Shadows," in a variety of measures, comprising eleven cantos, marked by sustained thought and much delicate fancy. Two hymns, of which he is author, find a place in the United Presbyterian Hymnal. He was an eloquent and fluent preacher, dearly beloved by his own people, and justly esteemed by the whole community.

JESSIE MARGARET KING,

A discriminating, graphic, and vivacious prose-writer, well known to all readers of the *Dundee Evening Telegraph* under the *nom de plume* of "Marguerite," was born at Bankfoot, in the Parish of Auchtergaven, in 1862, and received her education at the village school there. As a child she was delicate, but very studious, and a great reader. Her father, a man of remarkable intelligence, encouraged her in her studies; and every now and then a box of miscellaneous reading—magazines, reviews, etc.—would come by carrier's cart from Perth, where her uncle, Mr. James Sprunt, of esteemed memory, was editor of the *Perthshire Advertiser*. Teaching promised to be her future career; but she had only just entered Sharp's Institution, Perth, when her father fell ill, and this altered all the family plans. After a lingering illness, her father died, and two years subsequently, after having been employed for some time in an office in Bankfoot, Miss King received an appointment in the *Dundee Advertiser* office, and shortly afterwards obtained a responsible and important position on the staff of the *Evening Telegraph*, with which paper she is still connected. A prize essayist in several of the annual competitions connected with the Free Church's "Welfare of Youth" scheme, Miss King on one occasion distinguished herself by carrying off the first prize in both the junior and senior sections. To poetry she has applied her pen less frequently than to prose, but her contributions in this way, which have appeared under various *noms de plume*, in the *People's Friend* and elsewhere, show that she possesses a faculty for verse worthy of more assiduous cultivation.

DUNCAN KIPPEN,

Born in Crieff on the 28th of June 1831, the only son of the late John Kippen, shoemaker there, is quite a man of mark in various aspects of his life and character.

In the whole district of Strathearn there is no one better versed in the local history and topography, " Crieff—Its Traditions and Stories," being very largely from his pen. In musical matters he has been an enthusiast almost from his infancy, and besides knowing the subject theoretically and historically in every detail, he was for many years a teacher of vocal and instrumental music, has written numerous articles on the subject, and is himself the composer of many beautiful and distinctly original melodies, which have been published, set to words also written by himself. Mr. Kippen conducted the choir in Crieff Parish Church during the famous organ controversy, which extended from 1865 to 1867, when Dr. Cunningham introduced instrumental music into the church service. He has many a good-humoured and instructive story to tell of that animated struggle, as he has also of many other things which have happened in the district within his day and generation. Mr. Kippen's rare fund of humour, his familiarity with local history and tradition, his love of music and story-telling powers, secured to him the kindly interest of the late Sir William Keith Murray of Ochtertyre, than whom Scotland has seldom seen a finer specimen of the good old country gentleman; and it was he who led the famous local band which frequently performed at Ochtertyre house a number of years ago. Editor of "The Sacred Chorister," containing a varied selection of music for use in churches, he is Inspector of Poor for the Parish of Crieff, and has cultivated a taste for literature. For more than thirty years he has maintained a corresponding connection with the Press, and contributed articles to the *People's Journal*, *People's Friend*, and other publications. His songs contained in this work, selected from quite a number, mostly on local subjects, have been separately set to music and published in large sheet form with pianoforte accompaniments.

JOHN M'CULLOCH,

A well-known native of Crieff, who was a frequent writer of prose and verse, died at his residence in Comrie Street there, on the 27th March, 1891, aged 76. In his youth John learned the shoemaking trade, and on the completion of his apprenticeship went to Glasgow, where he remained until about twelve years ago. But though absent for so long, he continually kept up an intimate connection with his old friends, and informed himself regularly regarding the passing events of his native place. After a time he commenced to write interesting notices of men and things as they were in his youthful days, over the signature of "St. Mungo." These articles caused much interest, and he had the pleasure of seeing them appear in various leading periodicals. Latterly he wrote under the *nom de plume* of "Barnkittoch," this being the name of a small hamlet to the west of Crieff, near Milnab, not a vestige of which now remains. Several of his poetical and prose pieces were made popular in Crieff by the faultless reciting of the late Robert Laurence, a supreme favourite being always "Auld Johnnie Shaw," which finds a place in our treasury of the county's verse-idylls.

REV. J. R. MACDUFF, D.D.

Rev. John R. Macduff, D.D., a voluminous writer of popular religious works, and a poet of refined quality, is the second son of Alexander Macduff of Bonhard, and was born in 1818. He received the principal part of his education at the High School of Edinburgh, and studied for the Church in the University of that city, being for three years a student of the illustrious Dr. Chalmers. He was licensed as a minister of the Established Church in 1842, and the same year received the charge of the parish of Kettins, near Coupar Angus. Subsequently he was translated to St. Madocs, in the Carse of Gowrie, and latterly to Sandyford, in the west end of Glasgow, where he ministered for fifteen years, and became well known as one of the most talented preachers in the Church. Dr. Macduff received the honorary degree of D.D. from both the Universities of Glasgow and New York. In 1871 he resigned the laborious duties of a city clergyman, and has since resided at Chislehurst, in Kent, devoting himself to religious authorship, a department of work in which he has scarcely a compeer. His "Memories of Patmos," "Sunsets on the Hebrew Mountains," "Memories of Bethany," "The Parish of Taxwood," and other works from his pen, have attained an immense circulation, and are greatly appreciated on both sides of the Atlantic. A volume of his poems and hymns, "The Gates of Praise," was published by James Nisbet & Co., in 1875, the contents of which entitle our author to a prominent place amongst the religious poets of his country.

DUNCAN MACINTYRE.

Donacha Ban, or Fair-haired Duncan, the Burns of Gaelic poetry, was born in Glenorchy, in Argyleshire, on the 20th of March, 1724. In his early life he was employed as a forester by the Earl of Breadalbane; and on the outbreak of the Rebellion in 1745 he joined the Breadalbane Fencibles, and (though at heart a strict adherent of the Stuarts), marched with his regiment to the battle of Falkirk. For more than one-half of his long, and not uneventful, career, Duncan Ban dwelt among his native hills, haunting the "Misty Glen" at all hours, and composing his mountain music. Sometimes he travelled throughout the country collecting subscriptions for his poems, and during these expeditions was invariably dressed in the Highland garb; having a checked bonnet, over which hung a large bushy tail of a wild animal; a badger's skin, fastened by a belt, in front; a hanger by his side, and a soldier's wallet strapped to his shoulders. Wherever he went he was recognised by his peculiar appearance, and was kindly received. Duncan never made a song or poem, long or short, which was not set to a tune, and he first sang them himself, as he wandered to and fro amid his native wilds. For years they floated about in the poet's mind to music of their own, and from being sung by their author, many of them were carried from mouth to mouth until they reached the Hebrides. When forty-four years of age, he dictated his poems to a clergyman, who wrote them down with a view to their publication in book form. This was in 1768, and in the same year the book was printed in Edinburgh. A second edition appeared in 1790; and a third, with some additional pieces, in 1804. For six years he was a sergeant in the Breadalbane Fencibles, and when that regiment was disbanded in 1799, he procured, by the influence of the Earl of Breadalbane, a place in the City Guard of Edinburgh, those poor old veterans so sagely described by Fergusson in "Leith Races"—

"Their stumps, erst used to filabegs,
　Are dight in spatterdashes,
Whase barkent hides scarce fend their legs,
　Frae weet and weary splashes
　　O' dirt that day!"

He was then seventy-five years old. About this time he composed a quaint, long rhyme in praise of Dunedin, or Edinburgh; and the poem, although not one of his inspired productions, is deeply interesting from its quaint touches of wandering realism. He remained in the City Guard till about 1806, when, having saved a few pounds from his wages and the profits of his published poems, he was enabled to retire and spend his remaining years without toil of any kind. He was eighty-four years old when he died. On the 19th of May, 1812, he was buried in the Greyfriars Burying-ground, Edinburgh, and a number of years ago a monument was raised to his memory in Glenorchy. "All good judges of Celtic poetry agree," says Macintyre's biographer, in Reid's *Bibliotheca Scoto-Celtica*, "that nothing like the purity of his Gaelic and the style of his poetry has appeared in the Highlands since the days of Ossian."

CHARLES MACKAY, LL.D.

One of the most popular poets of the present century, Dr. Charles Mackay, was a native of Perth, and was born in 1814. He received the rudiments of his education in London, after which he was sent to a school at Brussels, and from thence to Belgium and Germany. In 1834, after the publication of a small volume of poems, which attracted considerable attention, he became connected with the *Morning Chronicle*. Ten years later he succeeded Mr. Weir in the editorship of the now defunct *Glasgow Argus*—then a leading organ of Liberal opinion in the commercial capital of Scotland; and in 1848 the University of Glasgow bestowed on him the degree of LL.D. After conducting the *Argus* with ability and success for a period of three years, he received the appointment of editor of the *Illustrated London News*, and returned to the Metropolis, where, with the exception of a brief sojourn in America, he continued to reside, till his death a little more than a year ago. To even name all Dr. Mackay's published works would occupy more space than we can afford here to devote to that purpose. As a poet, journalist, and general writer, he worked laboriously; and gave to the world in book-form what in quantity and quality would constitute no mean library. As a song-writer he has been highly successful. His verse is exceedingly sweet, flowing, and melodious, and his skill in music has given him a command over the resources of rhythm to which few contemporary song-writers have attained. Some of the most successful of his lyrics were set to tunes, also composed by himself. His best known song is "Cheer, boys, cheer." The second in popular favour being "John Brown; or a Plain Man's Philosophy," beginning—

" I've a guinea I can spend,
    I've a wife, and I've a friend,
And a troop of little children at my knee, John Brown;

I've a cottage of my own
With the ivy overgrown,
And a garden with a view of the sea, John Brown."

By the production of "Voices from the Crowd," he achieved the honourable position of "the Poet of the People."

ALEXANDER MACLAGAN,

The writer of many well-known Scottish lyrics, including "Hurrah for the Thistle," "We'll ha'e nane but Highland Bonnets Here," "Dinna ye Hear it?" "Tibby and the Laird," "My Auld Granny's Leather Pouch," etc., was born at Bridgend, Perth, on the 3rd of April, 1811. When five years old he was taken to Edinburgh by his father, and during the remainder of his life his headquarters continued in the capital. Mr. Maclagan was early apprenticed to a trade, and when he first became known as a writer of songs was a journeyman plumber. In 1829, while yet an apprentice, he became a contributor to the *Edinburgh Literary Journal*, then under the editorship of Mr. Henry Glassford Bell. As a contributor to that publication, he was introduced to Professor Wilson, William Motherwell, and the Ettrick Shepherd, who severally commended his verses. In 1844 Maclagan published a collected edition of his poems, which attracted the favourable notice of Lord Jeffrey, who invited the poet to his residence, and in many ways proved his benefactor. The last letter his Lordship wrote was one addressed to Maclagan, dated 4th January, 1850, and bore kindly reference to a new volume entitled "Sketches from Nature and other Poems," which he was about to publish. Soon after Lord Jeffrey's death Maclagan found a new patron and friend in Lord Cockburn, who procured him a junior clerkship in the office of the Inland Revenue, Edinburgh. In 1851 he was entertained by a number of his admirers at a public dinner in the hall attached to Burns' cottage, and more recently a similar compliment was extended to him in his native town. His third publication—

"Ragged and Industrial School Rhymes"—appeared in 1854. Two years later he had conferred on him a civil list pension of £30 per annum. His last publication was a handsome quarto volume, richly illustrated, entitled "Balmoral: Songs of the Highlands, and other Poems," which was dedicated by permission to Her Majesty the Queen. He died at Edinburgh in 1879. The late Tom Maclagan, of Music Hall celebrity, we may mention, was a son of the deceased poet.

Alexander Maclagan possessed a genuine lyrical faculty, and few minor bards of his day have a fairer chance of obtaining a permanent place in the minstrelsy of his native land.

JAMES MACLAGGAN,

Was born at Ballechan, in the parish of Logierait, in the year 1728. He was educated at the University of St. Andrews, and after being licensed as a preacher of the Gospel, was appointed to the Chapel-of-Ease at Amulree (made a parish in 1871). Subsequently he received a chaplaincy in the 42nd (Black Watch), and accompanied the regiment to the United States, where he was present in several engagements during the war of 1776-82. After discharging the duties of military chaplain for the long period of twenty-five years, Mr. Maclaggan was presented to the parish of Blair Athole, where he died in the course of the year 1805. He published anonymously a Collection of Gaelic Songs, and during his service with the regiment he composed a number of war lyrics and poems, many of which still remain in manuscript. He was a thorough Gaelic scholar; and is reported to have received, while settled in the Highlands, from the recitations of various persons, large portions of the poetry of Ossian prior to Macpherson's publications.

PETER M'NAUGHTON,

One of the best Gaelic scholars of recent times, and a poet of approved ability, was born on the farm of

Middleton of Tulliepowrie in the year 1814. In early life he engaged in farm work, and started shopkeeping on his own account in the village of Inver in his twenty-fourth year. Here he remained until 1874, when he crossed the river to Grandtully, where he built a house and business premises, and where with the assistance of two of his sons, he carried on with much success the business of a general merchant, until his death, on the 1st of January, 1889.

With a natural bent for the acquisition of knowledge, Mr. M'Naughton in his boyhood read with avidity every book he could lay his hands on. In his old age he was still an omnivorous reader, and a keen political economist, as well as a loving and intelligent student of nature. He composed many original poems and ballads which have never been printed, and are not likely to be. The great literary work of his life, and the one by which he will certainly be remembered, being a metrical translation of Ossian in the peculiar measure of the original. Macpherson's translation, without being strictly literal, is in prose, which does not preserve the measure of Ossian's verse,—a great want to one conversant with the Gaelic. Macgregor's and Clark's translations are more literal than that of Macpherson's, but neither of them attempts to preserve the rhythmic cadence of the original. To accomplish this in some measure was Mr. M'Naughton's ambition, as well as that of many enthusiastic admirers of Ossian who encouraged him in the work. It was an arduous task, but he succeeded even beyond expectation; and his work, published by Blackwood & Sons in 1887, has been highly commended by competent critics.

DAVID M. MAIN,

Editor of "A Treasury of English Sonnets," was a son of the late Mr. Main, Banker, Doune, one of whose daughters is the wife of Mr. Smart, R.S.A. He was trained to commercial life in Glasgow; but his literary inclinations led him about a dozen years ago to devote his undivided attention to the compilation of the great work on English sonnets, with which his name will be permanently identified. When engaged on this task he went south to Manchester, and also to London, ransacking the treasures in the British Museum and spending several months in the library of his friend, Mr. Alexander Ireland, of the *Manchester Examiner*, who took a warm personal interest in the scheme which his young fellow-countryman was prosecuting with so much zeal and enthusiasm. When the "Treasury" at length appeared in a noble volume, the external appearance of which harmonised with the value of its contents, it was at once accepted by the best authorities as the standard work on the subject—not only the choicest collection of English sonnets, but the most perfect in respect to editing, every page containing evidence of the most profound learning as well as of the most exquisite taste. Mr. Dante Rossetti, perhaps the greatest authority on the sonnet, pronounced the work a gem of the first water, and showed his respect for it by executing an illuminated title-page of great beauty for the copy which the editor presented to his mother. Shortly after the appearance of the "Treasury," Mr. Main settled as a bookseller in Royal Exchange Square, Glasgow, devoting himself especially to high-class literature. Of a highly sensitive nature, and never over robust constitution, his health broke down just on the eve of his projected marriage; and after two years, during which he was almost dead to the world, he died at Doune on the 19th January, 1888. Mr. Main had a fine gift as a poet, and was the author of several exquisite sonnets, two of which, by the permission of his relatives, are included in this work.

DAVID MALLET.

Chiefly known to present day readers as the author of the plaintive and beautiful ballad of "William and Margaret," David Mallet, or Malloch, was the son of a small innkeeper in Crieff, and was born in the year 1700. Educated at Aberdeen and Edinburgh Universities, he acted for a time as an unsalaried tutor in the family of Mr. Home of Dreghorn, near Edinburgh, after which he entered the family of the Duke of Montrose as tutor and travelling companion to his sons, with a salary of £30 per annum. In 1723 he accompanied his pupils to London, and changed his name from Malloch to Mallet, as more euphonious. Next year he produced his pathetic ballad of "William and Margaret," and published it in Aaron Hill's *Plain Dealer*. The ballad commanded considerable attention, and afforded him an introduction to the literary society of the Metropolis, which included such names as Young and Pope. The latter introduced him to Bolingbroke, who in turn, on the poet's death, found a willing instrument in Mallet for traducing the memory of his friend. Mallet—though we regret to say it of a Perthshire poet—was one of those mean creatures who always worship a rising and turn their back on a setting sun. By his very considerable talents, his management, and his address, he soon rose in the world. He was appointed Under-Secretary to the Prince of Wales, with a salary of £200 a year. In conjunction with Thomson, the poet of the "Seasons," to whom he was really kind, he wrote, in 1740, "The Masque of Alfred," in honour of the birthday of the Princess Augusta. In this dramatic composition, which was afterwards altered by Mallet, and produced at Drury Lane in 1751, the national song of "Rule Britannia" first appeared; a song which, as Southey said, will be the political hymn of Great Britain as long as she maintains her political power. Whether written by Thomson or Mallet is not known with certainty, but the consensus of critical opinion is that the lyric breathes the higher inspiration and more manly spirit of Thomson. Mallet's first wife, of whom nothing is recorded, having died, he married the daughter of Lord Carlisle's steward, who brought him a fortune of £10,000. Both she and Mallet gave themselves out as Deists. This was partly owing to the latter's intimacy with Bolingbroke, to gratify whom he heaped abuse upon Pope in a preface to the "The Patriot King," and was rewarded by

Bolingbroke leaving him the whole of his works and MSS. These he afterwards published, and exposed himself to the vengeful sarcasm of Johnson, who said that Bolingbroke was a scoundrel and a coward—a scoundrel to charge a blunderbuss against Christianity; and a coward, because he durst not fire it himself, but left a shilling to a beggarly Scotsman to draw the trigger after his death. Mallet ranked himself among the calumniators, and, as it proved, murderers of Admiral Byng. He wrote a life of Lord Bacon, in which, it was said, he forgot that Bacon was a philosopher, and would probably, when he came to write the life of Marlborough, forget that he was a general. His "Life of Bacon" is now utterly forgotten. The Duchess of Marlborough left £1000 in her will between Glover and Mallet to write a life of her husband. Glover threw up his share of the work, and Mallet engaged to perform the whole, to which besides he was stimulated by a pension from the second Duke of Marlborough. He got the money, but when he died it was found he had not written a line of the work. In his latter days he held the lucrative office of Keeper of the Book of Entries for the port of London. He died on the 21st of April, 1765.

Dastardly, mean, and unscrupulous, as a man, David Mallet is no credit to Perthshire and Scotland; yet, as the author of "William and Margaret," and the older set of "The Birks of Invermay," his name will live with the language in which these are written.

SIR WILLIAM STIRLING-MAXWELL, BART.

A Perthshire man in every respect, except in the mere accident of his birth, the late Sir William Stirling-Maxwell was born at Kenmure House, near Glasgow, in March, 1818. He was the only son of Mr. Archibald Stirling of Keir, the representative of an old and wealthy Perthshire family, his mother being a daughter of Sir John Maxwell, Bart., of Pollok, Renfrewshire. He was educated at Trinity College, Cambridge, where he graduated B.A. in 1839, and M.A. in 1843. On the death of his father in 1847, he succeeded to the estates of Keir and Calder, and on the death of his uncle, Sir John Maxwell, in 1866, the Pollock estate fell into his hands, bringing with it the title, which he did more to honour than he was honoured by. Sir William married in 1865 Lady Anna Maria Melville, third daughter of the eighth Earl of Leven and Melville, who died from the results of a sad accident in 1874, leaving two sons, the eldest of whom is the present master of Keir and Pollock. Three years subsequently he was wedded to the Hon. Mrs. Norton, the fashionable novelist, but very soon had to mourn her loss also. Sir William himself died at Venice in 1878. With natural artistic tastes, refined by study and travel, he made many important contributions to critical and historical literature. Among his best known works are "Annals of the Artists of Spain," 1848; "Cloister Life of Emperor Charles V.," 1852; "Velazquez and his Works," 1855; and his Essays concerning Proverbs, etc., and the Arts of Design. His only volume of verse, "Songs of the Holy Land," composed chiefly during a visit to Palestine, and from which our extracts are mainly taken, was published in 1846.

In addition to the honour of representing Perthshire in Parliament from 1852 to 1865, and being returned again in 1872, Sir William Stirling Maxwell was elected Rector of St. Andrews University in 1863, when he received the degree of LL.D., and was honoured with the same high office by the University of Edinburgh in 1872. Three years later, he was elected Chancellor of the University of Glasgow, as successor to the late Duke of Montrose. He was Chairman of the Scottish Education Board, and held the high rank of a Knight of the Thistle.

GRÆME REID MERCER,

Of Gorthy, the oldest representative of the "Red Mercers,"—the younger branch of the Mercer family, whose parent stem, known as the "Black Mercers," is now merged in the person of the Dowager Marchioness of Landsdowne—died in October, 1886, at the age of 74. Mr. Mercer took little or nothing to do with parochial concerns, but in local political affairs he displayed much interest, and on the occasion of contested elections in Perthshire, was wont to figure in a poetic capacity, by expressing his well known old Tory views of men and measures, through the medium of satirical epigrams and amusing versicles. He was also of an antiquarian turn, and, in the matter of genealogy in particular, was unsurpassed for knowledge relating to Perthshire families. His collection of antiquarian and other literature was exceptionally fine, and in the Register House in Edinburgh, as in the social circles of the Metropolis, the late Laird of Gorthy was a familiar figure. The song in this collection is said to be about the only non-political thing of the kind that issued from his pen.

DAVID MILLAR,

Author of "The Tay: A Poem"—a noble song of a truly noble stream—whose fame, though it deserves to embrace the limits of his native land, has not extended much beyond the limited scene of his song, was born at Newburgh, in Fife, in 1803. Here he spent his early years, indulged in his literary pursuits, married, and did business, till in 1840 he went to Perth, having been offered a situation on the staff of the *Perthshire Advertiser*. In early life he was fond of poetry and literature, and the pages of the *Fife Herald* were often enriched with his verse, and other articles, which were highly esteemed. That Mr. Millar had a keen appreciation of the charms of nature was shown in his "Saturday Afternoon Rambles," in the *Fife Herald*, in which he described the enthusiasm he felt as he roamed on the shores of the Tay, wandered in the glens around Lindores, or climbed the slopes of the Fifian Ochils. While in connection with the *Perthshire Advertiser*, he twice a year travelled through the greater part of Perthshire and adjoining counties, and collected a store of antiquarian and legendary lore, which he embodied in "Walks in the Country," published from time to time in the *Perthshire Advertiser*. His poem, "The Tay," appeared in 1850. On the Saturday previous to his decease he returned from his spring journey to the Highlands, apparently in good health and spirits; but during Sunday night he was suddenly seized with an alarming illness, and on Monday evening the Poet of the Tay, the interesting topographer and antiquarian, the kind-hearted friend and cheerful companion, whose gladsome face, merry laugh, and free genial disposition, were fitted to interest and delight every sensitive bosom, closed his mortal career and finished the journey of life, aged sixty-two years. This was in the spring of 1865. A prominent personal characteristic of Mr. Millar's was, we have been told by one who knew him well, a shrinking modesty in regard to his own productions. Until the publication of his poem "The Tay"—the labour almost of his life—was announced, his most intimate friends did not know that such a work had been on the anvil. Had he shown his hand earlier, in all probability his poem would have had a much more extensive circulation, and might have enjoyed a popularity more nearly approximate with its merit. It is a really valuable contribution to the national literature; and singing as it does the natural beauties of each "bosky bank and flowery brae" that adorns his "youthful muse's favourite theme;" and reciting so many interesting legendary and historical tales associated with the banks and bosom of the first river in the country, it is a poem that should be known and read by all who are proud to claim Scotland as the land of their birth.

Poor David Millar! he loved his native Tay, and sang her many-tinted glories cheerily and well. There is, however, a sigh for every song, and for every smile a tear. The concluding lines tell a sad tale:—

"The song that rose in gladness sinks in grief!
Fair Tay, thou'rt beautiful, but most unkind!
Though weak its numbers, was there nought but death
To recompense my love? I tried to bind
A chaplet round thy brow, and thou hast twined
For mine a cypress wreath! My fair, my gay,
My glad-souled boy! and didst thou, trusting find
Her lauded charms were trustless? Away!
A shadow's o'er thee now, ingrate but glorious Tay!"

REV. D. G. MITCHELL.

Born in the parish of Strachan, in Kincardineshire, in September, 1863, David Gibb Mitchell received his early education at Longforgan Public School, and has spent the most, as well as the happiest of his days, so far, on the braes of the Carse of Gowrie. "My heart swells," he writes, "as I look back on my laddie days. How bright, how happy, how real! In the glen I had nae bairnies to play wi', and so I was forced to become Nature's bairn. I threw myself into her arms, and she nursed me and taught me from her own lips. The birds in the woods became my companions. I learned all their names, and got familiar with their habits. I knew on what trees to find them, and felt as happy in their presence as on my mother's knee. With all of us this page in the book of memory, recording scenes and little incidents of early days, is often, often read. The stories of ghosts and hobgoblins—making our hair stand on end—of witches and warlocks, and many other such-like *screids*, related round the big log-fire on a winter's night, were so imprinted upon the imagination and memory that they continue fresh to the end of life."

In his youth he was employed for a time as a clerk with the Caledonian Railway Company, and latterly as a junior clerk in a carpet factory in Dundee, but all the while was secretly preparing at the night schools for college: and in two years from the time he left the day-school he entered as a student at the University of

St. Andrews. Before leaving college he took his degree in classics, was 5th prizeman in the class of Moral Philosophy, and was in the honours' list in Logic and English Literature. In 1886 he entered the Free Church Divinity Hall in Edinburgh, and in the following summer was sent to take charge of a mission station in Orkney. At the end of the succeeding session he was appointed missionary to the New College Students' Mission in Edinburgh. Subsequently he acted for a time as assistant to the Rev. Dr. M'Tavish, Inverness, and a year or two ago was appointed colleague and successor to the Rev. James Smith, Cramond, near Edinburgh, a position which he occupies with credit and acceptancy.

Mr. Mitchell was, by virtue of his musical and poetical abilities, a prime favourite with his fellow-students at College. For these, and the higher gifts and graces befitting his position as a minister of the Gospel, he is, we are glad to know, held in equal esteem by the good people of the Free Kirk of Cramond. Poetry has been a subject of by-play, rather than one of study with him, yet many of his poems are instinct with grace and beauty of thought, whilst some of his lighter efforts, like "Och, Hey, Hum," are of the happiest possible turn.

WILLIAM MURRAY,

Born at Finlarig, Breadalbane, in May, 1834, emigrated to Canada in his youth, and has been connected for a great many years with the well-known and extensive dry goods store of Messrs. A. Murray and Co., Hamilton, Ontario. He is the author of many pleasing and vigorous songs and poems on Scottish subjects, some of the latter being of considerable length and unusual good quality. Although frequently pressed by his friends to issue a collection of the creatures of his imagination in book-form, he has, thus far, refrained from gratifying their desire. "While Mr. Murray has never tasted of matrimonial joys," says Mr. John D. Ross, in his *Scottish*

Poets in America, "his lot in life is by no means an unhappy one. He enjoys a large circle of friends, is respected by all, and is ever ready to lend assistance wherever and whenever required. He is the author of many poems which deserve to be better known than they now are, and we hope that he will yet be induced to place a collection of his writings in a permanent form before the public."

CAROLINA, BARONESS NAIRNE,

After Burns, indisputably the greatest song-writer that Scotland has produced, was the third daughter of Laurence Oliphant, Esq. of Gask, and his spouse (who was also his cousin) Margaret Robertson, a daughter of Duncan Robertson of Struan, and was born in "The Auld House," which she afterwards celebrated in song, on the 16th of July, 1766. In her youth she was singularly beautiful, being known in her native district by the poetical designation of "The Flower of Strathearn"; and not less remarkable was she for the precocity of her intellect than for the elegance of her person. Descended from two old Jacobite families, and herself named in honour of Prince Charles Edward, her earlier sympathies received a strong bias in favour of the exiled race of Stuart, which in course of time found expression in such songs as "We hae a Croon without a Head," "Wha'll be King but Charlie?" "The Auld House," and "He's ower the Hills that I lo'e weel," and others. In the application of her talents, she was influenced by another incentive. A loose ribaldry tainted the songs and ballads which circulated among the peasantry, and she was convinced that the diffusion of a more wholesome minstrelsy would elevate the moral tone of the community. Thus, while still in her teens, she began to purify the older melodies and to compose new songs, which were ultimately destined to occupy an ample share of the national heart. On one occasion, about this time, her brother Laurence, entertaining the Gask tenantry at dinner, when called upon for a song, gave with much spirit a new version of a hitherto rude country song, "The Ploughman," which he said he had received from the writer. The song was received with warm approbation, and was speedily set to the old music and published. Thus encouraged, the "Flower of Strathearn" proceeded in her self-imposed task; and added song to song with remarkable rapidity and success, at the same time keeping her personality studiously concealed. To the early period of her career, in which she composed "The Ploughman," it is worth noting, there also belongs "The Laird o' Cockpen," which soon afterwards was followed by "The Land of the Leal" and some of her best known songs. Carolina Oliphant, in her hey-day, like the celebrated "Tibbie Fowler," had many suitors for her hand—"wooin' at her, pooin' at her" —but gave the preference to her second cousin, Captain William Murray Nairne (who but for an attainder had been fifth Lord Nairne), to whom she was married on 2nd June, 1806. Captain Nairne had obtained the office of Assistant Inspector General of Barracks in Scotland, with the brevet rank of Major. His official duties implied a residence in Edinburgh, and thither Mrs. Nairne repaired with her gallant husband. In the capital the Nairnes were known but to a select number of friends, and even these were kept in utter ignorance of her ladyship's poetical inclinations; yea, Major Nairne himself, it is said, was uninformed of his wife's habit of song-writing, and of the fact that she had composed "The Land o' the Leal." It was sometime previous to 1821 that the talented authoress entrusted to a single gentlewoman in Edinburgh the secret of her authorship. "In that year," writes Dr. Charles Rogers, "Mr. Robert Purdie, a music-seller in the capital, resolved to publish a series of the more approved national songs, accompanied by suitable melodies. Several ladies of musical tastes were solicited to render their assistance to the undertaking; and among others the gentlewoman who had been the depository of Lady Nairne's secret. Informed by this friend of Mr. Purdie's project, our authoress consented to render every assistance, on her *incognito* being preserved. The condition was readily acceded to; and though the publication of 'The Scottish Minstrel' extended over three years, and our authoress had several personal interviews and much correspondence with the publisher and his editor, Mr. Robert Archibald Smith, both these individuals remained ignorant of her real name. She had assumed the signature 'B. B.' in the 'Minstrel,' and in her correspondence with Mr. Purdie, who appears to have been entertained by the *discovery*, communicated in confidence, that the name of his contributor was 'Mrs. Bogan of Bogan,' and by this designation he subsequently addressed her." The "Scottish Minstrel" was completed in 1824, in six royal octavo volumes, but up to this time the real identity of the authoress of some of the choicest items in its contents had not leaked out. To the end of her days, indeed, Lady Nairne scrupulously preserved her *incognito*. As in the case of Lady Anne Barnard, she saw the popular creations of her Muse attributed to others, but this seemed to give her no annoyance. She experienced much gratification in finding her simple minstrelsy supplanting the coarse and demoralising rhymes of a former period; and this knowledge she preferred to fame. It was not until after her death that the first collection of her songs was printed and published, with her name on the title-page—"Lays from Strathearn; by Carolina, Baroness Nairne,"—which was followed, in 1868, by the full collection of her poetical writings, edited, with a memoir, by the late Dr. Charles Rogers.

By an Act of Parliament, which received the Royal sanction in June, 1824, Major Nairne was restored to his rank in the peerage, and the authoress of "The Land o' the Leal" became the Baroness Nairne. She was left a widow, with one son, on the 9th of July, 1830. The remaining years of her life, most of which she spent on the Continent, were marked by Christian zeal and philanthropy. She died in the mansion house of Gask, on Sunday, the 26th October, 1845, at the advanced age of seventy-nine years.

It is worth noting here that Niel Gow approved of Miss Oliphant's dancing, and when the great fiddler saw her on the floor at the County balls, he said, "He *drew* his bow." To realize the value and extent of her contributions to the national minstrelsy, it is only necessary to mention by name "The Land o' the Leal," "The Laird o' Cockpen," "Caller Herrin'," "The Auld House," "The Hundred Pipers," "The Rowan Tree," "Wha'll be King but Charlie?" "He's owre the Hills that I loe we'el," "Will ye no come back again?" and "The Women are a' gane Wud," every song of which stands in the front rank of popularity, affording proof for our claim made at the outset, that, after Burns, Lady Nairne is the greatest song-writer which our song-hallowed, song-loving country has yet produced.

WILLIAM NEISH

Is a native of the "lang toun" of Auchterarder, the "braes roun' aboot" which he has celebrated in one of the two songs from his pen which we have been able to find room for in this collection. Born on the 16th of July, 1867, Mr. Neish became a railway clerk, and served in the Clearing Houses at various junctions in Scotland until 1889, when he received an appointment in the head office in London, where he is likely to be permanently employed. He has not written much, but has a decided gift for lyrical composition.

JOHN NELSON,

Now resident in Syracuse, America, was born in Dunning, about 1810. He left his native land more than fifty years ago, but still retains a warm nook in his heart for dear auld Caledonia, and has contributed many pieces of a patriotic character to the newspapers and journals of the day.

ALEXANDER NICOL,

For sometime, more than a hundred years ago, schoolmaster at Collace, and author of "The Rural Muse; or a Collection of Miscellany Poems, both Comical and Serious," printed at Edinburgh in 1753, was, as we gather from the introductory pages of his book, born and bred on the estate of Pitcur, near Coupar Angus. In the course of the dedication of his volume to "The Honourable James Halyburton, of Pitcur, Esq., Member of Parliament for Orkney and Shetland, and Colonel in the Third Regiment of Foot Guards, etc," the author says—" To screen my weak performances from the malice and detraction of uncharitable readers, made me to seek shelter from them under the shadow of your protection; hoping it will not derogate anything from your honour, though I cannot say they are worth your notice; but, having your countenance, they will be acceptable to all into whose hands they shall come. And though I had been as famous an author as Virgil or Horace I could expect none but yourself to be my Mæcenas, seeing I was born and brought up within your inheritance; therefore you will excuse and pardon me for presuming to trouble you with such insignificant trifles, which yet, if at your leisure hours you may deign to cast your eyes on, though they do not satisfy, may divert you. For my former performances have been taken notice of by men of honour and learning, and the more, because I never had any education, and your honourable father was my best of many friends. The Right Honourable the late Lord Gray was the first that took notice of me, upon Monorgon's recommendation, with several other worthy gentlemen. At length the Right Honourable the Earl of Morton encouraged me, so that I grew ambitious to appear in publick; and applying to the present Lord Gray, he accepted of my dedication, which made my heart as light as a feather. And now once more I am revived by you. There are some so puft up with pride that such as I cannot get access unto them; but I do not reckon these persons of honour, but rather fools; and commonly such have no other character; for pride never dwells with virtue and a good character; otherwise you might have repulsed me after this manner :—

Thou punie fool, think'st thou that we
Regard ought that's perform'd by thee ?
Thou and thy *Rural Muse* may go
To vulgar sots, that nothing know,
But to converse with sheep and cattle ;
And unto them your nonsense rattle."

The dominie must have been a bit of a character in his day. And that he rode an ever-willing and sprightly Pegasus is evident. Within the scope of the "Rural Muse" we find "A Bundle of Flowers for Children : Being Verses on the most remarkable men and women mentioned in the Bible ; " "The Broken Laird Repair'd ; a comical tale in five Cantos ; " and "King Solomon's Book of Ecclesiastes, in Metre." Here we see some lines "On receiving a compliment from the Right Honourable the Lord Kinnaird," there a dissertation on " Mrs. Ogilvie's Chariot Wheel Sinking on the Brink of the River Spey ; " now it is an acrostic on Robert Hunter of South Ballo, then an elegy on his old friend Johnie Galla. The "City of Dundee" comes in for a share of his attention, and his remarks on that "ancient city, famed for arms and arts," are not devoid of interest.

ROBERT NICOLL,

Popularly known and esteemed as "Scotland's second Burns," was born at Little Tulliebeltane, in the parish of Auchtergaven, on the 7th of January, 1814, of "decent, honest, God-fearing parents." His mother, Grizel, or Grace Fenwick, a daughter of the venerable Seceder "Elder John," of whom the poet sings frequently and with much affection, and who seems to have been a remarkable woman, was his first and almost only teacher. By her aid—lent in the brief intervals of her domestic duties—Robert could read the New Testament by the time he was five years old. At this period of his life a sad calamity befel the household. His father —until then a farmer in comfortable circumstances— had become security for a large amount to a relative, who failed and absconded. Mr. Nicoll's ruin was the immediate consequence; and with his wife and children he left the farmhouse, and became a day-labourer on the fields he had lately rented. Robert Nicoll was thus from his earliest recollections the son of a very poor man, the inmate of a very lowly cottage home, and (the first-born having died early) the eldest of a struggling family. Like many men who have risen to distinction, he used to attribute his success to maternal influences exercised upon his youthful mind. "My mother," he says in one of his letters, "was in her early years an ardent book-woman. When she became poor her time was too precious to admit of its being spent in reading, and I generally read to her while she was working, for she took care that the children should not want education." Would that all mothers were animated with the same ambition, and the slur of *compulsory* education were lifted from off the character of our country! When six years old Robert was sent to the parish school, about three miles distant, to learn "countin' and wreatin';" attending school in winter, and herding cows during the summer months. No doubt it was while "a laddie herdin' kye" that he imbibed the germs of many of his songs and poems, and laid the foundation of what he afterwards expressed in "Youth's Dreams:"—

"I thought the little burnies ran,
  An' sang the while to me;
To glad me flowers cam' on the earth,
  An' leaves upon the tree;
An' heather on the muirland grew,
  An' tarns in glens did lie;
Of beauteous things like these I dreamed,
  When I was herdin' kye."

At thirteen he began to scribble down his thoughts in verse. At seventeen he was apprenticed to the grocery trade in Perth. Here he found access to storehouses of knowledge. By the kindness of a gentleman in Perth he got the use of the Public Library, and read with delight Milton's prose works, Locke's works, and some of

Bentham's treatises, and in the course of one summer Smith's "Wealth of Nations" several times through. During the run of his 'prentice time he attached himself to a debating society in Perth, wrote poetry on the North Inch, and stories in his fireless lodgings. One story he sent to the editor of *Johnstone's Edinburgh Magazine*, and had the pleasure of seeing it in print under the title of "Jessie Ogilvy." The publication of this story determined his future vocation. He decided to live by his pen, despite the entreaties of his old aunt, who said—"Dinna be an author, Robert; they're aye puir." On the expiry of his apprenticeship he went to Edinburgh, seeking he scarcely knew what, and after rolling about for some time in "a swither" as to what he should try, he proceeded to Dundee, and there opened a circulating library in Castle Street. The venture did not prove a successful one, but the nature of the business afforded him considerable time for devotion to literary exercises; and he did not idle himself. In a letter about this time he says—"No wonder I am busy: I am at this moment writing poetry; I have almost a volume of a novel written. I have to attend the meeting of the Kinloch Monument Committee; write some half-dozen articles for the *Advertiser*; and, to crown all, I have fallen in love." The young lady with whom he fell in love, and whom he afterwards married, was Miss Alice Suter, a niece of the then editor of the *Dundee Advertiser*. In his twenty-first year he published his "Poems and Lyrics," five editions of which have since appeared. They were well received by his friends and the press, but brought him no pecuniary assistance. On leaving Dundee, Nicoll again betook himself to Edinburgh, and there, through the influence of Mr. Tait, the publisher, succeeded in procuring the editorship of the *Leeds Times*, a Radical newspaper of the broadest type, at a salary of £100 per annum. The work was one the nature of which he had long sighed to obtain, and he threw his whole soul into it; but, never constitutionally robust, he soon broke down under the severe strain of editorship, and, though with great reluctancy, was obliged to relinquish the duties. He believed that breathing his native air and a look of his mother would soon restore him; and with his fond wife he hurried to his native land—but to die. He reached the house of his friend, Mr. Johnstone, in Edinburgh, and died there, "unstained and pure at the age of twenty-three," on the 9th of December, 1837. His remains were interred in the churchyard of North Leith, whither they were followed by a numerous and respectable assemblage, consisting chiefly of gentlemen connected with the press in Edinburgh.

Some of Nicoll's songs, such as "Bonnie Bessie Lee," and "My Auld Mither Dee'd in the Year Auchty-Nine," have attained a popularity only surpassed by those of Burns and Lady Nairne. But it is not in the production of popular song that his main strength lies; and not here is to be found the secret of his fame. His writings are cherished because, as he says himself "I have written my heart in my poems; and rude and unfinished, and hasty as they are, it can be read there."

WILLIAM NICOLL,

A younger brother of the author of "Bonnie Bessie Lee," was born at Little Tulliebeltane, in the year 1817, and after a brief existence, spent partly in Perth, Glasgow, and Edinburgh, he died in the latter city in 1855. In person, we are told, he was rather above the middle height, was fair complexioned, and had deep, grey eyes. In manners, he was affable, insinuating, and sprightly; in social life, warm and unsuspicious, though somewhat violent in his attachments, and merciless in his denunciations. He was a dutiful son, an affectionate brother, and a firm friend. In politics he was, like his better-known and more highly gifted brother, an extreme Radical; fervid and sincere, and ever ready to cross swords with a political opponent. He also longed to see "the warld better yet," and delighted in "the glorious privilege of being independent." William Nicoll's poetry certainly does not equal his brother's in any sense, but he is, nevertheless, a sweet, and true son of song. He sleeps in the same grave with his brother in North Leith Churchyard.

PETER NORVAL,

For nearly forty years schoolmaster of Collace, and who died only a year or two ago, added to many well-known mental, professional, and literary acquirements, a fine gift of lyrical composition, and left behind him in the world a handful of songs and ballads, several of which are worthy of a place in any and every collection of Scottish lyrical poetry.

Mr. Norval was a native of Fifeshire, and in that county began his professional career. After a short term of service in the Parish School of Kinnoull he was appointed schoolmaster of Collace. In addition to being schoolmaster, he held the situation of registrar of births, etc., for the parish, and had been more than once complimented by the Registrar-General for his fine penmanship and order in registration duties. He was one of the first among parochial teachers who, after the passing of the Education Act, qualified for having his school examined by Her Majesty's Inspector for Privy Council grant, and he held a certificate of the 1st class. By his old pupils, many of whom have distinguished themselves in various walks of life, and occupy positions of trust and usefulness in the country, and by all who came within the influence of his kindly, magnetic character, the memory of Mr. Norval will be cherished with deep and lasting affection. "Not only as a schoolmaster was he loved and admired," said the *Perthshire Constitutional* at the time of his death. "The same ever-ready sympathy and desire to help were evinced in his daily conduct outside the school. Though he did not mix much in company—he was too much a student for that —yet his obliging disposition and happy temperament were known always to be depended on, and not a few sought his society at the schoolhouse, his services as land measurer, and his counsel in their difficulties.

Possessed of a retentive memory and a highly-cultured mind, he had amassed vast stores of learning, which were ever ready for the benefit of others. His intellectual excellence was known and appreciated; he was an artist, too, of no mean order, with a creative genius which found expression also in poetry and music. He will be long remembered as a true gentleman."

Mr. Norval's death occurred in the end of June after a very brief illness. He had been the victim of heart disease, and a sharp cold contracted in the course of a visit to the Edinburgh International Exhibition of 1886 cut him off in his sixty-sixth year.

CAROLINE OLIPHANT, THE YOUNGER,

Born at Gask on the 16th January 1807, was the youngest of the eight children of Laurence Oliphant, brother of the authoress of "The Land o' the Leal." In youth she was volatile and gay, fond of novel-reading and seeing the world, and her early education is described as having been desultory. In the course of her teens, however, she became studious, and before she had reached the age of twenty had settled into an exemplary and sincerely Christian lady. She was a great admirer of Robert Hall, and read and studied the Scriptures in the original tongues. Writing of her now, a friend remarks, "I envy Caroline her talent, which shines in all she says or does; and still more the heavenly direction given to it. Never was the character of holiness and purity more legibly inscribed on any mortal." In 1826 the Oliphant's left Gask for Clifton, and Caroline died there, after a lingering illness, in the presence of the Baroness Nairne and other members of the family, on the 9th of February, 1831. She wrote many hymns and poems, only a few of which have been printed.

REV. JAMES PAUL,

Free Church minister of Lochlee, Forfarshire, was born in the village of Longforgan, in 1859. He studied at Edinburgh University, and distinguished himself by taking quite a number of scholarships. He began to write verses when about sixteen, and in his student days was a frequent contributor to the Dundee newspapers. For some time he wrote the Edinburgh Letter for the *Fifeshire Journal*, in the form of racy and vigorous notes, entitled "Echoes from Edina," and afterwards contributed to the same journal a series of clever humorous papers under the heading of "Havers frae Hoolitneuk." He has also written for various Christmas Annuals; and poems and articles from his pen, sometimes over his own name, but more frequently over the *nom de plume* of "White Tie," have appeared at intervals in the columns of the *Glasgow Weekly Citizen*, the *Ladies Journal*, and other periodical publications.

JOHN PAUL,

Presently engaged as an overseer in the firm of Messrs. Baxter, Dundee, was born on 20th October, 1853, at Woodside, St. Madoes, in the Carse of Gowrie. When he was three years of age his parents removed to the village of Longforgan, and at the Parish School there he received the best education the honest dominie could afford, which, we know, comprised "little Latin and less Greek." Leaving school in the spring of 1869, he apprenticed himself to the trade of a joiner in the village of Abernyte; and here, busy during the day in his calling, his evenings were spent either in examining the natural beauty of his surroundings, or trying to frame his thoughts into good form through the vehicle of verse.

In 1873 he removed to Dundee, and, as we have said, is now employed there. Mr. Paul is quite the centre of a little coterie of working men with poetical and theological leanings; but perhaps in no connection is he better known in Dundee than with the Sabbath forenoon meetings held week by week for the poorer classes of children, at which gatherings a visit from John Paul creates quite a sensation. He possesses a peculiar gift in his dealing with the bairns, and it does one's heart good to see how eagerly the wee eyes glisten and the young heads lean forward to listen to the " old, old story" so winningly told by our poetic friend.

This work is very near his heart, and did you take the liberty of upbraiding him with giving thus the cold shoulder to his first love of poetry, he would not be slow in answering that the bairns had stolen his heart away, and what was in him of the poet is giving place to the Children's Missionary. Mr. Paul is possessed of good literary gifts which are largely called forth in the manufacture of essays for debating societies, and such like, in which he takes a hearty interest. A few years ago he was successful in carrying off the first prize medal at Edinburgh which the Church of Scotland Young Men's Guild had offered for essays, and quite recently his name was announced as the winner of a five pound prize for the best poem expressive of patriotic love for the Church of Scotland.

JOHN MACLEAY PEACOCK,

Was born at Kincardine, Perthshire, in 1817, and died, of heart disease, in Glasgow, in 1877. In his early manhood he travelled a good deal in search of employment, and was at times engaged in shipbuilding yards throughout England, Ireland, and Scotland. He worked for several years in Spain, and spent some of his happiest days in that romantic land, to which his Muse has paid a fervent tribute. After being married he settled in Birkenhead where he was for some years employed in a large shipbuilding yard, and afterwards commenced business as a newsagent. Towards the close of his life he accepted a situation as gate-keeper in a foundry in Glasgow, and died there as described.

A volume of his "Poems and Songs," published in 1864, and which lies before us, proves his possession of a fine lyrical faculty, as well as the power of sustained thought and poetical expression. There is a smack of Burns in these lines :—:

"The wide world yet will see the time
 Whan want an' wae will pass awa',
An' men o' every creed an' clime
 Bear kindly love for ane an' a'."

ALICE PRINGLE,

Authoress of "Greycliff Hall, and other Poems," published by Messrs. Dunn & Wright, Glasgow, in 1878, is a daughter of the late Rev. Dr. William Pringle of the United Presbyterian Church, Auchterarder, who is remembered as an elegant writer, an effective platform speaker, and a man of rare scholarly attainments. To a pleasing gift of verse Miss Pringle adds an elocutionary talent of no mean order, and for a time she enjoyed considerable repute as a public reader. Some years ago she removed to England, and where, we presume, she continues to reside.

WILLIAM PYOTT,

Born at Ruthven, in Forfarshire, on the 29th August, 1851, has lived nearly all his days in Blairgowrie. His father, a native of Blair, was a mill overseer; and although no great scholar, was what is familiarly termed "a widely read man." To his sister, Mary, William regards himself primarily indebted for the warm love of poetry early engendered in his breast. On washing days, when his mother was busy, this sister would take him away to the braes, and beguile his thoughts from home by gathering wild flowers, and sitting down and repeating old ballads to him. Before he went to school, he was familiar with all the more stirring episodes in the lives of Wallace and Bruce, and had formed a love for books. The little education he ever got he received at a school at Craig Mill, Rattray, kept for half-time children. In his twelfth year, he was sent to work in one of the flax mills in Blair, and to the present day has continued to work and reside in that district. For many years he worked as a cloth-lapper, but recently, was appointed to the more congenial situation of colporteur of the district, in which office he is widely esteemed for his obliging disposition, intelligence, and general excellence of character.

A volume of his poems and songs, first published at Blairgowrie in 1869, is now in its third edition, and deservedly popular.

WILLIAM RICHARDSON,

Son of the Rev. James Richardson, was born in the Manse of Aberfoyle on the 1st October, 1743. Partly educated at the local school, he went to Edinburgh University and studied with a view to entering the Church, but before he had completed his theological course he entered the family of Lord Cathcart as tutor, and remained there until, through his patron's influence as Lord Rector, he succeeded Professor Muirhead in the Chair of Humanity at Glasgow University. A frequent contributor to various magazines, Professor Richardson wrote many critical examinations of Shakespeare's plays, "The Indian's Tragedy," and several volumes of poetry. He died in 1814.

ALEXANDER ROBERTSON,

The thirteenth laird of Struan of that family, a celebrated Jacobite Chief, and a poet, was born in the year 1668. He was educated for the Church, and with this view entered the University of St. Andrews; but succeeding to the family estate in his twentieth year, he joined Dundee in the Highlands, and aspired to a military career. He fought under Dundee at Killiecrankie, under Mar at Sheriffmuir, and under Prince Charlie at Culloden. Was twice tried, once imprisoned, and twice banished. His sister Margaret planned his escape from prison; his first sentence of banishment and confiscation was remitted by Queen Anne, the second by George the First, and in 1746 the Court of Oyer and Terminer failed to prove his connection with the last Rebellion. When age and its accompanying infirmities prevented Struan from taking part in the activities of the field, he indulged his peculiar fancy of decorating his house with poetical inscriptions. Over every gateway, door, and passage, appropriate lines were written in gold letters, all characteristic and pat in their application.

He died at his house, Mount Alexander, in Rannoch, aged 81. A volume of his poems was published not long after his death, and a second appeared at Edinburgh, in 1785, the latter containing also the "History and Martial Achievements of the Robertsons of Strowan." His effusions—some of them pious—many of them able —all of them clever—are in large part too plain spoken for presentation in these more finical times. Struan is thought to have suggested some hints to Sir Walter Scott for the portrait of Bradwardine in "Waverley."

WILLIAM ROBERTSON (page 192),

Born in Longforgan, in the Carse of Gowrie, in 1808, has been for many years a working gardener in Broughty Ferry. He was forty years old before he blossomed into verse, but a deal of fragrant bloom has fallen from him in his old age. A collection of his poems and songs published a few years ago went speedily out of print. He has long been a frequent and welcome contributor to the *Dundee Evening Telegraph* and the *People's Journal*.

WILLIAM ROBERTSON (page 330),

Although born in Dundee, was in a very important sense a Perthshire man, as well as a Perthshire poet. His father was a native of Old Rattray, and lived until beyond middle life in and about that district; whilst his mother was born in Strathbraan, and when a young girl moved eastward with her family to Blairgowrie, where she met her "marrow." Mr. Robertson served an apprenticeship to the provision trade in Dundee, and afterwards acted for some years as a clerk in a mill there. By and by he obtained the situation of salesman to the Auchtergaven Provision Society in Bankfoot, an office which he continued to discharge until shortly before his death, on the 1st of February, 1891. While a young man in Dundee he found his chief delight in the study and practice of music, but on his removal to the country a new life was opened up to him, and, inspired by the beauty of his sylvan surroundings, he gave his attention more particularly to the cultivation of a natural gift of poesy. For a number of years he was a frequent and welcome contributor to various local periodical publications, including the *People's Journal*, and his poems and songs, invariably sweet and pleasing, are frequently instinct with deep religious feeling. Mr. Robertson was a man of an amiable and devout Christian character, whose memory will be cherished for many years by the good folks of the parish of Auchtergaven.

MARGARET STEWART SANDEMAN.

Though much more widely known and esteemed for the fervent beauty and activity of her Christian life and character, Mrs. Stewart Sandeman of Springland, shared with her maternal aunt, the authoress of "The Land o' the Leal," the true poetic gift, and merits no insignificant place in the bead-roll of native poetesses. Poetry, however, it is clearly evident from reading the record of her life, by her daughter, the late Mrs. Barbour, she never pursued as an art, but simply employed as a ready and pleasant vehicle for the transmission to paper of the more imposing thoughts and feelings of her life. Truly, was she thus "a poetess by Nature made." Mrs. Sandeman was the daughter of Dr. Alexander Stewart of Bonskeid, and was born in the Watergate, Perth, in February, 1803. She succeeded her father in the possession of the estates, thus representing an old line of the "Stewarts," which for five hundred years had passed from father to son. Her mother, Marjory Anne Mary Oliphant of Gask, was the eldest sister of Carolina, afterwards Baroness Nairne. At the age of seventeen she married Mr. Glass Sandeman, a great-grandson of John Sandeman, who founded the religious body known as the Glassites, by whom she had a family of six sons and three daughters. Mr. Sandeman died more than thirty years ago at Montpelier, in France, but sleeps in Greyfriars, Perth. Three of Mrs. Sandeman's sons still survive her, the youngest being Colonel Frank Stewart Sandeman of Stanley House. Her daughter, the late Mrs. Barbour of Bonskeid, the authoress of "The Way Home" and other popular religious books, finds a place in this work. In Mrs. Sandeman were displayed many of the characteristics of the old Jacobite family of Gask, and her mind was richly stored with traditions and memories of a bygone age, which she delighted in contrasting and connecting with those of the present day. Of great literary taste she was, as we have already said, gifted with true poetic instincts. At an early age she was powerfully impressed by the spirit of the Christian religion, and during her life became intimately associated with many of the foremost promoters of evangelistic work. Her beautiful residence on the banks of the Tay, looking across on the North Inch of Perth, held an ever open door to the poor and needy worker in "the vineyard," and besides receiving strength and encouragement from her kind and prudent counsel, they very frequently were helped from the store of her worldly substance. During the last forty years of her life, Mrs. Sandeman kept a diary, entitled "Pro and Con," in which passing events of public and religious interest were regularly chronicled, together with personal criticisms and remarks thereon, frequently in verse. The last entry in the book was made by her own hand a few hours before her death, which took place in the beginning of March, 1883.

D. H. SAUNDERS,

Widely known as a lecturer and writer on social and political subjects, was born at Craig Mill, Rattray, on 2nd August, 1835. He succeeded his father as a flax spinner in Blairgowrie, and a number of years ago removed to Dundee, where in addition to conducting a mercantile business, he maintains a regular and systematic connection with the local press; his contributions to the *People's Journal* over the signature of "A Christian Democrat" being widely read and deservedly much esteemed. An occasional contributor to the magazines of the day, his ballad of "Donald MacInroy" is extracted from an old number of *Chambers' Journal*.

ALEXANDER M. SCOTT,

A youthful lyric poet of considerable promise, was born on the farm of Cordon, near Abernethy, on 20th July, 1866, but has spent the greater part of his yet brief career at Byres, near the village of Guildtown, in the parish of St. Martins. On leaving school at the age of fourteen he wrought for a year and a half at field work on the neighbouring farms, and thereafter went to Perth and began his apprenticeship as a compositor in the *Perthshire Advertiser* office, where, after three years absence in Edinburgh, he is presently employed. His contributions have appeared in the *Perthshire Magazine*, the *People's Journal, Dundee Weekly News*, and *People's Friend*.

JAMES C. SHAIN.

"James Shain was a poet, and a very gallant one," writes Mr. P. R. Drummond, "for out of his thirty-five published poems, twenty-five are devoted to 'woman!' and kissing, sobbing, and tear-shedding are the staple virtues." Mr. Shain half a century ago conducted a sort of "Do-the-boys Hall" in a wretched and sunless old building at the foot of the High Street of Perth, where he also lent books to those who were disposed to read. Where he was born or died has not been recorded.

ANDREW SHARPE,

Was a shoemaker to trade, and spent a goodly portion of his earthly career in or about Perth. Besides beating leather on a lapstone, he played the German flute and taught it, painted landscapes, and taught drawing, and composed love songs and sang them. Despite all these accomplishments, however, his life was one long, hard struggle with poverty. He died at Bridgend, Perth, on the 5th of February, 1817, and lies buried on the sunny side of the old church of Kinnoull. An upright slab marks the spot, and bears this quaint but expressive epitaph, written by himself some years before his death :—

"Halt for a moment, passenger, and read,
Here Andrew dozes in his daisied bed;
Silent his flute, and torn off the key;
His pencils scatter'd, and his Muse set free."

Also this addition by his wife :—

"An affectionate husband, a faithful friend, and an *honest man.*"

JAMES SIM,

In the closing years of the last, and the opening years of the present century, was a labouring man on the estate of Ballathie, in the parish of Kinclaven. Subsequently he resided for a few years in Carolina Place, Wolfhill, but when or where he was born or died no one seems to know. A worthy and well-known Perthshire farmer, who was born and bred on the estate of Ballathie, and whose "well-worn clay" we recently followed to the kirkyard of his native Kinclaven, once told us that he remembered "poet Sim," as he was called, quite well. He was an oldish man when our informant was a boy at school, in the early years of the century, and was of a taciturn disposition generally, but waxed voluble on occasions, and had a reputation for apt, humorous, and satirical repartee. Under the title of "Poems on various

Subjects, Local and General," Sim issued a volume of his rhymed ware in 1811. The book, which extends to 70 pages, was printed by James Crerar, Perth, and seems to have been largely bought up by subscription. The names of his subscribers are given in the back end of the booklet, and are arranged in parishes. And the first name on the list for Auchtergaven is, curiously enough, that of Grizel Fenwick, Robert Nicoll's mother, although Robert was not born until three years afterward. Looking over the names under Kinclaven we find M'Kendrick, Sim, Burns, Cram, Galletly, Foot, Watson, Ford, and Lamb; and under Cargill, Martin, Bannerman, Fenwick, Pirney, Young, Pringle, Thomson, Irvine, Taylor, and Howie predominating, as they still, with one or two exceptions, continue to do in these respective parishes. Sim, with a courage worthy of his calling, lays down, in the opening poem of the book, his plan of poetic censorship, and thus :—

"My theme shall be, since I've begun,
  To pity the oppress'd,
Wi' comic hearts I'll mak' guid fun,
  An' mourn wi' the distress'd.

Whae'er to virtue is inclin'd
  I'll by his merit prize him;
But where a puppy I do find
  I'll try to undisguise him."

So far as it is now possible to guess, "Poet Sim" fearlessly and freely carried out his self-imposed task of patron and protector of the local virtues, for there is in the course of the volume abundance of both praise and blame of the lieges. The results of his moral censorship were, we are afraid, however, not always for the best, since, in sermonizing others, he neglected to keep his own tongue clean.

DAVID MITCHELL SMITH,

A naturalized Perthshire man, and a poet of fine taste and variety of fancy, was born at Bullionfield, near

Dundee, in 1848. When he was yet a child the family removed to the neighbourhood of Kirriemuir, and David was educated at the Parish School of that busy little northern community. On receiving a fair rudimentary education, he commenced the serious business of life as a Railway Company's clerk, at which he continued for a period of fourteen years. Subsequently he entered the service of the Forfar Water Commissioners, where he remained until more than a dozen years ago, when he found employment as a clerk in Messrs. Pullar's Dye Works, Perth. Personally Mr. Smith is a man of sterling and unassuming character—the stuff that most true poets as well as true men are made of—and holds the pursuit of the Muses as quite a secondary consideration when set against the more practical duties of life. Still, loving the tuneful sisters with his whole heart, he finds sweet solace in their society, and manifests their influence in finely measured poem and sweet sounding song. He is a frequent and esteemed contributor to the poetical columns of several local newspapers and national literary journals, and gives fair promise of inscribing his name well up on the fame-scroll of his country. His writings disclose an ardent love of nature, and warm sympathy with the purest and noblest aspirations of the human heart.

JOHN SMITH,

A well-known inhabitant of the thriving little town of Alyth, was born there in the year 1838. When a youth he served an apprenticeship to the wholesale and retail drapery trade in Edinburgh. After filling various situations as a draper, he repaired to Glasgow where he entered the employment of the well-known firm of Messrs. Arthur & Co. This firm Mr. Smith represented in part of Perth and Forfarshire for a period of twelve years, when he retired. Since the year 1873 he has conducted on his own account a successful business in Alyth. He has in his time written and published a great many poetical pieces, and is well-known to newspaper readers by the *nom de plume* of "Auld C." His effusions have, each and every one, it is clearly evident, been written at the instigation of passing fancy, and without any attempt at elaboration, but they are none the less engaging on that account. We have seen them as they passed through the fanners of the local press and have frequently admired them for their pith, point, and pungency—qualities by no means common in the writings of the "occasional contributor." A volume of his "Poems and Lyrics," published in 1888, is locally held in high esteem, as it deserves.

CHARLES SPENCE,

Was born at Cockerhall, under the southern shoulder of Glendoick Hill, in the year 1779. In the early part of the present century he was well-known in the village of Rait, parish of Kilspindie, where he followed the dual vocation of mason and sculptor, and carried on for many years a pretty extensive business in that line. He was of middle height, broad shouldered and muscular in appearance. His face, though browned from continued exposure, was of round and pleasant type, his features regular and well-formed, and his hair long and curly. Although his gait was rather stoical, and his manner abrupt, his well-formed features and genuine wit won for him the admiration of the fair sex, and his high appreciation of integrity, his love for the sublime, and his power of hurling the weighty weapon of sarcasm against actions of meanness and tyranny, gained him the respect of all who were brought into contact with him in every-day life. As an artist of the chisel, Spence has shown himself to have been no mere trifler, but one whose hand could portray in stone the imaginations of a gifted mind. In his representations of the mythical Mermaid of Dallela, and several characters from Burns— still to be seen at Fingask Castle—the peculiarities of their sculptor are displayed with surprising distinctness. His poetic genius may be said never to have dawned beyond the limits of his native locality further than in the few songs and poems which appeared in the *Tales of Scotland,* a weekly magazine published in Perth in 1845 and 1846, in the columns of which we find "Linn-ma-Gray" appearing on the 7th June, 1845, and in the same year "Keen blaws the blast," "The Jacobite Song," "My Love's Window," "Oh, Flora, your Charlie maun leave ye," "Bird o' the Buddin' Bush," "A Lump o' Gowd," "The Castle o' Balmanno," "My Jamie's Gane," and "The Laird of the Longies," which last leads us back into the 17th century, where we find the auld laird falling in love with Lizzie, the elder daughter of Alexander and Lady Lindsay of Evelick Castle, the heroine, some folks say, of the well-known song beginning "Will ye gang wi' me, Lizzie Lindsay?" "Keen blaws the blast" smacks of Tannahill's "Braes of Gleniffer," and is a song that would do no discredit to the well-earned fame of the sweet singer of Paisley.

Many of Spence's poems and songs—in most part the best—were never published, because, being a sarcastic sketcher of prevailing customs and individual idiosyncrasies, such pieces as "Shanet and Rory," and "Jock o' Whitebank," etc., he could not allow to be brought before the public during his lifetime. Spence, it is said, gave all his MSS. many years ago to the late Mr. Porter, schoolmaster of Moneydie, who was to have published them at his death, but unfortunately Porter died before Spence, and the MSS. are supposed to have been lost. The poet spent a part of his later days in the hermit-like abode known as the "Auld Lint Mill"—a weird-looking and dilapidated building—a little above the village of Rait, where he lived surrounded by specimens of his own handicraft, and sustained himself in a frugal manner by the manufacture of small articles of wicker-work, etc. When too old to work, he went to reside with his son in Manchester, where he died on the 14th December, 1869, at the advanced age of ninety years.

THOMAS STEVEN,

Ex-chief magistrate, Blairgowrie, a man of cultured tastes and great business capacity, was born there sixty-seven years ago. He has been a master builder in Blair for more than forty years, undertaking large building contracts all over the country; and besides holding the honorary and responsible position of chief magistrate for about a dozen years, he has been a J. P. for the County, Chairman of the School Board, and for a life-time has been—as he still continues to be—altogether a man of "light and leading" in the community.

Mr. Steven is widely known as an intense and intelligent admirer of Tennyson, Matthew Arnold, and Wordsworth. His own dallyings with the Muses, neither few nor unimportant, have been conducted in the brief intervals of an active business and public career, perhaps the best of his poetical writings are buried away in the newspaper files of thirty and forty years ago.

JAMES STEWART

Was born in Paul Street, Perth, in the year 1801, his father, Duncan Stewart, being for many years overseer in Provost Wright's Brewery in North Methven Street. Young Stewart's education was of the meanest order; though, we are told, he was a good reader and a fair penman. At twelve years of age he was apprenticed to the shoemaking trade, with a Mr. M'Lean in George Street. During the run of his 'prentice time he was a close reader, and devoted every spare moment to the acquisition of knowledge, and the improvement of his mind. About 1826 he proceeded to Crieff, where he found employment, and remained upwards of two years. From Crieff he migrated to Dunkeld, and, with the exception of about a year spent in his native city, "wrought at the shoon" there until the date of his death. In the beginning of the month of March, 1843, he was invited to Perth in order to be present at a friend's wedding. He came; but the weather was bad, and he seems to have caught a severe cold while on the road, which ultimately produced inflammation. He was present at the wedding festivities, and appeared to be in his usual health—as certainly he was in his best spirits. Next morning he was taken alarmingly ill, and was immediately removed to the County and City Infirmary, where he died after two days illness. He was interred in the Greyfriars' Burying-ground at Perth.

In person, Stewart was a little under the middle height, and what is called round-shouldered, which gave him the appearance of having a slight stoop in his gait. His features were, if anything, small, but well formed, regular, and pleasing. A soft smile ever played about his lips. He had deep grey, sparkling eyes, an ample brow, and a massive square and compact head. In manner he was generally retired and meditative, and had such power of self-absorption, that, when the muse was on him, he could sit in the midst of a dozen hammers beating on as many lapstones, nor hear any part of the loud-voiced conversation of his fellow-workmen, or question or remark they might address to him. He cherished a sturdy, somewhat haughty independence, was to some extent the victim of "thochtless follies," particularly "dissipation's balefu' glammorie," but had a kindly, unselfish heart, which gained him the respect of all with whom he came in close contact.

Fourteen years after his death, Stewart's poems and songs, under the title of "Sketches of Scottish Character," and prefixed by a well-written memoir, were published in his native city. The largest poem in the collection, and the most ambitious, is "The Eden of North" (unfinished), but "Birnam" is perhaps the most polished and finished of his productions. In the book are many exquisite photographs of Scottish characters, such as "Fouscanhaud," "The Tailor o' Monzie," "Barley Geordie," "Benjie the Bookman," and "Duncan Ker," while "Mary Rose" (the last piece he wrote), "Grannie and her Oes," "The Herd Lassie," and "Our Little Jock," are the admiration of every lover of Scottish song. The last named is inimitable in its way, and enjoys a widespread popularity. It has been often imitated, but, so far as we have seen, never equalled.

JOHN JOSEPH SMALE STEWART,

The son of a Perthshire soldier, was born about 1838, while his father was with his regiment in Ireland, but was brought up at Lochearnhead, where his father on retiring from the army wrought for a time as a gardener, and latterly occupied the position of police inspector for the district. At the age of sixteen he went to serve on Her Majesty's Ship, *Cumberland*, then under command of Captain Seymour, and after cruising for some time sailed for Bermuda, and thence to Halifax and Nova Scotia. He took part in the Russian War, and after being discharged returned home for a brief season. Subsequently, after voyaging to various parts of the world, he took a farm in Australia, and for some years, along with a brother, was a successful farmer. Ultimately he settled as a schoolmaster at Tamarara, near Hooker's Bay, where he still resides, enjoying much popularity as a teacher and a citizen of the world.

SARAH JANE STEWART,

A sister of the subject of the foregoing notice, was born at St. Fillans in the autumn of 1845. With a view to fitting her for a professional career, Sarah received the full educational course of the local school. Her mother dying suddenly, however, and her father following her into the silent land in little more than a year thereafter, her prospects in life were changed, and she had to go out to service. In the winter of 1877 she became the wife of the late Mr. John Hyslop, the well-known Kilmarnock postman-poet; author of "The Dream of a Masque and other Poems," and her wedded career was one of unbroken happiness. Since she was fourteen years old Mrs. Hyslop has cultivated, as opportunity afforded, a natural and true poetic gift, and has written many tender heart-warming poems and songs, which have been widely circulated and esteemed.

WILLIAM STEWART.

For the few biographical particulars of the author of the really clever song "The Witch on the Brae," printed as anonymous in "The Book of Scottish Song," and elsewhere, we are indebted to the late Mr. P. R. Drummond of Perth, who, in his appreciative and interesting sketches of "Perthshire Poets," has introduced not a few waifs and strays of song which might otherwise have glided all unnoticed down the drumly stream of Time and been utterly lost in the wide ocean of oblivion.

Mr. Drummond says, "Of all those whom it is my intention to place on this list, I knew William Stewart best, although I neither knew when he was born, nor where he was born; how long he lived, nor the nature of his death. He was for many years an English teacher in Perth, first as assistant to Mr. Hindmarsh, next in a private school of his own in Athole Street, and eventually in the English department of the Perth Seminaries. During his earlier days of teaching, his mother kept his house, and a cosey couple they were. Mrs. Stewart looked upon her son as the paragon of teachers and men, and he looked upon his mother as the model of all mothers since the era of Mother Eve. They had many friends, kept a good table, and William was to some extent a diner-out. He was very lame, and always used a crutch, yet active and full of vitality. He did not sing, but those who have been at his table will remember with what gusto he recited 'The Witch on the Brae.' He never boasted of being the author, but his intimate friends knew that such was the fact. . . .

Mr. Stewart married rather late in life, and afterwards became a changed man. During his later days a cloud came over his existence, the density of which he kept to himself. His wife died a few years after their marriage, and he did not survive her long."

"The Witch on the Brae" is somewhat suggestive of Robert Nicoll's "Janet," although there is nothing in the songs to show that the one writer in any way borrowed from the other.

JOHN TAYLOR,

An artist and poet of approved taste and fancy, was born near Huntingtower, Perth, in 1837. His father, James Taylor, born at Mains of Nairne, near the "Auld House" of Gask, in 1813, possessed a happy "knack" of rhyming, and gained several prizes in poetic competitions. A song of his, "The Banks o' Tay," indeed, would have found a place in this work, but for the fact that so many pieces have been crowded out for want of space. His mother belonged to an old Perthshire stock, said by the family traditions to be connected with the Dalhousies. One relative was Lord Provost of Perth about the beginning of the century, and another was a royal chaplain, and minister of St. Enoch's, Glasgow, for about forty years. In 1840 the Taylor family removed to Glasgow, where the father died in 1875, and where John, and a sister who live together, still reside. In the course of his teens our artist-poet became a pupil teacher and Queen's scholar in the Free Normal Seminary in Glasgow, and on leaving it, in 1857, was engaged for a few years as a tutor in England. Subsequently, he paid two lengthy visits to France, studying art, and during the first of these (in 1860), painted several pictures in Paris. In 1862 he exhibited in the Glasgow Fine Art Institute a series of outline drawings, illustrative of Longfellow's poem "Excelsior," which have been greatly admired for their ideal beauty as well as for the delicate and finished character of the work. Mr. Taylor continued to accept engagements as a visiting master, teaching drawing, etc., in several higher class schools, till 1867, when he finally gave up teaching. For many years he has been a busy worker, employing alternately the brush, the pencil, and the pen; now sending a picture to one or other of the principal exhibitions, a drawing to a magazine, or a poem, a song, or a sketch to the *People's Friend*, or some other of the various periodicals with which he is connected. Some of Mr. Taylor's songs, set to music by himself, are exceedingly happy, and need to be better known only, we think, to become popular.

WILLIAM THOMAS TOVANI,

Co-editor of the *Auchterarder Chronicle*, and author of "My Edelweiss," and other stories, was born at Ardoch on the 27th October, 1863. When ten years old he went to reside with his brother at Tullibardine, where he "passed through his standards," and acted for several years as a pupil-teacher. Subsequently, he entered the University of St. Andrews, where he studied for three sessions, when his health broke down, and he was compelled to seek the invigorating influences of rural occupation for a season. In 1888 Mr. Tovani started the *Perthshire Magazine*, which recently had to succumb for want of support, and certainly deserved a better fate. Two-thirds of the first volume he wrote himself, and in the latter days of the publication, when Mr. J. Cuthbert Hadden, of Edinburgh, had assumed the editorship, he still maintained a warm if not active interest in the welfare of the happily-conceived serial. Presently Mr. Tovani resides in Auchterarder, and is the chief partner of the publishing firm of Messrs. Tovani & Company.

DAVID WEBSTER,

Was a native of Dunblane, and was born on the 25th September, 1787. He was at first destined for the Church, but, his father dying and leaving a family of eight children, of whom David was second eldest, the future poet was apprenticed to the less enviable occupation of handloom weaving. This he learned at Paisley, and continued to prosecute, short intervals excepted, until his death on 22nd January, 1837. Dr. Rogers says—"His life was much chequered by misfortune. Fond of society, he was led to associate with some dissolute persons, who professed to be admirers of his genius, and was enticed by their example to neglect the concerns of business for the delusive pleasures of the tavern." Such has been the sad fate of, alas! too many of the bardic clan, who, whatever may be said in their favour—and there is often much—have lacked that "prudent, cautious, self-control," which, according to Burns, "is wisdom's root."

M. BUCHANAN WHITE.

A frequent and welcome contributor of prose and verse to various magazines and literary periodicals, Miss M. Buchanan White is a daughter of the esteemed Dr. Buchanan White of Perth. She received her education at home, under the superintendence of her mother, and her acquaintance with many of the most picturesque districts of the Scottish Highlands, in which her parents have been wont to sojourn every summer, has no doubt tended to strengthen her inborn love for nature, as it has frequently inspired her muse to picture in glowing verse the beauty of flower and leaf, of hill and glen, and loch and lea.

Nothing in book-form has yet emanated from her pen, but it is the desire and expectation of her many friends and admirers in the "Fair City," and elsewhere, that she will, ere the world is much older, place a volume of her collected verse in their hands, to be cherished for its own sweet sake.

JOHN WHITE, LL.D.,

Was born at Inchcoonings, in the parish of Errol, in 1807, and received his elementary education at the Parochial School of St. Madoes and at the Grammar School of Perth. From thence he went to St. Andrews University, where he passed through the arts classes, etc. After this he taught in Edinburgh for two years, and in 1834 was appointed Commercial and Mathematical Master in Irvine Academy. This post he held with distinction until 1866, when he retired on account of his health. Dr. White is known in the West of Scotland as one of the foremost mathematical teachers of the day, and it was on account of his success and fame as such that the Senatus of Glasgow University, in 1867, conferred upon him the honorary distinction of LL.D. In the town of Irvine, where he is greatly respected and esteemed, he spends the evening of his life in cultured ease, singing a song betimes, and, under the charm of a lively fancy, feeling as young sometimes as when he climbed the hill of Kinnoull and raced on the banks of the Tay more than seventy years ago.

ROBERT WHITTET,

Author of "The Brighter Side of Suffering and Other Poems," is a native of Perth, and was born in 1829. Early in life he learned the printing trade, and, after working for some years as a journeyman printer in Aberdeen and Edinburgh, he returned to Perth, and started in business there on his own account. Eventually a poetical desire for a life of "rural felicity" took possession of his mind, and in 1869 he "pulled up stakes" and went out to America, where he purchased a plantation of some four hundred acres in Virginia, close by the old city of Williamsburg. The venture proved a disaster, whereupon Mr. Whittet found his way to the city of Richmond, the capital of the Southern Confederacy, and took up his original business of printing. For a time here the struggle for existence proved pretty keen, but fortune at length deigned to smile upon him, and now the printing and publishing firm of Whittet & Shepperson, of which he has the honour to be senior partner, is widely and favourably known. Mr. Whittet is possessed of poetical gifts of the highest order, and owns an unquestionable right to the title of a true poet. The superb volume of his poems published in 1882— "the product of odd half-hours and occasional wanderings by the wayside," as he tell us—has elicited the highest praise from critics on both sides of the Atlantic.

WILLIAM WILSON,

A native of Crieff, was born on Christmas Day, 1801. At an early age he was imbued with a passionate love of poetry, derived from his mother, who sang with great beauty the old Jacobite songs and ballads of his native land. His parents being of the industrial class, and in indigent circumstances, young Wilson was early devoted to a life of manual labour. While employed in a factory in Dundee some of his poetical compositions were brought under the notice of Mrs. Grant of Laggan, who interested herself in his behalf, and enabled him to start in business as a coal merchant. He married early in life, and in his twenty-fifth year removed to Edinburgh. "There was," wrote Dr. Robert Chambers, "at this time something very engaging in his appearance; a fair open countenance, ruddy with the bloom of health; manners soft and pleasing." In the same year of his removal to the Scottish capital he lost his young and devoted wife. He married again, in 1830, a Miss Sibbald, a lady of superior connections in the county of Roxburgh. When thirty-two years of age he removed to the United States, and settled at Poughkeepsie, on the Hudson, where he engaged in the business of bookselling and publishing, which he continned to prosecute till his death, August 25, 1860.

During his residence in the New World he occasionally contributed in prose and verse—and, as a rule, anonymously—to various American periodicals, and now and then sent a paper or poem to *Blackwood* or *Chambers' Journal*. Most of the recent collections of Scottish songs, such as "Whistle Binkie," Blackie's "Book of Scottish Song," and the "Modern Scottish Minstrel," contain selections from Wilson's many fine songs, the best known—and deservedly so—being "Jean Linn" and "Auld Johnny Graham," while several of his songs have been published in sheet form, set to music also composed by himself. Hew Ainslie, his brother poet, and who has since followed our subject into the land of shadows, thus wrote, a few years ago, to James Grant Wilson, the son of his poet friend:—"Having summered and wintered it for many long years with your dear father, I ought to know something of the base and bent of his genius, though, as he hated all shams and pretensions, a very slight acquaintance with him showed that independence and personal manhood, as, 'wha daur meddle wi' me,' were two of his strong features, while humour, deep feeling, and tenderness, were prominent in all he said or wrote. And oh! the pity that he did not give us more 'Jean Linns' and 'Auld Johnny Grahams' in his native tongue. I loved him as a man, a poet, and a brother; and I had many proofs that my feelings were reciprocated."

JOHN YOUNG,

A distinguished citizen of Perth, where he has practised for many years as a civil engineer and architect. John Young, author of "Selina, and Other Poems," was born at Pitfour, in the parish of St. Madoes, in the year 1826. He received his early education at the Parish School and afterwards at the Perth Academy. At a very early age he evinced a passion for poetry and romance; and, whilst steadily pursuing the arduous studies of his profession, became an occasional contributor to the poetical columns of the local newspapers. Besides enjoying a well-established reputation amongst civil engineers, he is well known as a lover of the fine arts, and an advanced student of natural science. As an evidence of his keen interest in the latter study, it may be mentioned that in 1879 he published a handsome volume of his poems in aid of funds for the erection of a museum for the natural history of Perthshire. He was for eleven years honorary secretary to the Perthshire Society of Natural Science, and many of his most enjoyable bits of verse were composed in connection with the excursions of that Society, and as bard of the Perthshire Mountain Club, "Selina," from which his volume takes its main title, is a narrative poem of seventy-seven stanzas, evincing considerable descriptive power and poetic feeling. But we readily confess to a preference for his shorter efforts, of which he has produced a great variety, "from grave to gay, from lively to severe."

FINIS.